Table Of Contents

Translations for Classically Speaking Selections:
        Chekhov: Constance Garnett
        Ibsen: William Archer, Christopher Martin
        Rostand: Christopher Martin
        Strindberg: Christopher Martin

Shakespeare Text and Line References:
        The Riverside Shakespeare Complete Works

Cover credits:
        Ginger Grace and Sheridan Crist, Aeschylus' *Oresteia*.
        Alberto Tore and Paul Meacham, Marlowe's *Edward II*.
        Productions by Christopher Martin, CSC Repertory.
        Photos by Gerry Goodstein.

"Who the hell wants to hear actors talk?"

Harry Warner, 1927
(On the release of the first talking picture: *The Jazz Singer*)

INTRODUCTION
to the second edition

All actors come to the table with the ability to use their pronunciation of English, influenced by their personal heritage or region of origin, to their advantage to portray characters from circumstances or regions of the world similar to their own.

Actors from New Jersey may be able to step straight into *The Sopranos* with no adjustment to their everyday speech. The same is true for Russian immigrants now living in the Brighton Beach section of Brooklyn one hears on *Law and Order* with Slavic-accented English, and the many young actors and actresses who are at ease playing characters with sounds typified by their contemporary pronunciation of "fershURE" or "AHHsome".

But, these same accents and dialects[1] can prove a liability when trying to accurately portray individuals with backgrounds and life experiences uniquely different from one's own. In order to play a *variety* of characters convincingly and believably, actors often need to train and expand their repertoire of skills.

Classically Speaking offers an approach for American actors who wish to explore sound beyond their habitual speech, fine-tune their ability to hear and identify subtle variations in sounds and dialects, and to develop the flexibility and skills necessary to adjust their speech to the particular demands of a wider range of characters and material.

The extensive Neutral American section could also serve advanced speakers of English as a Second Language (**ESL**), as well as English speakers from countries other than the US, including those from Canada, Australia, New Zealand, South Africa, Ireland and Great Britain, among others.

---

[1] The terms 'dialect' and 'accent' are traditionally applied from one's point of view—though the terms are very often used interchangeably. 'Dialect' refers to variations within one's native or first language, while 'accent' refers to variations within one's non-native language. For example, someone with American English as a first language would study a French or Russian accent and a Boston dialect.

2

Neutral American Speech
(NAS)

[handwritten: Most Practical]

⌐Neutral American is the most practical dialect an actor can study.⌐ Sometimes referred to as General American, it is spoken without regionalisms that identify an actor's specific point of origin or 'home' sounds. When effectively incorporated, the actor—and therefore the character—is not revealed as explicitly Southern, Mid-Western, or from Boston, New York, Chicago, Tennessee, New Hampshire, Texas, etc. He/she is therefore 'neutral'.

Though very few people actually speak pure Neutral American in their everyday lives, it is commonly used:

[handwritten: Most Commonly used]

* when a particular region of the country is unspecified in the text

* when clear, well-spoken sounds are required, rather than under-articulated speech, or slang

* when actors from various parts of the country need to convincingly play members of the same family

* in classical plays, when more formal classical dialect is not required

* in voiceovers and commercials involving upscale characters, pricey items, or well-articulated spokespersons.

Overall, Neutral American is very useful when attempting to increase one's flexibility and marketability. Many agents prefer their clients to have this dialect in their 'arsenal', and see it as a sign of a well-trained[1] actor. It is the standard against which most dialects and accents are compared in teaching materials for American-English speaking actors.

Rhythm Highlighters

The Neutral American section gives special focus to the Rhythm Highlighters, which address general rhythmic issues for well-spoken American English, before delving into the specific spoken sounds of English in detail. Rhythm Highlighters include: linking words in order to avoid glottal attack,

---

[1] Though vocal production is out of the scope of this text, it is a crucial element in one's training. As a designated Linklater voice teacher, the core of my training and teaching revolves around the methods expressed in Kristin Linklater's *Freeing the Natural Voice*. Actors may also wish to explore the work of many other wonderful voice/singing teachers, including: Roy Hart, Patsy Rodenburg, Cicely Berry, Catherine Fitzmaurice, Nova Thomas, and Keith Buhl, to name a few.

stressed syllables and their relationship to operative or key words, noun/verb variations, the use of weak and strong forms, prefixes, suffixes, syllabic endings, inflection, pause, literary devices, and scansion.

This material is crucial, for rhythmic variations not only promote more intelligible speech, but encourage corresponding changes in pitch, inflection, and musicality necessary for interesting, well-spoken speech choices.

Most importantly, Neutral American rhythms and sounds serve as the foundation for learning the second and third dialects covered in this book: Classical American and Standard British.

Classical American – Well spoken

This dialect offers an intermediate option between well-pronounced Neutral American and Standard British. It builds upon Neutral American, blending additional rhythmic and sound elements, which result in more formal or heightened speech without sounding British to an American ear.

Classical American can be used to indicate well-spoken, non-contemporary speech for plays set in another time or place, or to establish class or character distinctions from Neutral American Speech. It can be used when a language other than English would be spoken by the character, as in the French, Italian and Spanish plays of Molière, Pirandello or Lorca.

Classical American might also be suitably applied to the verse plays of Shakespeare, translations of the Ancient Greeks, or 19th century prose classics of Strindberg, Ibsen, and Chekhov, among others.

As previously noted, no one dialect is capable of fulfilling every requirement, and there are always variables to be considered when determining the appropriate speech or dialect for a particular production. These include:

* What is the director's concept?
* What specific time or place is being represented?
* Are there 'class' distinctions within the play?
* Do any of the characters require foreign accents?
* Do any of the actors speak with accents?
* How much rehearsal time is scheduled?
* How experienced and trained is the cast?

4

Elements selected for inclusion in the Classical American section are based on conversations with directors, actors, students, and my own experience as an actor, teacher and spectator. A certain degree of flexibility is implied, as choices should offer support for the particular reality being created on stage or screen.

Mid-Atlantic Stage speech known as **Mid-Atlantic** was popular during the mid 20th Century, and is often taught in acting schools and universities. It is almost indistinguishable from Standard British (RP), and many actors, directors, and members of the audience find it objectionable for this reason.

But, if a more British-English sound is desired, if historical characters are being played, or if British and American actors are appearing together in the same production, this dialect could be appropriate, and is covered, *in brief*, at the end of Classical American. [1]

Standard British (RP)

Upper & Middle Class

Standard British is the dialect traditionally spoken by the English upper and upper-middle classes. Also referred to as RP or Received Pronunciation, it is the name given to the speech instruction 'received' by students enrolled in public boarding schools. In an odd twist, public school in Britain is what is referred to in America as private school.

Today, Standard British is often considered too formal, rigid, or old-fashioned, as the contemporary characteristics of upper/upper-middle class speech in Britain have become more flexible and varied. But for period plays, including those of the 19th century Shaw and Wilde, or Restoration playwrights Congreve and Farquhar, among others, the formality and precision of Standard British is certainly appropriate.

It is also beneficial for American actors to know Standard British as a foundation on which to build their study of foreign accents. Many people worldwide who have learned English as a second language have been taught by speakers of Standard British, and this is reflected in their spoken English sounds.

---

[1] For a detailed rendering of Mid-Atlantic dialect, also known as Eastern Standard, see Edith Skinner's *Speak With Distinction*.

Accompanying CD

The accompanying CD contains over 300 audio selections, including a dozen monologues from Shakespeare, Wilde, Congreve, and Shaw spoken by fourteen professional actors, illustrating all sound changes in Neutral American, Classical American, Mid-Atlantic, and Standard British dialects.

International Phonetic Alphabet
(IPA)

The brief Overview that follows serves to introduce the International Phonetic Alphabet, and provide enough information on the consonant and vowel sounds to complete the IPA practice material and exercises.

Devised in 1888 by the International Phonetic Association, this system for representing spoken sounds—one symbol per sound—offers a much more reliable method of representing and comparing spoken sounds than alphabetical spelling. Letters of the alphabet in English can present difficulties when one is attempting to decipher, compare, or accurately represent pronunciation. For example, 'a' in the *spelling* of the following words represents seven *different* pronunciations:

f<u>a</u>ther, im<u>a</u>ge, <u>a</u>ny, c<u>a</u>t, sof<u>a</u>, t<u>a</u>lk, <u>a</u>te

Transcribing, notating, or writing using the International Phonetic Alphabet can help eliminate confusion in pronunciation, as there is one phonetic symbol to represent each sound of spoken English. Thus, seven different symbols would be used to notate the seven sounds represented by the letter 'a' in the words above.

Learning IPA symbols may take some effort, but there is a wonderful pay-off for the professional actor. Neutral American Speech is used as the basis from which other accents and dialects are learned. Sound adjustments necessary in switching from one dialect to another are often written in phonetics. It is also enormously useful to be able to use phonetic markings in one's script in advance of a cold reading or audition, or when researching and studying a role.

It is also possible to transcribe vowel and diphthong sounds with symbols that indicate the length or duration of the sound. Knowledge of the intrinsic lengths of vowels and diphthongs can be extremely useful for actors

6

with English as a second language. Approximating the rhythm of American English is important for increased intelligibility. Duplicating it is crucial for complete neutrality.

Studying the lengths of sounds can also provide a useful tool for actors who habitually swallow or clip their sounds, and/or shy away from expressing themselves through open-throated vowels and diphthongs. Length guidelines are outlined at the end of the Overview, followed by words which have been transcribed in IPA with length markings, transcription practice material, and an answer key. Length guidelines are restated and demonstrated with sample words, in applicable vowel and diphthong chapters. That said: use of length indicators with the IPA symbols is *optional*.

Practice

Dialects covered in *Classically Speaking* are presented in detail for a reason. The English-speaking public is more astute than actors might imagine when it comes to recognizing slight variations in speech sounds. (After all, we have all grown up sounding like the people around us.) So, when making sound adjustments, actors need to be precise and consistent to convince a discerning audience.

This can pose a challenge for actors. Some may begin with speech patterns very close to Neutral, so the need to make adjustments or changes will be small—a 'tweak' to one sound or two may suffice. Others may need to acquire an entirely new 'vocabulary' of sounds in order to possess the skills necessary for playing a wider range of characters and roles. If this describes you, don't worry—actors may have to work to learn your dialect in the future.

If you are going to be successful, you will need to integrate a new set of sound skills, which requires: practice. Think sports—for instance, basketball. More specifically, think about learning to *dribble* a basketball. Beginners can feel awkward and complain of a mechanical lack of freedom, because they need to look at the ball in order to keep from losing it. Even Michael Jordan had to keep his eye on the ball at first.

But practice results in increased muscle memory and skill level. The dribbler begins to be able to scan the court with only partial attention directed toward the ball. Soon, the player can dribble, running full-speed from one end of the court to the other, seemingly unconscious of the basketball itself. Eventually, the player can take (and make!) that shot while being agressively pursued by a member of the opposing team.

The same applies to learning a dialect well enough that it becomes an unconscious part of oneself. Practice, muscle memory, attention to detail, and more practice is required to ensure that the new sounds become an intrinsic part of oneself and therefore, one's character. This will happen with time.

[handwritten: To Perfect dialects]

In the meantime. . . practice!

Limited Class Time?

If there is not time to study the Neutral American section in full, I suggest covering the Overview on pages 10-38, the Rhythm Highlighters on pages 48-89, and the following specific **sound checks**, which can be found in the vowel and consonant chapters on the pages listed.

These elements were spotlighted in the previous edition of *Classically Speaking* and, although there are other sounds in Neutral American that might need attention, this 'check list' provides focus if time is short.

All of the individual issues listed below are demonstrated on the CD and are phonetically marked on the printed Shakespeare monologues, which are included at the end of Neutral American.

[handwritten: Make note-cards!]

Issue	Page
/e/ (g<u>e</u>t) before 'm' or 'n' *Audio 12*	105-111
/æ/ (th<u>a</u>t), relaxed and non-nasal *Audio 13*	112-117
/ɔ/ (<u>a</u>ll) vs. /ɑ/ (f<u>a</u>ther) sounds *Audio 21*	148-156
/aɪ̆/ (m<u>y</u>) before a voiceless consonant *Audio 24*	165-170
/ʊə̆/ (p<u>oo</u>r) diphthong *Audio 30*	191-194
/n, d, t, l/ tip of tongue placement *Audio 35*	208-218
Voiceless stop-plosives before a pause or silence *Audio 36A*	221-224
Voiced stop-plosives before a pause or silence *Audio 36B*	225-231
Consonant /r/ and 'dr', 'tr', 'str' combinations *Audio 49A,B,C*	294-302
Shakespeare Monologues *Audio 50, 51, 52*	320-325

OVERVIEW

&

INTERNATIONAL PHONETIC ALPHABET (IPA)

Selections for Recording

The following selections can be recorded at the beginning of study and re-recorded periodically to measure progress.

Rhythm Highlighters:

1. Arthur's amazing agent arranged the appointment.

2. If you have time to spare, become a volunteer.

3. We feel we must contest the results of the contest.

4. I'd like a part in a film, a commercial, and a mini-series.

5. The agency closed its door at the end of the day.

6. This machine takes nickels, dimes, quarters, or silver dollars.

7. They expect to reduce prescription costs before December.

8. What fearless statesman made that important statement?

9. Prudence, the students didn't meet at the center, they couldn't.

Vowels and Diphthongs:

10. I really feel that Neal is ideal for the part.

11. Phil is a little bit exhausted from his trip to the village.

12. Jenny was compelled to delve into the books on the shelves.

13. When apprehended, the criminal pretended to surrender.

14. Sandy and Jan were happy when cast in *As You Like It*.

15. The nervous, surly, underworld character cursed Sherlock.

16. Dr. Tull consulted another physician about his ulcer.

17. Julian, you know the rule. No mint juleps at the school's pool.

18. Wouldn't you rather wear wool in the woods in winter?

19. Olivia O'Neill drew the oasis pictured in the hotel's brochure.

20. Saul became lost in thought while drawing with chalk.

21.   Father commented on the calming effect of the sonatas.

22.   Hail the mailmen, both male and female.

23.   The bright sign shuts off each night, at midnight.

24.   Mr. Doyle prefers oysters broiled, not parboiled.

25.   If you lose your foothold, Joel, grab ahold of that boulder.

26.   Scowling and growling could befoul your reputation.

27.   Oh dear, here comes the peerless financier from Erie.

28.   Are you aware that's an unfair comparison, Gary?

29.   I'm curious, are you sure you're getting health insurance?

30.   Four more reporters poured into the Georgia courtroom.

31.   Arthur and Charlotte have a harmonious relationship.

32.   The fire was completely doused by powerful summer showers.

Consonants:

33.   DAD doesn't talk to DANNY until the end of Act Two.

34.   Tammy tailgated Tommy's truck and took out a tail light.

35.   "Ask the actors where they studied acting," he asked.

36.   We figure that singer has the strongest singing voice.

37.   Jill gave Bill the cold shoulder and felt a little guilty.

38.   Vincent travels to Venice on Friday, November fifth.

39.   What's the earth's length, width and breadth, Mr. Smithy?

40.   Rachel has a fondness for rich chocolate chip snacks.

41.   Pianists need the strongest fingers, wrists, and fists.

42.   We didn't wake up William, Watson—did you?

43.   Yes, yogurt and yellow onions promote youthfulness.

44.   The drunken driver drove into the tractor trailer's trunk.

45.   Go straight. Route sixty-six is obstructed by construction.

46.   She lisps each time she eats six-packs of crispy crisps.

Diagram of the Head
with
Speech Articulators and Related Structures

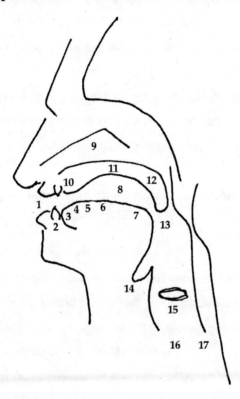

1. lips	10. alveolar ridge
2. teeth	(front of hard palate)
3. tongue tip	11. hard palate
4. tongue blade	12. soft palate
5. tongue front	13. uvula
6. tongue middle	14. epiglottis
7. tongue back	15. vocal folds
8. mouth	16. trachea
9. nasal cavity	17. esophagus

CONSONANT OVERVIEW

The sounds of English can be divided into two major categories: vowels and consonants. They are differentiated by how sound is formed and used. Vowels are formed when an uninterrupted stream of air is released through the mouth. Consonants are formed when the breath is impeded either partially or fully, during the course of its forward release through the mouth or nose. The release is influenced by one or more of the articulators (lips, teeth, tongue, hard palate, soft palate), which come together and result in the formation of a particular consonant.

Clearly spoken consonants and consonant combinations are crucial for understanding the specific spoken word. Open-throated vowels, diphthongs, and triphthongs are especially effective in communicating emotional content.

> *I understand a fury in your words,*
> *But not the words.*
>
> (Othello: IV, ii, 32)

Consonant sounds are either voiced or voiceless. Voiced consonants require vocal fold vibration. Many have a 'partner' sound that is made precisely the same way but without vibration of the vocal folds. This results in a voiceless or whispered sound. These pairs of sounds are called cognates. For example, the voiced and voiceless sounds 'd' and 't' form a cognate pair.

Voiced consonant endings are an important element in clear verbal communication. Vocal fold vibration needs to be maintained through the end of a word that finishes with a voiced consonant, or the voiceless partner may be inadvertently spoken instead. For example, energetically speak the word 'fee_d_'. If you heard yourself say 'fee_t_' instead of 'fee_d_', then voicing was not maintained through the end of the word, and voiceless 't' was spoken instead of 'd'.

Final consonant voicing also influences the length of the preceding vowel sound and therefore affects the rhythm of the word. Energetically speak the words 'fee_t_' *and* 'fee_d_'. Be sure to voice the 'd' ending. Notice how the vowel sound is longer when it precedes the voiced consonant 'd' in the word 'fee_d_' than when it precedes voiceless 't' in the word 'fee_t_'.

Clarity (handwritten, left margin)

So, if the director or the audience cannot understand you, clarify your intentions *and* your voiced endings.

Some accents—German, for example—use the voiceless 'partner' sound instead of the voiced, in certain instances. It can be beneficial to know voiced and voiceless partners before beginning accent study.

Consonants are generally divided into four distinct groups, according to the manner in which the air is modified and the place where it is modified during the course of sound production. These sound categories are listed below and summarized in the chart on page 17.

Stop-Plosives

add to notecards (handwritten, left margin)

/t d/   /p b/   /k g/
(to**t** **did**)   (po**p** **bib**)   (**c**ap **g**ap)

When forming these sounds, the outgoing air is always completely stopped between two articulators, which initiates a build-up of air pressure. The stop element of /t d/ is formed by pressing the tip of the tongue against the alveolar or gum ridge, just behind the upper teeth. The stop element of /p b/ sounds is formed by enlivened contact between the upper and lower lips (referred to as bi-labial) and the stop of /k g/ is formed by energized contact between the back of the tongue and the front of the soft palate or velum. Air is then either exploded or not, depending on the sound that follows the plosive.

If voiceless plosives are followed directly by another *consonant*, then only the stop element is articulated, notated in IPA by / ˌ / following the /tˌ pˌ kˌ/. The following words are marked for demonstration.

Stop only: tˌrim   pˌlay   kˌlutˌz   thatˌ man

If voiceless plosives are followed directly by a *pause, silence, vowel,* or *diphthong*, then stop and aspiration elements are articulated, notated by / ʰ / after the /tʰ pʰ kʰ/.

Stop, then aspirate: tʰoo   pʰeekʰ   pʰipʰe   aftʰer workʰ

Voiced partners are not phonetically marked for aspiration in IPA with either / ʰ / or / ˌ /, though the criteria for articulating the stop, or the stop and plosive, is identical. See pages 221-231 for more detail.

Continuants

When speaking continuants, the articulators maintain their position throughout the duration of the sound. Continuants are divided into three sub-groups: nasal, lateral, and fricative, and offer a wonderful contrast in rhythm with the stop-plosives. See pages 232-247 for more detail.

nasal continuants

/ m /   / n /   / ŋ /
(**mom**)   (o**n**)   (si**ng**)

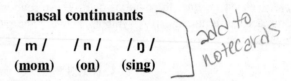

The articulators maintain their position when speaking these three sounds, which are released out the nose. All three are voiced and have no voiceless partners. See pages 232-247 for more detail.

lateral continuant

/ l / (**l**i**ly**)

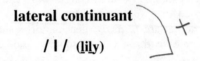

This voiced continuant sound is the only consonant sound in Neutral American that releases laterally, over the sides of the tongue. See pages 248-254 for more detail.

fricative continuants

/ f v /   / θ ð /
(lea**f** lea**ve**)   (ba**th** ba**the**)

/ s z /   / ʃ ʒ /
(bu**s** bu**zz**)   (ru**sh** rou**ge**)

/ h / (**h**e)

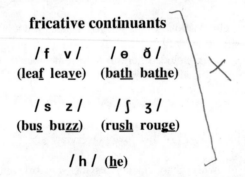

These nine sounds, four cognate pairs and voiceless 'h', maintain their position while breath is directed through an opening formed by the speech articulators narrow enough to cause emission of a friction-like sound. See pages 255-284 for more detail.

Affricates

/ t͡ʃ   d͡ʒ /
(ri**ch** ri**dge**)

    There are two affricates, one cognate pair, which consist of the short stop element from the stop-plosives /t, d/, and the longer fricative continuants /ʃ, ʒ/, blended together to sound as one. These sounds are represented in the words and corresponding IPA symbols, above. See pages 285-288 for more detail.

Glides

/ w /   / j /   / r /
(**w**e) (**y**ou) (red)

    Glides begin in one position then quickly and seamlessly flow into the vowel sound that always follows. They do not quite fit the definition of consonants, sounds that are formed when the air is stopped or impeded during the course of its release through the mouth or nose. Glides are sometimes referred to as 'semi-vowels'.

    The three gliding sounds occur only before vowels and never as the last sound of a word. In addition, if the shape and position for the glide is maintained too long, a vowel sound can be formed instead of the consonant.

    The slight friction sound formed when producing the consonant /r/ allows its classification as both a fricative continuant and glide. A case can be made for either. It is included here to help remember that, like the other two glides, consonant /r/ is always followed by a vowel sound, and is never the last sound of a word. See pages 289-302 for more detail on the three glides.

    Note. An 'r' in the spelling can also represent a vowel sound. This is introduced on pages 20-21 of the Vowel Overview.

    The following chart categorizes the way or manner in which air is modified during formation of the consonant sound, in CAPITAL LETTERS. The next line notes the IPA symbol and includes a sample word containing the voiced sound, followed by a word with the voiceless partner sound, if one exists. A short description summarizes the place where the sound is modified when spoken, followed by a short summary word in the right column. Unless noted

otherwise, the tongue tip rests down behind the lower front teeth when producing the sound.

The reader now has enough information to transcribe the words listed on page 29 using IPA symbols. All contain the vowel sound / i / (we).

Consonant Chart for Neutral American				
voiced		**voiceless**		
STOP-PLOSIVES				
d feed	t	feet	tongue tip contacts the upper gum ridge	Alveolar
b cab	p	cap	both lips articulate against each other	Bilabial
g pig	k	pick	back of tongue contacts the soft palate	Velar
CONTINUANTS				
Nasal				
m mom	*none*		both lips articulate against each other	Bilabial
n nine	*none*		tongue tip contacts the upper gum ridge	Alveolar
ŋ sing	*none*		back of tongue contacts the soft palate	Velar
Lateral				
l well	*none*		tongue tip contacts the upper gum ridge	Alveolar
Fricative				
v leave	f	leaf	lower lip contacts edge of upper front teeth	Labio-dental
ð bathe	θ	bath	tongue tip contacts edge of upper front teeth	Dental
z buzz	s	bus	tongue tip points toward upper gum ridge	Alveolar
ʒ beige	ʃ	bash	tongue blade points toward upper gum ridge	Alveolar
	h	he	space between the vocal folds	Glottal
AFFRICATES				
dʒ ridge	tʃ	rich	tongue tip contacts the upper gum ridge	Alveolar
GLIDES				
w went	hw	why[1]	both lips round	Bilabial
j you	*none*		tongue front arches toward the hard palate	Lingua-palatal
r red	*none*		tongue tip points toward upper gum ridge	Alveolar

---

[1] The voiceless partner is spoken in Classical American and, occasionally, in Standard British.

VOWEL OVERVIEW

Vowels are formed when an uninterrupted stream of air is released through the mouth. The releasing air involves vibration of the vocal folds, which is referred to as voicing. Vibration, or voicing, can be felt externally by placing your fingertips on your throat while saying: *ahhhhh.*

Vowels are designated as **front, mid**, or **back**, depending on the area of the tongue that is actively arched during sound formation. This, in combination with the shape formed as a result of the position of the lower jaw and the lips, determines which vowel sound is actually spoken.

Parts of the Tongue

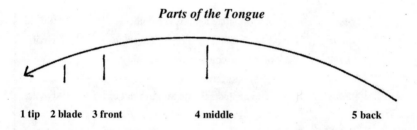

1 tip   2 blade   3 front   4 middle   5 back

Overall Position of the Tongue Arch

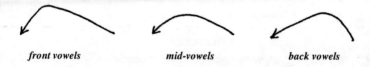

front vowels   *mid-vowels*   *back vowels*

The very tip of the tongue touches the back of the lower front teeth during vowel production and the soft palate is raised. This helps insure a complete lack of nasality on all vowel sounds as they release through the mouth, not the nose. An exception to the tip of the tongue placement occurs in the formation of Neutral American vowels and diphthongs of 'r', which are introduced on page 20-21 and 23-24.

Front Vowels

The first, most closed front vowel is: /i/ (w<u>e</u>). To form the specific shape necessary for speaking this sound, the jaw is mostly closed, the tip of the tongue rests down behind the lower teeth, the front of the tongue arches high toward the front of the hard palate, and the lips are slightly spread.

If the jaw is allowed to relax progressively more open as the tongue tip rests behind the lower teeth, the arch of the tongue begins to flatten, the spreading of the cheeks decreases, and the shapes necessary for forming the remaining three Neutral American front vowels: /ɪ/ (w<u>i</u>ll), /e/ (g<u>e</u>t), /æ/ (th<u>a</u>t) are formed.

If the jaw drops and the tongue arch flattens slightly more than for the /æ/ (th<u>a</u>t) sound, the front vowel represented by the symbol /a/ is formed. Though /a/ is not spoken as a vowel in NAS, it *is* spoken as the first sound of the diphthong in the words: m<u>y</u> and n<u>ow</u>, represented by the corresponding IPA symbols: /aɪ̆/ and /aŏ/.

This is the sound that can be heard in some Bostonian's pronunciation of '*pahk the cahr in Hahvahd yahd*' or in certain southerner's pronunciation of pi*e* and by*e* where the second part of the sound is dropped. It is also spoken as a vowel in several accents and dialects, including Spanish and Irish. Since this sound is not used on its own as a vowel in Neutral American, there is no truly appropriate sample word. See page 422 for further discussion of this sound.

Key words to help remember Neutral American front vowels:

i   ɪ   e   æ   (a)
W<u>e</u>   w<u>i</u>ll   g<u>e</u>t   th<u>a</u>t   (*laugh—in some dialects*).

Additional sample words:

i   h<u>e</u>, s<u>ee</u>, tr<u>ea</u>t, ach<u>ie</u>ve, rec<u>ei</u>ve, p<u>eo</u>ple, debr<u>i</u>s, fl<u>ea</u>s

ɪ   <u>i</u>t, <u>i</u>sn't, b<u>ui</u>lding, <u>i</u>mage, b<u>u</u>sy, w<u>i</u>ndow, w<u>i</u>ng, w<u>o</u>m<u>e</u>n

e   b<u>e</u>t, m<u>a</u>ny, qu<u>e</u>st, s<u>ai</u>d, d<u>ea</u>f, ag<u>ai</u>n, t<u>e</u>mper, sh<u>e</u>pherd

æ   h<u>a</u>t, c<u>a</u>sh, pl<u>ai</u>d, s<u>a</u>ck, p<u>a</u>l, m<u>a</u>n, l<u>a</u>mb, m<u>a</u>ngle, r<u>a</u>nk

(a)   *none*

(handwritten marginalia: Lesson for 11)

Phonetic symbols are usually placed between slashes / / in order to avoid confusing them with alphabetical letters, though slashes are sometimes eliminated when their absence will not cause confusion.

Mid-Vowels

It is necessary to understand stressed syllables before discussing the mid-vowels. A stressed syllable is that part of a word which receives the strongest emphasis. This is marked in IPA by / ' / before the stressed[1] syllable. It is used here, in combination with bolding, for emphasis and clarity.

(handwritten marginalia: stress vs unstress)

The vowel sound in the stressed syllable of a word is generally *louder*, *longer*, and *higher* in pitch than those in the unstressed syllable(s), which offers a rhythmic contrast within the syllables of a word. A one-syllable word is considered stressed, even though there is no other syllable in the word to offer contrast, and it is not usually notated with a phonetic marker.

Mid-vowels, also known as central vowels, are formed with the jaw partially open, the middle of the tongue arching in the middle of the mouth, the soft palate raised, and the lips in a neutral position. Though in reality there are four mid-vowel sounds in Neutral American, they can be thought of as two sounds that both have a longer and shorter duration, and corresponding IPA symbols to reflect this duration or stress.

Vowel of 'r'. The first two mid-vowels that are differentiated by their duration or stress contain the letter 'r' in the spelling[2]. These sounds are illustrated by the spellings 'ER' and 'er', indicating a longer and shorter duration of the sound. This is reflected in IPA by the use of two different phonetic symbols, which can be thought of as rhythm markers.

(handwritten marginalia: ER = longer)

When the 'ER' sound occurs in the stressed syllable and is longer in duration, as in: '**bur**ning, '**wor**thy, '**Ear**nest, and con'**cur**, it is represented phonetically by /ɝ/.

(handwritten marginalia: Shorter version)

When the 'er' sound occurs in the unstressed syllable and is shorter in duration, as in '**fath**er, '**sug**ar, '**act**or, and per'**suade**, it is represented by /ɚ/.

---

[1] Stressed syllable markings used throughout this book are based on speaking sounds, rather than observing technical rules or dividing syllables according to spelling. See pages 57-61.

[2] Exception: 'colonel' is pronounced with /ɝ/ even though there is no 'r' in the spelling.

The tip of the tongue curls back from the lower teeth when forming Neutral American /ɝ/ and /ɚ/. This curling back, or retroflexion, results in 'r' coloring of the vowel, notated by the small 'curl' or 'tail' on the IPA symbol. Though mid-vowels do not require lip rounding, some people do round slightly when speaking these two sounds.

The word 'murmur' contains these vowels in the stressed and unstressed syllables and is transcribed: /'mɝmɚ/. Speak the word 'murmur' out loud. The lower jaw will drop to a slightly more open position for stressed /ɝ/ than it does for unstressed /ɚ/.

The two remaining mid-vowels are illustrated by the spellings 'UH' and 'uh', which indicate a longer and shorter duration of the sound. This is reflected in IPA by the use of two different symbols, which can be thought of as rhythm markers. When the 'UH' sound occurs in the stressed syllable and is longer in duration, as in 'money, 'public, tough, it is represented in IPA by /ʌ/.

When the 'uh' sound occurs in an unstressed syllable and is shorter in duration, as in: 'sofa, 'Nina, pu'blicity, a'mazed, it is represented in IPA by /ə/. Unstressed /ə/ (uh) is also often used in weak forms of words (see pages 65-72).

The word 'above' contains this sound in both stressed and unstressed[1] syllables, and is transcribed: /ə'bʌv/. Speak the word 'above' out loud. The lower jaw will drop to a slightly more open position for stressed /ʌ/ than for unstressed /ə/.

Key words to help remember the mid-vowels

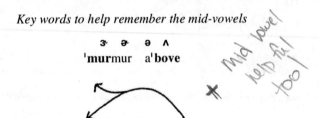

ɝ ɚ ə ʌ

'murmur   a'bove

The tongue tip points up toward the alveolar ridge on /ɝ/ and /ɚ/. The tongue tip rests down behind the lower teeth for /ʌ/ and /ə/. This is represented in the diagram, above.

---

[1] Unstressed syllables of words with 'un' prefixes (as in unhappy and unpleasant) and compound words (as in understood and teacup) are often transcribed with /ʌ/ rather than /ə/.

Back Vowels

Back vowels are made with the back of the tongue arching in relation to the raised soft palate, the tip of the tongue down behind the lower teeth, and the lips in a rounded position. The back of the tongue arch is very low and the lips are <u>un</u>rounded for /ɑ/ (f<u>a</u>ther), the most open back vowel sound.

The jaw is most closed, with the tongue arch most high, and the lips most rounded for /u/ (wh<u>o</u>) and, as the lower jaw opens more and the tongue arch drops, the shapes necessary for the /ʊ/ (w<u>ou</u>ld), /o/ (<u>o</u>'mit), /ɔ/ (<u>a</u>ll), and /ɑ/ (f<u>a</u>ther) sounds are formed[1].

Key words to help remember the back vowels:

u   ʊ   o   ɔ   (ɒ)[2]   ɑ

Wh<u>o</u> w<u>ou</u>ld <u>o</u>'mit <u>a</u>ll (*h<u>o</u>nest*) f<u>a</u>thers?

Additional sample words:

u	**who**	t<u>wo</u>, w<u>oo</u>, bl<u>ue</u>, gr<u>ew</u>, j<u>u</u>do, gl<u>oo</u>my, s<u>ui</u>t
ʊ	**would**	p<u>u</u>t, sh<u>ou</u>ld, t<u>oo</u>k, w<u>o</u>lf, b<u>oo</u>gie-w<u>oo</u>gie
o	**<u>o</u>'mit,**	<u>o</u>'asis, <u>o</u>'bese, <u>o</u>'dometer, <u>O</u>'hio, <u>o</u>'pacity
ɔ	**<u>a</u>ll**	cl<u>aw</u>, s<u>au</u>ce, w<u>a</u>ll, st<u>a</u>lk, l<u>o</u>ng, d<u>o</u>g, <u>o</u>ff[3]
(ɒ)	*none*	(*see footnote #2*)
ɑ	**f<u>a</u>thers**	t<u>o</u>p, <u>o</u>dd, cl<u>o</u>bber, w<u>a</u>tch, b<u>o</u>tch, R<u>o</u>ger

---

[1] There is much discrepancy on how to represent the 'oh' sound in phonetics. Some dictionaries use /o/ in all positions in a word, some use /oʊ/, which represents two blended vowel sounds, and some make a distinction in the sound in stressed and unstressed syllables. Short /o/ is used in the Neutral American section of *Classically Speaking* to represent this sound in the unstressed first syllable, which occurs infrequently. This use facilitates the introduction of this sound along with the other vowels, and highlights the importance of rhythm in well-pronounced speech. The symbol /oʊ/ is used to represent this sound in all other positions in a word.

[2] The symbol /ɒ/ represents another back vowel sometimes referred to as the 'honest' sound. There is variation in opinion, among dictionaries and speech teachers alike, on the use of this sound and symbol in Neutral American. (I feel most Neutral American speakers do not use this sound, and teaching it as part of Neutral American Speech can be counter productive—especially for ESL actors studying NAS—since short, slightly lip-rounded /ɒ/ is often indicative of an accent or dialect. That said, there is difference in opinion....so listen to your teacher.) The /ɒ/ sound is included in the sentence above and in the vowel chart, so that the reader has an idea where this sound fits in with the other back vowels for future Classical American and Standard British study.

[3] Spellings to help differentiate /ɔ/ (<u>a</u>ll) and /ɑ/ (f<u>a</u>ther) words can be found on pages 148-149.

Diphthongs

Sounds composed of two of the previously covered vowels, seamlessly blended together to sound as one, are referred to as diphthongs.

Stress is on the first element of all diphthongs, the second element is rhythmically shorter as notated by / ˘ / over the second element in the IPA symbol. Altogether, there are ten diphthongs, which are generally divided into two groups:

(a)   potentially long diphthongs: /eĭ/ (h<u>ey</u>), /aĭ/ (m<u>y</u>), /ɔĭ/ (b<u>oy</u>), /oŭ/ (g<u>o</u>), /aŭ/ (n<u>ow</u>)

(b)   diphthongs of 'r' which have the short /ɚ/ (er) sound as their second element: /ɪɚ/ (h<u>ere</u>'s), /eɚ/ (th<u>eir</u>), /ʊɚ/ (p<u>oor</u>), /ɔɚ/ (sp<u>or</u>ts), /aɚ/ (c<u>ar</u>)

Key words to help remember the potentially long diphthongs:

eĭ   aĭ   ɔĭ   oŭ   aŭ
H<u>ey</u> m<u>y</u> b<u>oy</u> g<u>o</u> n<u>ow</u>.

Key words to help remember the diphthongs of 'r':

ɪɚ   eɚ   ʊɚ   ɔɚ   aɚ
H<u>ere</u>'s th<u>eir</u> p<u>oor</u> sp<u>or</u>ts c<u>ar</u>.

Additional sample words containing **diphthongs**:

eĭ	<u>ai</u>d, <u>ei</u>ght, sl<u>ay</u>		ɪɚ	<u>ear,</u> st<u>ee</u>r, t<u>ie</u>r
aĭ	<u>I</u>, sk<u>y</u>, g<u>ui</u>de, m<u>i</u>ght		eɚ	<u>air</u>, wh<u>ere</u>, h<u>eir</u>s
ɔĭ	pl<u>oy</u>, g<u>oi</u>ter, <u>oy</u>ster		ʊɚ	s<u>ure</u>, y<u>our</u>, mat<u>ure</u>
oŭ	fl<u>ow</u>, c<u>o</u>de, d<u>ough</u>		ɔɚ	sh<u>ore</u>, w<u>ar</u>t, fl<u>oor</u>
aŭ	c<u>ow</u>, h<u>ou</u>se, l<u>ou</u>nge		aɚ	<u>are</u>, sc<u>ar</u>f, g<u>uar</u>d

Triphthongs

A triphthong is three vowel sounds blended to sound as one. There are two triphthongs that both have short /ɚ/ (er) as the third element: /aɪɚ/ (fi<u>re</u>), /aʊɚ/ (p<u>ower</u>). Depending on the rhythmic demands of the text, they can also be spoken as diphthongs followed by a vowel: /aɪ ɚ/ (fi<u>re</u>) or /aʊ ɚ/ (p<u>ower</u>).

Diphthongs and triphthongs share the same attributes as pure vowel sounds: all are voiced, and are formed by an uninterrupted flow of air vibrating the vocal folds and releasing through the mouth.

The pure vowels that combine and blend are reflected in the phonetic symbols that represent each diphthong. For example, the /ɪɚ/ (h<u>ere</u>) diphthong begins in the position and shape for /ɪ/ and then blends seamlessly into /ɚ/. A smooth movement from the shape of the first element through the shape of the second element results in each particular diphthong.

The first element is longer, louder, and usually more open, than the second and third elements. The shorter second and third elements are notated phonetically by a little unstressed symbol / ˘ / as a reminder of the rhythmic difference within the sound.

Key words to help remember the two possible triphthongs:

aɪɚ   aʊɚ

fi<u>re</u>   p<u>ower</u>

Additional sample words containing triphthongs:

aɪɚ   <u>ire</u>, exp<u>ire</u>, M<u>y</u>er, enqu<u>ire</u>, ch<u>oir</u>s, fr<u>iar</u>

aʊɚ   h<u>our</u>, <u>our</u>, dev<u>our</u>, sh<u>ower</u>, emp<u>ower</u>ing

The Vowel Chart

The following chart diagrams the shape and position of the articulators when forming Front, Mid and Back vowel sounds: lips (spread, neutral or rounded), lower jaw (most closed to most opened—from top to bottom on the chart), tongue arch (high, mid, low—from top to bottom on the chart). The left side of the chart reflects the front of the mouth, the right side, the back.

Vowel Chart

Front	Mid or Central	Back
Lips slightly spread **Lower jaw most closed**	**Lips neutral** **Lower jaw most closed**	**Lips most rounded** **Lower jaw most closed**
High i w<u>e</u> ↓ ɪ w<u>i</u>ll		u wh<u>o</u> **High** ʊ w<u>ou</u>ld ↓
Mid e g<u>e</u>t ↓	ɝ **ER** ɚ <u>er</u> ə <u>uh</u>	o <u>o</u>'mit **Mid** ↓
↓	ʌ **UH**	ɔ <u>a</u>ll ↓
æ th<u>a</u>t **Low** a* l<u>au</u>gh*		ɒ* h<u>o</u>nest* ɑ f<u>a</u>thers **Low**
Lips neutral **Lower jaw most open**	**Lips neutral** **Lower jaw most open**	**Lips unrounded on /ɑ/** **Lower jaw most open**

Vowel, Diphthong and Triphthong Sound Relationships

All words begin with 'p' to focus on vowel, diphthong and triphthong sounds.

Front	Mid or Central	Back
i p<u>ea</u>		u p<u>ooh</u>
ɪ ɪɚ p<u>i</u>t, p<u>ier</u>		ʊ ʊɚ p<u>u</u>t, p<u>oor</u>
e eɪ eɚ p<u>e</u>t, p<u>ay</u>, p<u>air</u>	ɝ 'p<u>er</u>son	o oʊ p<u>o</u>'etic, 'p<u>oe</u>m
æ p<u>a</u>t	ɚ p<u>er</u>'suade	ɔ ɔɪ ɔɚ p<u>aw</u>, p<u>oi</u>se, p<u>ore</u>
a* aɪ aɪɚ aʊ aʊɚ	ə p<u>u</u>'blicity	ɒ* p<u>o</u>sh*
p<u>ass</u>*, p<u>ie</u>, p<u>yre</u>, p<u>ow</u>, p<u>ower</u>	ʌ 'p<u>u</u>blic	ɑ ɑɚ p<u>a</u>, p<u>ar</u>

* Symbols and sample words followed by an asterisk represent sounds spoken in Classical American and/or Standard British, not Neutral American Speech.

IPA SYMBOLS
AND SAMPLE WORDS

VOWELS

All Voiced

Front

/i/	w<u>e</u>, s<u>ee</u>
/ɪ/	w<u>i</u>ll, <u>i</u>s
/e/	g<u>e</u>t, <u>e</u>nd
/æ/	th<u>a</u>t, <u>a</u>pple
/a/*	l<u>au</u>gh*

Mid

/ɝ/	**ER**, **'p<u>er</u>**son
/ɚ/	<u>er</u>, p<u>er</u>**'suade**
/ə/	<u>uh</u>, p<u>u</u>'**bl**icity
/ʌ/	**UH**, **'p<u>u</u>**blic

Back

/u/	wh<u>o</u>, bl<u>ue</u>
/ʊ/	w<u>ou</u>ld, h<u>oo</u>k
/o/	<u>o</u>'**mit,** <u>o</u>'asis
/ɔ/	<u>a</u>ll, cl<u>aw</u>
/ɒ/*	h<u>o</u>nest*
/ɑ/	f<u>a</u>thers, dr<u>a</u>ma

DIPHTHONGS

/eɪ̆/	h<u>ey</u>, <u>a</u>ge
/aɪ̆/	m<u>y</u>, <u>eye</u>
/ɔɪ̆/	b<u>oy</u>, <u>oi</u>l
/oŭ/	g<u>o</u>, <u>o</u>nly
/aŭ/	n<u>ow</u>, <u>ou</u>t
/ɑŭ/*	n<u>ow</u>*

CONSONANTS

	Voiced		Voiceless	
/d/	<u>d</u>i<u>d</u>, fee<u>d</u>	/t/	<u>t</u>o<u>t</u>, fee<u>t</u>
/b/	<u>b</u>i<u>b</u>, ca<u>b</u>	/p/	<u>p</u>o<u>p</u>, ca<u>p</u>
/g/	<u>g</u>ap, pi<u>g</u>	/k/	<u>c</u>ap, pi<u>ck</u>
/m/	<u>m</u>o<u>m</u>, hi<u>m</u>		
/n/	<u>n</u>i<u>n</u>e, o<u>n</u>		
/ŋ/	si<u>ng</u>, ri<u>ng</u>er		
/l/	<u>l</u>i<u>l</u>y, we<u>ll</u>		
/v/	<u>v</u>est, lea<u>v</u>e	/f/	<u>f</u>ee, lea<u>f</u>
/ð/	<u>th</u>em, ba<u>th</u>e	/θ/	<u>th</u>ing, ba<u>th</u>
/z/	<u>z</u>oo, bu<u>zz</u>	/s/	<u>s</u>ue, bu<u>s</u>
/ʒ/	a<u>z</u>ure, bei<u>g</u>e	/ʃ/	<u>sh</u>u<u>sh</u>, ba<u>sh</u>
		/h/**	<u>h</u>e, <u>h</u>ate
/dʒ/	<u>judg</u>e, ri<u>dg</u>e	/t‚ʃ/	<u>ch</u>ur<u>ch</u>, ri<u>ch</u>
/w/	<u>w</u>ent, <u>w</u>e	/hw/*	<u>wh</u>y*
/j/	<u>y</u>ou, <u>y</u>ellow		
/r/	<u>r</u>ed, p<u>r</u>etty		

DIPHTHONGS AND TRIPHTHONGS OF 'R'

/ɪɚ̆/	h<u>ere</u>'s, <u>ear</u>
/eɚ̆/	th<u>eir</u>, <u>air</u>
/ʊɚ̆/	p<u>oor</u>, t<u>our</u>
/ɔɚ̆/	sp<u>orts</u>, <u>oar</u>
/ɑɚ̆/	c<u>ar</u>, <u>are</u>
/aɪɚ̆/	f<u>ire</u>, p<u>yre</u>
/aŭɚ̆/	p<u>ower</u>, h<u>our</u>
/ɑŭɚ̆/*	p<u>ower</u>*

---

* Sounds represented by these symbols and words are *not* covered in Neutral American, but are included for sound changes introduced in Classical American and Standard British.

** Technically, there is a voiced /ɦ/ that occurs between two vowel sounds. Voiced /ɦ/ and voiceless /h/ are nearly indistinguishable, and only /h/ is used throughout this book.

INTERNATIONAL
PHONETIC ALPHABET

Study & Practice

1. Make flashcards of the phonetic symbols.

2. Write words, phrases, or sentences in IPA. See if others can read out loud what has been written.

3. Make up and speak 'nonsense' sounds, words, or phrases out loud. See if others can transcribe what is being said in IPA. The speaker must be very clear and careful to repeat the 'nonsense' sound, word or phrase exactly the same each time it is spoken.

4. Divide the class into teams, one player from each team at the blackboard. A word, author's name, play title, etc. is spoken out loud and must be transcribed correctly for the team to get a point. The transcription can be timed as a race, or not, and can also be done with or without partners. The transcription can be done for Neutral American, Classical American, or Standard British.

5. Make up BINGO cards with the IPA symbols instead of letters of the alphabet. Call out the sounds represented by the symbols. Otherwise, the game is played just like BINGO.

6. HANGMAN can be played with phonetic symbols instead of the letters of the alphabet.

7. Crossword Puzzles. Create crossword puzzles with the answers in IPA transcription.

8. Phonetic Pillows. The brain child of Louis Colaianni, these wonderful pillows are made in the shape of the IPA symbols. They can be tossed, caressed, and used in ways which encourage a kinesthetic exploration of sound.

SAMPLE WORDS TRANSCRIBED IN IPA

Remember: one-syllable words are considered stressed.

1. read / rid /
2. sting / stʰɪŋ /
3. thug / θʌg /
4. then / ðen /
5. calf / kʰæf /
6. whisk / wɪskʰ /
7. fudge / fʌdʒ /
8. worth / wɝθ /
9. book / bʊkʰ /
10. soothe / suð /
11. thunder / ˈθʌndɚ /
12. wealthy / ˈwelθi /
13. hanger / ˈhæŋɚ /
14. longer / ˈlɔŋgɚ /
15. turning / ˈtʰɝnɪŋ /
16. girder / ˈgɝdɚ /
17. attend / əˈtʰend /
18. pleasure / ˈpˌleʒɚ /
19. reaches / ˈritˌʃɪz /
20. things / θɪŋz /

21. loved / lʌvd /
22. wished / wɪʃtʰ /
23. banks / bæŋkˌs /
24. fluffed / flʌftʰ /
25. paused / pʰɔzd /
26. clutches / ˈkˌlʌtˌʃɪz /
27. snoozed / snuzd /
28. lumped / lʌmpˌtʰ /
29. bearded / ˈbɪɚdɪd /
30. faced / feɪstʰ /
31. annoyed / əˈnɔɪd /
32. pounded / ˈpʰaʊndɪd /
33. blindly / ˈblaɪndli /
34. partners / ˈpʰaɚtˌnəz /
35. orthodox / ˈɔɚθədakˌs /
36. sharing / ˈʃeɚrɪŋ /[1]
37. approached / əˈpˌroʊtˌʃtʰ /
38. admiring / ədˈmaɪɚrɪŋ /
39. orchards / ˈɔɚtˌʃədz /
40. kimonos / kʰɪˈmoʊnoʊz /

---

[1] When a vowel or diphthong of 'r' is followed immediately by another vowel or diphthong, a linking consonant /r/ is usually inserted in between, smoothly blending them together. Speakers are often unaware they are using a linking /r/. See page 294 for consonant /r/ and page 300 for additional information on linking with consonant /r/.

IPA TRANSCRIPTION

Consonants and one vowel: / i / (we)

This page is useful if you have studied the consonant IPA symbols. Just add the / i / (we) vowel sound and you can transcribe all of the following words.

Remember: think *sounds* not spelling!

1.   see   _____

2.   tea   _____

3.   Lee   _____

4.   she   _____

5.   fee   _____

6.   bee   _____

7.   bead   _____

8.   ease   _____

9.   each   _____

10.   creek   _____

11.   thee   _____

12.   sleep   _____

13.   jeep   _____

14.   yeast   _____

15.   weave   _____

Answer key page 37

IPA TRANSCRIPTION

Consonants and three vowels: / i / (w<u>e</u>), / u / (wh<u>o</u>), / ɑ / (f<u>a</u>ther)

Numbers 1-15: What is the word written in IPA? Numbers 16-30: Transcribe using IPA consonant symbols and the three vowels listed above.

1.	/tʰu/	~~too~~	16.	me	/mi/
2.	/waʃ/	wash	17.	ah	/æh/
3.	/bruz/	bruise	18.	you	/iu/
4.	/mit‚s/	meets	19.	top	/tɑp/
5.	/dak‚s/	ducks	20.	beat	/bit/
6.	/ˈfluzi/	floosy	21.	spa	/spɑ/
7.	/pʰivd/	peeved	22.	keys	/kis/
8.	/dʒun/	June	23.	glue	/ɡlu/
9.	/bluz/	blues	24.	these	/θiz/
10.	/blatˌʃ/	blotch	25.	thief	/θef/
11.	/blitˌʃ/	bleach	26.	rules	/ruʊlz/
12.	/ˈkˌripʰi/	creepy	27.	John's	/ʒɑns/
13.	/ʃak‚s/	snake	28.	sheets	/sits/
14.	/ˈkˌwizi/	queasy	29.	wheezy	/wizi/
15.	/pʰutˌʃ/	pooch	30.	choosy	/tʃuz/

Useful Guidelines:

1. When an 's' is added to the end of a noun making it plural or possessive, or to the end of a third-person singular verb, the 's' is pronounced /z/ when the sound directly preceding it is voiced, as in: dogs, ribs, cows, Phil's, Brad's, Sue's, runs, plays.

2. A stressed syllable is that part of a word which receives the strongest emphasis. This is marked in IPA by a / ' / symbol before the stressed syllable, as in numbers 6, above. One-syllable words are considered stressed but are not notated with a phonetic marker.

Note. If you can't tell what syllable is stressed, place your hand on the underside of your chin. The jaw is usually most open on the vowel sound of the stressed syllable, though there are some exceptions. If you are still having difficulty, try over-stressing various syllables. The 'correct' pronunciation will probably become more obvious.

Answer key page 37

IPA TRANSCRIPTION

Consonants and Front Vowels

key words: we will get that

Numbers 1-15: Transcribe using IPA consonant symbols and the four front vowel sounds. Numbers 16-30: What is the word that's written in IPA? IPA symbols page 26.

#	Word	Answer	#	IPA	Answer
1.	he	/hi/	16.	/fænz/	fans
2.	yes	/jɛs/	17.	/henz/	hens
3.	bad	/bæd/	18.	/rɪŋz/	rings
4.	fish	/fɪt/	19.	/tʰɪmz/	tims
5.	gym	/gɪm/	20.	/milz/	meals
6.	path	/pæθ/	21.	/bæŋkˌs/	banks
7.	Jack's	/ʒæks/	22.	/grif/	greif
8.	when	/wɛn/	23.	/ʃitˌs/	sheets
9.	wrist	/rɪst/	24.	/drɪld/	drilled
10.	seeds	/sidz/	25.	/wɪʃtʰ/	wished
11.	quest	/kwɛst/	26.	/pʰækˌtʰ/	packed
12.	thinks	/θɪnks/	27.	/pʰend/	pend
13.	matches	/mætsɛs/	28.	/θæŋkˌtʰ/	thanked
14.	bleached	/blitʃɛd/	29.	/siðd/	seethed
15.	teething	/tiθŋ/	30.	/ˈskˌritˌʃɪz/	screeches

Useful Guidelines:

1. When an 's' is added to the end of a noun making it plural or possessive, or to the end of a third-person singular verb, the 's' is pronounced /z/ when the sound directly preceding it is voiced, as in: dogs, ribs, cows, Phil's, Brad's, Sue's, runs, plays.

2. When a word ends in /s, z, t∫ or dʒ/ and 'es' is added to make the word plural or possessive, a separate syllable ending in /ɪz/ is formed, as in: losses, quizzes, batches, judges.

3. When 'ed' is added to the end of a verb, the 'ed' ending is pronounced as /t/ if the sound directly preceding the 'ed' is a voiceless consonant, as in: picked, washed, leafed, sipped, priced.

Answer key page 37

IPA TRANSCRIPTION

Consonants and Mid-Vowel Concentration

key words: 'murmur a'bove

Numbers 1-10 and 17-25: Transcribe using IPA consonants, front, and mid-vowel symbols. Numbers 11-15 and 26-30: What is the word that's written in IPA?

1.	ton	/tənl/	16.	actors	/æktors/
2.	thus	/ðəs/	17.	worst	/wɚst/
3.	pizza	/pitsn/	18.	hermit	/hɚmɪt/
4.	thrust	/θrəst/	19.	fevers	/fivɚs/
5.	attack	/ntæk/	20.	cursed	/kɚst/
6.	sunny	/snni/	21.	blurbs	/blɚbs/
7.	junked	/jʌnked/	22.	observed	/əb sɚved/
8.	among	/nmɔng/	23.	churlish	/tʃɚɪʃ/
9.	anemic	/nnimɪk/	24.	PERmits	/ˈpɚmɪts/
10.	undone	/nndən/	25.	perMITS	/pɚˈmɪts/
11.	/əˈtʃiv/	achieve	26.	/ˈtˌreʒəz/	treasures
12.	/θʌmz/	thumbs	27.	/ˈkʰʌvəd/	covered
13.	/ˈdʒʌstʰɪs/	justice	28.	/ˈθʌndə/	thunder
14.	/ˈbʌsɪz/	buses	29.	/ˈfɝ ðəd/	furthered
15.	/əˈgenstʰ/	against	30.	/ˈdʒʌmpʰəz/	jumpes

Useful Guideline:

A stressed syllable is that part of a word which receives the strongest emphasis, marked in IPA by a / ' / symbol before the stressed syllable as in: / 'blidɪŋ / (bleeding). One-syllable words are considered stressed, but are not usually notated with a phonetic marker.

Note. Having trouble? Place your hand on the underside of your chin; the jaw is usually most open on the vowel of the stressed syllable, though there are some exceptions. For another approach, try over-stressing various syllables. The 'correct' pronunciation will probably be more obvious to you.

Answer key page 37

IPA TRANSCRIPTION

Consonants and Back Vowel Concentration

key words: wh<u>o</u> w<u>ou</u>ld <u>o</u>'mit[1] <u>a</u>ll f<u>a</u>thers

Numbers 1-13 and 19-31: Transcribe using the IPA symbols for consonants, back vowels, and the front vowel in 'w<u>i</u>ll'. Numbers 14-18 and 32-36: What is the word transcribed in IPA?

1. fall /fɔl/
2. loft /lɔft/
3. pull /pʊl/
4. rude /rud/
5. chop /tʃɑp/
6. talk /tɔlk/
7. tock /tɔk/
8. lose /luzl/
9. obese /obis/
10. song /sɔŋg/
11. could /kʊld/
12. moth /mɔθ/
13. rouge /ruʒ/
14. /stʰʊd/ stood
15. /watʃ/ watch
16. /kɾʊkʰ/ crook
17. /swav/ suave
18. /sam, salm/ Sam

19. dogs /dɔgs/
20. blahs /blɑhs/
21. goods /gʊds/
22. tossed /tɔsd/
23. Rob's /rɔbs/
24. squalls /skwɔls/
25. clauses /klɔses/
26. Brook's /brʊks/
27. cruises /kruses/
28. fawned /fɔned/
29. viewed /vɪwld/
30. longed /lɔŋgd/
31. cooked /kʊked/
32. /spˌjud/ spewed
33. /bukˌtʰ/ bucket
34. /stʰupˌtʰ/ stooped
35. /batˌʃtʰ/ botched
36. /lɔntˌʃtʰ/ bunched

---

[1] Remember, /o/ is used in the unstressed first syllable, only. See pages 148-149 for spelling guidelines for /ɔ/ (<u>a</u>ll) sounds. A complete list of phonetic symbols appears on page 26.

Answer key page 38

(handwritten margin notes:)
ɪ ɪ e æ
wе will get that
ʊ ʊ ɔ ə ɑ
Who would omit all bothers

eɪ ɑɪ ɔɪ oʊ ɑʊ
Hey my boy go now
ɪɚ eɚ ʊɚ ɔɚ ɑɚ
Here's their poor sports car.

ə bove
ʌ
ɝ ɚ
murmur

ɔɪɚ
ɑʊɚ

IPA TRANSCRIPTION

Consonants and Diphthongs

key words: h**ey** m**y** b**oy** g**o** n**ow**

Numbers 1-15 and 21-35: Transcribe using the IPA consonant, vowel, and diphthong symbols. Numbers 16-18 and 36-38: What is the word that is transcribed in IPA?

1. bay /beɪ/
2. joy /dʒɔɪ/
3. line /lɑɪn/
4. cope /koʊp/
5. out /ɑʊt/
6. bribe /brɑɪb/
7. poise /pɔɪz/
8. grade /greɪd/
9. town /tɑʊn/
10. boil /bɔɪl/
11. wild /wɑɪld/
12. stove /stoʊv/
13. price /prɑɪs/
14. groin /grɔɪn/
15. south /sɑʊθ/
16. /greɪv/ grave
17. /roʊg/ rogue
18. /əd'vɑɪs/ advise

19. Roy's /rɔɪz/
20. goats /goʊts/
21. Dave's /deɪvz/
22. moist /mɔɪst/
23. doubts /dɑʊts/
24. crimes /krɑɪmz/
25. raged /reɪdʒd/
26. Mike's /mɑɪks/
27. bolsters /boʊlstɚ/
28. stages /steɪdʒez/
29. toasted /toʊsted/
30. striped /strɑɪpt/
31. avoided /ʌvɔɪded/
32. croaked /kroʊkt/
33. sliding /slɑɪdɪŋ/
34. /ɪn'geɪdʒd/ engaged
35. /'grɑʊndɪd/ grounded
36. /pʰɚ'lɔɪnd/ purloined

Answer key page 38

IPA TRANSCRIPTION power ɔʊɚ

Consonants, Diphthongs and Triphthongs of 'r'

key words: here's their poor sports car / fire power

Transcribe using the IPA consonants and vowels, and the diphthongs and triphthongs of 'r'.

#	Word	IPA	#	Word	IPA
1.	bear	/beɚ/	19.	spear	/spIɚ/
2.	short	/ʃɔɚt/	20.	hearts	/hɑɚts/
3.	chart	/tʃɑɚt/	21.	mature	/mʌtʊɚ/
4.	we're	/wIɚ/	22.	square	/skweɚ/
5.	tour	/tʊɚ/	23.	restore	/ristɔɚ/
6.	clear	/klIɚ/	24.	perspire	/pɝˈspɔɪɚ/
7.	fair	/feɚ/	25.	shower	/ʃaʊɚ/
8.	snort	/snɔɚt/	26.	parsley	/pɑɚsli/
9.	harsh	/hɑɚʃ/	27.	sworn	/swɔɚn/
10.	pour	/pʊɚ/	28.	cowers	/kaʊɚz/
11.	snarls	/snɑɚlz/	29.	wearable	/weɚəbl/
12.	retorts	/ritɔɚts/	30.	remarked	/rimɑɚkt/
13.	assure	/ʌʃʊɚ/	31.	deplores	/dɪplɔɚz/
14.	abhors	/æbʊɚz/	32.	charming	/tʃɑɚmɪŋ/
15.	glares	/gleɚz/	33.	transpire	/trænspɔɪɚ/
16.	career	/kʌrIɚ/	34.	prayers	/preɚz/
17.	orders	/ɔɚdɚz/	35.	starched	/stɑɚtʃt/
18.	argues	/ɑɚguz/	36.	conspire	/kʌnspɔɪɚ/

Answer key page 38

IPA TRANSCRIPTION

All Sounds[1] in the key words:

we will get that

'murmur a'bove

who would o'mit all fathers

hey my boy go now

here's their poor sports car

fire power

1. chairs /tʃeɚz/
2. echos /ekoz/
3. sneers /snɪɚz/
4. market /maɚket/
5. portly /pɔɚtli/
6. sincere /sɪnsɪɚ/
7. shining /ʃaɪnɪŋ/
8. employed /emplɔɪd/
9. Queen /kwin/
10. implied /ɪmplaɪd/
11. hollow /halo/
12. clowns /klaʊnz/
13. patches /paetʃez/
14. winked /wɪnkt/
15. modified /madəfaɪd/

16. foil /fɔɪl/
17. cubes /kjubz/
18. spies /spaɪz/
19. surely /ʃoʊrli/
20. overt /ovɝt/
21. baked /beɪkt/
22. trousers /traʊzəz/
23. strokes /stroʊks/
24. witches /wɪtʃez/
25. authors /ɔθɚt/
26. smudged /smʌdʒd/
27. neighbors /neɪbəz/
28. half hour /half aʊɚ/
29. movie star /muvi staɚ/
30. performance /pɝtʃʊmens/

---

[1] A complete list of phonetic symbols appears on page 26. Remember, /o/ is used in the unstressed first syllable only. Spelling guidelines for /ɔ/ (all) can be found on pages 148-149.

Answer key page 38

ANSWER KEY

Page 29—one vowel

1. /si/
2. /tʰi/
3. /li/
4. /ʃi/
5. /fi/
6. /bi/
7. /bid/
8. /iz/
9. /it̩ʃ/
10. /k̩rikʰ/
11. /ði/
12. /slipʰ/
13. /dʒipʰ/
14. /jistʰ/
15. /wiv/

Page 30—three vowels

1. to
2. wash
3. brews
4. meets
5. docks
6. floozy
7. peeved
8. June
9. blues
10. blotch
11. bleach
12. creepy
13. shocks
14. queasy
15. pooch
16. /mi/
17. /ɑ/
18. /ju/
19. /tʰapʰ/
20. /bitʰ/
21. /spʰɑ/
22. /kʰiz/
23. /glu/
24. /ðiz/
25. /θif/
26. /rulz/
27. /dʒɑnz/
28. /ʃit̩s/
29. /ˈwizi/
30. /ˈt̩ʃuzi/

Page 31—front vowels

1. /hi/
2. /jes/
3. /bæd/
4. /fɪʃ/
5. /dʒɪm/
6. /pʰæθ/
7. /dʒæk̩s/
8. /wen/
9. /rɪstʰ/
10. /sidz/
11. /k̩westʰ/
12. /θɪŋk̩s/
13. /ˈmæt̩ʃɪz/
14. /blit̩ʃtʰ/
15. /ˈtʰiðɪŋ/
16. fans
17. hens
18. rings
19. Tim's
20. meals
21. banks
22. grief
23. sheets
24. drilled
25. wished
26. packed
27. penned
28. thanked
29. seethed
30. screeches

Page 32—mid-vowels

1. /tʰʌn/
2. /ðʌs/
3. /ˈpʰit̩sə/
4. /θrʌstʰ/
5. /əˈtʰækʰ/
6. /ˈsʌni/
7. /dʒʌŋk̩tʰ/
8. /əˈmʌn/
9. /əˈnimɪkʰ/
10. /ʌnˈdʌn/
11. achieve
12. thumbs
13. justice
14. busses
15. against
16. /ˈæk̩tʰɚz/
17. /wɝstʰ/
18. /ˈhɝmɪtʰ/
19. /ˈfivɚz/
20. /kʰɝstʰ/
21. /blɚbz/
22. /əbˈzɝvd/
23. /ˈt̩ʃɚlɪʃ/
24. /ˈpʰɝmɪt̩s/
25. /pʰəˈmɪt̩s/
26. treasures
27. covered
28. thunder
29. furthered
30. jumpers

ANSWER KEY

Page 33—back vowels

1. /fɔl/	19. /dɔgz/		
2. /lɔftʰ/	20. /blɑz/		
3. /pʰʊl/	21. /gʊdz/		
4. /rud/	22. /tʰɔstʰ/		
5. /t‚ʃɑpʰ/	23. /rɑbz/		
6. /tʰɔkʰ/	24. /sk‚wɔlz/		
7. /tʰakʰ/	25. /ˈk‚lɔzɪz/		
8. /luz/	26. /brʊk‚s/		
9. /oˈbis/	27. /ˈk‚ruzɪz/		
10. /sɔŋ/	28. /fɔnd/		
11. /kʰʊd/	29. /vjud/		
12. /mɔθ/	30. /lɔŋd/		
13. /ruʒ/	31. /kʰʊk‚tʰ/		
14. stood	32. spewed		
15. watch	33. booked		
16. crook	34. stooped		
17. suave	35. botched		
18. psalm	36. launched		

Page 34—diphthongs

1. /beĭ/	19. /rɔĭz/		
2. /dʒɔĭ/	20. /goŭt‚s/		
3. /laĭn/	21. /deĭvz/		
4. /kʰoŭpʰ/	22. /mɔĭstʰ/		
5. /aŭtʰ/	23. /daŭt‚s/		
6. /braĭb/	24. /k‚raĭmz/		
7. /pʰɔĭz/	25. /reĭdʒd/		
8. /greĭd/	26. /maĭk‚s/		
9. /tʰaŭn/	27. /ˈboŭlstʰɚz/		
10. /bɔĭl/	28. /ˈstʰeĭdʒɪz/		
11. /waĭld/	29. /ˈtʰoŭstʰɪd/		
12. /stʰoŭv/	30. /st‚raĭp‚tʰ/		
13. /p‚raĭs/	31. /əˈvɔĭdɪd/		
14. /grɔĭn/	32. /k‚roŭk‚tʰ/		
15. /saŭθ/	33. /ˈslaĭdɪŋ/		
16. grave	34. engaged		
17. rogue	35. grounded		
18. advice	36. purloined		

Page 35—diphth/triphthongs of 'r'

1. /beɚ/	19. /spʰɪɚ/		
2. /ʃɔɚtʰ/	20. /haɚt‚s/		
3. /t‚ʃaɚtʰ/	21. /məˈt‚ʃʊɚ/		
4. /wɪɚ/	22. /sk‚weɚ/		
5. /tʰʊɚ/	23. /rɪˈstʰɔɚ/		
6. /k‚lɪɚ/	24. /pʰəˈspʰaĭɚ/		
7. /feɚ/	25. /ʃaŭɚ/		
8. /snɔɚtʰ/	26. /ˈpʰaɚsli/		
9. /haɚʃ/	27. /swɔɚn/		
10. /pʰɔɚ/	28. /kʰaŭɚz/		
11. /snaɚlz/	29. /ˈweɚrəbl/		
12. /rɪˈtʰɔɚt‚s/	30. /rɪˈmaɚk‚tʰ/		
13. /əˈʃʊɚ/	31. /dɪˈp‚lɔɚz/		
14. /əbˈhɔɚz/	32. /ˈt‚ʃaɚmɪŋ/		
15. /gleɚz/	33. /t‚rænsˈpʰaĭɚ/		
16. /kʰəˈrɪɚ/	34. /p‚reɚz/		
17. /ˈɔɚdɚz/	35. /stʰaɚt‚ʃtʰ/		
18. /ˈaɚgjuz/	36. /kʰənˈspʰaĭɚ/		

Page 36—all sounds

1. /t‚ʃeɚz/	16. /fɔĭl/
2. /ˈekʰoŭz/	17. /k‚jubz/
3. /snɪɚz/	18. /spʰaĭz/
4. /ˈmaɚkʰɪtʰ/	19. /ˈʃʊɚli/
5. /ˈpʰɔɚt‚li/	20. /oˈvɝtʰ/
6. /sɪnˈsɪɚ/	21. /beĭk‚tʰ/
7. /ˈʃaĭnɪŋ/	22. /ˈt‚raŭzɚz/
8. /ɪmˈp‚lɔĭd/	23. /st‚roŭk‚s/
9. /k‚win/	24. /ˈwɪt‚ʃɪz/
10. /ɪmˈp‚laĭd/	25. /ˈɔθɚz/
11. /ˈhaloŭ/	26. /smʌdʒd/
12. /k‚laŭnz/	27. /ˈneĭbɚz/
13. /ˈpʰætˌʃɪz/	28. /hæf aŭɚ/
14. /wɪŋk‚tʰ/	29. /ˈmuvi stʰaɚ/
15. /ˈmadəfaĭd/	30. /pʰəˈfɔɚmənz/

VOWEL & DIPHTHONG
LENGTH

Note: This section has been included especially for those students with English as a second language. (Previous word lists can be transcribed with dots for length. See the answer keys on pages 44-45, which are marked for length.)

All vowel sounds are intrinsically longer in stressed syllables, especially in words that are **operative** or **key** to the meaning.

But, there are five sounds that have the potential to be much longer in comparison to the others.

Five of thirteen vowels
can be classified either long, half-long, or short

These five vowels can be remembered by the line:

A̲ll dr̲ama u̲ses the̲se wo̲rds!

Long

In a stressed syllable:

(a)   before a voiced[1] consonant: t̲all, c̲alm, sh̲oes, tr̲ees, w̲orld

(b)   as the last sound of the word: s̲aw, h̲a! d̲o, fl̲ee, bl̲ur

$$\text{ɔː} \quad \text{ɑː} \quad \text{uː} \quad \text{iː} \quad \text{ɜː}$$

In IPA, the double dots, or colon, indicate full-length.

---

[1] Voiced and voiceless consonants are listed on pages 17 and 26.

Half-Long

In a stressed syllable:

(a)   before a voiceless consonant within a word (very common): awful, chopping, boost, leashing, perk

(b)   before another vowel sound within a word (less common): sawing, doing, seeing

(c)   before a voiced consonant followed by a voiceless consonant (much less common): salt, burnt

ɔ· ɑ· u· i· ɝ

In IPA, the single dot indicates half-length.

Short

In an unstressed syllable:

(a)   (less common) audacity, nuance, unique, methinks, Mercutio[1]

In unstressed weak[2] forms:

(b)   (very common) you, do, he, me, she, be, we, the, her, were

ɔ ɑ u i ɝ·

In IPA, no dots are used.

The eight remaining vowels are always classified as short

These are included in the line:

ʌ ɚ ʊ ə o eɪ æ
Mother took a poetics class[3].

---

[1]   With very few exceptions, 'er' in an unstressed syllable is transcribed /ɚ/.

[2]   Weak forms are covered on pages 65-72.

[3]   The word 'a' is pronounced with the weak form, a very short 'uh' sound. 'Poetics' is pronounced with pure /o/ in the unstressed first syllable.

Diphthong Length

Diphthongs are two vowel sounds blended to sound as one. The first element is stressed and is therefore longer, louder, and more open than the rest of the sound. This is especially important to remember when lengthening or stressing a diphthong in an operative or key word in order to make a point.

Five Diphthongs Classified Long[1]

These five diphthongs can be remembered by the line:

eˑĭ· aˑĭ· ɔˑĭ· oˑŭ· aˑŭ·

H<u>ey</u> m<u>y</u> b<u>oy</u> g<u>o</u> n<u>ow</u>.

One dot follows each element of a long diphthong in IPA.

In the <u>stressed</u> syllable:

(a)   as the last sound of the word: d<u>ay</u>, wh<u>y</u>, ah<u>oy</u>, n<u>o</u>, n<u>ow</u>

(b)   before one or more voiced consonants within the word: g<u>a</u>ve, s<u>i</u>ze, s<u>oi</u>l, h<u>o</u>me, imp<u>ou</u>nd.

Short Diphthongs

These **same** five diphthongs are classified short in all other instances. In addition, **diphthongs and triphthongs of 'r'**, which are represented by the phrases *'here's their poor sports car'* and *'fire power'*, are always categorized as short and never transcribed with dots.

    Note. The practice transcription words on pages 29-36 can be transcribed with or without length markers. If you choose to transcribe with dots for length, use the answer key on pages 44-45.

---

[1] It is my experience that insisting a diphthong must be in the stressed *first* syllable of a word in order to be considered long overcomplicates, and serves as an ineffective learning tool for most actors, whether English is their first or second language. Therefore, for actors, I advocate the simplified version of the guideline listed above.

SOUND COMPARISONS

(transcribed in IPA with initial 'b' and with dots for length)

Remember: one-syllable words are considered stressed.

Front Vowels

/iː/ (we) as in: bean /biːn/
/ɪ/ (will) as in: bin /bɪn/
/e/ (get) as in: Ben /ben/
/æ/ (that) as in: ban /bæn/

Mid-Vowels

/ɜː/ (ER) as in: burn /bɜːn/
/ɚ/ (er) as in: burner /'bɜːnɚ/
/ə/ (uh) as in: Buddha /'buːdə/
/ʌ/ (UH) as in: bun /bʌn/

Back Vowels

/uː/ (who) as in: boon /buːn/
/ʊ/ (would) as in: book /bʊk/
/o/ (o'mit) as in: bodega /bo'deˑɪˑgə/
/ɔː/ (all) as in: ball /bɔːl/
/ɑː/ (fathers) as in: bomb /bɑːm/

Diphthongs

/eˑɪˑ/ (hey) as in: bay /beˑɪˑ/
/aˑɪˑ/ (my) as in: bye /baˑɪˑ/
/ɔˑɪˑ/ (boy) as in: boy /bɔˑɪˑ/
/oˑʊˑ/ (go) as in: bone /boˑʊˑn/
/aˑʊˑ/ (now) as in: bow /baˑʊˑ/

/ɪɚ/ (here) as in: beer /bɪɚ/
/eɚ/ (their) as in: bear /beɚ/
/ʊɚ/ (poor) as in: boor /bʊɚ/
/ɔɚ/ (sports) as in: bore /bɔɚ/
/ɑɚ/ (car) as in: bar /bɑɚ/

Triphthongs

/aɪɚ/ (fire) as in: buyer /baɪɚ/
/aʊɚ/ (power) as in: bower /baʊɚ/

SAMPLE WORDS TRANSCRIBED IN IPA

(transcribed with dots for length[1], aspiration, and linking 'r')

1.	freed	/ friːd /	21.	gloved	/ glʌvd /
2.	sling	/ slɪŋ /	22.	pushed	/ pʰʊʃtʰ /
3.	young	/ jʌŋ /	23.	thanks	/ θæŋkˌs /
4.	them	/ ðem /	24.	coughs	/ kʰɔˑfs /
5.	half	/ hæf /	25.	pauses	/ ˈpʰɔːzɪz /
6.	whim	/ wɪm /	26.	touched	/ tʰʌtˌʃtʰ /
7.	ridge	/ rɪdʒ /	27.	bruised	/ bruːzd /
8.	mirth	/ mɝˑθ /	28.	zeros	/ ˈzɪɚˑroŭz /
9.	sugar	/ ˈʃʊgɚ /	29.	appeared	/ əˈpʰɪɚd /
10.	smooth	/ smuːð /	30.	thumped	/ θʌmpˌtʰ /
11.	under	/ ˈʌndɚ /	31.	poised	/ pʰɔˑɪ̆ˑzd /
12.	deathly	/ ˈdeθli /	32.	Martha's	/ ˈmɑɚ̆θəz /
13.	singer	/ ˈsɪŋɚ /	33.	quietly	/ ˈkˌwaˑɪ̆ˑətˌli /
14.	finger	/ ˈfɪŋgɚ /	34.	disgraced	/ dɪsˈgreɪstʰ /
15.	falling	/ ˈfɔːlɪŋ /	35.	tornados	/ tʰɔɚ̆ˈneˑɪ̆ˑdoŭz /
16.	server	/ ˈsɝˑːvɚ /	36.	compared	/ kʰəmˈpʰeɚ̆d /
17.	drama	/ ˈdrɑːmə /	37.	grounded	/ ˈgraˑŭˑndɪd /
18.	measured	/ ˈmeʒɚd /	38.	questions	/ ˈkˌwestˌʃənz /
19.	patches	/ ˈpʰætˌʃɪz /	39.	telephones	/ ˈtʰeləfoŭnz /
20.	strings	/ stˌrɪŋz /	40.	perspiring	/ pʰəˈspʰaɪ̆ɚ̆rɪŋ /

---

[1] Remember: one-syllable words are considered stressed.

ANSWER KEY: transcribed with dots for length

Page 29—one vowel

1. /si:/
2. /tʰi:/
3. /li:/
4. /ʃi:/
5. /fi:/
6. /bi:/
7. /bi:d/
8. /i:z/
9. /i·tˌʃ/
10. /kˌri·kʰ/
11. /ði:/
12. /sli·pʰ/
13. /dʒi·pʰ/
14. /ji·stʰ/
15. /wi:v/

Page 30—three vowels

1. to (too, two)
2. wash
3. brews (bruise)
4. meets (meats)
5. docks
6. floozy
7. peeved
8. June
9. blues
10. blotch
11. bleach
12. creepy
13. shocks
14. queasy
15. pooch
16. /mi:/
17. /ɑ:/
18. /ju:/
19. /tʰɑ·pʰ/
20. /bi·tʰ/
21. /spʰɑ:/
22. /kʰi:z/
23. /glu:/
24. /ði:z/
25. /θi·f/
26. /ru:lz/
27. /dʒɑ:nz/
28. /ʃi·tˌs/
29. /ˈwi:zi/
30. /ˈtˌʃu:zi/

Page 31—front vowels

1. /hi:/
2. /jes/
3. /bæd/
4. /fɪʃ/
5. /dʒɪm/
6. /pʰæθ/
7. /dʒækˌs/
8. /wen/
9. /rɪstʰ/
10. /si:dz/
11. /kˌwestʰ/
12. /θɪŋkˌs/
13. /ˈmætˌʃɪz/
14. /bli·tˌʃtʰ/
15. /ˈtʰi:ðɪŋ/
16. fans
17. hens
18. rings
19. Tim's
20. meals
21. banks
22. grief
23. sheets
24. drilled
25. wished
26. packed
27. penned
28. thanked
29. seethed
30. screeches

Page 32—mid-vowels

1. /tʰʌn/
2. /ðʌs/
3. /ˈpʰi·tˌsə/
4. /θrʌstʰ/
5. /əˈtʰækʰ/
6. /ˈsʌni/
7. /dʒʌŋkˌtʰ/
8. /əˈmʌn/
9. /əˈni:mɪkʰ/
10. /ʌnˈdʌn/
11. achieve
12. thumbs
13. justice
14. busses
15. against
16. /ˈækˌtʰɚz/
17. /wɜ·stʰ/
18. /ˈhɜ·mɪtʰ/
19. /ˈfi:vɚz/
20. /kʰɜ·stʰ/
21. /blɜ·bz/
22. /əbˈzɜ·vd/
23. /ˈtˌʃɜ·lɪʃ/
24. /ˈpʰɜ·mɪtˌs/
25. /pʰɚˈmɪtˌs/
26. treasures
27. covered
28. thunder
29. furthered
30. jumpers

ANSWER KEY: transcribed with dots for length

Page 33—back vowels

1. /fɔːl/	19. /dɔːgz/
2. /lɔ·ftʰ/	20. /blɑːz/
3. /pʰʊl/	21. /gʊdz/
4. /ruːd/	22. /tʰɔ·stʰ/
5. /tˌʃɑ·pʰ/	23. /rɑːbz/
6. /tʰɔ·kʰ/	24. /skˌwɔːlz/
7. /tʰɑ·kʰ/	25. /ˈkˌlɔːzɪz/
8. /luːz/	26. /brʊkˌs/
9. /oˈbi·s/	27. /ˈkˌruːzɪz/
10. /sɔːŋ/	28. /fɔːnd/
11. /kʰʊd/	29. /vjuːd/
12. /mɔ·θ/	30. /lɔːŋd/
13. /ruːʒ/	31. /kʰʊkˌtʰ/
14. stood	32. spewed
15. watch	33. booked
16. crook	34. stooped
17. suave	35. botched
18. psalm	36. launched

Page 34—diphthongs

1. /beˈɪ̆·/	19. /rɔˈɪ̆·z/
2. /dʒɔˈɪ̆·/	20. /goʊ̆tˌs/
3. /lɑˈɪ̆·n/	21. /deˈɪ̆·vz/
4. /kʰoʊ̆pʰ/	22. /mɔɪstʰ/
5. /aʊ̆tʰ/	23. /daʊ̆tˌs/
6. /brɑˈɪ̆·b/	24. /kˌrɑˈɪ̆·mz/
7. /pʰɔˈɪ̆·z/·	25. /reˈɪ̆·dʒd/
8. /greˈɪ̆·d/	26. /maɪ̆kˌs/
9. /tʰɑ·ŭ·n/	27. /ˈboˈʊ̆·lstʰə·z/
10. /bɔˈɪ̆·l/	28. /ˈstʰeˈɪ̆·dʒɪz/
11. /waˈɪ̆·ld/	29. /ˈtʰoʊ̆stʰɪd/
12. /stʰo·ŭ·v/	30. /stˌraɪpˌtʰ/
13. /pˌraɪ̆s/	31. /əˈvɔˈɪ̆·dɪd/
14. /grɔˈɪ̆·n/	32. /kˌroʊ̆kˌtʰ/
15. /saʊ̆θ/	33. /ˈslaˈɪ̆·dɪŋ/
16. grave	34. engaged
17. rogue	35. grounded
18. advice	36. purloined

Page 35—diphth/triphthongs of 'r'

1. /beɚ̆·/	19. /spʰɪɚ̆·/
2. /ʃɔɚ̆tʰ/	20. /haɚ̆tˌs/
3. /tˌʃaɚ̆tʰ/	21. /məˈtˌʃʊɚ̆·/
4. /wɪɚ̆·/	22. /skˌweɚ̆·/
5. /tʰʊɚ̆·/	23. /rɪˈstʰɔɚ̆·/
6. /kˌlɪɚ̆·/	24. /pʰɚ̆ˈspʰaɪɚ̆·/
7. /feɚ̆·/	25. /ʃaʊ̆ɚ̆·/
8. /snɔɚ̆·tʰ/	26. /ˈpʰaɚ̆·sli/
9. /haɚ̆·ʃ/	27. /swɔɚ̆·n/
10. /pʰɔɚ̆·/	28. /kʰaʊ̆ɚ̆·z/
11. /snaɚ̆·lz/	29. /ˈweɚ̆·rəbl̩/
12. /rɪˈtʰɔɚ̆·tˌs/	30. /rɪˈmaɚ̆·kˌtʰ/
13. /əˈʃʊɚ̆·/	31. /dɪˈpˌlɔɚ̆·z/
14. /əbˈhɔɚ̆·z/	32. /ˈtˌʃaɚ̆·mɪn/
15. /gleɚ̆·z/	33. /tˌrænˈspʰaɪɚ̆·/
16. /kʰəˈrɪɚ̆·/	34. /pˌreɚ̆·z/
17. /ˈɔɚ̆·dɚ·z/	35. /stʰaɚ̆·tˌʃtʰ/
18. /ˈaɚ̆·gjuz/	36. /kʰənˈspʰaɪɚ̆·/

Page 36—all sounds

1. /tˌʃeɚ̆·z/	16. /fɔˈɪ̆·l/
2. /ˈekʰoʊ̆z/	17. /kˌjuːbz/
3. /snɪɚ̆·z/	18. /spʰaˈɪ̆·z/·
4. /ˈmaɚ̆·kʰɪtʰ/	19. /ˈʃʊɚ̆·li/
5. /ˈpʰɔɚ̆tˌli/	20. /oˈvɚ·tʰ/
6. /sɪnˈsɪɚ̆·/	21. /beɪ̆kˌtʰ/
7. /ˈʃaˈɪ̆·nɪŋ/	22. /ˈtˌraˈʊ̆·zɚ·z/
8. /ɪmˈpʰˌlɔˈɪ̆·d/	23. /stˌroʊ̆kˌs/
9. /kˌwiːn/	24. /ˈwɪtˌʃɪz/
10. /ɪmˈpʰˌlaˈɪ̆·d/	25. /ˈɔ·θɚ·z/
11. /ˈhɑːloʊ̆/	26. /smʌdʒd/
12. /kˌlaˈʊ̆·nz/	27. /ˈneˈɪ̆·bə·z/
13. /ˈpʰætˌʃɪz/	28. /hæf aʊ̆ɚ̆·/
14. /wɪŋkˌtʰ/	29. /ˈmuːvi stʰaɚ̆·/
15. /ˈmɑːdəfaɪd/	30. /pʰɚ̆ˈfɔɚ̆·məns/

NEUTRAL AMERICAN DIALECT

AUDIO SELECTIONS▶
Carman Lacivita and Patricia Fletcher

RHYTHM HIGHLIGHTERS

"Contenting myself with the certainty that Music, in its various modes of metre, rhythm, and rhyme, is of so vast a moment in Poetry as never to be wisely rejected—is so vitally important an adjunct, that he is simply silly who declines its assistance…"

(Edgar Allan Poe: The Poetic Principle)

The following items accentuate or highlight the rhythmic qualities inherent in spoken English, and are crucial for effectively playing well-pronounced characters or adjusting contemporary speech to the demands of classical texts.

Rhythm Highlighters pertaining to specific vowels and consonants are covered in specific sound sections, including:

Linking

To Avoid Glottal Attack and Glottal Fry

Many speakers, especially younger contemporary actors, have a habit of interrupting the formation of initial vowel sounds with a **glottal** stop, or sudden closing of the space between the vocal folds in the throat. Tensing the vocal folds in this manner explodes the breath and initiates vowel sounds with a slight popping noise, giving them a harsh, choppy quality.

Note: You may be familiar with the glottal pronunciation of 'better', 'butter' and 'bottle' in the *Cockney* dialect, when the medial consonant /t/ is replaced by a glottal stop.

This approach to initiating sound is especially common in actors speaking with emphasis or expressing themselves while in a highly emotional state. But vowels exploded from the glottis in the throat are much less open, clear, informative, or expressive than those uninterrupted in their release through an open throat. Also, undue stress placed on the vocal mechanism from continued use of glottal attacks can contribute to serious vocal problems.

To break the habit of beginning vowel production with a glottal stop, try **linking** the vowel that begins a word to the last sound of the previous word. This will help avoid the initial 'pop' and promote an uninterrupted, forward release of breath and sound through the mouth.

AUDIO 1▶ **linking words to avoid glottal attacks**

To show‿an‿unfelt sorrow‿is‿an‿office
Which the false man does‿easy.

(Macbeth: II, iii, 136)

There‿are such‿a lot‿of vulgar‿and‿ unpleasant‿and‿offensive
people‿among the‿other civilians.

(Chekhov: Three Sisters)

Come, come‿away!
The sun‿is high, and we‿outwear the day.

(Henry V: IV, ii, 62)

The symbol for linking to the previous word: / ‿ / is used in the remaining practice phrases in this section, though linking is ultimately at an actor's discretion. I suggest marking your own script until the habit of linking sounds is firmly established. Do not link with an 'r' sound if there is no 'r' in the spelling, see **intrusive 'r'** on pages 129-130 and pages 153-154.

PHRASES linking words to avoid glottal attacks

1.	saying yes‿or no	6.	today‿it‿isn't
2.	paying for‿Adam	7.	someone‿else‿is
3.	wherever you‿are	8.	closing‿all doors
4.	going with‿Annie	9.	knowing‿about‿it
5.	thinking‿of‿Evelyn	10.	filling‿in‿all blanks

SENTENCES linking words to avoid glottal attacks

1. Take action!

2. What's in your eye?

3. Who is after you in line?

4. The animals are in cages.

5. Hiking isn't for everyone.

6. The IRS did what I asked.

7. Those apples are unwashed.

8. Benjamin left after auditioning.

9. They all lived happily ever after!

10. Has everyone already eaten dinner?

11. He asked to play a part in *Everyman*.

12. The opening night party is at Sardi's.

13. This sofa isn't comfortable anymore.

14. Japan and China are on our itinerary.

15. Do vocal warm-ups before all auditions.

16. They rehearsed every evening last week.

17. That idiomatic expression is everywhere.

18.   She's not exaggerating: they had eleven callbacks.

19.   Dad dreams of vacationing in the sun every February.

20.   They're both excellent actors and they're in my acting class.

When a vowel sound begins a sentence or new phrase, and there is no previous sound to link with, extra care and practice is required to avoid initiating sound with a glottal attack.

Gently place your hand on your throat and begin the <u>first</u> word in the pair below by elongating the initial 'h'. Notice the smooth flow of breath as it moves from the middle of the torso, up through the relaxed throat, carrying the vowel that follows 'h' through the mouth. Breathe. Speak the <u>second</u> word of the pair. Focus on repeating the sensation of a smooth, open-throated release of breath that carries sound through the mouth without any stoppage in the throat.

WORDS avoiding glottal attack on initial words

hi – eye	hit – it	hail – ale	heart – art
heat – eat	haul –all	ham – am	hand – and
hate – ate	hair – air	head – Ed	halter – alter
heel – eel	hive – I've	Henry – any	heave – even
hash – ash	hem – Emma	hamper – amp	heavy – Evan

Another approach is to form the *shape*[1] necessary to speak the initial vowel on an open-throated intake of breath. Then, smoothly release the vowel through that shape on a tension-free exhalation with no closing, catching, stopping, or interruption in the throat. This technique should be used for brief practice, not in everyday life or in performance.

The IPA symbol /ʔ/ below represents a glottal sound. It is used here as a reminder to avoid beginning with a glottal attack.

PHRASES linking and avoiding glottal attack on initial words

1.	ʔ as‿is	6.	ʔ always‿acting
2.	ʔ interesting‿image	7.	ʔ isn't‿alienated
3.	ʔ evening‿activities	8.	ʔ about‿an‿hour
4.	ʔ anything‿Edith‿asks	9.	ʔ outside‿at‿Evan's
5.	ʔ unaccountable‿action	10.	ʔ eventually‿interred

---

[1] Specific shapes necessary for forming all sounds are covered in the individual sound chapters.

SENTENCES linking and avoiding initial glottal attack on initial words

1. Avoid oysters.

2. Oliver exhausts.

3. Avery is an angel.

4. Embroider everything.

5. Insist on oil free ointment.

6. *As You Like It* ended early.

7. Ida idolizes opulent operas.

8. Evelyn's earrings are opaque.

9. Unsolicited advice is annoying.

10. Insight is extremely underrated.

11. Alvin Anderson's always invited.

12. Awesome adventures are often admired.

13. At eighty-eight, aging Abe is inexhaustible.

14. 'An eye for an eye' isn't an admirable outlook.

15. Arthur's amazing agent arranged the appointment.

16. Evening attire is expressly indicated on the invitation.

17. Intoxication inevitably evolves into obnoxious behavior.

18. After an hour, irate Irene still waited for an announcement.

. **Preventing glottal fry:** many contemporary speakers have a habit of tensing the muscles of the throat and stopping the release of breath, especially during vowel sounds at the ends of phrases or sentences—rather than continuing the forward release of breath and sound through an open throat through the end of the word and thought. The resulting raspy, throaty sound is sometimes referred to as a **glottal fry**.

Muscles of the throat, larynx, and outer abdominal area should remain relaxed during inhalation, and breath release should initiate from the middle of the torso, not from the throat and larynx. This forward release must continue, through the last sound of the last word, without any experience of forcing or squeezing on the final sounds.

EXERCISE Encourage a relaxed intake of breath. Then, as you release breath from your center and speak the following phrases, gently move your hands up near either side of your throat, then out away from your throat—wider than your outer shoulders. All the while, picture width and accompanying spaciousness in your throat—through which you release the spoken phrase. Promote the image/feeling: the longer the spoken line, the more available space in the throat.

PHRASES avoiding glottal fry before a pause

1.	day after day	6.	over here
2.	filled with joy	7.	sure, sure
3.	what a wise guy	8.	feeling the fire
4.	seeing eye to eye	9.	his mother and father
5.	showing him the way	10.	more and more and more

SENTENCES avoiding glottal fry before a pause

1. Are you sure?

2. Well, that was a blooper.

3. How do you save money?

4. I've been waiting forever!

5. When are you going to yoga?

6. I'd love to be cast in that movie.

7. It's time we all went to see a play.

8. Let's get a banana split; we'll share!

9. We were sequestered during jury duty.

10. We met the author last November, remember?

11. Acting class meets on Monday and Wednesday.

12. Did they say that dog is called Emma, or Emily?

13. Do you have time to spare? Consider being a volunteer.

14. He's likely to earn enough to buy a house in the country.

15. Take a shower, comb your hair, then meet me at the diner.

NEUTRAL AMERICAN TEXT **avoiding glottal attack / glottal fry.** *Mark the following for linking. Speak out loud without glottal attack or fry.*

That is very nice and dutiful of him.

(Ibsen: Ghosts)

I was afraid that you might hate me.

(Chekhov: The Seagull)

Even so must I run on, and even so stop.

(King John: V, vii, 67)

Who is smoking such horrible cigars here?

(Chekhov: The Cherry Orchard)

Affection makes him false, he speaks not true.

(Romeo and Juliet: III, i,177)

It's exactly a year ago that Father died, isn't it?

(Chekhov: Three Sisters)

Sweet blowse, you are a beauteous blossom sure.

(Titus Andronicus: IV, ii, 72)

If we obey them not, this will ensue:
They'll suck our breath, or pinch us black and blue.

(Comedy of Errors: II, ii, 191)

Yes, her father is a pretty thorough scoundrel, one must do him
the justice to say so.

(Chekhov: The Seagull)

And most, dear actors, eat no onions nor garlic, for we are to utter
sweet breath.

(A Midsummer Night's Dream: IV, ii, 42)

True, madam; he, of all the men that ever my foolish eyes look'd
upon, was the best deserving a fair lady.

(The Merchant of Venice: I, ii, 117)

That long avenue that runs straight, straight as an arrow, how it
shines on a moonlight night.

(Chekhov: The Cherry Orchard)

MOTHER GOOSE RHYMES avoiding glottal attack and glottal fry

HUMPTY DUMPTY	Humpty Dumpty sat on a wall,
	Humpty Dumpty had a great fall;
	All the King's horses and all the King's men
	Couldn't put Humpty together again.

HUMPTY DUMPTY

Humpty Dumpty sat on a wall,
Humpty Dumpty had a great fall;
All the King's horses and all the King's men
Couldn't put Humpty together again.

HOT CROSS BUNS

Hot cross buns! Hot cross buns!
One a penny, two a penny,
Hot cross buns!
If you have no daughters,
Give them to your sons;
One a penny, two a penny
Hot cross buns.

HODDLEY, PODDLEY

Hoddley, poddley, puddle and fogs,
Cats are to marry the poodle dogs;
Cats in blue jackets and dogs in red hats,
What will become of the mice and the rats?

OLD MOTHER HUBBARD

Old Mother Hubbard
Went to the cupboard,
To fetch her poor dog a bone;
But when she got there
The cupboard was bare,
And so the poor dog had none.

THE PUMPKIN EATER

Peter, Peter pumpkin eater,
Had a wife and couldn't keep her;
He put her in a pumpkin shell,
And there he kept her very well.

TWINKLE, TWINKLE

Twinkle, twinkle, little star,
How I wonder what you are!
Up above the world so high,
Like a diamond in the sky.

JACK-A-NORY

I'll tell you a story
About Jack-a-Nory,
And now my story's begun;
I'll tell you another
About his brother,
And now my story is done.

CLASSICALLY SPEAKING   RHYTHM HIGHLIGHTERS linking

From **THE FALL OF THE HOUSE OF USHER**

Edgar Allan Poe

I struggled to reason off the nervousness which had dominion over me. I endeavored to believe that much, if not all of what I felt was due to the bewildering influence of the gloomy furniture of the room— of the dark and tattered draperies, which, tortured into motion by the breath of a rising tempest, swayed fitfully to and fro upon the walls, and rustled uneasily about the decorations of the bed. But my efforts were fruitless. An irrepressible tremor gradually pervaded my frame; and, at length, there sat upon my very heart an incubus of utterly causeless alarm. Shaking this off with a gasp and a struggle, I uplifted myself upon the pillows, and, peering earnestly within the intense darkness of the chamber, hearkened—I know not why, except that an instinctive spirit prompted me—to certain low and indefinite sounds which came, through the pauses of the storm, at long intervals, I knew not whence.

SUNDOWN

Henry Wadsworth Longfellow

The summer sun is sinking low;
Only the tree-tops redden and glow:
Only the weathercock on the spire
Of the neighboring church is a flame of fire;
    All is in shadow below.

O beautiful, awful summer day,
What hast thou given, what taken away?
Life and death, and love and hate,
Homes made happy or desolate,
    Hearts made sad or gay!

On the road of life one mile-stone more!
In the book of life one leaf turned o'er!
Like a red seal is the setting sun
On the good and the evil men have done,--
    Naught can to-day restore!

Key Words
& Stressed Syllables

English is a wonderfully rhythmic language, composed of varying combinations of stressed and unstressed syllables within words, and stressed and unstressed words within phrases and sentences. Recognizing stress patterns and understanding the contribution stress makes to rhythm, inflected speech and clarity of expression, can increase the likelihood an actor will be sensitive to a character's rhythmic delivery when interpreting any text, from Shakespeare to Beckett to Mamet.

I would define, in brief, the Poetry of words as

'The Rhythmical Creation of Beauty'.
(Edgar Allan Poe: The Poetic Principle)

Syllables. A one-syllable word contains only one vowel sound, as in 'tea', one diphthong sound, as in 'tie', or one triphthong sound, as in 'tire'. Though a word like 'fame' has two letters that are associated with vowel sounds, the final 'e' is silent. Remember to consider sound, not spelling.

If a one-syllable word is **operative** or **key** to the meaning being expressed, the entire word will be emphasized or stressed. Any contrast in stress will be between this one-syllable word and other less important words in the sentence. One possible choice, demonstrated on Audio 2 and marked below, follows.

AUDIO 2► **stressing key words**

To think upon my **pomp** shall be my **hell**.
(2 Henry VI: II, iv, 27)

Do all men **kill** the things they do not **love**?
(The Merchant of Venice: IV, i, 66)

'Tis **he**. **Slink** by, and **note** him.
(As You Like It: III, ii, 252)

CLASSICALLY SPEAKING   **RHYTHM HIGHLIGHTERS** stress

Read through the following sentences and notice how meaning and implication change, depending on the word receiving stress.

> **Chris**, I don't want pizza now.
> Chris, **I** don't want pizza now.
> Chris, I **don't** want pizza now.
> Chris, I don't **want** pizza now.
> Chris, I don't want **pizza** now.
> Chris, I don't want pizza **now**.

As you see, actors need to choose carefully, placing stress on words that clearly communicate their point. This usually involves: nouns, action verbs, adjectives and adverbs, though it is not usually necessary to stress more than one word per phrase, or unit of thought. Stressing too many words can cause as much confusion and lack of clarity as stressing too few.

When an operative or key word contains more than one syllable, as in: 'crying', 'prefer', or 'peaceful', the vowel sound in the stressed syllable is usually contrasted (or highlighted) by making it louder, longer, and higher in pitch than the rest of the word. This is influenced by many variables, including the thought being communicated, and the emotional life and intention of the speaker.

Paying attention to stressed syllables, especially in key words and phrases, is a useful way to add variety, musicality, and increased intelligibility to one's speech and to avoid a monotone delivery.

A stressed syllable in a word can be notated in IPA by placing a / ' / mark in front of it; **bolding** will also used for additional clarity. Selections in Audio 3, below, are marked with both to reflect the speakers' choices. When working with a microphone, stress is subtler than when speaking for the stage.

AUDIO 3▶ **stressed syllables of key words**

> Just sitting here 'prat**tling** with Miss 'Ju**lie**.
> > (Strindberg: Miss Julie)
>
> **Think** you I am no 'stronger than my **sex**,
> Being so 'father'd and so 'husbanded?
> > (Julius Caesar: II, i, 296)
>
> The **tongues** of 'dying **men**
> En'force a'ttention like deep 'harmony.
> > (Richard II: II, i, 5)

As previously stated, stressed syllable markings used throughout this book are based on pronunciation, rather than observing technical rules or dividing syllables according to spelling combinations.

a'**wake**   '**fla**vor   de'**mure**ly

ri'**dic**ulous   unin'**ten**tional   respecta'**bil**ity

The contrast in rhythm and pitch between the stressed and unstressed syllables in the words 'awake' and 'flavor' could be represented:

a'**wake**   short ^LONG   tuh ^TUM

'**fla**vor   ^LONG short   ^TUM tuh

Energetically speak the following words. Notice if the vowel of the *stressed* syllable is louder, longer, and higher in pitch than the vowel(s) in the unstressed syllable(s).

WORDS with stressed syllables marked

re'**ply**	'**trai**tor	a'**pplaud**	de'**ny**
'**fad**ing	'**poi**son	a'**lar**ming	'**chim**ing
'**sat**isfied	'**morn**ing	de'**tained**	'**in**tercom
com'**plain**	'**poun**ding	com'**pressed**	un'**nat**ural
re'**spon**sive	de'**stroyed**	'**ban**ishment	'**pros**perous

Hint: If you are having difficulty discerning the stressed syllable, place your hand on the underside of your chin. The jaw is usually most open on the vowel sound of the stressed syllable. If you are still having difficulty, try over-stressing various syllables. The 'correct' choice will probably become more apparent.

WORDS with stressed syllables unmarked

robber	avenue	serial	sailor
soberly	contain	about	patent
account	allowed	media	dignity
lionized	limerick	absurd	display
deceived	legislate	limestone	libretto
belonging	bachelor	turpentine	particle
chaperone	probably	inscrutable	equality

NEUTRAL AMERICAN TEXT key words, stressed syllables. *Underline your choice key words and speak aloud, with attention to stressed syllables. Find a balance: stressing too many words is as unclear as stressing too few.*

I've been <u>thinking</u> of setting up a new line of <u>business</u>.

(Ibsen: Ghosts)

Fie, my lord, fie! A soldier, and afeard?

(Macbeth: V, i, 36)

Nina, how strange it is that I should be seeing you. Why would you not let me see you?

(Chekhov: The Seagull)

Alas! Yes, family life is certainly not always so pure as it ought to be.

(Ibsen: Ghosts)

We turn up our noses at one another, but life is passing all the while.

(Chekhov: The Cherry Orchard)

DOCTOR PINCH. Give me your hand and let me feel your pulse.
ANTIPHOLUS.   There is my hand, and let it feel your ear.

(The Comedy of Errors: IV, iv, 52)

I may neither choose who I would, not refuse who I dislike; so is the will of a living daughter curb'd by the will of a dead father.

(The Merchant of Venice: I, ii, 23)

GREMIO.   O this learning, what a thing it is!
GRUMIO.   O this woodcock, what an ass it is!

(The Taming of the Shrew: I, ii, 159)

From THE CASK OF AMONTILLADO

Edgar Allan Poe

The thousand injuries of Fortunato I had borne as best I could; but when he ventured upon insult, I vowed revenge. You, who so well know the nature of my soul, will not suppose, however, that I gave utterance to a threat. *At length* I would be avenged; this was a point definitively settled—but the very definitiveness with which it was resolved, precluded the idea of risk. I must not only punish, but punish with impunity. A wrong is unredressed when retribution overtakes its redresser. It is equally unredressed when the avenger fails to make himself felt as such to him who has done the wrong.

From **THE TAMING OF THE SHREW**

William Shakespeare

Choose your key words carefully, in order to make the following conversation clear.

LUCENTIO.	Pray you sit down,
	For now we sit to chat as well as eat.
PETRUCHIO.	Nothing but sit and sit, and eat and eat!
BAPTISTA.	Padua affords this kindness, son Petruchio.
PETRUCHIO.	Padua affords nothing but what is kind.
HORTENSIO.	For both our sakes, I would that word were true.
PETRUCHIO.	Now, for my life, Hortensio fears his widow.
WIDOW.	Then never trust me if I be afeard.
PETRUCHIO.	You are very sensible, and yet you miss my sense:
	I mean Hortensio is afeard of you.
WIDOW.	He that is giddy thinks the world turns round.
PETRUCHIO.	Roundly replied.
KATHERINE.	Mistress, how mean you that?
WIDOW.	Thus I conceive by him.
PETRUCHIO.	Conceives by me! how likes Hortensio that?
HORTENSIO.	My widow says, thus she conceives her tale.
PETRUCHIO.	Very well mended. Kiss him for that, good widow.
KATHERINE.	"He that is giddy thinks the world turns round":
	I pray you tell me what you meant by that.
WIDOW.	Your husband, being troubled with a shrew,
	Measures my husband's sorrow by his woe:
	And now you know my meaning.
KATHERINE.	A very mean meaning.
WIDOW.	Right, I mean you.
KATHERINE.	And I am mean indeed, respecting you.
PETRUCHIO.	To her, Kate!
HORTENSIO.	To her, widow!
PETRUCHIO.	A hundred marks, my Kate does put her down.
HORTENSIO.	That's my office.
PETRUCHIO.	Spoke like an officer. Ha' to thee, lad!

Drinks to Hortensio.

(V, ii, 10-37)

CLASSICALLY SPEAKING   **RHYTHM HIGHLIGHTERS stress**

Noun / Verb Variations

There are words whose stress and meaning can vary depending on their use as nouns, verbs, or adjectives. Some words commonly used as both nouns and verbs follow.

Nouns	Verbs
1st syllable stressed)	(2nd syllable stressed)
LONG short TUM tuh	short LONG tuh TUM
'compound	com'pound
'content	con'tent
'contest	con'test
'contract	con'tract
'contrast	con'trast
'convert	con'vert
'defect	de'fect
'discourse	dis'course
'extract	ex'tract
'frequent	fre'quent
'import	im'port
'insult	in'sult
'object	ob'ject
'perfect	per'fect
'permit	per'mit
'pervert	per'vert
'present	pre'sent
'produce	pro'duce
'progress	pro'gress
'project	pro'ject
'rebel	re'bel
'record	re'cord
'subject	sub'ject
'survey	sur'vey
'suspect	su'spect
'torment	tor'ment

AUDIO 4▶ **noun / verb variations**

And tor**'ment** each other to death?

(Strindberg: Miss Julie)

Fancy—to be able to write on such a **'subj**ect as that!

(Ibsen: Hedda Gabler)

Come, come, dis**'patch,** the Duke would be at dinner.

(Richard III: III, iv, 94)

SENTENCES noun / verb variations

1. Don't subject me to studying that subject.

2. Let me present you with this lovely present.

3. She's a rebel who rebels against everything!

4. I feel I must contest the results of the contest.

5. You insult by reading from that book of insults.

6. Vanilla extract is extracted from the vanilla bean.

7. For the record, I recorded my first record in 1970.

8. I suspect that the suspect is still living in Manhattan.

9. I am content after hearing the contents of the review.

10. I will defect to the other side unless you correct this defect.

NEUTRAL AMERICAN TEXT noun / verb variations. *Mark the stressed syllable of words that vary between noun and verb, and speak aloud.*

The object and the pleasure of mine eye.

(A Midsummer Night's Dream: IV, i, 170)

I cannot project mine own cause so well.

(Antony and Cleopatra: V, ii, 121)

Content yourself. God knows I lov'd my niece.

(Much Ado About Nothing: V, i, 87)

CLASSICALLY SPEAKING   RHYTHM HIGHLIGHTERS noun/verb

O, that record is lively in my soul!

(Richard II: I, i, 30)

And to the nightingale's complaining notes
Tune my distresses and record my woes.

(The Two Gentlemen of Verona: V, iv, 5)

A woman sometimes scorns what best contents her.

(The Two Gentlemen of Verona: III, i, 93)

Thus was I, sleeping, by a brother's hand
Of life, of crown, of queen, at once dispatch'd.

(Hamlet: I, v, 74)

Let's follow him, and pervert the present wrath
He hath against himself.

(Cymbeline: II, iv, 151)

And mark what object did present itself
Under an old oak, whose boughs were moss'd with age
And high top bald with dry antiquity.

(As You Like It: IV, iii, 103)

First, heaven be the record to my speech,
In the devotion of a subject's love.
Tend'ring the precious safety of my prince,
And free from other misbegotten hate,
Come I appellant to this princely presence.

(Richard II: I, i, 30)

I know a wench of excellent discourse,
Pretty and witty; wild, and yet, too, gentle;
There will we dine. This woman that I mean,
My wife (but, I protest, without desert)
Hath often times upbraided me withal.

(The Comedy of Errors: III, I, 109)

It is a melancholy of mine own, compounded of many simples
extracted from many objects.

(As You Like It: IV, i, 15)

(handwritten, left margin) 2 Pronunciations!

Weak Forms

Weak forms, sometimes referred to as vowel reductions, are specific words that have two pronunciations; a strong form (sf), which uses a longer, more prominent vowel sound, and a weak form (wf), which uses a shorter vowel sound. In most cases, the vowel in the weak form of a word is the short /ə/ (uh) sound, also known as the 'schwa' sound.

Articles, auxiliary verbs, pronouns (including personal, possessive and demonstrative), prepositions and connectives all have weak forms. Using weak forms helps rhythmically focus attention onto more important or informative key words, while maintaining a relaxed, conversational rhythm.

The following is marked as spoken in the audio selection.

AUDIO 5▶ weak forms

> tə   ə   əz   əz   ə
> To **wake** a **wolf** is as **bad** as **smell** a **fox**.
>
> (2 Henry IV: I, ii, 155)

>   ə   əv   ðəts   ðə
> There 's not a **note** of **mine** that' s **worth** the 'noting.
>
> (Much Ado About Nothing: II, iii, 55)

>   ðə   əv ðə
> 'Memory, the 'warder of the **brain**.
>
> (Macbeth: I, vii, 65)

ARTICLES: The choice of weak form in this case depends on the first sound of the word that <u>follows</u> the article.

Strong form			Weak form
a	eĭ	followed by a consonant sound use	ə
an	æn	followed by a vowel sound use	ən

The weak form of the word 'a', /ə/, prevails unless 'a' is being stressed to make a point. In that uncommon instance /eĭ/ is spoken. Compare:

Weak form   I'd like a <u>ticket</u>.

Strong form   I'd like <u>a</u> ticket.

          ə   ə
Sometime a horse I'll be, sometime a hound,
 ə   ə   ə
A hog, a headless bear, sometime a fire.
(A Midsummer Night's Dream: III, I, 108)

Remember: The article **'a'** is not used (in writing or speaking) before words that begin with a vowel; **'an'** is used, in either its strong or weak form.

PHRASES *'a'* followed by consonants / *'an'* followed by vowels

	/ə/	/ə/	/ən/	/ən/
1.	a key	a jolt	an ant	an altar
2.	a box	a fact	an exam	an oboe
3.	a talk	a date	an event	an action
4.	a play	a song	an addict	an actress
5.	a script	a thing	an animal	an umpire
6.	a snack	a bottle	an excuse	an opinion
7.	a check	a printer	an emotion	an illusion
8.	a knock	a chorus	an audition	an incident
9.	a couch	a change	an umbrella	an evening
10.	a movie	a promotion	an intention	an argument

SENTENCES *'a'* followed by consonants / *'an'* followed by vowels

1. Give me a break.

2. That was an exciting event.

3. It's an exact duplicate of a very old antique.

4. What an inspired thought; that's a great idea!

5. An ounce of prevention is worth a pound of cure.

6. I'll have a piece of cake with a scoop of ice cream.

7.   I have a feeling an announcement will be made soon.

8.   Creating an artistic environment is a challenging job.

9.   As a matter of fact, I'd like to buy a ticket for a hit show.

10.   They had a great time on an ocean liner in the Caribbean.

Strong form		**Weak form**
the ði	when followed by a consonant sound use	ðə
	when followed by a vowel sound use	ði (or) ðɪ

ðə

SHYLOCK. *Is that the law?*

ði

PORTIA.   *Thyself shalt see the‿act.*

(The Merchant of Venice: IV, i, 314)

PHRASES 'the' followed by consonants and vowels

	/ðə/	/ðə/	/ði/ or /ðɪ/	/ði/ or /ðɪ/
1.	the way	the job	the‿item	the‿ad
2.	the cast	the day	the‿ache	the‿act
3.	the sink	the fish	the‿extra	the‿end
4.	the play	the one	the‿apple	the‿eyes
5.	the time	the best	the‿author	the‿actor
6.	the craft	the wait	the‿energy	the‿oven
7.	the news	the truth	the‿opening	the‿action
8.	the notes	the stage	the‿audition	the‿interest
9.	the place	the worst	the‿intention	the‿address
10.	the boxer	the traffic	the‿academic	the‿argument

SENTENCES 'the' followed by consonants and vowels

1.   The agency closed its door at the end of the day.

2.   The sign-in sheet at the audition was full by 6 a.m.

3.   The attorney couldn't defend the criminal's actions.

4.   Delaying the shooting was the last thing he wanted.

5.   The last time we visited the theatre, the lights went out.

6.   The waitress brought the coffee first, then the dessert.

7.   The knives and forks were all purchased just for the event.

8.   The singers scheduled a vocal warm-up before the concert.

9.   All the entertainers were applauded at the end of the show.

10.   The reading was a huge success; the actors were wonderful.

AUXILIARY VERBS. The verbs in the following list are commonly used either alone in a sentence as the main verb, or in combination with another verb as auxiliary verb.

am	are	can	could	do	does
had	has	have	must	was	should

When used alone as the main verb, as in the second column, the strong form is spoken and the word is stressed. When used as the auxiliary verb, as in the third column, the weak form is used to focus attention onto the more descriptive main verb that comes after, which is stressed. Phonetic transcription of strong and weak forms is included above the word, below. *Read across.*

VERB	**Strong Form**	**Weak Form**
	æm	əm
am	Yes I **am**!	I am **here**.
	ɑɚ̃	ɚ
are	You **are**?	Bob and Tim are **gone**.
	kæn	kən
can	They **can**.	They can **leave**.
	kʊd	kəd
could	We **could**.	We could **see** that.
	du	də (or dʊ)
do	You **do**?	What do you **want**?
	dʌz	dəz
does	He **does**.	Does it **work**?
	hæd	həd (or əd)
had	I wish I **had**.	I wish I had **known**.
	hæz	həz (or əz)
has	Yes, he **has**.	He has been **hurt**.

	həv	həv (or əv)
have	They **have** it!	What have you **seen**?
	mʌst	məst (or məs)
must	**Must** I?	I must **tell** you something.
	ʃud	ʃəd (or ʃd)
should	I **should**.	I know I should **wait**.
	wʌz	wəz
was	He **was**.	He was **hired**.

PRONOUN	**Strong Form**	**Weak Form**
	ðem	ðəm (or ðm̩)
them	Tell **them**.	Tell them to **wait**.
	ʌs	əs
us	It's for **us**.	Give us **room**.
	sʌm	səm (or sm̩)
some	I'd like **some**.	I'd like some **tea**.

An exception occurs in the weak form of the words: you, me, he, her, she, we. The vowel sound in the weak form of these words remains the same as in the strong form, only shorter. Pronouns are not generally stressed in Shakespeare; their weak forms are often used instead, as in the following:

$$\overset{i}{}\qquad\overset{u}{}$$

With duty and desire we follow you.

(A Midsummer Night's Dream: I, i, 127)

PREPOSITION	**Strong Form**	**Weak Form**
	æt	ət
at	Who do you look **at**?	Look at **you**.
	fɔ˞	fə˞
for	What **for**?	It's for **Rob**.
	frʌm	frəm
from	Where's he **from**?	He's from **town**.
	ʌv	əv
of	What do you think **of**?	I think of **you**.

	tu	tə
to	Who does this go **to**?	He wants tʊ[1] **go**.
	ɪntu	ɪntə
into	What are you **into**?	Get intʊ **bed**.

CONNECTIVE[2] **Strong Form**		**Weak Form**
	æn	ənd
and	I'd like pie **and**[3] cake!	I'd like ham ənd **eggs**.
	æz	əz ə
as	What did I go **as**?	I went əs ə **cow**.
	bʌt	bət
but	No **buts** about it.	I have nothing bət **fun**.
	ɔɚ	ɚ
or	I said chicken **or** fish.	Do you like it ɚ **not**.
	ðæt	ðət
that	I know **that**!	I know ðət you **went**.
	ðæn	ðən
than	It's nicer **than**…	It's nicer ðən **what**?

The following words have no weak form: in, just, on, wasn't, when and get ('git' is not the weak form of 'get').

Speak the following sentences using the **bolded** word with its weak form (which has a strikethrough) and strong form (which is underlined). Notice how the use of the weak form can rhythmically focus attention onto the more important word in the sentence.

SENTENCES weak and strong forms

1. **(can)**   Cən you believe it? Yes, I <u>can</u>.

2. **(does)**   Dəs it matter what he <u>does</u> for a living?

---

[1] When 'to' is followed by a consonant sound, the weak form /tə/ is an option. When 'to' is followed by a vowel sound, the weak form /tʊ/ is an option. Actors sometimes glottalize the vowel that comes after when using /tʊ/. If this is the case, link with a short /u/ rather than /ʊ/.

[2] This section also includes conjunctions and demonstrative pronouns.

[3] When followed by a word beginning with a consonant sound, the /d/ is optional.

3. **(from)**   Where are you <u>from</u>? I'm fr~~o~~m New York.

4. (some)   I've had <u>some</u> day! Now, I need s~~o~~me rest.

5. (that)   They told me th~~a~~t I won; do you believe <u>that</u>?

6. (of)   I'm thinking ~~o~~f you; that's what I'm thinking <u>of</u>.

7. **(must)**   We m~~u~~st go to a show sometime; we really <u>must</u>!

8. (was)   I w~~a~~s going to confirm it. Really, I <u>was</u>.

9. (had)   I wish I h~~a~~d known. I really wish I <u>had</u>.

10. (for)   Who's that <u>for</u>; is it fo~~r~~ you?

NEUTRAL AMERICAN TEXT weak forms. *Draw a line through words with weak forms or write the appropriate IPA symbol above the weak form word. Speak out loud, highlighting key words.*

~~A~~ new <u>bonnet</u> ~~and~~ ~~a~~ new <u>parasol</u>!

(Ibsen: Hedda Gabler)

Brilliant! You should have been an actor!

(Strindberg: Miss Julie)

It is the part of men to fear and tremble.

(Julius Caesar: I, iii, 54)

Soft you; a word or two before you go.

(Othello: V, ii, 338)

From time to time I have acquainted you...

(The Merry Wives of Windsor: IV, vi, 8)

Condemning some to death and some to exile.

(Coriolanus: I, vi, 34)

In peace there's nothing so becomes a man
As modest stillness and humility.

(Henry V: III, i, 3)

What a delight it is to have you again, as large as life, before
my very eyes!

(Ibsen: Hedda Gabler)

From **THE PURLOINED LETTER**

Edgar Allan Poe

Why, the fact is, we took our time, and we searched *everywhere*. I have had long experience in these affairs. I took the entire building, room by room; devoting the nights of a whole week to each. We examined, first, the furniture of each apartment. We opened every possible drawer; and I presume you know that, to a properly trained police-agent, such a thing as a *'secret'* drawer is impossible. Any man is a dolt who permits a 'secret' drawer to escape him in a search of this kind.

THE RAINY DAY

Henry Wadsworth Longfellow

The day is cold, a nd dark, and dreary;
It rains, and the wind is never weary;
The vine still clings to the mouldering wall,
But at every gust the dead leaves fall,
And the day is dark and dreary.

My life is cold, and dark, and dreary,
It rains, and the wind is never weary,
My thoughts still cling to the mouldering Past,
But the hopes of youth fall thick in the blast,
And the days are dark and dreary.

Be still, sad heart! and cease repining;
Behind the clouds is the sun still shining;
Thy fate is the common fate of all,
Into each life some rain must fall,
Some days must be dark and dreary.

Inflection

The continuous rising and falling of pitch, or notes, when speaking is referred to as **intonation**. The change of pitch *within* a vowel or diphthong sound itself is called **inflection**.

Most of us inflect constantly in our daily lives in order to make ourselves clearly understood, to transmit our point of view, and to get what we want. Inflection is one of the keys to expressiveness. Some actors have difficulty applying this natural response to text. The following may be useful.

(a)   A change in pitch, sliding from a lower to a higher note within a vowel sound, constitutes a **rising inflection**. Most often, this change of pitch reflects questioning:

↗

yeeEEES?

It can also imply hesitation, insincerity, surprise, uncertainty, suspense, etc.

(b)   If the pitch within the vowel or diphthong slides from a higher to lower note, it is referred to as a **falling inflection**:

↘

NOOooo!

and can reflect finality, condemnation, belligerence, bossiness, avoidance, etc.

(c) ·   If the pitch is sustained or elongated without inflecting either up or down, this is referred to as a **level inflection**:

→

Weeell!

and can express indecision, disinterest, wariness, etc.

(d)   Finally, any combination of rising and falling notes within the vowel or diphthong sound is referred to as a **double** or **circumflex inflection**, which can include rising, then falling, as in:

↗↘

heeEEEeey

or falling, then rising, as in:

↘↗

HEEeeeEEY

This can offer a wonderful expression of flirtation, sarcasm, evasion, reluctance, even *double-entendre* (two ways of interpreting what is being said, one of which is usually 'naughty' – and very popular in Shakespeare).

> MARIA. *My lady will hang thee for thy absence.*
>
> ↗↘
>
> CLOWN. *Let her hang me! He that is well <u>hang'd</u> in this world*
> *needs to fear no colors.*
>
> (Twelfth Night: I, v, 3)

AUDIO 6► inflection on operative or key words

↘   ↘↗

What! my dear Lady Disdain, are you yet living?

(Much Ado About Nothing: I, i, 123)

↘

My pride fell with my fortunes.

(As You Like It: I, ii, 260)

↘↗   ↘↗   →↘   ↘

Eleven widows and nine maids is simple coming-in for one man.

(The Merchant of Venice: II, ii, 162)

Notice how your inflection shifts as you speak the words on the following page from various points of view. For example, speak the word:

'why'

really *questioning* to get an answer. . . why? Then speak the same word again, this time *challenging* the person to give you a good reason, once again *flirting* for attention, and yet again, *ignoring* the listener and their response. Your inflections were probably very different in each case.

Speak the following words allowing inflection to aid in communicating your point of view. Choose a meaning for yourself or, if you wish, follow the point of view suggested by the sentence in parenthesis—without actually reading the sentence out loud.

PHRASES **inflecting within the vowel or diphthong of key words**

1. so (What do you think? *or* What of it!)

2. see (I knew I was right. *or* Doesn't this look great?)

3. fame (I'm not interested in fame! *or* I <u>long</u> for fame.)

4. fine (Can't you see it's <u>not</u> fine? *or* I feel great!)

5. oh (Maybe I know, maybe I don't. *or* You scared me!)

6. mine (Are you crazy; that's not mine. *or* Eat your heart out.)

7. stay (I wish you would leave. *or* Never leave.)

8. how (Nothing is possible. *or* I don't understand.)

9. those (Do you think <u>I</u> would want <u>those</u>? *or* I choose those.)

10. true (Great guess, you sexy thing. *or* That can't be true.)

An upward inflection is *not* required at the end of a sentence when the question asked is rhetorical and the answer implied, as in: "Well, isn't it a nice day?"

SOUND CHECK: inflecting on lists. Speaking lists with an upward, level, or even double inflection can be a useful way of subtly communicating that there is a list in progress. Downward inflection usually communicates finality and is especially useful on the last item, but can be misleading if used after every item.

Read the following lists using a downward inflection before each comma. Notice how the train of thought is interrupted and the meaning obscured. Then read again, using an upward, level, or double inflection before each comma and a downward inflection to finish the sentence.

SENTENCES **inflecting on lists**

1. No dogs, cats, birds, or reptiles allowed inside.

2. We need lettuce, tomatoes, and pears for the salad.

3. Bob, Lisa, Cathy, Janice, and Dave haven't paid yet.

4. David, Daniel, Dylan, Don, or Douglas: who are you?

5. She had her hair washed, dried, and set for forty dollars?

6.   We saw London, Paris, Rome, and Venice; then flew home.

7.   Was our appointment for Monday, Tuesday, or Wednesday?

8.   Knives, forks, spoons, salt, pepper, and napkins are included.

9.   Loud yelling, screaming, swearing, and cursing are forbidden.

10.   The machine accepts nickels, dimes, quarters, or silver dollars.

NEUTRAL AMERICAN TEXT inflection. *Speak the following, allowing inflection to aid in communicating your point of view. Remember to lift the inflection on lists.*

Who's there?

(King John: V, vi, 1)

Oh, not at all.

(Ibsen: Ghosts)

How now, my lords? What, all unready so?

(1 Henry VI: II, i, 38)

Do you not remember, lady, in your father's time, a Venetian, a scholar and a soldier, that came hither?

(The Merchant of Venice: I, ii, 112)

The day is hot, and the weather, and the wars, and the King, and the Dukes; it is no time to discourse.

(Henry V: III, iii, 106)

Oh, that's a brave man! he writes brave verses, speaks brave words, swears brave oaths, and breaks them bravely.

(As You Like It: III, v, 40)

You're bolder, more honest, deeper than we are, but think, be just a little magnanimous, have pity on me.

(Chekhov: The Cherry Orchard)

They say there is divinity in odd numbers, either in nativity, chance, or death.

(The Merry Wives of Windsor: V, i, 3)

You have beauty, grace, nobility, charm—when it pleases you—and the flame you rouse in a man won't ever be put out.

(Strindberg: Miss Julie)

From **SHADOW—A PARABLE**

Edgar Allan Poe

The year had been a year of terror, and of feelings more intense than terror for which there is no name upon the earth. For many prodigies and signs had taken place, and far and wide, over the sea and land, the black wings of the Pestilence were spread abroad. To those, nevertheless, cunning in the stars, it was not unknown that the heavens wore an aspect of ill; and to me, the Greek Oinos, among others, it was evident that now had arrived the alternation of that seven hundred and ninety-fourth year when, at the entrance of Aires, the planet Jupiter is conjoined with the red ring of the terrible Saturnus. The peculiar spirit of the skies, if I mistake not greatly, made itself manifest, not only in the physical orb of the earth, but in the souls, imaginations, and meditations of mankind.

From **ALICE IN WONDERLAND**

Lewis Carroll

Tied around the neck of the bottle was a paper label, with the words "DRINK ME" beautifully printed on it in large letters.

It was all very well to say "Drink me," but the wise little Alice was not going to do *that* in a hurry. "No, I'll look first," she said, "and see whether it's marked '*poison*' or not"; for she had read several nice little stories about children who had got burnt, and eaten up by wild beasts, and other unpleasant things, all because they *would* not remember the simple rules their friends had taught them: such as, that a red-hot poker will burn you if you hold it too long; and that, if you cut your finger *very* deeply with a knife, it usually bleeds; and she had never forgotten that, if you drink much from a bottle marked "poison," it is almost certain to disagree with you, sooner or later.

However, this bottle was *not* marked "poison," so Alice ventured to taste it, and finding it very nice (it had, in fact, a sort of mixed flavour of cherry-tart, custard, pine-apple, roast turkey, toffy, and hot buttered toast), she very soon finished it off.

Pause

Perhaps the most rhythmically useful tool available when speaking is silence. A pause is cessation of speech (silence) in the middle or end of verbalization for any number of reasons, the most popular – breathing!

Speak the following sentence, which is written without punctuation. Make sure any pause taken for breath does not interfere with the 'unit of thought' or idea being expressed.

I have of late but wherefore I know not lost all my mirth forgone all custom of exercises and indeed it goes so heavily with my disposition that this goodly frame the earth seems to me a sterile promontory this most excellent canopy the air look you this brave o'erhanging firmament this majestical roof fretted with golden fire why it appeareth nothing to me but a foul and pestilent congregation of vapors.

(Hamlet: II, ii, 295)

Some playwrights are extremely precise in their use of punctuation; for example, Harold Pinter, Edward Albee, and David Mamet. When ignored, it is to the actor's detriment.

The punctuation is very useful in the following:

TESMAN. *What... are you staring at?*

PAUSE.

Hedda... ?

HEDDA. *The leaves. They're so yellow... withered.*

TESMAN. *Well, it is September.*

PAUSE.

HEDDA. *Think of it! September... already.*

SILENCE.

(Ibsen: Hedda Gabler)

Sometimes pauses are needed in order to avoid confusion and are thus used for **clarity**. Parentheses are used in the following example to delineate pauses:

*I do affect the very ground (which is base) where her shoe (which is
baser) guided by her foot (which is basest) doth tread.*

(Love's Labor's Lost, I, ii, 167)

There is often a slight pause within a line of verse called a **caesura**,
indicated by **/** in the sample below. The line may or may not be marked with
punctuation, but a caesura can serve to clarify the thought or offer a pause for
dramatic effect:

*He talks to me **/** that never had a son.*

(King John: III, iv, 91)

AUDIO 7▶ dramatic pause

Some rise by sin, and some by virtue **/** fall.

(Measure for Measure: II, i, 38)

Just think: Midsummer Day, in a stifling train, packed in with
that mob of families all gaping at me; train stalled in the station,
when you want **/** to fly!

(Strindberg: Miss Julie)

The inaudible and noiseless foot **/** of time.

(Twelfth Night: V, iii, 4)

Changes in the pace, speed, or tempo of the delivery, coupled with
pauses, can be a very effective tool for breaking up established patterns and
adding dramatic effect.

Some actors, gifted with an internal sense of rhythm, have perfect
'timing' and possess an innate feeling for precisely when to begin or end a line,
phrase, laugh, or pause. But there are also some purely technical considerations
that can be helpful.

A longer 'dramatic' pause can be used as a set-up before an important
idea, or for underscoring a point after an idea has been introduced. But such
dramatic pauses must be earned. There is a direct relationship between one's
pace and energy when speaking and the amount of time 'earned' that can be
'spent' on a pause. In other words, actors should establish an enlivened delivery
first, so they have something with which to balance the length of the pause.

The slower the pace, the shorter the pause; the quicker the pace and higher the energy level, the more time earned for an engaging pause.

It is important to remember that pausing is not emptiness in time and space. The thought must continue. The character stops for a reason—to decide what to say next, to allow something to settle in, to recover his/her composure, etc. The pause is related to the moments before and after and must reflect that by being filled.

When a pause occurs in the middle of a thought, an upward, double or even level inflection immediately preceding the pause can subtly communicate that the speaker is not yet finished, and can increase the time 'earned' for the pause.

It is often effective to 'break' the pause by returning to speech on a lower pitch, especially if upward inflection was used immediately before pausing, while being sensitive to the need to re-establish or 'pick up' the pace.

In summary, 'pace', 'pitch', then 'pause' are the technical underpinnings, but any pause should be driven and substantiated by the character's wants and needs as expressed through the text.

NEUTRAL AMERICAN TEXT pause and dramatic pause. *Decide where a dramatic pause might be possible, mark the text, and then speak the text aloud.*

It's your duty **/** to go on the stage.

(Chekhov: The Seagull)

Thou art, as you are all, a sorceress.

(The Comedy of Errors: IV, iii, 66)

You surely do not suppose that I have nothing better to do than to study such publications as these?

(Ibsen: Ghosts)

You argue like a man who has had enough. You are satisfied and so you are indifferent to life, nothing matters to you. But even you will be afraid to die.

(Chekhov: The Seagull)

Uncle, what could be more hopeless and stupid than my position?

(Chekhov: The Seagull)

From **THE MASQUE OF THE RED DEATH**

Edgar Allan Poe

The "Red Death" had long devastated the country. No pestilence had ever been so fatal, or so hideous. Blood was its Avatar and its seal—the redness and the horror of blood. There were sharp pains, and sudden dizziness, and then profuse bleeding at the pores, with dissolution. The scarlet stains upon the body and especially upon the face of the victim, were the pest ban which shut him out from the aid and from the sympathy of his fellow-men. And the whole seizure, progress and termination of the disease, were the incidents of half an hour.

From **THREE SUNDAYS IN A WEEK**

Edgar Allan Poe

A very "fine old English gentleman," was my grand-uncle Rumgudgeon, but unlike him of the song, he had his weak points. He was a little, pursy, pompous, passionate semicircular somebody, with a red nose, a thick skull, a long purse, and a strong sense of his own consequence. With the best heart in the world, he contrived, through a predominant whim of contradiction, to earn for himself, among those who only knew him superficially, the character of a curmudgeon. Like many excellent people, he seemed possessed with a spirit of tantalization, which might easily, at a casual glance, have been mistaken for malevolence. To every request, a positive "No!" was his immediate answer; but, in the end—in the long, long end—there were exceedingly few requests which he refused. Against all attacks upon his purse he made the most sturdy defense; but the amount extorted from him, at last, was generally in direct ratio with the length of the siege and the stubbornness of the resistance. In charity no one gave more liberally or with a worse grace.

LITERARY DEVICES

An immortal instinct, deep within the spirit of man, is thus, plainly, a sense of the Beautiful. This it is which administers to his delight in the manifold forms, and sounds, and odors, and sentiments amid which he exists.

(Edgar Allan Poe: The Poetic Principle)

Increased sensitivity to the palate of sounds and rhythms that make up spoken words and phrases can be promoted through an awareness of the following commonly used literary devices.

Rhyme

Rhyme is the reoccurrence of the same last sound, or last few sounds, in two or more words.

AUDIO 8 A▶ **rhyme**

The time is out of joint – O cursed sp<u>ite</u>,
That ever I was born to set it r<u>ight</u>!

(Hamlet: I, v, 188)

Your hands than mine are quicker for a fr<u>ay</u>;
My legs are longer though, to run aw<u>ay</u>.

(A Midsummer Night's Dream: III, ii, 342)

Mount, mount, my soul! thy seat is up on h<u>igh</u>,
Whilst my gross flesh sinks downward, here to d<u>ie</u>.

(Richard II: V, v, 112)

Assonance

Reoccurrence of vowel or diphthong sounds within two or more words or syllables is called assonance.

AUDIO 8 B▶ assonance

A ho<u>rse</u>! a ho<u>rse</u>! my kingdom <u>for</u> a ho<u>rse</u>!

(Richard III: V, iv, 7)

To w<u>ee</u>p is to make l<u>e</u>ss the d<u>e</u>pth of gr<u>ie</u>f.

(3 Henry IV: II, i, 85)

L<u>i</u>ght, seeking l<u>i</u>ght, doth l<u>i</u>ght of l<u>i</u>ght begu<u>i</u>le.

(Love's Labor's Lost: I, i, 77)

Alliteration

Alliteration is the reoccurrence of the initial consonant sounds in two or more words.

AUDIO 8 C▶ alliteration

<u>B</u>less thee, <u>B</u>ottom! <u>b</u>less thee!

(A Midsummer Night's Dream: III, i, 118)

I will not <u>st</u>ruggle, I will <u>st</u>and <u>st</u>one-<u>st</u>ill.

(King John: IV, i, 76)

This <u>m</u>usic <u>m</u>ads <u>m</u>e; let it sound no <u>m</u>ore.

(Richard II: V, v, 61)

Consonance

Consonance is the reoccurrence of medial or ending consonant sounds, not necessarily preceded by the same vowel sounds, in two or more words.

AUDIO 8 D▶ consonance

Gra<u>ce</u> me no gra<u>ce</u>, nor un<u>cle</u> me no un<u>cle</u>.

(Richard II: II, iii, 87)

That which ha<u>th</u> made them drunk ha<u>th</u> made me bold;
What ha<u>th</u> quench'd them ha<u>th</u> given me fire.

(Macbeth: II, ii, 1)

O fle<u>sh</u>, fle<u>sh</u>, how art thou fi<u>sh</u>ified!

(Romeo and Juliet: II, iv, 37)

Anaphora

Anaphora refers to the repetition of words at the beginning of two or more clauses. Repetition of words should be noted anywhere in the sentence.

AUDIO 8 E▶ **anaphora**

<u>Past</u> hope, <u>past</u> cure, <u>past</u> help!

(Romeo and Juliet: IV, i, 45)

<u>O</u> sleep! <u>O</u> gentle sleep!

(2 Henry IV: III, i, 5)

You care not who sees your <u>back</u>. Call you that <u>back</u>ing of your friends? A plague upon such <u>back</u>ing!

(1 Henry IV: II, iv, 149)

Onomatopoeia

Words in which the sounds suggest the meaning are onomatopoeic.

AUDIO 8 F▶ **onomatopoeia**

<u>Fight</u> till the <u>last gasp</u>.

(1 Henry VI: I, ii,127)

<u>Gallop apace</u>, you <u>fiery</u>-<u>footed</u> steeds.

(Romeo and Juliet: III, ii, 1)

<u>Blow</u>, winds, and <u>crack</u> your cheeks! <u>rage</u>! <u>blow</u>!

(King Lear: III, ii, 1)

Imagery

Imagery refers to the use of words that create vivid pictures or images in the mind of the listener. See all previous entries, along with the following.

AUDIO 8 G▶ **imagery**

At first the infant,
Mewling and puking in the nurse's arms.

(As You Like It: II, vii 143)

> Thou elvish-mark'd, abortive, rooting hog!
>
> (Richard III: I, iii, 227)
>
> They have made worms' meat of me.
>
> (Romeo and Juliet: III, i, 107)

Simile

A simile is a figure of speech which compares two things using the words 'like' or 'as'.

AUDIO 8 H▶ simile

> They will eat like wolves and fight like devils.
>
> (Henry V: III: vii, 150)
>
> ...therefore think him as a serpent's egg,
> And kill him in the shell.
>
> (Julius Caesar: II, i, 32)
>
> Therefore my age is as a lusty winter,
> Frosty, but kindly.
>
> (As You Like It: II, iii, 52)

Metaphor

A metaphor is a figure of speech which compares two things without using the words 'like' or 'as'.

AUDIO 8 I▶ metaphor

> Why then the world's my oyster,
> Which I with sword will open.
>
> (The Merry Wives of Windsor: II, ii, 3)
>
> I had rather be a dog, and bay the moon.
>
> (Julius Caesar: IV, iii, 27)
>
> Tigers, not daughters.
>
> (King Lear: IV, ii, 40)

SCANSION

CELIA.   *Didst thou hear these verses?*
ROSALIND.   *O yes, I heard them all, and more too, for some of them*
had in them more feet than the verses would bear.

(As You Like It: III, ii, 162)

A brief overview of what can be a rather extensive study follows.

Text can be divided into two major groups depending on its rhythmic pattern, or the arrangement of stressed syllables, unstressed syllables, and silence.   **Prose** is text which has no structured rhythmic pattern; ordinary dialogue would qualify as prose.   **Verse** is text which has a definite rhythmic pattern that can be analyzed, as in a limerick or selection from *Mother Goose*. The process of analyzing the rhythmic pattern of verse is called **scansion**.

When scanning or analyzing the rhythmic pattern, one unit of the pattern is referred to as a **foot**, much like a measure in music; while **meter** refers to how many feet, or units, comprise the verse line.

The underlying rhythmic pattern (or feet) used by Shakespeare and his contemporaries is an unstressed/stressed arrangement of syllables, which is called 'iambic'.   This iambic foot repeats five times per metrical line.   Penta refers to 'five', thus the classification: **iambic pentameter**.

*/ unstressed, **stressed** /*

*/ It's **use** / ful **just** / re**lax** / and **read** / a**long** /.*

AUDIO 9 A► **iambic pentameter**

*/ If **mu** / sic **be**/ the **food** / of **love**, / play **on**! /*

(Twelfth Night: I, i, 1)

> Now **cracks** a **noble heart**. Good **night**, sweet **prince**,
> And **flights** of **angels sing** thee **to** thy **rest**!
>
> (Hamlet: V, ii, 359)
>
> Now **all** the **youth** of **England are** on **fire**,
> And **silken dalliance in** the **wardrobe lies**.
>
> (King Henry V: II, Chorus, 1)

Note. Often the unstressed pulse of the foot is a weak form, syllabic ending, prefix, or suffix of a word. The stressed pulse of the foot is often the stressed syllable of an operative or key word.

Scanning text can help the actor find the underlying iambic rhythm but it should not be 'played', or be too obvious during performance. It can also vary and is open to interpretation.

For example, though the first entry in **Audio 9A** above scans for an underlying iambic pattern, the actor might choose, after examination, to stress the last two words in order to make an emphatic point, in the same way singers might offer their interpretation of a musical selection after having studied the musical score.

Scansion is a tool for exploration. Examining variations or changes in the iambic rhythm of a line can be a useful aid in understanding meaning and determining how to communicate the point most effectively.

Sometimes characters may share the five feet of the iambic verse line:

AUDIO 9 B▶ **sharing a five foot iambic line**

1ˢᵗ MURDERER.
/ But who / did bid / thee join / with us? /
3ʳᵈ MURDERER.   / Macbeth. /

(Macbeth: III, iii, 1)

DIANA.
/ She then / was ho / nest.
BERTRAM.   So / should you / be.
DIANA.   No. /

(All's Well That Ends Well: IV, ii, 11)

KING JOHN
Death.
HUBERT
/ My lord? /
KING JOHN   / A grave. /
HUBERT   / He shall / not live. /
KING JOHN   / Enough. /

(King John: III, iii, 65)

VARIATION ON THE THEME: when the iambic meter is broken by the use of other metric feet, including:

Feet with two beats or syllables (other than iambic):

Trochaic: stressed/unstressed rhythm: / ' ⌣ /
Pyrrhic: unstressed, unstressed: / ⌣ ⌣ /
Spondaic: stressed, stressed: / ' ' /

Feet with three beats or syllables:

Anapestic: unstressed, unstressed, stressed: / ⌣ ⌣ ' /
Dactylic: stressed, unstressed, unstressed: / ' ⌣ ⌣ /

Many words in English are trochees, with the stress falling on the first syllable of the word: **fa**vor, **see**ing, etc. When they are preceded by short one-syllable words (such as articles, connectives, or prepositions) iambic rhythms are formed, as in: a **fa**vor, not **see**ing **clear**ly.

TROCHAIC OPENING refers to a common variation in the iambic opening of a line, when the first syllable of the opening foot is stressed, rather than the second.

Compare: the trochaic opening of the 2nd line against the fully iambic 1st line below:

⌣ / ⌣ / ⌣ / ⌣ / ⌣ / ⌣
The ve / nom cla / mors of / a jea / lous wo / man[1]

/ ⌣ ⌣ / ⌣ / ⌣ / ⌣ /
Poison / more dead / ly than / a mad / dog's tooth.

(Comedy of Errors: V, i, 69)

---

[1] See feminine endings, which are covered on page 89.

***AUDIO 9 C▶* trochaic opening**

/ ‿ ‿ / ‿ / ‿ / ‿ /
Stiffen / the si /news, con / jure up / the blood.

(Henry V: III, i, 7)

/ ‿ ‿ / ‿ / ‿ / ‿ /
Never, / O ne / ver, do / his ghost / the wrong.

(2 Henry IV: II, iii, 39)

/ ‿ ‿ / ‿ / ‿ / ‿ /
Horses / did neigh, / and dy / ing men / did groan.

(Julius Caesar: II, ii, 23)

MASCULINE ENDING refers to a line that ends with a stressed syllable, as in the typical iambic line:

How green / you are / and fresh / in this / old world!

(King John: III, iv, 144)

FEMININE ENDING refers to a line that ends with an unstressed syllable. Feminine endings finish the fifth foot giving the line 11 syllables in total, instead of 10.

For ho/nor tra/vels in /a strait/so na rrow,
Where one but goes abreast.

(Troilus and Cressida: III, iii, 154)

CAESURA refers to a slight pause within the five-foot line, usually after the 2nd or 3rd foot, which may or may not be marked with punctuation, but can serve to clarify the line and thought:

***AUDIO 9 D▶* caesura**

A little more than kin, / and less than kind.

(Hamlet: I, ii, 64)

France friend with England, / what becomes of me?

(King John: III, i, 35)

Men prize the thing ungain'd / more than it is.

(Troilus and Cressida: I, ii, 289)

FRONT VOWELS

See Overview pages 18-26

/ i / (w<u>e</u>)

Form the shape for speaking the first front vowel /i/ (w<u>e</u>) by closing the lower jaw almost completely, placing the tip of the tongue down behind the lower teeth, arching the front of the tongue high and forward toward the front of the hard palate, slightly spreading the cheeks and lips, and releasing sound through the mouth.

AUDIO 10▶ /i/ (w<u>e</u>)

      i

S<u>ea</u>l then, and all is done.

(Antony and Cleopatra: IV, xiv, 49)

      i   i   i   i

To w<u>ee</u>p with them that w<u>ee</u>p doth <u>ea</u>se some d<u>ea</u>l.

(Titus Andronicus: III, i, 244)

          i   i   i

The King is sickl<u>y</u>, w<u>ea</u>k, and melanchol<u>y</u>,

                 i

And his physicians fear him mightil<u>y</u>.

(Richard III: I, i, 136)

WORDS /i/ (w<u>e</u>)

Initial	Medial	Final
? eel	sleep	me
? easy	reach	key
? even	mean	knee
? each	grease	handy
? Eden	speech	weepy

The symbol /?/ is a reminder not to glottalize the initial vowel.

RHYTHM TRACK This vowel is one of five[1] that can be categorized as long, half-long, or short depending on its position in the word and the sounds that follow. Notice the variation in the length[2] of this sound, *reading across*:

long /i:/	long /i:/	half-long /i·/	short /i/
me	meal	meek	slimy
pea	peal	peach	lippy
see	seed	seat	sassy
bee	bean	beast	baby
agree	green	Greek	angry

This sound is **long /i:/** in a stressed syllable:

(a)   when it's the last sound of the word

(b)   when it's followed by a voiced consonant

PHRASES long /i:/

1.	cedar tree	6.	freed eagles
2.	yes, please	7.	green leaves
3.	mean thieves	8.	illegal to ski
4.	agrees to clean	9.	breathing easily
5.	seems reasonable	10.	team's achievement

This sound is **half-long /i·/** in a stressed syllable when followed by a voiceless consonant.

PHRASES half-long /i·/

1.	no sheets	6.	tired feet
2.	seeks Keith	7.	takes a peek
3.	peace on earth	8.	day at the beach
4.	dog on a leash	9.	washes with bleach
5.	fond of peaches	10.	filled with disbelief

This sound is **short /i/** when in an unstressed syllable or when used in the weak form of: he, me, she, we, be. Short /i/ is often represented by the spelling 'y' in an unstressed syllable at the end of a word.

---

[1] The five vowels that can be categorized long, half-long or short can be remembered from the line: 'All drama uses these words'. The eight other vowels, which are always categorized as short, can be remembered from the phrase: 'Mother took a poetics class'.

[2] Length indicators, or dots, used in IPA notation are optional (see pages 39-40). This section is marked to promote increased awareness and to aid those studying lengths.

PHRASES short /i/

1.	no vacancy	6.	my balcony
2.	awfully good	7.	joined Equity
3.	given priority	8.	filled a cavity
4.	what a rivalry	9.	very gracefully
5.	not particularly	10.	lots of activity

elongating but more natural - **Note: /i/ (we) is not marked for length from this point on.**

SENTENCES /i/ (we) various lengths

1. Steve, you're bleeding.

2. Truthfully, there's no vacancy.

3. He's leaving this evening it seems.

4. The carpet needs to be steam cleaned.

5. I believe you're my team leader, Deena.

6. Police caught the thieves fleeing the scene.

7. Overeating is not the only cause of obesity.

8. That was the creepiest movie I've ever seen!

9. I need to have this completed by this evening.

10. Teaching Edith how to water-ski was tedious.

11. There's no fee. Every human being gets in free.

12. Let's eat! I'd like an omelet with cheese, please.

13. Remembering to breathe helps me speak more clearly.

14. Lisa grieved over her beagle's death from heart disease.

15. She needs anesthesia for that medical procedure, I believe.

SOUND CHECK #1: /i/ **before the consonant /l/.** The back of the tongue should remain relaxed and uninvolved while moving the tongue tip from behind the lower teeth to touch the upper gum ridge on /il/ combinations, so that /j/ is not inserted between the two sounds. In other words, speak 'eel', not 'ee**juh**l'.

WORDS /i/ before /l/

feel	veal	keel	seal
real	deal	zeal	he'll
peel	we'll	steal	spiel
appeal	unreal	squeal	meal
feeling	Camille	genteel	ideal

PHRASES /i/ before /l/

1.	real appeal	6.	reeling it in
2.	break the seal	7.	feels the ordeal
3.	squeals at eels	8.	peals of laughter
4.	wheels and deals	9.	the meal of meals
5.	kneeling on steel	10.	shouldn't steal seals

SENTENCES /i/ before /l/

1.   I feel Neil is ideal for the part.

2.   They're optimistic and audition with zeal.

3.   We'll meet after the show, if you feel like it.

4.   Did you ever see 'Let's Make a Deal' on TV?

5.   That teal cashmere sweater feels great in the cold.

6.   That's by one of my favorite authors: Eugene O'Neill.

7.   The actor slipped on the banana peel, to peals of laughter.

8.   Her head was reeling and she almost keeled over on stage.

9.   What an ordeal, I broke my heel in the middle of the scene.

10.   Leigh was cast as MISS BEALE in the Broadway production.

NEUTRAL AMERICAN TEXT /i/ (we). *Mark the following and then speak out loud.*

/i/ before /l/:

                      i   i

The day will steal upon thee suddenly.

(Middleton & Rowley: The Changeling)

O now doth Death line his dead chaps with steel.

(King John: II, i, 352)

We must be brief when traitors brave the field.

(Richard III: IV, iii, 57)

Oh—ideals, ideals! If only I were not such a coward!

(Ibsen: Ghosts)

He'll learn before he quickly turns his heel,
That he's been booted face to face—with steel!

(Rostand: Cyrano de Bergerac)

Bow, stubborn knees, and heart, with strings of steel,
Be soft as sinews of the new-born babe!

(Hamlet: III, iii, 70)

/i/ various positions:

As in this world there are degrees of evils,
So in this world there are degrees of devils.

(Webster: The White Devil)

All that we see or seem
Is but a dream within a dream.

(Poe: A Dream Within a Dream)

Oh sin foul and deep!
Great faults are winked at when the Duke's asleep.

(Tourneur: The Revenger's Tragedy)

QUEEN.   Why seems it so particular with thee?
HAMLET. Seems, madam? Nay, it is, I know not "seems".

(Hamlet: I, ii, 75)

Methought I heard a voice cry, "Sleep no more!
Macbeth does murder sleep"—the innocent sleep,
Sleep that knits up the ravell'd sleeve of care.

(Macbeth: II, ii, 32)

/ ɪ / (wɪll)

The shape necessary for speaking the second front vowel /ɪ/ is nearly identical to that of the previous front vowel /i/. The jaw is mostly closed with the tongue tip resting down behind the lower teeth. The front of the tongue is arched high toward the front of the hard palate, and the lips and cheeks are slightly spread. When speaking /ɪ/, the articulators are slightly more open and relaxed with the tongue arched slightly lower.

AUDIO 11 A▶ /ɪ/ (wɪll)

I'll kɪll hɪm; by thɪs sword, I wɪll.

(Henry V: II, i, 100)

Soft stɪllnɛss and the night
Bɛcome the touchɛs of sweet harmony.

(The Merchant of Venice: V, i, 56)

The wɪll, the wɪll! we wɪll hear Caesar's wɪll!

(Julius Caesar: III, ii, 139)

WORDS /ɪ/ (wɪll)

Initial	Medial	Final
? if	fist	*
? itch	sing	*
? isn't	dish	*
? India	bring	*
? interest	million	*

Note: * this sound does not occur in the final position in NAS.

RHYTHM TRACK Sounds can be of various lengths and the time spent on the expression of any spoken sound is, hopefully, linked to an actor's intention or point of view. That said, /ɪ/ (wɪll) is short, crisp, and bright, especially in comparison to /i/ (wɛ).

PHRASES /ɪ/ (wi̱ll)

1.	invi̱sible i̱nsides	6.	li̱ttle bi̱t of gi̱n
2.	bri̱sk si̱ster Li̱nda	7.	i̱nclined to wi̱n
3.	chi̱ps and mi̱nt di̱p	8.	mi̱ssi̱ng i̱nsects
4.	Mi̱ss Bri̱tt's i̱nsti̱nct	9.	shi̱pped on a whi̱m
5.	i̱mmensely i̱mproved	10.	si̱ppi̱ng pi̱nk dri̱nks

SOUND CHECK #1 Rhythm Highlighter: use unstressed /ɪ/ prefixes. A prefix is a small group of letters added to the *beginning* of a base word, or root, that affects the meaning. Several prefixes have more than one pronunciation in contemporary American speech. The advantage of using /ɪ/ (wi̱ll) instead of /i/ (we̱), /ə/ (u̱h) or /e/ (ge̱t), is that it highlights the contrast in rhythm and musicality between the unstressed and stressed syllables, while keeping the prefix short, forward in the mouth, and clear.

AUDIO 11 B▶ /ɪ/ prefix

      ɪ
And now re'**mains**

         ɪ
That we find out the cause of this e'**ffect**,

         i
Or rather say, the cause of this '**de**fect,

  ɪ   ɪ
For this e'**ffect** de'**fec**tive comes by cause.

                         (Hamlet: II, ii, 100)

          ɪ   ɪ
There, at the moated grange, re'**sides** this de'**jec**ted Mariana.

                       (Measure for Measure: III, i, 264)

        ɪ   ɪ   ɪ
I will not ex'**cuse** you, you shall not be ex'**cus'd**, ex'**cu**ses shall

                   ɪ
not be admitted, there is no ex'**cuse** shall serve, you shall not

 ɪ
be ex'**cus'd**.

                         (2 Henry IV: V, i, 4)

This variation in rhythm and pitch within the word can be represented:

	LONG			**TUM**
short		(*or*)	tuh	

WORDS /ɪ/ (w**i**ll) **prefix** (common spellings left column)

be	be'**come**, be'**fore**, be'**friend**, be'**hoove**, be'**jewel**, be'**reft**
de	de'**cline**, de'**crease**, de'**part**, de'**rive**, de'**stroy**, de'**tain**
e	e'**ffect**, e'**llipse**, e'**longate**, e'**lude**, e'**quate**, e'**quip**, e'**rase**
i	i'**llicit**, i'**lliterate**, i'**magine**, i'**mmune**, i'**rrational**, i'**talics**
ne	ne'**gate**, ne'**glect**, ne'**gotiate**, ne'**farious**, ne'**matic**
pre	pre'**caution**, pre'**cede**, pre'**clude**, pre'**dict**, pre'**fer**, pre'**vent**
re	re'**bel**, re'**cede**, re'**cite**, re'**cline**, re'**flect**, re'**form**, re'**lated**
se	se'**clude**, se'**cure**, se'**date**, se'**duce**, se'**lect**, se'**rene**

/sɪkjuʌ/

PHRASES /ɪ/ (w**i**ll) **prefix**

NO GLOTTALS!

1.	re'**peat** after me	6.	no de'**cep**tion
2.	be'**hind** the door	7.	re'**hear**sing now
3.	pre'**fers** pre'**ven**tion	8.	i'**llegal** de'**ten**tion
4.	re'**strain** from e'**rup**ting	9.	be'**fore** or be'**tween**
5.	i'**maginative** negoti'**ation**	10.	precipi'**tation** tonight

Use the short /ɪ/ (w**i**ll) sound instead of the /e/ (g**e**t) sound in the following prefixes:

ɪ

| **em** | em'**balm**, em'**barr**assed, em'**bark,** em'**brace** |

ɪ

| **en** | en'**cour**age, en'**joy**, en'**liven**, en'**trenched** |

When 'ex' in the prefix is followed by a *voiceless* consonant, the prefix is pronounced /ɪks/ as in ex'pense. When 'ex' in the prefix is followed by a *voiced* sound, the prefix is pronounced /ɪgz/ as in ex'act.

later, *flutter*, *later*

ex	**ɪks**	ex'**pense**, ex'**cel**, ex'**pend**, ex'**plore**, ex'**tent**
ex	**ɪgz**	ex'**act**, ex'**alt**, ex'**amine**, ex'**ample**, ex'**haust**

ADDITIONAL PHRASES /ɪ/ (wɪll) prefix

1.	ex'**amines** it	6.	always ex'**act**
2.	em'**braces** her	7.	ex'**plained** later
3.	too ex'**haus**ting	8.	not an ex'**cep**tion
4.	en'**joy**ing living	9.	overly ex'**pen**sive
5.	ex'**pelled** at once	10.	carefully em'**balmed**

SENTENCES /ɪ/ (wɪll) prefix

1. If he recovers, he'll present the award.

2. The fire was immediately extinguished.

3. The reclusive farmer began to feel lonely.

4. Be exact when you examine the evidence.

5. She was determined to attend the premiere.

6. Can you explain why you refused to reply?

7. I thought that demented species was extinct.

8. I prefer you refrain from referring to your notes.

9. The expressive performance was strangely seductive.

10. Bill isn't prepared to take a salary reduction in December.

SOUND CHECK #2 Rhythm Highlighter: use /ɪ/ in unstressed suffixes and word endings. A suffix is a small group of letters added to the *end* of a base word, or root, that affects the meaning. Using the short /ɪ/ (wɪll) sound highlights the contrast in rhythm and musicality between the stressed and unstressed syllables. Common spellings include: 'i' (ing, ish, ity, ive), 'a' (age, ate) and 'e' (ed, et, es, ess, est, less, ness).

AUDIO 11 C▶ /ɪ/ suffix

Thou ˈbasest thing, avoid hence, from my sight!

(Cymbeline: I, i, 125)

To be furious

Is to be ˈfrighted out of fear.

(Antony and Cleopatra: III, xiii, 194)

How sharper than a serpent's tooth it is

To have a ˈthankless child!

(King Lear: I, iv, 288)

This variation in rhythm and pitch can by represented:

LONG short   (*or*)   **TUM** tuh

WORDS /ɪ/ (wi̱ll) suffix (common spellings left column)

ing	ˈdoing, ˈgoing, ˈsaying ˈseeing, ˈtalking, ˈwriting
ish	ˈbookish, ˈchildish, ˈgreenish ˈselfish, ˈsqueamish
ity	caˈpacity, luminˈosity, raˈpacity, veˈracity
ive	creˈative, exˈpressive, ˈmissive, ˈpassive, proˈgressive
age	ˈbaggage, ˈmarriage, ˈpassage, ˈsavage, ˈscrimmage
ate[1]	ˈaggregate, ˈfortunate, iˈmmediate, ˈpassionate
ed	inˈfected, ˈheeded, ˈplanted, ˈpleaded, proˈtected
et	ˈbasket, ˈcarpet, ˈcloset, ˈmarket, ˈpicket, ˈpocket
es	ˈbreezes, ˈcrushes, ˈmisses, ˈpauses, ˈprices, ˈwishes

---

[1] When the 'ate' ending occurs in words used as *verbs*, it is often pronounced /eɪt/ (ate) as in: estim<u>ate</u>, intim<u>ate</u>, advoc<u>ate</u>. For example: "Estim<u>ate</u> the price".

(handwritten annotation: 1 prìncéss / 2 prìnce̦s)

ess	'hostess, 'shepherdess, 'sorceress, 'waitress
est	'biggest, 'boldest, 'happiest, 'luckiest, 'smartest
less	'careless, 'helpless, 'sleepless, 'thoughtless, 'useless
ness	'fondness, 'friendliness, 'goodness, 'happiness

PHRASES /ɪ/ (wi̱ll) suffix

1.	my 'goodness	6.	quite 'hopeless
2.	what au'dacity	7.	an 'average day
3.	very 'passionate	8.	'falling to 'pieces
4.	not the 'cheapest	9.	trans'mitted di'seases
5.	'nothing 'granted	10.	placed on the 'cabinet

SENTENCES /ɪ/ (wi̱ll) suffix

1. Rummage through the closet.

2. After marriage, they took a pilgrimage.

3. The actress received massive media coverage.

4. Goodness, we're hopelessly and helplessly lost.

5. She loved that snippet of lighthearted dialogue.

6. That is the rarest of jewels: in fact, it's priceless.

7. He's decisive and perceptive, though a bit peevish.

8. The corporate executive was immediately promoted.

9. The ineffective faucet was made of the weakest materials.

10. Damage from the storm that ravaged the area was minimal.

SPECIAL ATTENTION Remember to speak /ɪ/ (wi̱ll) *not* /i/ (we̱):

(a)   when 'ing' occurs in the root of a word

(b)   in 'ing' suffixes

There should be no 'off-glide' or addition of an 'uh' sound, on the final voiced /ŋ/ 'ng'. See additional practice on page 246.

WORDS /ɪŋ/ 'ing' in the root

ring	rink	sing	kink
ting	fink	king	slink
ping	pink	ding	minx
thing	mink	wing	brink
Ming	think	bring	shrink

FALSTAFF. *Go, you thing, go.*
HOSTESS. *Say, what thing? what thing?*
FALSTAFF. *What thing? why, a thing to thank God on.*
HOSTESS. *I am no thing to thank God on... I am an honest*
man's wife.

(1 Henry IV: III, iii, 115)

WORDS /ɪŋ/ 'ing' suffix

¹**ar**guing	¹**offering**	¹**gesturing**	¹**ra**vaging
¹**me**nacing	¹**fa**voring	¹**cantering**	¹**emp**tying
ex¹**pecting**	¹**banishing**	¹**pon**dering	¹**hun**gering

PHRASES /ɪŋ/ 'ing' suffix

1. needs ¹**watering**
2. seen ¹**wan**dering
3. a little ¹**worry**ing
4. heard ¹**mur**muring
5. very en¹**light**ening
6. just ¹**visi**ting
7. ¹**shivering** a bit
8. always ¹**lis**tening
9. fond of ¹**revel**ing
10. lights are ¹**dim**ming

SENTENCES /ɪŋ/ 'ing' suffix (see also: poetry of *Southey* on page 312)

1. Why is everyone loitering?

2. I'm thinking of practicing more.

3. They've stopped eating fattening foods.

4. He's busy entertaining visiting relatives.

5. She was comforting a whimpering puppy.

6. It can be discouraging, but don't stop auditioning.

7. I love watching and listening to actors rehearsing.

8. The plot is unraveling in the most interesting way.

9. They've just finished furnishing their new apartment.

10. The performance was so boring, I felt like walking out.

SOUND CHECK #3: /ɪ/ (w<u>i</u>ll) and /i/ (w<u>e</u>) before /l/. Distinguish between the longer, energized /i/ sound and the shorter, slightly more relaxed /ɪ/ sound before the consonant /l/ in the following words. *Read across.*

/ɪl/	/il/	/ɪl/	/il/
fill	feel	mill	meal
pill	peel	dill	deal
hill	heal	village	veal
kill	keel	Bill	Beale
nil	kneel	Jill	congeal

PHRASES /ɪ/ (w<u>i</u>ll) before /l/

1. st<u>i</u>ll sk<u>i</u>lled
2. thr<u>i</u>lled J<u>i</u>ll
3. one m<u>i</u>llion
4. st<u>i</u>ll ch<u>i</u>lling
5. dr<u>i</u>lling for oil
6. sp<u>i</u>lt m<u>i</u>lk
7. d<u>i</u>ll pickles
8. s<u>i</u>lly W<u>i</u>lliam
9. sp<u>i</u>lled the p<u>i</u>lls
10. f<u>i</u>lled to the h<u>i</u>lt

SENTENCES /ɪ/ (w<u>i</u>ll) before /l/

1. Little Lily is a brilliant downhill skier.

2. Bill thrills to the trill of whippoorwills.

3. Will's skill at writing with a quill pen is nil.

4. Do they make chlorophyll pills from daffodils?

5. When building a kiln, don't use unskilled labor.

6. Until the film, I knew zilch about the Vanderbilts.

7. I still feel guilty about spilling milk on the silk quilt.

8. Jill got a chill on the plane coming back from Brazil.

9. I still haven't seen *The Amityville Horror* or *Kill Bill*.

10. Sounds from drilling at the mill are shrill in Louisville.

NEUTRAL AMERICAN TEXT /ɪ/ (wɪll). *Mark the following and then speak out loud.*

/ɪ/ before /l/:

        I   I   I   I

Error i' th' bill, sir, error i' th' bill!

(The Taming of the Shrew: IV, iii, 145)

I'll gild the faces of the grooms withal,
For it must seem their guilt.

(Macbeth: II, ii, 53)

At morn—at noon—at twilight dim—
Maria! thou hast heard my hymn!
In joy and woe—in good and ill—
Mother of God, be with me still!

(Edgar Allan Poe: Hymn)

Achilles will not to the field to-morrow.

(Troilus and Cressida: II, iii, 162)

/ɪ/ prefixes and suffixes:

But let us give him burial as becomes.

(Titus Andronicus: I, i, 347)

You shall offend him and extend his passion.

(Macbeth: III, iv, 56)

Falling in, after falling out, may make them three.

(Troilus and Cressida: III, i, 103)

Thou grumblest and railest every hour on Achilles.

(Troilus and Cressida: II, i, 32)

Why, what a gorgeous bonnet you've been investing in!

(Ibsen: Hedda Gabler)

Oh, his relations have entirely washed their hands of him.

(Ibsen: Hedda Gabler)

He made confession of you,
And gave you such a masterly report
For art and exercise in your defense,
And for your rapier most especial.

(Hamlet IV, vii, 95)

There is no tarrying here.

(Troilus and Cressida: II, iii, 258)

The least allusion to the...cartilage...
Alas, may prove a fatal sacrilege!

(Rostand: Cyrano de Bergerac)

The lowest and most dejected thing of fortune.

(King Lear: IV, i, 3)

Shall the Orphanage buildings be insured or not?

(Ibsen: Ghosts)

I'll assume you were merely exaggerating, or engaging in
what's commonly known as flattery.

(Strindberg: Miss Julie)

Singing, or howling, braying, barking, all
As their wild fancies prompt 'em.

(Middleton & Rowley: The Changeling)

You men of Cyprus, let her have your knees.
Hail to thee, lady! and the grace of heaven,
Before, behind thee, and on every hand,
Enwheel thee round!

(Othello: II, i, 84)

Truly, shepherd, in respect of itself, it is a good life; but in respect that
it is a shepherd's life, it is naught. In respect that it is solitary, I like it
very well; but in respect that it is private, it is a very vile life. Now in
respect it is in the fields, it pleaseth me well; but in respect it is not in
the court, it is tedious.

(As You Like It: III, ii, 13)

Shall I tell you a lie? I do despise a liar as I do despise one that is
false, or as I despise one that is not true.

(The Merry Wives of Windsor: I, i, 68)

O villain, villain! His very opinion in the letter. Abhorred villain!
unnatural, detested, brutish villain! worse than brutish! Go, sirrah,
seek him; I'll apprehend him. Abominable villain! Where is he?

(King Lear: I, ii, 75)

/ e / (g<u>e</u>t)

Form the shape for the third front vowel **/e/** (g<u>e</u>t) by opening the lower jaw slightly more than for the second front vowel **/ɪ/**, resting the tip of the tongue down behind the lower front teeth, and arching the front of the tongue half-high. The lips and cheeks remain almost neutral as this short, bright sound releases forward through the mouth. Remember: all vowels release through the mouth and are spoken with the soft palate raised in well-pronounced NAS.

AUDIO 12 A▶ **/e/ (g<u>e</u>t)**

>   e   e
> Is there <u>a</u>ny way to show such fri<u>e</u>ndship?
>
> > (Much Ado About Nothing: IV, i, 263)
>
> e   e
> B<u>e</u>nefactors? Well; what b<u>e</u>nefactors are they?
>
> > (Measure for Measure: II, i, 51)
>
>   e   e
> Urge me no more, I shall forg<u>e</u>t mys<u>e</u>lf;
>   e   e
> Have mind upon your h<u>ea</u>lth; t<u>e</u>mpt me no farther.
>
> > (Julius Caesar: IV, iii, 35)

WORDS /e/ (g<u>e</u>t)

Initial	Medial	Final
? ebb	best	*
? edge	guess	*
? ethics	desert	*
? Edgar	feather	*
? efforts	impression	*

Note: The following words are spoken with **/e/** (g<u>e</u>t): any, many, egg, leg, beg, keg, pleasure, measure, length, strength.

RHYTHM TRACK The vowel **/e/** (g<u>e</u>t) is a short, clear, bright sound spoken with the tongue arched forward in the mouth to avoid a dull, lax sound.

PHRASES /e/ (g<u>e</u>t)

1.	b<u>e</u>tter l<u>e</u>verage	6.	h<u>e</u>sitates to st<u>e</u>p
2.	r<u>e</u>sting y<u>e</u>sterday	7.	<u>e</u>thically corr<u>e</u>ct
3.	cost <u>e</u>ff<u>e</u>ctiveness	8.	d<u>e</u>adly sch<u>e</u>dule
4.	impr<u>e</u>ssive sk<u>e</u>tch	9.	l<u>e</u>ngth and str<u>e</u>ngth
5.	p<u>e</u>ssimistic pr<u>e</u>sident	10.	v<u>e</u>getables on l<u>e</u>ttuce

SENTENCES /e/ (l<u>e</u>t)

1. Are we there yet, Chester?

2. Leslie felt she needed to stretch.

3. You're correct, I detest that smell.

4. This extra soft Kleenex is the best.

5. I confess I'd love to play MACBETH.

6. I was impressed with everyone's integrity.

7. Which pirate is known for his peg leg, Leonard?

8. Check with Esther before you order refreshments.

9. The effects of red pepper on insects are legendary.

10. It was alleged that the detective never studied the evidence.

SOUND CHECK #1: /e/ (get) before 'm' or 'n'. Use neutral /e/ (g<u>e</u>t) rather than /ɪ/ (w<u>i</u>ll) before 'm' and 'n' in the *stressed* syllable of a word. This is an important sound check for those from parts of the South and Mid-West. Remember: *unstressed* 'en' and 'em' prefixes are spoken with /ɪ/. See page 97.

AUDIO 12 B▶ /e/ (g<u>e</u>t) before 'm' or 'n'

       e
I do believe he's tr<u>e</u>mbling.

          (Strindberg: Miss Julie)

    e   e   e
Rem<u>e</u>mber who comm<u>e</u>nded thy yellow stockings.

          (Twelfth Night: II, v, 153)

      e   e   e
Good g<u>e</u>ntle youth, t<u>e</u>mpt not a desperate man.

          (Romeo and Juliet: V, iii, 59)

WORDS /e/ (get) before 'm' or 'n'

gems	cents	event	spent
blend	hence	defend	bench
empty	rented	lament	gentle
amend	expend	avenge	empire
quench	attempt	slender	prevent

COMPARE /ɪ/ (will) and /e/ (get) *Read across.*

/ɪ/ (will)	/e/ (get)	/ɪ/ (will)	/e/ (get)
sin	send	fin	fen
pin	pen	tin	ten
kin	Ken	bin	Ben
Linda	lender	pinnacle	pencil
mimic	member	since	sentence

PHRASES /e/ (get) before 'm' or 'n'

1.	defensive measures	6.	remembering Ben
2.	lending them again	7.	embassy's remedy
3.	commendable ending	8.	sense of adventure
4.	spending every penny	9.	send many men then
5.	pens for his eminence	10.	vendors renting tents

Rhyming sounds can sometimes be useful when trying to distinguish if one is speaking /e/ before 'm' and 'n', as in the following exercise.

WORDS /e/ (get) sounds in the following should 'rhyme' *Read across.*

/e/	ever	/e/	empty, emblem, emperor, empathy
/he/	heck	/he/	hem, hemisphere, hemp, hemlock
/me/	met	/me/	memo, member, remember, memory
/te/	test	/te/	tempo, temperature, tempest, temporary
/fe/	fetch	/fe/	fen, fender, defending, defensive
/se/	set	/se/	send, sent, sentence, senator, sensitive
/pe/	pest	/pe/	pen, pencil, pensive, pendant
/we/	west	/we/	when, went, Wendy, wench
/me/	mess	/me/	men, meant, mend, mention, mental
/de/	desk	/de/	den, dent, dense, Denny, dental
/be/	best	/be/	Ben, bench, bent, benefits, beneficial
/te/	Tess	/te/	ten, tense, attend, attention, tennis

SENTENCES /e/ (g<u>e</u>t) before 'm' or 'n'

1. Erin was involved in a fender bender.

2. Cayenne pepper can offend the senses.

3. Have you ever watched *The Avengers*?

4. The letter was marked 'return to sender'.

5. Transcend the need for vengeance, Wendy.

6. My dentist promotes preventative measures.

7. The ill-tempered superintendent is condescending.

8. Benny, we recommend ending your overspending.

9. Penny's performance was mentioned in the review.

10. Intense penguins can stand at attention indefinitely.

11. Ken and I are no longer members of the tennis club.

12. Emmett dislikes defense and prefers playing offense.

13. Friends asked me for a sentence of exactly ten words.

14. Theatre companies generally accept tax-exempt status.

15. The musical tones blended during the lovely crescendo.

16. When apprehended, the criminal pretended to surrender.

17. Jen spoke endlessly of a gentlemanly tenor from Denver.

18. The apprentice should be commended; he's indispensable.

19. *Agamemnon* will not be extended; it will end in November.

20. How many men are invited to the convention in Tennessee?

Len and Ken's Adventure

Len and Ken, both in their late twenties, have been best friends since elementary school. Last December, intent on adopting a pet together, they went to Wendy's Veterinary Medical Center. Emma, an immensely contented French Bulldog, now resides with Len and Ken in their rented penthouse in the east seventies.

SOUND CHECK #2: /e/ before /l/. Arch the tongue forward in the mouth in order to avoid a dull, lax vowel sound when speaking /el/ combinations.

bell	cell	fell	gel
hell	Nell	tell	yell
smell	shell	expel	quell
propel	Ravel	dwell	retell
compel	dispel	personnel	unwell

PHRASES /e/ before /l/

1.	self-help	6.	a cappella
2.	sells jelly	7.	Elmer Fudd
3.	felt svelte	8.	Helen's fella
4.	dinner bell	9.	farewell to elves
5.	health and wealth	10.	blond bombshell

SENTENCES /e/ before /l/

1. Do tell, Mel, who rang the bell?

2. Twelve elk became unwell eating elm trees.

3. Anyone remember *The Lawrence Welk Show*?

4. Cornell tightened his belt, then felt like belching.

5. Ed was compelled to delve into the books on the shelf.

6. Well, when overwhelmed with jealousy, elephants yell.

7. It's a delicate situation, so Ellen's walking on egg shells.

8. Tell Mr. Roosevelt mademoiselle has had a fainting spell.

9. In a nutshell, our motel is the worst in the commonwealth.

10. Nell's clientele prefer *Velvet* hair gel; it penetrates the cells.

NEUTRAL AMERICAN TEXT /e/ (get). *Mark the following and then speak out loud.*

/e/ before 'm' or 'n':

           e

I will be mild and gentle in my words.

(Richard III: IV, iv, 161)

110

If we shadows have offended,
Think but this, and all is mended.

(A Midsummer Night's Dream: V, i, 423)

O, it is excellent
To have a giant's strength; but it is tyrannous
To use it like a giant.

(Measure for Measure: II, ii, 107)

L. MACBETH.
Did not you speak?
MACBETH.　　　　　When?
L. MACBETH.　　　　　　　Now.
MACBETH.　　　　　　　　　As I descended?

(Macbeth: II, ii, 16)

QUEEN.　　Hamlet, thou hast thy father much offended.
HAMLET.　Mother, you have my father much offended.

(Hamlet: III, iv, 9)

That ever-living man of memory,
Henry the Fifth.

(1 Henry VI: IV, iii, 51)

Ah, let me live in prison all my days,
And when I give occasion of offense,
Then let me die, for now thou hast no cause.

(3 Henry VI: I, iii, 43)

What, sir, not yet at rest? The King's a-bed.
He hath been in unusual pleasure, and
Sent forth great largess to your offices.

(Macbeth: II, i, 12)

And turning to his men,
Quoth our brave Henry then,
'Though they be one to ten,
Be not amazéd.
Yet have we well begun,
Battles so bravely won
Have ever to the sun
By fame been raiséd.

(Michael Drayton: Ballad of Agincourt)

No longer session hold upon my shame,
But let my trial be mine own confession.
Immediate sentence then, and sequent death,
Is all the grace I beg.

(Measure for Measure: V, i, 371)

/e/ before /l/:

Who lives and dares but say thou didst not well
When I was got, I'll send his soul to hell.

(King John: I, i, 271)

The bell invites me.
Hear it not, Duncan, for it is a knell,
That summons thee to heaven or to hell.

(Macbeth: II, i, 62)

SCROOP.　　Both young and old rebel,
　　　　　　And all goes worse than I have power to tell.
K. RICHARD.　Too well, too well thou tell'st a tale so ill.

(Richard II: III, ii, 119)

If you did wed my sister for her wealth,
Then for her wealth's sake use her with more kindness:
Or if you like elsewhere, do it by stealth.

(The Comedy of Errors: III, ii, 5)

Hear the sledges with the bells –
Silver bells!
What a world of merriment their melody foretells!
How they tinkle, tinkle, tinkle,
In the icy air of night!
While the stars that oversprinkle
All the heavens seem to twinkle
With a crystalline delight;
Keeping time, time, time,
In a sort of Runic rhyme,
To the tintinnabulation that so musically wells
From the bells, bells, bells, bells,
Bells, bells, bells –
From the jingling and the tinkling of the bells.

(Edgar Allan Poe: The Bells)

/ æ / (th<u>a</u>t)

Form the shape for the fourth front vowel /æ/ (th<u>a</u>t) by resting the tip of the tongue down behind the lower teeth and dropping the lower jaw substantially more open than for the previous /e/ (g<u>e</u>t) sound. This will lessen the front tongue arch noticeably to a low, almost flat position in relationship to the hard palate. The cheeks and lips remain neutral but energized as sound releases forward through the mouth.

AUDIO 13▶ /æ/ (th<u>a</u>t)

(weak form or æ)   æ   æ
The princess shall have her castle.

(Ibsen: The Master Builder)

æ (or weak form)   æ
I <u>a</u>m not bound to please thee with my <u>a</u>nswers.

(The Merchant of Venice: IV, i, 65)

æ   æ
Things p<u>a</u>st redress are now with me p<u>a</u>st care.

(Richard II: II, iii, 171)

WORDS /æ/ (th<u>a</u>t)

Initial	Medial	Final
? after	slap	*
? actor	habit	*
? assets	traffic	*
? agitate	attack	*
? aspirin	casting	*

RHYTHM TRACK Although /æ/ (th<u>a</u>t) is classified as short, it is generally longer than either /ɪ/ (w<u>i</u>ll) or /e/ (g<u>e</u>t) when spoken.

Note: If Spanish is your first language, position the front tongue arch slightly higher and more forward than for the Spanish pronunciation represented by the letter 'a'. The jaw may also need to close slightly more.

PHRASES /æ/ (th<u>a</u>t)

1.	scr<u>a</u>tchy p<u>a</u>tch	6.	f<u>a</u>shionable <u>a</u>ds
2.	<u>a</u>ctually <u>a</u>cting	7.	st<u>a</u>cks of sn<u>a</u>cks
3.	h<u>a</u>ppy <u>a</u>crob<u>a</u>ts	8.	dis<u>a</u>strous j<u>a</u>cket
4.	<u>a</u>thletic <u>a</u>ctivity	9.	enthusi<u>a</u>stic cl<u>a</u>pping
5.	p<u>a</u>ckage to <u>A</u>frica	10.	h<u>a</u>bit of st<u>a</u>shing c<u>a</u>sh

---

SOUND CHECK #1: Speak the vowel /æ/ rather than /ẽæ/ diphthong by keeping the throat, tongue, cheeks, and jaw relaxed as the tongue arches low in the mouth. Some speakers from the Great Lakes area, NYC, Boston, etc. 'slide' from /e/ to /æ/ while over-tensing the articulators. This results in a bright, nasal diphthong represented by /ẽæ/. The wavy line over /ẽ/ represents nasality.

Breathe in, then speak the following words on the releasing breath. The throat, tongue, cheeks, and jaw should remain relaxed, with the tongue arched low. You can also pinch your nose during the vowel to check that sound is releasing through the mouth, not the nose. Sound *should* release through the nose on /m n ŋ/, so do not pinch your nose on those sounds.

WORDS speak the pure vowel /æ/ rather than /ẽæ/ diphthong

Jack	crash	batch	task
sassy	nasty	faster	gasp
apple	savage	tablet	sadly
match	Athens	lavish	black
casting	laughter	passive	master

PHRASES speak the pure vowel /æ/ rather than /ẽæ/ diphthong

1.	<u>a</u>fter th<u>a</u>t	6.	h<u>a</u>ppy d<u>a</u>ds
2.	b<u>a</u>d tr<u>a</u>ffic	7.	l<u>a</u>st S<u>a</u>turday
3.	M<u>a</u>tt's st<u>a</u>sh	8.	h<u>a</u>ppen to <u>a</u>sk
4.	b<u>a</u>ck tr<u>a</u>cking	9.	l<u>a</u>cks the f<u>a</u>cts
5.	tr<u>a</u>ctor coll<u>a</u>psed	10.	sm<u>a</u>shed gl<u>a</u>sses

SENTENCES speak the pure vowel /æ/ rather than /ẽæ/ diphthong

1. Perhaps Jack is an insomniac.

2. Cathy, let's practice chatting in Latin.

3. Jack's black cat sat basking in the sun.

4. Wear something practical (but not tacky).

5. After the accident, they took drastic action.

6. We were hired to enact the historical battle.

7. What's that scratching sound, Mr. Thatcher?

8. Brad, your socks are attractive, but don't match.

9. Actually, overacting can detract from the scene.

10. They ran out of gas on the way to the track meet.

11. Collect the facts before preparing your income tax.

12. Congratulations; your advertisement is fascinating.

13. The fragile sound of distant bagpipes was a bit magical.

14. As an actor, Maxwell is a craftsman; he's great at accents.

15. I'm baffled how they photographed workers on the scaffold.

SOUND CHECK #2 special case: /æ/ before 'm', 'n', 'g', 'ng', 'nk' need not be a pure vowel sound in NAS[1], but it should not be overly tense or nasalized.

/æn/	/æm/	/æg/	/æŋ/	/æŋk/	/æŋg/
man	slam	tag	rang	rank	angle
frantic	lamb	rags	hang	stank	dangle
fanned	clams	ragged	slang	blank	bangle
bandage	champ	snagged	clang	Hank	mangle
standard	damage	haggard	banged	thanks	strangle

PHRASES /æ/ relaxed (th_a_t) before / n, m, g, ŋ, ŋk, ng /

1. angry Danny
2. campus prank
3. clanging tanks
4. pampered Annie
5. unmanageable bags
6. drank brandy
7. bankrupt Hank
8. fancy planning
9. anxious to thank
10. Thanksgiving ham

---

[1] Classical American dialect does require pure /æ/. See pages 349-352 for instructional material.

SENTENCES /æ/ relaxed (th<u>a</u>t) before / n, m, g, ŋ, ŋk, ŋg /

1. Nancy stared blankly.

2. What's the plan, Chan?

3. Brand saw the damage firsthand.

4. Did Blanche escape the avalanche?

5. Thankfully, I have a fantastic landlady.

6. Who won the break dancing championship?

7. That anchorman's office is overly cramped.

8. Can we wrangle Yankee tickets for Sammy?

9. The telegram advised Ann: see France firsthand.

10. The band cancelled; they all have swollen glands.

11. The champion's remarks are considered sacrosanct.

12. Hank's Mustang vanished while he was in the bank.

13. Our clan formed a caravan and drove to the Grand Slam.

14. The man in command of expanding Disneyland is grand.

15. Are you sure camcorders are banned in the theatre? I am.

æ
For stony limits ꞌ*c<u>a</u>nnot hold love out.*

(Romeo and Juliet: II, ii, 67)

Stress is usually placed on the second syllable of the word 'cannot' in contemporary material and on the first syllable of the word in classic text, as in the selection from *Romeo and Juliet*, above.

SOUND CHECK #3: speak pure, open /æ/ before /l/. The tongue tip contacts the upper gum ridge and does not protrude between the teeth on /l/.

---

shall	alp	pal	scalp
value	aloe	talon	alpine
tallow	ballot	callow	gallop
scallop	gallon	gallows	valiant
morale	callous	salvage	shallow

PHRASES clear /æ/ before /l/

1.	v<u>a</u>lley girls	4.	v<u>a</u>liant g<u>a</u>l
2.	s<u>a</u>lad dressing	5.	f<u>a</u>lcon's t<u>a</u>lons
3.	It<u>a</u>lian b<u>a</u>llads	6.	C<u>a</u>lifornia can<u>a</u>l

SENTENCES clear /æ/ before /l/

1. Psychoanalysis demands confidentiality, Allen.

2. Sally is expected at the rally on Valentine's Day.

3. Valerie maintains her vitality by cutting calories.

NEUTRAL AMERICAN TEXT /æ/ (th<u>a</u>t). *Mark the following and speak out loud.*

/æ/ before 'm', 'n', 'g', 'ng', 'nk':

æ

How well I underst<u>an</u>d her, if only she knew!

(Chekhov: The Cherry Orchard)

Rage like an angry boar chafed with sweat?

(The Taming of the Shrew: I, ii, 202)

Why not face matters as they stand?
Perhaps m'sieur finds it a trifle…grand?

(Rostand: Cyrano de Bergerac)

Everyone can master a grief but he that has it.

(Much Ado About Nothing: III, ii, 28)

CASSIUS.   Stand ho!
BRUTUS.   Stand ho! Speak the word along.
1 SOLDIER.   Stand!
2 SOLDIER.   Stand!
3 SOLDIER.   Stand!

(Julius Caesar: IV, ii, 32)

O, my offense is rank, it smells to heaven.

(Hamlet: III, iii, 36)

Post back with speed, and tell him what hath chanc'd.

(Julius Caesar: III, I, 287)

EMILIA.   What will you give me now
            For that same handkerchief?
IAGO.   What handkerchief?
EMILIA.   What handkerchief?
            Why, that the Moor first gave to Desdemona.

(Othello: III, iii, 305)

/æ/ various positions:

Ay me, unhappy,
To be a queen, and crown'd with infamy!

(2 Henry VI: III, ii, 70)

Wast thou mad,
That thus so madly thou didst answer me?

(The Comedy of Errors: II, ii, 11)

We are glad the Dauphin is so pleasant with us,
His present and your pains we thank you for.
When we have match'd our rackets to these balls,
We will in France, by God's grace, play a set
Shall strike his father's crown into the hazard.
Tell him he hath made a match with such a wrangler
That all the courts of France will be disturb'd
With chaces. And we understand him well.

(Henry V: I, ii, 259)

And thereof came it that the man was mad.

(The Comedy of Errors: V, i, 68)

For that matter, he was away from home himself—he was traveling.

(Ibsen: Hedda Gabler)

Rats!
They fought the dogs and killed the cats,
And bit the babies in the cradles,
And ate the cheeses out of the vats,
And licked the soup from the cooks' own ladles,
Split open the kegs of salted sprats,
Made nests inside men's Sunday hats,
And even spoiled the women's chats
By drowning their speaking
With shrieking and squeaking
In fifty different sharps and flats.

(Robert Browning: Pied Piper of Hamelin)

MID-VOWELS

See Overview pages 18-26

/ ɝ / (ER)

Form the shape for the stressed mid-vowel /ɝ/ (ER) by relaxing the jaw half open, arching the middle of the tongue high near the hard palate, lifting the *tip* up behind the alveolar ridge and curling it slightly back, as sound releases through the mouth. Rounding the lips is not necessary, though many people do.

The tongue tip rests down behind the lower front teeth for all vowels, diphthongs, and triphthongs, *except* those that contain the strong or weak vowels of 'r': /ɝ/ (ER), /ɚ/ (er).

AUDIO 14► stressed /ɝ/ (ER)

I see thee compass'd with thy kingdom's **pearl**.

(Macbeth: V, ix, 22)

Th'ob**'serv'd** of all ob**'ser**vers, quite, quite down!

(Hamlet: III, i, 154)

My **w<u>or</u>ds** fly up, my thoughts remain below:
W<u>or</u>ds without thoughts never to heaven go.

(Hamlet: III, iii, 97)

WORDS stressed /ɝ/ (ER)

Initial	Medial	Final
? 'err	'learn	'sir
? 'irk	'purple	'fur
? 'urge	'thirsty	'stir
? 'early	'person	in'fer
? 'earth	re'hearsal	con'cur

RHYTHM TRACK: This sound can be categorized as long, half-long, or, in rare instances, short.[1] This depends on its position in the word and the sounds that follow. Notice the variation in lengths while *reading across*:

long /ɝː/	long /ɝː/	half-long /ɝ·/	half-long /ɝ·/
infer	fern	firth	flirt
blur	blurb	blurt	burp
burr	burn	birth	burst
purr	perm	purse	perch
were	worm	worth	worst

This sound is **long /ɝː/** in a stressed syllable:

(a)   when it is the last sound of the word

(b)   when it is followed by a voiced consonant

PHRASES long /ɝː/

1.	girls in a hurry[2]	6.	swirl and twirl
2.	too early to worry	7.	girlish mermaid
3.	encouraged courage	8.	nourishing curry
4.	surge in subservience	9.	currant preserves
5.	thoroughly concerned	10.	conservative journal

This sound is **half-long /ɝ·/** in a stressed syllable when followed by a voiceless consonant.

PHRASES half-long /ɝ·/

1.	perky worker	6.	purple circle
2.	reimburse Percy	7.	birthday shirt
3.	lurching curtsey	8.	worship dessert
4.	perfect rehearsal	9.	cursing merchants
5.	immersed in work	10.	search for a purpose

---

[1] Length indicators (or dots) used in IPA notation are optional (see pages 39-40). This section is marked to promote increased awareness and to aid those studying lengths.
[2] Many words in these phrases are pronounced with the stressed vowel /ɝː/ before the consonant /r/ in Neutral American Speech, as in hurry: /ˈhɝːri/.

A slightly **shorter** /ɜ/ can be spoken in weak forms of 'her', 'were' and 'sir'. In almost all other cases, the short version of this sound represented by the symbol /ə/ is spoken in unstressed syllables. The following selection contains the weak form of /ɜ/, fully-long stressed /ɜ:/, and the unstressed vowel /ə/.

weak forms: ɜ (or) ə   ɜ: ə ə
> They w<u>ere</u> villains, m<u>urderers</u>. The will, read the will!

(Julius Caesar: III, ii, 156)

Note: /ɜ/ (ER) is not marked for length from this point on.

SENTENCES /ɜ/ (ER) various lengths

1. Turn the toast before it burns.

2. You certainly deserved first prize.

3. Blackbirds chirped in the birch tree.

4. Burt splurged on tickets to the circus.

5. He asserts that nursing is worthy work.

6. Do crossword puzzles use code words?

7. Certainly, surgeons must be reimbursed.

8. The most overworked interns are in research.

9. I'm concerned. We need more rehearsal time.

10. This superb herb dressing isn't sold commercially.

11. Her blurred version of events concerned the attorney.

12. It was confirmed. Someone hacked into the network.

13. Detergent will wash that dessert off your favorite shirt.

14. I heard the colonel cursing when his job was terminated.

15. The anniversary circular was published Thursday the 30th.

SOUND CHECK #1: clear /ɜl/ combinations. Do not pull down or flatten the middle of the tongue as the <u>tip</u> moves to touch the upper gum ridge for /l/, or else /ə/ (<u>uh</u>) may be inserted between /ɜ/ and /l/. Speak 'girl' not 'giruhl'.

WORDS /ɝ/ before /l/

girl	early	purl	curl
hurl	pearl	surly	skirl
twirl	whirl	early	burly
world	unfurl	churl	furlough
Shirley	underworld	Merlin	Sherlock

PHRASES /ɝ/ before /l/

1. early bird
2. other worldly
3. old chorus girl
4. lovely showgirl
5. surly underworld

6. burly Earl
7. hurled pearls
8. the third world
9. thirsty cowgirl
10. mother-of-pearl

SENTENCES /ɝ/ before /l/

1. Earl was cast in *Hurly Burly*.

2. Shirley Temple had the curliest hair.

3. Swirl and twirl, they told the showgirl.

4. Were the sails furled or unfurled, sailor?

5. Pearls wrapped in burlap? That's absurd.

6. The directions instruct: knit one, purl two.

7. The whole world watched *That Girl* on TV.

8. The skirl of bagpipes was heard early today.

9. Sherlock cursed the surly underworld character.

10. We heard the whirr as the whirligig beetle whirled about.

NEUTRAL AMERICAN TEXT   stressed /ɝ/ (ER).   *Mark the following and speak out loud.*

/ɝ/ before /l/:

          ɝ   ɝ

Hector was stirring early.

(Troilus and Cressida I, ii, 51)

My master is of churlish disposition.

(As You Like It: II, iv, 80)

There is another comfort than this world.

(Measure for Measure: V, i, 49)

Be opposite with a kinsman, surly with servants.

(Twelfth Night: II, v, 149)

/ɜ/ various positions:

O, sir, content you;
I follow him to serve my turn upon him.

(Othello: I, i, 41)

Balm of hurt minds, great nature's second course,
Chief nourisher in life's feast.

(Macbeth: II, ii, 36)

Words spoke in tears
Are like the murmurs of the waters; the sound
Is loudly heard, but cannot be distinguished.

(Tourneur: The Revenger's Tragedy)

Put money in thy purse; follow thou the wars; defeat thy favor with an
usurp'd beard. I say put money in thy purse. It cannot be long that
Desdemona should continue her love to the Moor—put money in thy
purse—nor he his to her.

(Othello: I, iii, 339)

CASSIUS. When Caesar liv'd, he durst not thus have mov'd me.
BRUTUS. Peace, peace, you durst not so have tempted him.
CASSIUS. I durst not?
BRUTUS. No.
CASSIUS. What? durst not tempt him?
BRUTUS.   For your life you durst not.

(Julius Caesar: IV, iii, 58)

LEONTES. Once more, take her hence.
PAULINA. A most unworthy and unnatural lord
          Can do no more.
LEONTES.   I'll ha' thee burnt.
PAULINA.   I care not:
          It is a heretic that makes the fire,
          Not she which burns in't.

(The The Winter's Tale: II, iii, 112)

/ ɚ / (er)

Form the shape for speaking unstressed /ɚ / (er) by relaxing the jaw half open, slightly more than for stressed /ɝ/, arching the middle of the tongue high near the hard palate, lifting the tip up behind the alveolar ridge and curling it slightly back, while releasing sound through the mouth. Lip rounding is not required.

AUDIO 15▶ **short, unstressed /ɚ / (er)**

              ɚ   ɚ   ɚ

I said an 'eld<u>er</u> 'soldi<u>er</u>, not a 'bett<u>er</u>.

                ɚ

Did I say "'bett<u>er</u>"?

                 (Julius Caesar: IV, iii, 56)

              ɚ

I have no 'furth<u>er</u> with you.

                 (Coriolanus: II, iii, 173)

          ɚ   ɚ

I re'memb<u>er</u> him well, and I re'memb<u>er</u> him 'worthy of thy praise.

                 (The Merchant of Venice: I, ii, 120)

WORDS short, unstressed /ɚ/ (er)

Initial[1]	Medial	Final
*	cur'tail	'sister
*	sur'mise	'actor
*	ger'mane	'sugar
*	per'suade	'favor
*	fer'mentable	'theatre

RHYTHM TRACK /ɚ / (er) occurs in unstressed syllables and is, therefore, always short. It may help to think of /ɚ / (er) as a shorter, more relaxed /ɝ / (ER).

---

[1] The word 'urbane' *could* be placed here, though it's sometimes transcribed /ɝ/ (ER).

WORDS unstressed /ə/ (<u>er</u>)

water	over	diner	owner
never	cover	father	matter
savor	anger	traitor	mother
brother	either	singer	Virginia
remember	permission	perspective	neighbor

PHRASES unstressed /ə/ (<u>er</u>)

1.	old<u>er</u> surf<u>er</u>	6.	teach<u>er</u>'s sist<u>er</u>
2.	calling the wait<u>er</u>	7.	blist<u>er</u>ed fing<u>er</u>s
3.	wid<u>er</u> pap<u>er</u> cutt<u>er</u>	8.	fail<u>ure</u> to cens<u>ure</u>
4.	pict<u>ure</u> of glam<u>our</u>	9.	sculpt<u>ure</u>d leath<u>er</u>
5.	wond<u>er</u>ful struct<u>ure</u>	10.	both<u>er</u>some comput<u>er</u>

WORDS with stressed /ɝ/ (<u>ER</u>) and unstressed /ə/ (<u>er</u>)

'server	'turner	'girder	'stirrer
'cursor	'purser	'fervor	'Mercer
'bursar	'learner	'further	'burner
'furniture	'murder	dis'burser	'Herbert
'worshiper	'murmur	con'server	'pervert

SENTENCES unstressed /ə/ (<u>er</u>)

1. Expect better weather in November.

2. Do me a favor, please pass the sugar.

3. Hector registered for officer training.

4. Edgar is a tenured professor at Vassar.

5. The caterer sent dinner over via messenger.

6. That singer gave a spectacular performance.

7. Actors often think dinner tastes better after the show.

8. Do me a favor and audition Leonard for the tenor part.

9. I feel like seeing a lighter play, one filled with laughter.

10. Smother the mixture in vinegar, then cover and let simmer.

NEUTRAL AMERICAN TEXT unstressed /ɚ/ (<u>er</u>). *Mark the following and speak out loud.*

                          ɚ

Farewell, sweet lord, and sist<u>er</u>.

> (King Lear: III, vii, 21)

He hath a lady, wiser, fairer, truer,
Than ever Greek did couple in his arms.

> (Troilus and Cressida: I, iii, 275)

Suffer? I'll suffer you to be gone, I'll suffer you
To come no more; what would you have me suffer?

> (Tourneur: The Revenger's Tragedy)

Turned apostle now, our demon brother?
Smite one nostril, and he turns the other!

> (Rostand: Cyrano de Bergerac)

Thou'lt come no more,
Never, never, never, never, never.

> (King Lear: V, iii, 308)

Her father is no better than an earl,
Although in glorious titles he excel.

> (1 Henry VI: V, v, 37)

Never to be able to work again! Never—never! A living
death! Mother, can you imagine anything so horrible!

> (Ibsen: Ghosts)

Of course, I'm clever, cleverer than plenty of other people,
but happiness does not consist of merely being clever.

> (Chekhov: Three Sisters)

K. RICHARD. Should dying men flatter with those that live?
GAUNT.   No, no, men living flatter those that die.
K. RICHARD. Thou, now a-dying, sayest thou flatterest me.
GAUNT.   O no, thou diest, though I the sicker be.

> (Richard II: II, i, 88)

/ ə / (<u>uh</u>)

Form the shape for always short /ə/ (<u>uh</u>) by resting the tongue tip down behind the lower teeth, with the lips and cheeks relaxed in a neutral position, opening the jaw a little more than for /ɚ/ (<u>er</u>), and arching the middle of the tongue slightly toward the center of the mouth.

AUDIO 16 A▶ **short, unstressed**[1] **/ə/ (<u>uh</u>).**

  ə   ə ə   ə   ə ə
I <u>a</u>m **'Cinn<u>a</u>** th<u>e</u> poet, I <u>a</u>m **'Cinn<u>a</u>** th<u>e</u> poet.

                     (Julius Caesar: III, iii, 29)

 ə   ə   ə   ə
<u>A</u> proper man <u>a</u>s one shall see in <u>a</u> summer's day; <u>a</u> most
          ə
lovely **'gentle<u>man</u>**-like man.

             (A Midsummer Night's Dream: I, ii, 86)

      ə   ə
There's law <u>and</u> **'warr<u>ant</u>**, lady, for my curse.

                  (King John: III, i, 184)

WORDS short, unstressed /ə/ (<u>uh</u>).

Initial	Medial	Final
a'far	'legacy	'sofa
a'bout	con'trol	'Lisa
a'ffirm	com'pare	'diva
a'ttempt	'adamant	'salsa
a'ccount	mathema'tician	'pizza

Avoid a glottal attack on the first sound of the word in the first column.

RHYTHM TRACK The sound /ə/ (<u>uh</u>), sometimes referred to as the **'schwa'**, occurs in unstressed syllables and is always short. It is a shorter, more relaxed version of stressed /ʌ/ (<u>UH</u>). It is also spoken in many weak forms of words. Weak forms are covered in the Rhythm Highlighter section, pages 65-72.

---

[1] Possible weak forms using /ə/ (<u>uh</u>) are also marked.

WORDS short, unstressed /ə/ (<u>uh</u>)

<u>a</u>bout	ag<u>ai</u>n	agr<u>ee</u>	sof<u>a</u>
<u>a</u>rrest	arom<u>a</u>	<u>a</u>ffect	col<u>a</u>
<u>a</u>nnoy	f<u>a</u>cility	<u>a</u>head	Marth<u>a</u>
p<u>o</u>lice	ped<u>i</u>gree	leg<u>a</u>cy	c<u>a</u>daver
m<u>a</u>ternal	<u>a</u>shamed	t<u>o</u>night	sed<u>a</u>tive

PHRASES short, unstressed /ə/ (<u>uh</u>)

1.	<u>a</u>bove c<u>o</u>ntempt	6.	p<u>a</u>thetic <u>a</u>ward
2.	<u>a</u>fford<u>a</u>ble ag<u>ai</u>n	7.	agree<u>a</u>ble <u>a</u>ffect
3.	atroc<u>iou</u>s form<u>u</u>l<u>a</u>	8.	Atlant<u>a</u>, Georgi<u>a</u>
4.	c<u>o</u>nfirm c<u>o</u>mplaints	9.	<u>a</u>fraid or <u>a</u>nnoyed
5.	s<u>u</u>ppos<u>e</u>dly c<u>o</u>medic	10.	<u>A</u>meric<u>a</u>n diplom<u>a</u>

SOUND CHECK #1 Rhythm Highlighter: use /ə/ (<u>uh</u>) in unstressed suffixes and word endings. Highlight the contrast in rhythm and musicality between stressed and unstressed syllables by using short /ə/ on unstressed suffixes and word endings commonly spelled: 'ance', 'ence', 'ant', 'ent', 'ous', 'man', 'ment'.

AUDIO 16 B▶ /ə/ suffix and word endings

Here have we war for war and blood for blood,
Con'**trol**ment for con'**trol**ment: so answer France.

(King John: I, i, 19)

You could easily nab a husband one fine day! A rich
'**Eng**lishman, why not?

(Strindberg: Miss Julie)

Good '**sen**tences, and well pronounc'd.

(The Merchant of Venice: I, ii, 10)

     Though contemporary speakers often use the short /ɪ/ (w<u>i</u>ll) sound on the following suffixes, instead of the more traditional /ə/ (<u>uh</u>), it is useful to learn to distinguish /ɪ/ (w<u>i</u>ll) from /ə/ (<u>uh</u>) for future dialect study.

WORDS /ə/ schwa suffix (common spellings left column)

Suffix Schwas (handwritten annotation)

ance	a'cquaintance, 'arrogance, 'countenance, 'entrance, 'radiance, 'resonance, 'utterance
ence	'abstinence, 'eminence, 'essence, 'impudence, 'insolence, 'truculence, 'violence, 'virulence
ant	a'ssistant, 'dissonant, 'dominant, ex'travagant, lieu'tenant, 'petulant, 'recreant, 'servant, 'tenant
ent	'eloquent, 'excellent, fla'vescent, 'imminent, o'bedient, re'silient, 'regent, superin'tendent
ous	am'biguous, am'bitious, 'bigamous, 'copious, 'dangerous, 'marvelous, 'nervous, odo'riferous
man	'ottoman, 'Scotsman, de'liveryman, 'fisherman, 'Frenchman, 'henchman, 'statesman, 'doorman
ment	a'ppeasement 'argument a'rraignment, 'instrument, 'ligament, 'regiment, re'quirement, re'sentment

PHRASES /ə/ schwa suffix and word endings

1. the best 'postman
2. especially 'tenuous
3. tipping the 'doorman
4. wonderfully 'fragrant
5. well-known 'statesman
6. not 'prevalent
7. very ob'noxious
8. unnoticed 'absence
9. unreleased 'statement
10. offers some re'sistance

SENTENCES /ə/ schwa suffix and word endings

1. What a surprising development.

2. They enjoyed the absence of violence.

3. A glorious event is planned in remembrance.

4. The actor was paid a pittance for his appearance.

5. The assessment confirmed their interdependence.

6. What statesman was convicted of embezzlement?

7. He engendered resentment from the management.

8. His doorman works undercover for the government.

9. Prepayment was demanded at the restaurant's entrance.

10. A highwayman has taken up residence in the basement.

SOUND CHECK #2: **intrusive, unstressed vowel of 'r'.** When words end in the 'schwa' sound /ə/ (uh) and there is no 'r' in the spelling, do not add /ɚ/ (er). Pronounce 'sofa' not 'sofer'. Also, do not not link to another vowel sound by inserting the consonant /r/. Speak: The sofa is dirty. Not: The sofer‿is dirty.

WORDS final /ə/ (uh) with no intrusive /ɚ/ (er)

'aura	'quota	'pizza	'Russia
i'dea	'Linda	'Africa	'comma
a'rena	'melba	an'tenna	ba'nana
A'merica	'Emma	Ye'shiva	The'resa
no'stalgia	'Martha	am'brosia	'Georgia

PHRASES final /ə/ with no intrusive /ɚ/ (er) or linking /r/

1.	Cuba incident	6.	Martha isn't
2.	no idea about it	7.	diarrhea ends
3.	Aretha asks him	8	China involved
4.	seeing Lisa angry	9.	Australia advised
5.	media advertisements	10.	pasta isn't cooked

SENTENCES final /ə/ with no intrusive /ɚ/ (er) or linking /r/

1. Sophia is buying soda in the market.

2. Is the panda in the zoo pregnant yet?

3. Diana, are mimosas made with Coca Cola?

4. Zelda is a prima donna and loves her tiara.

5. Let's have pizza and watch the Oscars, Eva.

6. The saga of Attila in China is on TV tonight.

7. Nina's idea of traveling to Cuba is appealing.

8. Brenda and Emma are working on the agenda.

9. PORTIA isn't listed on the casting notice after all.

10. Cleopatra looks beautiful wearing magenta in the Sahara.

NEUTRAL AMERICAN TEXT   unstressed /ə/ (<u>uh</u>). *Mark the following and speak out loud.*

schwa suffixes, word endings, weak forms:

        ə   ə   ə ə   ə
My jud<u>g</u><u>ment</u> is the jud<u>g</u><u>ment</u> <u>of</u> th<u>e</u> law.

(Strindberg: The Father)

So every bondman in his own hand bears
The power to cancel his captivity.

(Julius Caesar: I, iii, 101)

It was the owl that shriek'd / the fatal bellman,
Which gives the stern'st good-night.

(Macbeth: II, ii, 3)

To the contrary I have express commandment.

(The The Winter's Tale: II, ii, 8)

A document in madness, thoughts and remembrance fitted.

(Hamlet: IV, v, 178)

Yes, my thoughtlessness had consequences, my dear Judge.

(Ibsen: Hedda Gabler)

My lord, I know not what the matter is, but to my judgment your
highness is not entertain'd with that ceremonious affection as you were
wont. There's a great abatement of kindness appears as well in the
general dependants as in the Duke himself also, and your daughter.

(King Lear: I, iv, 58)

AUTOLYCUS. I am robb'd sir…
CLOWN   . What, by a horseman, or a footman?
AUTOLYCUS. A footman, sweet sir, a footman.
CLOWN.   Indeed, he should be a footman by the garments he has
            left with thee. If this be a horseman's coat, it hath seen
            very hot service.

(The The Winter's Tale: IV, iii, 61)

/ ʌ / (UH)

Form the shape for stressed or strong /ʌ/ (UH) by resting the tongue tip down behind the lower teeth with the lips and cheeks relaxed and neutral, opening the jaw a little more than for /ə/ (uh), arching the middle of the tongue low in the mouth, and releasing sound through the mouth.

AUDIO 17▶ stressed /ʌ/ (UH)

            ʌ

Avaunt, you 'cullions!

(Henry V: III, ii, 20)

        ʌ   ʌ

If it were done, when 'tis done, then 'twere well

     ʌ

It were done quickly.

(Macbeth: I, vii, 1)

   ʌ

A'dultery?

            ʌ

Thou shalt not die. Die for a'dultery?

(King Lear: IV, vi, 110)

WORDS stressed /ʌ/ (UH)

Initial	Medial	Final
up	gum	*
'ugly	'trouble	*
'uncle	'wonder	*
'other	'chunky	*
'under	be'loved	*

Do not begin words in the initial column with a glottal attack.

RHYTHM TRACK Stressed /ʌ/ (UH) is classified as a short vowel, though it is longer than unstressed /ə/ (uh), which is also classified as short.

PHRASES /ʌ/ (<u>UH</u>)

1.	l<u>u</u>cky in l<u>o</u>ve	6.	<u>u</u>ncle in L<u>o</u>ndon
2.	b<u>u</u>tter cr<u>u</u>nch	7.	d<u>ou</u>ble or n<u>o</u>thing
3.	s<u>u</u>nny s<u>u</u>mmer	8.	c<u>o</u>mforting c<u>u</u>ddle
4.	j<u>u</u>st d<u>u</u>mb l<u>u</u>ck	9.	j<u>u</u>dged to be dr<u>u</u>nk
5.	br<u>u</u>nch or l<u>u</u>nch	10.	a m<u>o</u>nth of S<u>u</u>ndays

SENTENCES stressed /ʌ/ (<u>UH</u>)

1. I'm ready for my close-up.

2. Young Judd was stage-struck.

3. Speak up, Douglas, you're mumbling.

4. Gus signaled 'thumbs up' when he won.

5. Is your new puppy named Fluffy or Puffy?

6. The crumbling mummy was discovered in the sun.

7. Hundreds have wondered where thunder comes from.

8. They're casting for a handsome, honey-tongued lover.

9. I have a hunch it will take months to finish these puzzles.

10. Any discussion will involve dozens of cousins and brothers.

11. One impulsive summer crush is a must for any young adult.

12. Royal flush? Eyes fluttering, blood pumping—he's bluffing!

When 'un' is added as a prefix to the beginning of a word, it is spoken and transcribed in IPA with strong /ʌ/, even though the sound is technically in the unstressed syllable. Also, compound words are often transcribed with strong /ʌ/ in the unstressed syllable, for example: <u>u</u>nder'go, <u>u</u>nder'graduate, 'teac<u>u</u>p.

PHRASES /ʌ/ (<u>UH</u>) prefix and compound words

1.	<u>u</u>nlikely buyer	6.	<u>u</u>nsound advice
2.	<u>u</u>nearned inc<u>o</u>me	7.	<u>u</u>nvoiced ending
3.	<u>u</u>nfriendly waiter	8.	handc<u>u</u>ffed c<u>u</u>lprits
4.	<u>u</u>ndisciplined f<u>u</u>n	9.	<u>u</u>nhappy <u>u</u>nderneath
5.	<u>u</u>nwatered b<u>u</u>ttercups	10.	<u>u</u>nkempt and <u>u</u>nd<u>o</u>ne

SOUND CHECK #1: /ʌl/ (UHL) combinations. Relax the lower jaw open and speak strong, stressed /ʌ/ (UH) before bringing the tongue tip up to touch the gum ridge on /l/. Do not round the lips or /o/ may be spoken instead of /ʌ/.

dull	sulk	pulp	result
cull	hulk	ulcer	culture
skull	adult	pulse	ulcerous
culprit	consult	bulge	repulsive
vulture	impulse	dulcet	revulsion

PHRASES /ʌ/ before /l/

1. dull bulb
2. pop culture
3. sulking culprits
4. result of adultery
5. impulsive vulture
6. ultra dull
7. sullied hull
8. bulging seagulls
9. compulsive gulping
10. divulged his revulsion

SENTENCES /ʌ/ before /l/

1. Is mulch repulsive? Mull that over.
2. The culvert was flooded during the storm.
3. Skulking and sulking can give you ulcers.
4. Lullabies have such soothing dulcet tones.
5. Convulsions resulted in injury, they divulged.
6. All applicants to culinary school were insulted.
7. They found the cult culpable of occult practices.
8. Multinational cultural institutions were consulted.
9. The bulkhead rested on the fulcrum during repairs.
10. Mr. Tull won't divulge where the bulbs are planted.
11. I'd like to indulge my impulse to vacation on the gulf.
12. She felt sullen and vulnerable in the sultry evening air.
13. Adultery: the marriage nullified, the culprit pulverized.

NEUTRAL AMERICAN TEXT   stressed /ʌ/ (UH).   *Mark the following and speak aloud.*

/ʌ/ before /l/:

ʌl
Away you scullion!

(2 Henry IV, II, i, 59)

Sing in our sweet lullaby,
Lulla, lulla, lullaby, lulla, lulla, lullaby.

(A Midsummer Night's Dream: II, ii, 14)

Your pulsidge beats as extraordinarily as heart would desire.

(2 Henry IV: II, iv, 23)

No doubt the murd'rous knife was dull and blunt.

(Richard III, IV, iv, 227)

/ʌ/ various positions:

I am undone!

(The Merry Wives of Windsor: IV, ii, 41)

O coz, coz, coz, my pretty little coz, that thou didst know how many fathom deep I am in love!

(As You Like It: IV, i, 205)

O blood, blood, blood!

(Othello: III, iii, 451)

Finds brotherhood in thee no sharper spur?
Hath love in thy old blood no living fire?
Edward's seven sons, whereof thyself art one,
Were as seven vials of his sacred blood.

(Richard II: I, ii, 9)

Oh, nonsense! Your love touches me, but I can't reciprocate it—that's all.

(Chekhov: The Seagull)

1 WITCH. Here I have a pilot's thumb,
          Wrack'd as homeward he did come.
3 WITCH. A drum, a drum!
          Macbeth doth come.

(Macbeth: I, iii, 28)

BACK VOWELS

See Overview pages 18-26

/ u / (wh<u>o</u>)

Form the shape necessary for speaking the first back vowel sound /u/ (wh<u>o</u>) by closing the jaw almost completely, resting the tip of the tongue down behind the lower teeth, arching the back of the tongue high toward the front of the soft palate, sinking the cheeks, rounding the lips, and releasing sound through the mouth.

AUDIO 18▶ /u/ (wh<u>o</u>)

>   u
> Why, he is the Prince's jester, a very dull f<u>oo</u>l.
> *(Much Ado About Nothing: II, i, 138)*
>
>   u
> We cannot fight for love, as men may d<u>o</u>.
>   u   u
> We should be w<u>oo</u>'d, and were not made to w<u>oo</u>.
> *(A Midsummer Night's Dream: II, i, 241)*
>
>   u   u   u
> Draw thy t<u>oo</u>l, here comes tw<u>o</u> of the house of Montag<u>ue</u>s.
> *(Romeo and Juliet: I, i, 31)*

WORDS /u/ (wh<u>o</u>)

Initial	Medial	Final
ʔ Uzi	truth	two
ʔ oops	tomb	woo
ʔ ooze	move	blue
ʔ oodles	boom	stew
ʔ oomph	assume	canoe

CLASSICALLY SPEAKING   **NEUTRAL AMERICAN** /u/

RHYTHM TRACK This sound can be categorized as long, half-long or short depending on its position in the word and the sounds that follow.[1] Notice the variation in lengths. *Read across.*

long /u:/	long /u:/	half-long /u·/	short /u/
flu	floozy	flute	curfew
Jew	June	juice	statue
rue	room	Ruth	routine
shoe	shooed	shoot	cashew
taboo	booed	booth	boutique

This sound is **long /u:/** in a stressed syllable:

(a)　　when it's the last sound of the word

(b)　　when it's followed by a voiced consonant

PHRASES long /u:/

1.	true blue	6.	gloomy tomb
2.	brew booze	7.	choose cartoons
3.	wounded poodle	8.	imprudent shoes
4.	afternoon snooze	9.	drooling kangaroos
5.	zounds to you too	10.	concluded the review

This sound is **half-long /u·/** (who) in a stressed syllable when followed by a voiceless consonant.

PHRASES half-long /u·/

1.	loose suit	6.	brutes in boots
2.	oops, a blooper	7.	gruesome truth
3.	introducing Zeus	8.	exclusive troops
4.	shoots the jukebox	9.	juice, not vermouth
5.	plays hoops on the roof	10.	smooching pooches

Short /u/ (who) is spoken when in the unstressed syllable, or when used in the weak forms of the words 'do' and 'you'.

---

[1]　Length indicators (or dots) used in IPA notation are optional (see pages 39-40). This section is marked to promote increased awareness and to aid those studying lengths.

PHRASES short /u/

1.	superb duet	6.	unique statue
2.	routine tuition	7.	Cashew Avenue
3.	ubiquitous toupees	8.	Eugene's attitude
4.	humane throughout	9.	nephew's revenues
5.	stupendous museum	10.	unanimously united

Note: /u/ (who) is not marked for length from this point on.

SENTENCES /u/ various lengths

1. I'd like to see the duo on Tuesday.

2. Wear your new swimsuit in the pool.

3. Walking shoeless can be excruciating.

4. I'm amused and confused by their feud.

5. Is it inhumane to keep baboons in a zoo?

6. Where is Bloom Avenue? I haven't a clue.

7. They'll soon sue the unscrupulous cruise line.

8. Rumors forecasting doom and gloom are routine.

9. Does a ride in my aluminum canoe appeal to you?

10. In my youth, I swooned to the musical tunes of that group.

SOUND CHECK #1: /u/ **before the consonant /l/.** Maintain lip rounding as the tongue tip touches the upper gum ridge on /ul/ combinations. If the lips are released before the tongue tip touches the gum ridge, then /wə/ may be inserted between /u/ and /l/. In other words, speak 'pool' not 'poowuhl'.

WORDS /u/ before /l/ Only I syllable!

pool	tool	rule	fool
cool	mule	fuel	Julie
tulle	Julius	you'll	spool
carpool	who'll	school	ghoul
hooligan	molecule	toadstool	vestibule

PHRASES /u/ before /l/

1.	new ruler	6.	dirty pool
2.	cool shoes	7.	drooling mules
3.	round stool	8.	blue toadstools
4.	nobody's fool	9.	April Fool's Day
5.	against the rules	10.	Yuletide greetings

SENTENCES /u/ before /l/

1. Who'll stand on that footstool?

2. The stray cat let out a ghoulish mewl.

3. Susan was ridiculed by the hooligans.

4. Julian, the rule is no mint juleps in school.

5. The tulips in Istanbul were beautiful in June.

6. Mr. Buhl concluded it's too cool in the vestibule.

7. Use the spool of wire in the tool shed; it's foolproof.

8. The tulle trim came off her ballet costume at school.

9. Is there a swimming pool I can use while in Liverpool?

10. You'll examine DNA molecules to determine the gene pool.

> *This is the way we go to school,*
> *Go to school, go to school,*
> *This is the way we go to school,*
> *On a cold and frosty morning.*
>
> (Mother Goose: The Mulberry Bush)

NEUTRAL AMERICAN TEXT /u/ (who). *Mark the following and speak out loud.*

/u/ before /l/:

      ul   ul   ul
O fool, fool, fool!

(Othello: V, ii, 323)

Base muleteers of France!

(1 Henry VI: III, ii, 68)

I have some private schooling for you both.

(A Midsummer Night's Dream: I, i, 116)

MEDDLER. I find it small, no—even miniscule!
CYRANO. What's this? Subject me now to ridicule?

(Rostand: Cyrano de Bergerac)

BASTARD. Brief then; and what's the news?
HUBERT. O my sweet sir, news fitting to the night,
Black, fearful, comfortless, and horrible.
BASTARD. Show me the very wound of this ill news;
I am no woman, I'll not swound at it.

(King John: V, vi, 18)

I have a whole school of tongues in this belly of mine.

(2 Henry IV: IV, iii, 18)

PROTEUS. I gave this unto Julia.
JULIA. And Julia herself did give it me,
And Julia herself hath brought it hither.
PROTEUS. How? Julia?

(Two Gentlemen of Verona: V, iv, 97)

/u/ various positions:

Ah, foul shrewd news! Beshrew thy very heart!
I did not think to be so sad to-night.

(King John: V, v, 14)

That he's mad, 'tis true, 'tis true 'tis pity,
And pity 'tis 'tis true—a foolish figure.

(Hamlet: II, ii, 97)

At midnight, in the month of June,
I stand beneath the mystic moon.
An opiate vapor, dewy, dim,
Exhales from out her golden rim,
And, softly dripping, drop by drop,
Upon the quiet mountain top,
Steals drowsily and musically
Into the universal valley.

(Poe: The Sleeper)

/ ʊ / (w<u>ou</u>ld)

The shape for speaking the second, always-short back vowel sound /ʊ/ (w<u>ou</u>ld) is nearly identical to that of the previous back vowel /u/ (wh<u>o</u>). The jaw is mostly closed, the tongue tip rests down behind the lower teeth, the back of the tongue arches high, while the cheeks sink and the lips round. For the /ʊ/ (w<u>ou</u>ld) sound, however, the articulators are slightly more open and relaxed.

AUDIO 19▶ /ʊ/ (w<u>ou</u>ld)

                 ʊ

You took the moon at f<u>u</u>ll, but now she's changed.

(Love's Labor's Lost: V, ii, 214)

            ʊ   ʊ

What says my b<u>u</u>lly-r<u>oo</u>k?

(The Merry Wives of Windsor: I, iii, 2)

      ʊ   ʊ

Whose b<u>oo</u>kish rule hath p<u>u</u>ll'd fair England down.

(2 Henry VI: I, i, 259)

WORDS /ʊ/ (w<u>ou</u>ld)

Initial	Medial	Final
*	pull	*
*	foot	*
*	fully	*
*	shook	*
*	cushion	*

RHYTHM TRACK /ʊ/ (w<u>ou</u>ld) is short, especially compared with /u/ (wh<u>o</u>).

WORDS /ʊ/ (w<u>ou</u>ld)

put	bully	wool	full
good	hood	crook	poof
sugar	bullion	goody	bullet
pulpit	cookies	woman	could
barefoot	pudding	Pulitzer	forsook

PHRASES /ʊ/ (w<u>ou</u>ld)

1.	sugar c<u>oo</u>kies	6.	t<u>oo</u>k a b<u>u</u>llet
2.	st<u>oo</u>d in dark s<u>oo</u>t	7.	l<u>oo</u>ks cr<u>oo</u>ked
3.	w<u>ou</u>ld like Br<u>oo</u>ke	8.	c<u>ou</u>ld be a b<u>oo</u>king
4.	mist<u>oo</u>k the w<u>o</u>man	9.	g<u>oo</u>d s<u>u</u>gar p<u>u</u>dding
5.	l<u>oo</u>ks for g<u>oo</u>d b<u>oo</u>ks	10.	w<u>oo</u>den h<u>oo</u>ks sh<u>oo</u>k

SENTENCES /ʊ/ (w<u>ou</u>ld)

1. They're bullish on America.

2. The woman lost her footing.

3. You're hood's on crooked, Butch.

4. Could you, should you, would you?

5. He tripped on the cushion underfoot.

6. Tell us about your boyhood in Brooklyn.

7. My favorite store, Woolworth's, is kaput.

8. No one likes being called a goody-goody.

9. The woman misunderstood and pushed Brooke.

10. Should you bully the butcher when he's cooking?

11. He was in charge of finding firewood on the kibbutz.

12. Who is the good-looking man playing BOLINGBROKE?

13. The anchorwoman interviewed the barefooted onlookers.

SOUND CHECK #1: Compare the short, more open /ʊ/ (w<u>ou</u>ld) sound with the longer, more closed and energetically lip-rounded /u/ (wh<u>o</u>). *Read across.*

/ʊ/	/u/	/ʊ/	/u/
put	pool	cookie	kook
good	goose	hook	who
stood	stewed	book	booth
foot	food	shook	shoed
would	woo	look	Luke

PHRASES   short /ʊ/ (would) and longer /u/ (who)

1.	hooded statue	6.	shouldn't shoot
2.	barefoot Hugo	7.	cooked couscous
3.	womanly wooer	8.	rural route ruined
4.	pulling the pooch	9.	bulletproof booth
5.	brutal Miss Brooks	10.	good-looking Lucy

SENTENCES /ʊ/ (would) and /u/ (who)

1. Brooding isn't good for you.

2. They overtook the crooks in Utah.

3. Wooden spoons are best for cooking.

4. Rookie cops should use bulletproof vests.

5. Take a good look; then tell me if this is crooked.

SOUND CHECK #2: /ʊ/ (would) before /l/. Be sure to speak short /ʊ/ before the consonant /l/ in the following words, rather than the longer /u/ (who) sound.

---

bull	wool	pull	full
wolf	bullet	Fuller	fulfill
pulley	pulpit	fulsome	wolves

PHRASES /ʊ/ before /l/

1.	fully full	6.	wooly bully
2.	cries wolf	7.	Bulgarian bulls
3.	woman in wool	8.	pushed the pulpit
4.	pulling the pulley	9.	would see wolves
5.	books about bullets	10.	woolens from Wooster

SENTENCES /ʊ/ before /l/

1. Butch named his team the 'Brooklyn Bullets'.

2. Mr. Woolsey drinks nothing but hot bullion.

3. Was Sandra Bullock in *Dancing with Wolves*?

4. Fuller should fulfill his dream of selling cookies.

5. Wouldn't you prefer wearing wool in the woods in winter?

SOUND CHECK #3: Compare /ʊ/ (w<u>ou</u>ld) and /ʌ/ (<u>UH</u>). Speak /ʊ/ with the jaw mostly closed, the lips slightly rounded and the back of the tongue arched. Speak /ʌ/ with the jaw more open, the lips unrounded and the middle of the tongue slightly arched. *Read across.*

/ʊ/	/ʌ/	/ʊ/	/ʌ/
put	putt	could	cud
would	what	look	luck
bull	bulb	soot	such
stood	stud	book	buck
hook	Huck	shook	shucks

PHRASES /ʊ/ and /ʌ/

1. rushing br<u>oo</u>ks
2. l<u>oo</u>king for lunch
3. p<u>u</u>shed the punks
4. b<u>oo</u>ked a bus tour
5. the w<u>o</u>man wasn't
6. baref<u>oo</u>t ushers
7. puffing and p<u>u</u>lling
8. combustible b<u>u</u>llets
9. sh<u>ou</u>ldn't have sunk
10. c<u>oo</u>ked for customers

SENTENCES /ʊ/ and /ʌ/

1. You look lovely, Brooke.

2. I wonder if that's deadwood.

3. Crooks will be fully punished.

4. She held the bundle to her bosom.

5. We took the Chunnel into London.

NEUTRAL AMERICAN TEXT /ʊ/ (w<u>ou</u>ld). *Mark the following and speak out loud.*

/ʊ/ before /l/:

    ʊl   ʊl
Your w<u>ol</u>f no longer seems to be a w<u>ol</u>f
Than when she's hungry.

(Webster: The White Devil)

Some to the common pulpits, and cry out.

(Julius Caesar: III, i, 80)

/ʊ/ various positions:

Bless'd pudding!

(Othello: II, i, 253)

I grant I am a woman; but withal
A woman that Lord Brutus took to wife.
I grant I am a woman; but withal
A woman well reputed, Cato's daughter.

(Julius Caesar: II, i, 292)

Wake Duncan with thy knocking! I would thou couldst!

(Macbeth: II, ii, 71)

Upon my lips — in ambush, there, he stood —
My foe, a lackey; his sword, a log of wood!

(Rostand: Cyrano de Bergerac)

O Rosalind, these trees shall be my books,
And in their barks my thoughts I'll character,
That every eye which in this forest looks
Shall see thy virtue witness'd every where.

(As You Like It: III, ii, 5)

ELEANOR.   There's a good mother, boy, that blots thy father.
CONSTANCE. There's a good grandame, boy, that would blot thee.
AUSTRIA.   Peace!

(King John: II, i, 132)

I would the college of the Cardinals
Would choose him Pope and carry him to Rome

(2 Henry VI: I, iii, 61)

PAULINA. I say, I come
                From your good queen.
LEONTES. Good queen?
PAULINA. Good queen, my lord, good queen, I say good queen,
                And would by combat make her good, so were I
                A man...

(The The Winter's Tale: II, iii, 57)

/ o / (o̱'mit)

Form the shape for speaking the third back vowel sound, <u>unstressed</u> /o/ (o̱'mit), by opening the jaw and relaxing the articulators slightly more than for the previous /ʊ/ sound. The jaw will be half open, the tip of the tongue resting behind the lower teeth, the back of the tongue arched half-high toward the soft palate and the lips gently rounded in the shape of an 'o'.

AUDIO 20▶ /o/ (o̱'mit) in the first, unstressed syllable

>   o
> Beauty pro̱'voketh thieves sooner than gold.
>
> > (As You Like It: I, iii, 110)
>
>   o
> I would the gods had made thee po̱'etical.
>
> > (As You Like It: III, iii, 16)
>
>   o
> Farewell! O̱'thello's occupation's gone!
>
> > (Othello: III, iii, 357)

WORDS /o/ (o̱'mit) in the first, unstressed syllable

Initial	Medial	Final
o'mit	mo'saic	*
o'vert	do'main	*
o'mega	no'bility	*
o'vation	co'quette	*
o'mission	bro'chure	*

RHYTHM TRACK /o/ (o̱'mit) is short, and occurs in the unstressed first syllable—as the first sound of the word or as the vowel in the first syllable.[1] The diphthong /oʊ/ is spoken in all other instances. (Pure /o/ is common in many accents, including: Spanish, Irish, Italian and Scottish.)

---

[1] This sound is represented many ways in dictionaries: as a diphthong in all positions in a word, as a vowel in all positions, and as a vowel or diphthong depending on its stress in a word. It is presented here as a vowel sound in the first, unstressed syllable of a word for its rhythmic implications, and to introduce this sound in context with the vowels.

Short /ə/ (<u>uh</u>) is very often spoken instead of /o/ in Neutral American, especially in words that begin with 'o', 'co', 'do', 'po', 'pro', 'so' in the spelling:

object, oblige, oblivion, obscene, obscure, observe, occasion, occult, occur, offend, offense, official, Olympics, opinion, oppress, Othello, command, convert, domestic, dominion, polemic, police, polite, possess, potential, proceed, proclaim, produce, profess, profound, promote, pronounce, protrude, provoke, society, solemnity, solution

PHRASES initial unstressed /o/ (<u>o</u>'mit)

1.	beautiful <u>o</u>asis	6.	on pr<u>o</u>bation
2.	this N<u>o</u>vember	7.	finds great h<u>o</u>tels
3.	gorgeous l<u>o</u>cale	8.	check the n<u>o</u>tation
4.	seems gr<u>o</u>tesque	9.	h<u>o</u>listic viewpoints
5.	finding a v<u>o</u>cation	10.	cute k<u>o</u>ala sighting

SENTENCES initial unstressed /o/ (<u>o</u>'mit)

1. It's a very romantic locale.

2. They decided to cooperate.

3. Sophia always obeys the law.

4. She received a standing ovation.

5. Young O'Neill is Olympic material.

6. Opaque glass was omitted from the model.

7. The loquacious young man courted Odetta.

8. A donation was requested at Yosemite National Park.

9. The Oasis, a holistic hotel, is featured in the brochure.

10. Is there a relationship between ovarian cancer and obesity?

NEUTRAL AMERICAN TEXT initial unstressed /o/ (<u>o</u>'mit). *Mark the following and speak out loud.*

o
Most pleasing it is, and <u>o</u>doriferous.

(Middleton & Rowley: The Changeling)

What if we do omit
This reprobate till he were well inclin'd?

(Measure for Measure: IV, iii, 73)

If he bid you set it down, obey him.

(The Merry Wives of Windsor: IV, ii, 109)

Therefore omit him not, blunt not his love,
Nor lose the good advantage of his grace.

(2 Henry IV: IV, iv, 27)

But that's all one; omittance is no quittance.

(As You Like It: III, v, 133)

Then true noblesse would
Learn him forbearance from so foul a wrong.

(Richard II: IV, I, 119)

I induced you to resume the yoke of duty and obedience!

(Ibsen: Ghosts)

The following selections could be spoken with pure /o/ or /ə/.

I will proclaim thee, Angelo, look for't!

(Measure for Measure: II, iv, 151)

How all occasions do inform against me.

(Hamlet: IV, iv, 32)

And if we thrive, promise them such rewards
As victors wear at the Olympian games.

(3 Henry VI: II, iii, 52)

Yea, brother Richard, are you offended too?

(3 Henry VI: IV, i, 19)

When water-drops have worn the stones of Troy,
And blind oblivion swallow'd cities up.

(Troilus and Cressida: III, ii, 186)

Suppose they take offense without a cause?

(3 Henry VI: IV, i, 14)

/ ɔ / (<u>a</u>ll)

Form the shape for the fourth back vowel /ɔ/ (<u>a</u>ll) by resting the tip of the tongue down behind the lower teeth, opening the jaw substantially more than for the previous /o/ sound, dropping the back of the tongue arch to a half-low position, and very slightly sinking the cheeks, which will slightly round the lips. This sound is sometimes referred to as the 'claw' sound, as the articulators tend to take the shape of the written IPA symbol: /ɔ/.

AUDIO 21▶ /ɔ/ (<u>a</u>ll)

    ɔ   ɔ

I <u>a</u>lways dream I'm under a t<u>a</u>ll tree in a dark wood.

                          (Strindberg: Miss Julie)

       ɔ

Kill Cl<u>au</u>dio.

              (Much Ado About Nothing: IV, i, 289)

     ɔ   ɔ

And <u>o</u>ftentimes excusing of a f<u>au</u>lt
  ʌ   ɔ
Doth make the f<u>au</u>lt the worse by th' excuse.

                      (King John: IV, ii, 30)

WORDS /ɔ/ (<u>a</u>ll)

Initial	Medial	Final
ʔ awe	chalk	jaw
ʔ ought	flaunt	saw
ʔ awful	coffee	paw
ʔ always	sought	draw
ʔ August	daughter	thaw

The sound /ɔ/ is commonly represented by the spellings:

all	wall	tall	small	squall
alk	walk	balk	chalk	stalk
aw	law	saw	bawd	dawn
au	auction	sauce	daughter	audition

The sound /ɔ/ is also suggested[1] by the spellings:

og	log	smog	frog	dog
of(f)	often	soft	coffee	loft
os(s)	cross	toss	across	gloss
oth	cloth	moth	broth	froth
ong	song	belong	wrong	strong
ought	ought	bought	sought	fought

The word 'water' is pronounced with /ɔ/ (all), not /ɑ/ (father) in NAS.

RHYTHM TRACK This sound can be categorized as long, half-long or short, depending both on its position in the word and on the sounds that follow it.[2] Notice the variation in length of this sound in the following. *Read across.*

long /ɔː/	half-long /ɔ·/	short /ɔ/
ball	balk	albeit
awe	aught	Australia
awed	ought	autumnal
pawn	paucity	Paulina
cause	caught	Caucasian

This sound is **long /ɔː/** in a stressed syllable:

(a)   when it's the last sound of the word

(b)   when it's followed by a voiced consonant

PHRASES long /ɔː/

1.	gnawed paws		6.	flawed straws
2.	finds the cause		7.	implausible law
3.	bawdy Mr. Shaw		8.	clawed Claudius
4.	appalled by *Jaws*		9.	draws an audience
5.	applause, applause		10.	marauding alderman

---

[1] There is discrepancy and difference of opinion, among dictionaries and teachers alike, whether words are pronounced with /ɔ/ (all) or /ɑ/ (father). Some also suggest /ɒ/ as an option. Though there are a few exceptions to the guidelines presented above, they are included in an attempt to offer a manageable, recognizable organization of words by sound and spelling, for both well-pronounced characters and/or for classical text. These guidelines are then referred to, and systematically altered when moving on to the Classical American and Standard British dialects.

[2] Length indicators (or dots) used in IPA notation are optional. This section is marked to promote increased awareness and to aid those studying lengths.

This sound is **half-long /ɔ·/** in a stressed syllable when followed by a voiceless consonant.

PHRASES half-long /ɔ·/

1.	awful faucet	6.	cautions Austin	
2.	saucy sausage	7.	exhausting walk	
3.	caught talking	8.	awkwardly taught	
4.	brought hawks	9.	fraught with chalk	
5.	unlawfully sought	10.	awesome thoughts	

Short /ɔ/ is spoken when in the unstressed syllable.

WORDS short /ɔ/

already	augment	albeit	alright
austere	authentic	Almighty	Warsaw
Augustus	audacious	Australian	audition

Note: /ɔ/ (all) is not marked for length from this point on.

PHRASES /ɔ/ various lengths

1.	draws on cloth	6.	authentic talk	
2.	haunted walkway	7.	gawky authors	
3.	awkward songster	8.	enthralling waterfall	
4.	all the daughter saw	9.	wall covered in chalk	
5.	bought fresh prawns	10.	ought to be thoughtful	

SENTENCES /ɔ/ (all) various lengths

1. What an exhausting talk!

2. Claude, the offer is a fraud.

3. How often do you go walking?

4. Dawn, are you working offline?

5. Store the softest cloth in mothballs.

6. His brother-in-law is from Arkansas.

7. The entire audience coughed at once.

Keep "aw" long!

8. Does your dog travel abroad with you?

9. There's no alternative but to be cautious.

10. They launched the boat off the boardwalk.

11. You're stalling; please fix the faulty faucet.

12. Without chalk, Dawn could no longer draw.

13. Saul becomes lost in thought when drawing.

14. They talked and talked for hours over coffee.

15. Paula always serves sweet sausage in autumn.

16. The applause from the auditorium was audible.

17. That small saucepan is filled with scalding water.

18. That's an awful song coming from that automobile.

19. They were appalled when she wallpapered the office.

20. The cost is automatically deducted from your account.

Make ALL Legato—LINK!

SOUND CHECK #1: Distinguish between /ɔ/ (all) and /ɑ/ (father) sounds in the following. Refer to the spelling guidelines on the previous pages 148-149.

WORDS comparing /ɑ/ (father) and /ɔ/ (all) *Read across.*

/ɑ/	/ɔ/	/ɑ/	/ɔ/
wok	walk	Tom	talk
stop	stall	pot	pall
drop	draw	John	jaw
dock	dawn	lot	lawn
shop	Shaw	hock	hawk
bob	bauble	crop	crawl
sot	sought	tot	taught

PHRASES /ɑ/ (father) and /ɔ/ (all)

1. flawed clocks
2. moms talking
3. saw the drama
4. a small omelet
5. not applauding

6. calling John
7. fond of Paula
8. caught Donna
9. lots of drawings
10. awfully odd drama

Link!

_ = /ɔ/

SENTENCES /ɑ/ (f<u>a</u>ther) and /ɔ/ (<u>a</u>ll)

1. Lots of sm<u>a</u>ll t<u>o</u>ts <u>wa</u>lk and t<u>a</u>lk.

2. G<u>o</u>sh, F<u>a</u>lstaff's v<u>oi</u>ce is too s<u>o</u>ft.

3. <u>Au</u>drey set the w<u>o</u>k on the sidew<u>a</u>lk.

4. They c<u>a</u>lled 'bravo' after father's s<u>o</u>ng.

5. Not feeling well? Sip some h<u>o</u>t br<u>o</u>th.

6. What's c<u>au</u>sing the c<u>o</u>st of t<u>a</u>cos to rise?

   Chalk

7. Am I wr<u>o</u>ng? I th<u>ou</u>ght Tom lost his job.

8. They <u>o</u>ften c<u>a</u>ll Tom for a sm<u>a</u>ll donation.

9. Hot ch<u>o</u>colate is <u>a</u>lways good for business.

10. The disc jockey played that l<u>o</u>ng, l<u>o</u>ng s<u>o</u>ng.

11. Thousands of <u>a</u>ctors resp<u>o</u>nded to the cattle c<u>a</u>ll.

12. Robert was too n<u>au</u>seous to enjoy the panorama.

13. <u>Daw</u>n and D<u>o</u>n <u>a</u>lways look su<u>a</u>ve in silk pajamas.

14. Who's that on the <u>o</u>pposite sidew<u>a</u>lk, John or P<u>au</u>l?

15. The sonata w<u>a</u>fted through the <u>o</u>ffice building, c<u>a</u>lming[1] <u>a</u>ll.

Hush-a-bye, baby, on the tree top,
When the wind blows, the cradle will rock;
When the bough breaks, the cradle will fall;
Down will come baby, cradle and all.

(Mother Goose: Hush-a-Bye)

SOUND CHECK #2: /ɔ/ (<u>a</u>ll) before consonant /l/. Drop the jaw open to the shape and position for /ɔ/ rather than beginning this sound combination with the more closed /ʊ/ (w<u>ou</u>ld) shape. Also, maintain the sunken cheeks and tongue arch as the tongue tip touches the upper gum ridge for /l/ to avoid inserting short /ə/ (<u>uh</u>) or /wə/ (<u>wuh</u>) before /l/. Speak 'all' not 'ooall' or 'awuhll'.

---

[1] The spelling 'alm' in words such as calm, palm and psalm is usually pronounced /ɑm/ in NAS.

WORDS /ɔ/ before /l/

all	bawl	awl	ball
call	drawl	thrall	haul
hall	miscall	befall	brawl
carryall	basketball	fireball	install
disenthrall	downfallen	caterwaul	baseball

PHRASES /ɔ/ before /l/

1. salty meatballs
2. southern drawl
3. no wherewithal
4. small waterfalls
5. Rock of Gibraltar
6. urban sprawl
7. not enthralled
8. awful spitballs
9. almost waltzing
10. smelly mothballs

SENTENCES /ɔ/ before /l/

1. Is Walton's last name Dalton?

2. They stood eyeball-to-eyeball.

3. We called Saul to play handball.

4. It's not my fault Paul is stonewalling.

5. He was assaulted during the football free-for-all.

> *I know not whether Laws be right,*
> *Or whether Laws be wrong;*
> *All that we know who lie in gaol[1]*
> *Is that the wall is strong;*
> *And that each day is like a year,*
> *A year whose days are long.*
> (Oscar Wilde: Ballad of Reading Gaol)

SOUND CHECK #3: intrusive, unstressed vowel of 'r'. When a word ends in /ɔ/ and there is no 'r' in the spelling, do not add an /ɚ/ (er) sound or link with a consonant /r/. Example: pronounce 'saw' not 'sawer' and 'sawing' not 'sawring'.

---

[1] This word is pronounced: /dʒël/ (jail), and is British for jail.

WORDS /ɔ/ (<u>all</u>) with no intrusive /ɚ/ (<u>er</u>)

saw	law	caw	flaw
jaw	paw	claw	slaw
raw	awe	craw	draw
thaw	craw	maw	gnaw
braw	chaw	pshaw	straw

PHRASES /ɔ/ (<u>all</u>) with no intrusive /ɚ/ (<u>er</u>) or linking /r/

1.	jaw injury	6.	saw everything
2.	law issued	7.	pawing animals
3.	straw inside	8.	gnawing insects
4.	clawing monsters	9.	draw in the sand
5.	thawing ice cream	10.	flaw in materials

SENTENCES /ɔ/ (<u>all</u>), with no intrusive /ɚ/ (<u>er</u>) or linking /r/

1. She's in awe of musicians.

2. Is there a flaw in his reasoning?

3. Shawn's fond of drawing horses.

4. Her jaw is overly tense and painful.

5. We saw Elizabeth in *Dead Man Walking*.

6. The sound of clawing emanated from the shed.

7. The thought of gnawing on raw oysters is appalling.

8. What are the ingredients in cold slaw and potato salad?

9. The electricity shut off, thawing everything in the freezer.

10. Her daughter-in-law is withdrawing money from the bank.

NEUTRAL AMERICAN TEXT /ɔ/ (<u>all</u>). *Mark the following and then speak out loud.*

/ɔ/ before /l/:

ɔ
O, what a f<u>all</u> was there, my countrymen!

(Julius Caesar: III, ii, 190)

Don't talk, that's all.

(Chekhov: The Cherry Orchard)

She was as false as water.

(Othello: V, ii, 134)

Why, what a caterwauling dost thou keep!

(Titus Andronicus: IV, ii, 57)

I have decked the sea with drops full salt.

(The Tempest: I, ii, 155)

Yet all goes well, yet all our joints are whole.

(1 Henry IV: IV, i, 83)

All—all expired save thee—save less than thou:
Save only the divine light in thine eyes—
Save but the soul in thine uplifted eyes.
I saw but them—they were the world to me.
I saw but them—saw only them for hours—
Saw only them until the moon went down.

(Poe: To Helen)

And thou, O wall, O sweet, O lovely wall,
That stand'st between her father's ground and mine!
Thou wall, O wall, O sweet and lovely wall,
Show me thy chink, to blink through with mine eyne!

(A Midsummer Night's Dream: V, I, 174)

CROWD.   Boo! boo!
JODELET.   Yes, yes! And the same unto you all!
BELLEROSE. Time we all went home now—!
JODELET.   Clear the hall!

(Rostand: Cyrano de Bergerac)

ANGELO.   Condemn the fault and not the actor of it?
           Why, every fault's condemn'd ere it be done.
           Mine were the very cipher of a function,
           To fine the faults whose fine stands in record,
           And let go by the actor.
ISABEL.   O just but severe law!

(Measure for Measure: II, ii, 37)

/ɔ/ various positions:

I'll make them pay; I'll sauce them.

(The Merry Wives of Windsor: IV, iii, 8)

Thou dost usurp that title now by fraud,
For in that shell of mother breeds a bawd.

(Tourneur: The Revenger's Tragedy)

While you two talk this out, I'll go shave!

(Strindberg: Miss Julie)

He says, my lord, your daughter is not well.

(King Lear: I, iv, 50)

Conscience is but a word that cowards use,
Devis'd at first to keep the strong in awe.

(Richard III: V, iii, 309)

He calls us rebels, traitors, and will scourge
With haughty arms this hateful name in us.

(1 Henry IV: V, ii, 39)

Thou call'dst me dog before thou hadst a cause,
But since I am a dog, beware my fangs.

(The Merchant of Venice: III, iii, 6)

A small writer, particularly when he is not successful, seems to
himself clumsy, awkward, unnecessary...

(Chekhov: The Seagull)

KING.   To this point hast thou heard him
              At any time speak aught?
SURVEYOR.   He was brought to this
              By a vain prophecy of Nicholas Henton.

(Henry VIII: I, ii, 145)

When law can do no right,
Let it be lawful that law bar no wrong;
Law cannot give my child his kingdom here,
For he that holds his kingdom holds the law;
Therefore since law itself is perfect wrong,
How can the law forbid my tongue to curse?

(King John: III, i, 185)

/ ɑ / (f<u>a</u>ther)

Form the shape for the fifth back vowel /ɑ/ (f<u>a</u>ther) by resting the tip of the tongue down behind the lower front teeth, opening the lower jaw slightly more than for the previous back vowel sound /ɔ/ (<u>a</u>ll), relaxing the back of the tongue low in the mouth and releasing sound through the mouth with the lips <u>un</u>rounded. The muscles of the throat and cheeks remain relaxed throughout.

AUDIO 22▶ /ɑ/ (f<u>a</u>ther)

                                          ɑ

And through his cloak, his sword thrust out to m<u>o</u>ck

                    ɑ

The ruffled feathers of a strutting c<u>o</u>ck!

                  (Rostand: Cyrano de Bergerac)

                  ɑ

All this is nothing; you shall see an<u>o</u>n

              ɑ

A place you little dream <u>o</u>n.

            (Middleton & Rowley: The Changeling)

     ɑ   ɑ   ɑ

Oh, "f<u>a</u>ther," — "f<u>a</u>ther"! I never knew anything of f<u>a</u>ther.

                                (Ibsen: Ghosts)

WORDS /ɑ/ (f<u>a</u>ther)

Initial	Medial	Final
ˀ ox	sobs	*
ˀ on	palm	*
ˀ opt	drama	*
ˀ omelet	topping	*
ˀ obvious	common	*

RHYTHM TRACK This sound can be categorized as long, half-long or short depending on its position in the word and the sounds that follow.[1] Notice the variation in lengths while reading the words that follow out loud. *Read across.*

---

[1] Length indicators (or dots) used in IPA notation are optional (see pages 39-40). This section is marked to promote increased awareness and to aid those studying lengths.

long /ɑ:/	half-long /ɑ·/	short /ɑ·/
nod	not	nuance
rod	rot	(*occurs very rarely*)
mob	mop	
lodge	lots	
blond	block	

This sound is **long /ɑ:/** in a stressed syllable:

(a)   when it's the last sound of the word

(b)   when it's followed by a voiced consonant

PHRASES long /ɑ:/

1.	spa massage	6.	John's collie
2.	holiday lodge	7.	monstrous job
3.	modern college	8.	scholarly mom
4.	blond bombshell	9.	snobby robbers
5.	five-dollar omelet	10.	twenty-third Psalm

This sound is **half long /ɑ·/** in a stressed syllable when followed by a voiceless consonant.

PHRASES half-long /ɑ·/

1.	stocky doctor	6.	posh watches
2.	shot of Scotch	7.	lots of peacocks
3.	boxes of pasta	8.	forgotten operas
4.	shops in Washington	9.	yachts in the tropics
5.	improper stock option	10.	popular cotton socks

Short /ɑ/ is spoken in unstressed syllables, which occurs very rarely.

Note: /ɑ/ (father) is not marked for length from this point on.

SENTENCES /ɑ/ various lengths

1.   Mom shopped for pasta.

2.   It's impossible to contact Robert.

3.   The dropped stop watch stopped running.

4.   Solid dark chocolate is not considered toxic.

5.   Robin had a calming massage at the health spa.

6.   My father's cell phone is probably not turned on.

7.   The rockers feasted on hot popcorn, pasta, and nachos.

8.   They all raced nonstop around the block, then dropped.

9.   Manhattan co-ops are uncommonly expensive property.

10.   Tom will be waiting in the lobby at the Renaissance drama.

NEUTRAL AMERICAN TEXT /ɑ/ (f<u>a</u>ther). *Mark the following and speak out loud.*

/ɑ/ various positions:

                 ɔ
Discuss unto me, art thou officer,
         ɑ   ɑ
Or art thou base, c<u>o</u>mmon, and p<u>o</u>pular?
                               (Henry V: IV, i, 37)

It shall be call'd "Bottom's Dream," because it hath no bottom.
                           (A Midsummer Night's Dream: IV, i, 215)

Abjure this magic, turn to God again.
Ay, and Faustus will turn to God again.
To God? He loves thee not.
The God thou servest is thine own appetite.
                               (Marlowe: Doctor Faustus)

CASSIO. Welcome, Iago; we must to the watch.
IAGO.   Not this hour, lieutenant; 'tis not yet ten o' th' clock.
                               (Othello: II, iii, 12)

GRUMIO.   Knock, sir? whom should I knock? Is there any man
                has rebus'd your worship?
PETRUCHIO. Villain, I say, knock me here soundly.
GRUMIO.   Knock you here, sir? Why, sir, what am I, sir, that I
                should knock you here, sir?
PETRUCHIO. Villain, I say, knock me at this gate.
                          (The Taming of the Shrew: I, ii, 6)

LONG DIPHTHONGS

See Overview pages 18-26

/ eɪ̆ / (h<u>ey</u>)

Form **/eɪ̆/** (h<u>ey</u>) by beginning in the shape and position for the third front vowel **/e/** (g<u>e</u>t), then seamlessly blending into the second front vowel **/ɪ/** (w<u>i</u>ll). The jaw will close slightly and the front tongue arch will lift during the blend.

Stress is on the first element of all diphthongs. The second element is rhythmically shorter as notated by / ˘ / in the IPA symbol.

AUDIO 23▶ /eɪ̆/ (h<u>ey</u>)

>   eɪ̆   eɪ̆
> For the red blood r<u>eig</u>ns in the winter's p<u>a</u>le.
>
>   (The The Winter's Tale: IV, iii, 4)
>
>   eɪ̆   eɪ̆   eɪ̆
> I pr<u>ay</u> thee, good Hor<u>a</u>tio, w<u>ai</u>t upon him.
>
>   (Hamlet: V, i, 293)
>
>   eɪ̆   eɪ̆
> A wicked d<u>ay</u>, and not a holy d<u>ay</u>!
>
>   (King John: III, i, 83)

WORDS /eɪ̆/ (h<u>ey</u>)

Initial	Medial	Final
ʔ age	raid	day
ʔ aid	lake	hay
ʔ ace	faint	stay
ʔ ape	brain	relay
ʔ aim	praise	matinee

RHYTHM TRACK This sound can be categorized as long or short depending on its position in the word and the sounds that follow.

When the duration of the sound is long, a 'dot' follows each element of the symbol. Keep in mind that diphthongs consist of two blended vowels, so they can be wonderfully expressive, even when categorized as short.

This sound is **long /e·ĭ·/** in a stressed syllable:

(a)   when it's the last sound of the word

(b)   when it's followed by a voiced consonant

This sound is **short** in all other instances.

PHRASES long /e·ĭ·/

1.	bathes today	6.	snail mail
2.	displays rage	7.	plays at Shea
3.	explains to Dave	8.	made the grade
4.	pays for lemonade	9.	persuaded Wayne
5.	dismayed by the delay	10.	chained to the stage

PHRASES short /eĭ/

1.	dates Kate	6.	apes fate
2.	great shape	7.	erased mistakes
3.	wastes paste	8.	face with makeup
4.	eight debates	9.	displaced glaciers
5.	hates pancakes	10.	disgraceful skates

Note: /eĭ/ (pay) is not marked for length from this point on.

SENTENCES /eĭ/ various lengths

1.   Jane is off to Norway on Monday.

2.   Did you say 'checkmate', Lorraine?

3.   The gray fire escape is strangely shaped.

4.   Subway stations are being painted today.

5. The play received raves in all the daily papers.

6. Laurence Olivier was great in *The Entertainer*.

7. Grace, I'm midway through your essay on Spain.

8. Who is playing KATE in *The Taming of the Shrew*?

9. They gave first aid in the freight train at the station.

10. They were not 'on the same page' and were enraged.

11. There's no debate; Adrian is a great conversationalist.

12. Failure to obey was a grave mistake and chaos reined.

13. Everyone is acquainted with heartache; it's no disgrace.

14. Dr. Abe's patients are grateful and sing his praises daily.

15. By the way, Craig's application to the Navy was misplaced.

SOUND CHECK #1: **/eĭl/ combinations.** The middle and back of the tongue should remain relaxed and uninvolved when moving the tongue tip from its position resting down behind the lower teeth on **/eĭ/**, up to touch the upper gum ridge on **/l/**. Otherwise, an **/ə/** (<u>uh</u>) or **/jə/** (<u>yuh</u>) sound will be inserted before the **/l/**. In other words, speak 'hail' rather than 'hai**uh**l' or 'hai**yuh**l'.

/eĭl/	/eĭl/	/eĭl/	/eĭl/
jail	rail	nail	fail
flail	kale	dale	mail
scale	whale	snail	assail
ale/ail	sale/sail	inhale	they'll
tail/tale	gale/Gail	hail/hale	pail/pale

PHRASES /eĭ/ before /l/

1. the Holy Grail
2. tells great tales
3. needs an inhaler
4. raising pay scales
5. gray whale sighting
6. daily mail
7. veils on sale
8. the third rail
9. pale assailants
10. frail from ailments

SENTENCES /eĭ/ before /l/

1. Grades are pass/fail in Airedale.

2. If the ginger ale is stale, have a cocktail.

3. Hail the mailmen, both male and female.

4. Ms. Hale, what does studying Braille entail?

5. They tried to pay on a sliding scale, to no avail.

6. The trailer for the movie failed to generate sales.

7. Gale, you can't buy wholesale at Bloomingdales.

8. Abigail played FLORENCE NIGHTINGALE in pigtails.

9. The blackmailer was nailed by police and put in jail.

10. Evil Dale is impaled in the fairy tale, so good prevails.

NEUTRAL AMERICAN TEXT /eĭ/ (h<u>ey</u>). *Mark the following and speak out loud.*

/eĭ/ before /l/:

eĭ   eĭ   eĭ

"A s<u>ail</u>, a s<u>ail</u>, a s<u>ail</u>!"

(Othello: II, i, 51)

Let not search and inquisition quail.

(As You Like It: II, ii, 20)

PETRUCHIO. Whose tongue?
KATHERINE. Yours, if you talk of tales, and so farewell.
PETRUCHIO. What, with my tongue in your tail?

(The Taming of the Shrew: II, i, 216)

MACBETH.   If we should fail?
L. MACBETH.   We fail?
But screw your courage to the sticking place,
And we'll not fail.

(Macbeth: I, vii, 59)

All hail, Macbeth, hail to thee, Thane of Cawdor!

(Macbeth: I, iii, 49)

164

/eĭ/ various positions:

Or shall we give the signal to our rage.

(King John: II, i, 265)

Poor Cyrano! We must find a gentle way
To tell Roxanne. What does the doctor say?

(Rostand: Cyrano de Bergerac)

The grave doth gape, and doting death is near.

(Henry V: II, i, 61)

To solemnize this day the glorious sun
Stays in his course and plays the alchemist.

(King John: III, i, 78)

You lie, in faith, for you are call'd plain Kate,
And bonny Kate, and sometimes Kate the curst;
But Kate, the prettiest Kate in Christendom.

(The Taming of the Shrew: II, i, 185)

NYM.   You'll pay me the eight shillings I won of you at betting?
PISTOL.   Base is the slave that pays.

(Henry V: II i, 94)

Had he been ta'en, we should have heard the news;
Had he been slain, we should have heard the news.

(3 Henry VI: II, i, 4)

Reputation, reputation, reputation! O, I have lost my reputation!
I have lost the immortal part of myself, and what remains is bestial.
My reputation, Iago, my reputation!

(Othello: II, iii, 262)

Down, down I come, like glist'ring Phaëton,
Wanting the manage of unruly jades.
In the base court? Base court, where kings grow base,
To come at traitors' calls and do them grace.
In the base court, come down? Down court! Down king!

(Richard II: III, iii, 178)

/ aĭ / (my)

This diphthong is one of two in NAS that begins with the /a/ sound.

Form the first element /a/ by resting the tip of the tongue down behind the lower teeth, opening the jaw and flattening the tongue arch slightly more than for the fourth front vowel /æ/ (that), with the lips and cheeks neutral but energized. Then, seamlessly blend in the second front vowel /ɪ/, closing the lower jaw, lifting the front tongue arch, and slightly spreading the cheeks and lips.

Stress is on the first element of all diphthongs. The second element is rhythmically shorter as notated by / ˘ / in the IPA symbol.

AUDIO 24▶ /aĭ/ (my)

        aĭ   aĭ

The moon shines bright.

(The Merchant of Venice: V, i, 1)

        aĭ   aĭə   aĭ   aĭ aĭ

And you, like an iron stovepipe…your eyes like coals…

(Strindberg: Miss Julie)

        aĭ   aĭ

Alas, how life can trifle with itself!

(Two Gentlemen of Verona: IV, iv, 183)

WORDS /aĭ/ (my)

Initial	Medial	Final
ʔ ice	time	sky
ʔ Ida	dying	why
ʔ I've	primal	deny
ʔ icon	survive	reply
ʔ idea	implied	thigh

RHYTHM TRACK This sound can be categorized as long or short depending on its position in the word and the sounds that follow.

This sound is **long /a·ĭ·/** in a stressed syllable:

(a)   when it's the last sound of the word

(b)   when it's followed by a voiced consonant

This sound is **short** in all other instances, including unstressed weak forms of the words: 'I', 'my', 'thy'.

PHRASES long /a·ĭ·/

1.	applies dye	6.	surprised child
2.	provides a guide	7.	a sad goodbye
3.	describes the sign	8.	blinds his eyes
4.	hides French fries	9.	declined to cry
5.	reapplied with the guys	10.	slips and slides

PHRASES short /aĭ/

1.	not ice cream	6.	swiped bike
2.	likes the fights	7.	enticing item
3.	gripes about life	8.	might be spliced
4.	hikes to the turnpike	9.	likely to be indicted
5.	frightened the playwright	10.	delightful housewife

Note: /aĭ/ (my) is not marked for length from this point on.

SENTENCES /aĭ/ various lengths

1.   Bye-bye, Brian.

2.   The climate is fine in Shanghai.

3.   Simplify your life, what great advice!

4.   There wasn't a dry eye in the audience.

5.   You were a riot in *Private Lives*, McGuire.

6.   The sweet pineapple pie has finally arrived.

7.   I see it's inscribed, but what does that signify?

8. Guy arrives disguised, so he's not recognized.

9. What a triumphant recital; you're highly admired.

10. I'm standing-by in *The Prime of Miss Jean Brodie*.

11. I advise you to stop whining; whiners are despised.

12. The bride is marrying the pilot Friday evening at five.

13. Shall we wine and dine in Wyoming or Thailand, Ryan?

14. My advice? Lengthen your spine for improved alignment.

15. The way the sun is shining on this mild day is just sublime.

SOUND CHECK #1: /aĭ/ before a *voiceless* consonant. The jaw should be mostly open with a slight front of the tongue arch for the first element /a/, so that /ə/ (uh) is not spoken instead (for very well-pronounced characters or when speaking classical/poetic text). 'Rhyming' /aĭ/ sounds in the word pairs that follow may be useful for spotting variations in pronunciation. Also note, the second element of this diphthong, though rhythmically shorter, should not be eliminated. This is important for individuals from the South and Mid-west.

South=get rid of dipthong!

WORD PAIRS /aĭ/ before a voiceless consonant *Read across.*

tie/type	hi/hype	lie/life	vie/vice
pie/pike	my/mike	eye/ice	my/might
rye/right	fry/fright	why/wife	nigh/night

WORDS /aĭ/ before a voiceless consonant

life	rife	wife	strife
hike	like	plight	strike
pipe	right	spices	thrice
tight	stripe	device	slight
mighty	insightful	dislike	birthright

PHRASES /aĭ/ before a voiceless consonant

1.	so nice	6.	too tight
2.	she's bright	7.	not tonight
3.	the good life	8.	feisty advice
4.	more than likely	9.	iced or spiced
5.	height and might	10.	just delightful

SENTENCES /aĭ/ before a voiceless consonant

1. Can I play the spiteful sprite?

2. Have you seen *White Nights*?

3. What an extremely bright playwright.

4. Is there a hyphen in the word 'housewife'?

5. Most everyone dislikes cellulite; am I right?

6. No one will be on-site after midnight tonight.

7. It fell off the Eiffel tower and had to be spliced.

8. I didn't see the sign at night because of its height.

9. Swipe the card and the price of the item is sighted.

10. When cast as the fighter, he began taking vitamins.

11. It's unlikely the vice president will make this flight.

12. Would you like that tight little item in red or white?

13. The fishwife had a large pike caught in her windpipe.

14. In hindsight, it might have been better to avoid sunlight.

15. She priced the toy rifle for Mike but bought a kite instead.

SOUND CHECK #2: When /aĭ/ is followed immediately by /l/ within a word a short schwa may be inserted, with the resulting pronunciations: /aĭl/ *or* /aĭ əl/, depending on the rhythm of the text. The back of the tongue must remain relaxed and uninvolved so a /j/ (you) sound is not inserted between /aĭ/ and /l/ or between /aĭ/ and /əl/. Speak the word: 'wild' or 'wiuhld', *not* 'wiyyuhld'.

I'll	file	bile	dial
rile	trial	Nile	vile
pile	mild	wild	trial
awhile	guile	style	Lyall
while/wile	child	revile	denial

PHRASES /aɪ/ and /aɪ ə/ before /l/

1.	hair styling	6.	love child
2.	lot of smiles	7.	mile after mile
3.	fair and mild	8.	all Francophiles
4.	no crocodiles	9.	puerile behavior
5.	down the aisle	10.	wild on the Nile

SENTENCES /aɪ/ and /aɪ ə/ before /l/

1. The juvenile has style.

2. Are there crocodiles in the Nile?

3. What vile behavior, defiling the files.

4. Have that wild child be quiet for awhile.

5. The mild smile on the Mona Lisa beguiles.

6. Compile all reviews of *Buried Child* in a pile.

7. Kyle disguised himself, then tried to rile Lyle.

8. The reviled pedophile couldn't receive a fair trial.

9. I'll while away the time for awhile on a desert isle.

10. They cancelled their trip down the aisle, then reconciled.

NEUTRAL AMERICAN TEXT /aɪ/ (my). *Mark the following and speak out loud.*

/aɪ/ and /aɪ ə/ before /l/:

        aɪ

Will you be patient? Will you stay awhile?

(Julius Caesar: III, ii, 149)

O villain, villain, smiling, damned villain!
My tables—meet it is I set it down
That one may smile, and smile, and be a villain!

(Hamlet: I, v, 106)

O tiger's heart wrapp'd in a woman's hide!
How couldst thou drain the life-blood of the child?

(3 Henry VI: I, iv, 137)

The greater file of the subject held the Duke to be wise.

(Measure for Measure: III, ii, 136)

/aĭ/ before a voiceless consonant:

My wife, my wife! what wife? I have no wife.

(Othello: V, ii, 97)

Antonio, I am married to a wife
Which is as dear to me as life itself,
But life itself, my wife, and all the world,
Are not with me esteem'd above thy life.

(The Merchant of Venice: IV, i, 282)

/aĭ/ various positions:

Be silent while I write.

(Strindberg: The Father)

Why day is day, night night, and time is time.

(Hamlet: II, ii, 88)

O, sir, I find her milder than she was.

(Two Gentlemen of Verona: V, ii, 2)

In my mind's eye, Horatio.

(Hamlet: I, ii, 185)

Hath Romeo slain himself? Say thou but ay
And that bare vowel *I* shall poison more
Than the death-darting eye of cockatrice.
I am not I, if there be such an ay,
Or those eyes shut, that makes thee answer ay.
If he be slain, say ay, or if not, no.

(Romeo and Juliet: III, ii, 45)

Thou speakest aright;
I am that merry wanderer of the night.
I jest to Oberon and make him smile
When I a fat and bean-fed horse beguile.

(A Midsummer Night's Dream: II, i, 42)

That's a lie! I'm the one who broke it! Did he say that he did?
The swine!

(Strindberg: Miss Julie)

/ ɔĭ / (b<u>oy</u>)

Form /ɔĭ/ (b<u>oy</u>) by beginning in the shape and position for the fourth back vowel /ɔ/ (<u>a</u>ll) then seamlessly blending into the short, second front vowel /ɪ/ (w<u>i</u>ll). During the blend, the jaw will close slightly, the front tongue arch will lift, the lips will unround and slightly spread.

Take care not to begin this diphthong in the more closed, lip rounded shape and position of the back vowel /ʊ/ (w<u>ou</u>ld).

Stress is on the first element of all diphthongs. The second element is rhythmically shorter as notated by / ˘ / in the IPA symbol.

AUDIO 25▶ /ɔĭ/ (b<u>oy</u>)

ɔĭ
Thou lily-liver'd b<u>oy</u>!

(Macbeth: V, iii, 15)

ɔĭ
The King, I fear, is p<u>oi</u>son'd by a monk.

(King John: V, vi, 23)

ɔĭ
'Tis safer to be that which we destr<u>oy</u>
ɔĭ
Than by destruction dwell in doubtful j<u>oy</u>.

(Macbeth: III, ii, 6)

WORDS /ɔĭ/ (b<u>oy</u>)

Initial	Medial	Final
? oil	boil	joy
? oily	coin	soy
? oink	foible	ahoy
? oyster	doilies	destroy
? ointment	lawyer	employ

RHYTHM TRACK This sound can be categorized as long or short depending on its position in the word and the sounds that follow it.

This sound is **long /ɔ·ɪ·/** in a stressed syllable:

(a)   when it's the last sound of the word

(b)   when it's followed by a voiced consonant

This sound is **short** in all other instances.

PHRASES long /ɔ·ɪ·/

1.	avoids noise	6.	deployed Roy
2.	destroys toys	7.	enjoys St. Croix
3.	coins in tin foil	8.	conjoined in Troy
4.	recoils from boys	9.	spoiled and soiled
5.	annoyed in Illinois	10.	employed by Freud

PHRASES short /ɔɪ/

1.	Rolls Royce	6.	paranoid choice
2.	hoisting sails	7.	boisterous Joyce
3.	orders oysters	8.	moistened throat
4.	not boycotting	9.	voiced or voiceless
5.	stops in Detroit	10.	going to the Cloisters

Note: /ɔɪ/ (boy) is not marked for length from this point on.

SENTENCES /ɔɪ/ various lengths

1.   Boy oh boy!

2.   Joyce loves corduroy.

3.   Let's embroider in the foyer.

4.   Anoint joints with moist ointments.

5.   Is that consonant voiced or unvoiced?

6.   Join the boycott in the adjoining room.

7.   People with choices feel less exploited.

8.   Mr. Freud recoils from cleaning the toilet.

9.   Annoyingly, moist soil destroys old coins.

10. No longer embroiled in turmoil, he rejoiced.

11. Wrap the soybeans in tin foil or they'll spoil.

12. She enjoyed dancing on point at the Bolshoi.

13. Boyle was appointed to pinpoint the problem.

14. Do oysters become poisonous when boiled in oil?

15. Roy stopped using steroids. They destroyed his health.

SOUND CHECK #1: The first element of the diphthong /ɔɪ/ is /ɔ/ *not* the more closed, lip rounded /ʊ/. All of the words below begin with /ɔ/, as notated by the IPA symbols. Feel the relationship in shape between /ɔ/ in the words in the first and second columns, and the third and fourth columns. *Read across.*

/ɔ/	/ɔɪ/	/ɔ/	/ɔɪ/
awe	oyster	awe	oil
saw	soy	saw	soil
caw	coy	caw	coil
daw	doily	fall	foil
jaw	joy	jaw	join
raw	Roy	talk	toys
haw	hoist	haw	ahoy
law	loin	law	loyal
paw	poise	paw	point
naught	annoy	paw	poison

PHRASES /ɔ/ and /ɔɪ/

1. saw the soil
2. awful ointment
3. cautions and coy
4. unlawful loitering
5. taught to enjoy toys
6. lost lawyers
7. haughty 'ahoy'
8. annoying audition
9. Paul's appointment
10. bought for the boys

SOUND CHECK #2: When /ɔɪ/ occurs immediately before /l/ in the same word, it can also be pronounced /ɔɪ əl/. But the back of the tongue must remain relaxed and uninvolved, so /j/ (you) is not inserted between /ɔɪ/ and /l/ or between /ɔɪ/ and /əl/. Speak the word: 'oil' or 'oiuhl', not 'oiyyuhl.'

---

oil	coil	foil	moil
boil	toil	soil	broil
turmoil	spoil	voile	Boyle
parboil	quatrefoil	recoil	uncoil
embroil	counterfoil	despoil	Troilus

PHRASES /ɔ̆ɪ/ before /l/

1.	broiled in oil	6.	spoiled sausage
2.	coiled springs	7.	quatrefoil design
3. •	family turmoil	8.	embroiled in debate
4.	recoils from joy	9.	lovely voile material
5.	kept the counterfoil	10.	parboiled vegetables

SENTENCES /ɔ̆ɪ/ before /l/

1. Boil it in oil.

2. Wash all soiled doilies.

3. To the winner go the spoils.

4. Embroiled in the soiled toilet.

5. They toiled to uncoil the tin foil.

6. Disembroil yourself from Doyle.

7. Boyle's toiling over the broken boiler.

8. Have you seen *Foyle's War* on BBC America?

9. Mr. Doyle prefers oysters broiled, not parboiled.

10. Her royal blue voile dress was soiled in all the turmoil.

NEUTRAL AMERICAN TEXT /ɔ̆ɪ/ (b<u>oy</u>). *Mark the following and speak out loud.*

/ɔ̆ɪ/ before /l/:

         ɔɪ

Give us the f<u>oi</u>ls.

(Hamlet: V, ii, 254)

His soldiers fell to spoil.

(Julius Caesar: V, iii, 7)

So nightly toils the subject of the land.

(Hamlet: I, i, 72)

Like a hell-broth boil and bubble.

(Macbeth: IV, i, 19)

They clepe us drunkards, and with swinish phrase
Soil our addition.

(Hamlet: I, iv, 19)

/ɔĭ/ various positions:

Turn face to face and bloody point to point.

(King John: II, i, 390)

Whilst I am here on earth let me be cloyed
With all things that delight the heart of man.

(Marlowe: Doctor Faustus)

Sir, you of Troy, call you yourself Aeneas?

(Troilus and Cressida: I, iii, 245)

With her I liv'd in joy; our wealth increas'd
By prosperous voyages I often made.

(The Comedy of Errors: I, i, 39)

Hail, you anointed deputies of heaven!

(King John: III, i, 136)

LEONTES. What noise there, ho?
PAULINA. No noise, my lord, but needful conference.

(The The Winter's Tale: II, iii, 39)

There's a good grandame, boy, that would blot thee.

(King John: II, i, 133)

The violence of either grief or joy
Their own enactures with themselves destroy.
Where joy most revels, grief doth most lament;
Grief joys, joy grieves, on slender accident.

(Hamlet: III, ii, 196)

/ oŭ / (g<u>o</u>)

Form /oŭ/ (g<u>o</u>) by beginning in the shape and position for the third back vowel /o/, then seamlessly blending into the second back vowel /ʊ/ (w<u>ou</u>ld). The jaw will close a little, the back tongue arch will raise slightly, and the lips will round and energize during the blend.

Stress is on the first element of all diphthongs. The second element is rhythmically shorter as notated by / ˘ / in the IPA symbol.

AUDIO 26▶ /oŭ/ (g<u>o</u>)

>   oŭ   oŭ
> H<u>o</u>ld, h<u>o</u>ld, my heart,
>   oŭ   oŭ
> And you, my sinews, gr<u>ow</u> not instant <u>o</u>ld.
>
> (Hamlet: I, v, 93)
>
>   oŭ oŭ
> If he were mad, he would not plead s<u>o</u> c<u>o</u>ldly.
>
> (The Comedy of Errors: V, i, 273)
>
>   oŭ
> What a plague mean ye to c<u>o</u>lt me thus?
>
> (1 Henry IV: II, ii, 37)

WORDS /oŭ/ (g<u>o</u>)

Initial	Medial	Final
? oaf	close	go
? old	ghost	sew
? ode	home	crow
? own	bones	below
? oboe	moaning	dough

RHYTHM TRACK This sound can be categorized as long or short depending on its position in the word and the sounds that follow it.

This sound is **long /o·ŭ·/** in a stressed syllable:

(a)   when it's the last sound of the word

(b)   when it's followed by a voiced consonant

This sound is **short** in all other instances.

PHRASES long /o·ŭ·/

1.	stone cold	6.	drove home
2.	old clothes	7.	cajoled loans
3.	low plateau	8.	hasn't phoned
4.	circle the globe	9.	yoga explosion
5.	exposed his foes	10.	proposing to Joan

PHRASES short /oŭ/

1.	soaked coats	6.	boasting oaf
2.	hope to elope	7.	woeful notes
3.	smoky smoke	8.	hopeful folks
4.	revoked the vote	9.	coast to coast
5.	mostly unfocused	10.	emotional vote

Note: /oŭ/ (go) is not marked for length from this point on.

SENTENCES /oŭ/ (go) various lengths

1.   Who phoned, Joseph?

2.   Lois played the oboe at the opening.

3.   Nobody knows *Oklahoma* like Lowell.

4.   No, I want to go to work even if it's snowing.

5.   Rhoda was approached about taking over the role.

6.   Oh no! Who in the front row is so overly verbose?

7.   A video was made of the bold performance in Tokyo.

8.   The opinion poll is focusing on folks from Minnesota.

9.   Ms. De Soto hoped for a role in *Show Boat* in Sarasota.

10.   The pony was overexposed to the cold and almost froze.

> **SOUND CHECK #1: /l/, /lt/, and /ld/ endings.** Be sure to pronounce all of the consonant sounds in these combinations when they follow **/oŭ/**. The tongue tip should make contact with the hard palate behind the upper teeth and fully sound **/l/** before continuing on to the **/t/** or **/d/** sound that follows. *Read across.*

/oŭ/	/oŭl/	/oŭlt/	/oŭld/
Coe	coal	colt	cold
bow	bowl	bolt	bold
hoe	hole	holt	hold
mow	mole	molt	mold
doe	dole	dolt	doled

Thy prime of manhood daring, b<u>old</u>, and venturous.

(Richard III: IV, iv, 171)

PHRASES /oŭ/ before /l/, /lt/ and /ld/

1. not foret<u>old</u>
2. day-<u>old</u> s<u>ole</u>
3. t<u>old</u> to ref<u>old</u>
4. too <u>old</u> to sc<u>old</u>
5. p<u>o</u>lling p<u>o</u>llsters

6. ice-c<u>old</u> m<u>old</u>
7. loves marig<u>olds</u>
8. twice-t<u>old</u> to caj<u>ole</u>
9. reasons are twof<u>old</u>
10. w<u>o</u>n't withh<u>old</u> g<u>old</u>

SENTENCES /oŭ/ before /l/, /lt/ and /ld/

1. Behold the golden statue.

2. Scold Joe for undercooking the poultry.

3. They only sold shoes with hand-sewn soles.

4. Hold on a minute; that's not what I was told!

5. Members of the household revolted when blindfolded.

6. Grab ahold of the stone wall if you lose your foothold.

7. The shareholder was cajoled; then he sold to Mr. Dole.

8. The crowd was uncontrolled; we couldn't uphold the law.

9. Don't think me overbold, but I'd love the role of LEOPOLD.

10. The goalie maintained a stronghold between the goal posts.

NEUTRAL AMERICAN TEXT /oŭ/ (g<u>o</u>). *Mark the following and speak out loud.*

/oŭ/ before /l/, /lt/ and /ld/:

oŭ
And therefore fortify your h<u>o</u>ld, my lord.

(3 Henry VI: I, ii, 52)

Thy language is so bold and vicious.

(Middleton & Rowley: The Changeling)

And this, so sole and so unmatchable.

(King John: IV, iii, 52)

For here's the scroll
In which thou hast given thy soul to Lucifer.

(Marlowe: Doctor Faustus)

For many men that stumble at the threshold
Are well foretold that danger lurks within.

(3 Henry VI: IV, vii, 11)

When I desir'd him to come home to dinner,
He ask'd me for a thousand marks in gold:
"'Tis dinner-time," quoth I: "My gold!" quoth he.
"Your meat doth burn," quoth I: "My gold!" quoth he.
"Will you come?" quoth I: "My gold!" quoth he.

(The Comedy of Errors: II, i, 60)

Hold, hold! Zounds, he'll raise up a kettle of devils, I think anon.
Good my lord, entreat for me. 'Sblood, I am never able to endure
these torments.

(Marlowe: Doctor Faustus)

The bull, the primitive statue and oblique memorial of cuckolds.

(Troilus and Cressida: V, i, 54)

But he grew old—
This knight so bold—
And o'er his heart a shadow
Fell as he found
No spot of ground
That looked like Eldorado.

(Poe: Eldorado)

And by our holy Sabbath have I sworn
To have the due and forfeit of my bond.

(The Merchant of Venice: IV, i, 36)

Life is as tedious as a twice-told tale,
Vexing the dull ear of a drowsy man.

(King John: III, iv, 108)

Yet here, Laertes? Aboard, aboard, for shame!
The wind sits in the shoulder of your sail.

(Hamlet: I, iii, 55)

I have seen tempests when the scolding winds
Have riv'd the knotty oaks, and I have seen
Th' ambitious ocean swell, and rage, and foam,
To be exalted with the threat'ning clouds.

(Julius Caesar: I, iii, 5)

All that glisters is not gold,
Often have you heard that told;
Many a man his life hath sold
But my outside to behold.
Gilded tombs do worms infold.
Had you been as wise as bold,
Young in limbs, in judgment old,
Your answer had not been inscroll'd.
Fare you well, your suit is cold.

(The Merchant of Venice: II, vii, 65)

/oŭ/ various positions:

Here is a mourning Rome, a dangerous Rome,
No Rome of safety for Octavius yet;
Hie hence, and tell him so.

(Julius Caesar: III, i, 288)

O woe! O woeful, woeful, woeful day!
Most lamentable day, most woeful day
That ever, ever, I did yet behold!
O day, O day, O day, O hateful day!
Never was seen so black a day as this.
O woeful day, O woeful day!

(Romeo and Juliet: IV, v, 49)

/ aŭ / (n<u>ow</u>)

This diphthong is one of two in NAS that begins with the /a/ sound.

Form the first element /a/ by resting the tip of the tongue down behind the lower teeth, opening the jaw and flattening the tongue arch slightly more than for the fourth front vowel /æ/ (th<u>a</u>t), with the lips and cheeks neutral but energized. Then seamlessly blend in the second back vowel /ʊ/ (w<u>ou</u>ld) closing the lower jaw, lifting the back tongue arch, and rounding the lips.

Stress is on the first element of all diphthongs. The second element is rhythmically shorter as notated by / ˘ / in the IPA symbol.

AUDIO 27▶ /aŭ/ (n<u>ow</u>)

           aŭ
From north to s<u>ou</u>th —
                       aŭ
Austria and France shoot in each other's m<u>ou</u>th.

(King John: II, I, 413)

       aŭ   aŭ   aŭ   aŭ
Oh, th<u>ou</u>'rt a f<u>ou</u>l black cl<u>ou</u>d, and th<u>ou</u> dost threat

A violent storm!

(Webster: The White Devil)

      aŭ   aŭ   aŭ
O h<u>ou</u>nd of Crete, think'st th<u>ou</u> my sp<u>ou</u>se to get?

(Henry V: II, i, 73)

WORDS /aŭ/ (n<u>ow</u>)

Initial	Medial	Final
ʔ out	pounds	how
ʔ owl	without	cow
ʔ oust	founder	thou
ʔ ouch	rounding	brow
ʔ ounce	mountain	chow

Take care not to begin this diphthong with the /æ/ (th<u>a</u>t) sound. This results in a diphthong that is overly tense and nasal for Neutral American, but is spoken in some Southern and Midwestern dialects.

RHYTHM TRACK This sound can be categorized as long or short depending on its position in the word and the sounds that follow it.

This sound is **long /a·ŭ·/** in a stressed syllable:

(a)   when it's the last sound of the word

(b)   when it's followed by a voiced consonant

This sound is **short** in all other instances.

PHRASES /a·ŭ·/

1.	l<u>ou</u>d cr<u>ow</u>ds	6.	gr<u>ou</u>nd d<u>ow</u>n
2.	f<u>ou</u>nd ar<u>ou</u>nd	7.	r<u>ou</u>nd cr<u>ow</u>ns
3.	d<u>ow</u>dy in br<u>ow</u>n	8.	surr<u>ou</u>nd s<u>ou</u>nd
4.	ar<u>ou</u>sed the t<u>ow</u>n	9.	h<u>ow</u>l and gr<u>ow</u>l
5.	w<u>ow</u>s with ch<u>ow</u>der	10.	schn<u>au</u>zers all<u>ow</u>ed

PHRASES short /aŭ/

1.	sh<u>ou</u>t ab<u>ou</u>t	6.	st<u>ou</u>t sp<u>ou</u>t
2.	what a sn<u>ou</u>t	7.	<u>ou</u>t of cl<u>ou</u>t
3.	<u>ou</u>sted sp<u>ou</u>se	8.	d<u>ou</u>se the h<u>ou</u>se
4.	gr<u>ou</u>ch on the c<u>ou</u>ch	9.	p<u>ou</u>ting boy sc<u>ou</u>ts
5.	m<u>ou</u>sy-colored bl<u>ou</u>se	10.	looking <u>ou</u>t for tr<u>ou</u>t

Note: /aŭ/ (n<u>ow</u>) is not marked for length from this point on.

SENTENCES /aŭ/ (n<u>ow</u>) various lengths

1.   Our hound 'bow-wows' to go out.

2.   Now, how many ounces in a pound?

3.   Theatre in the round can be powerful!

4.   You're grounded! How does that sound?

5.   I can't vouch for powdered clam chowder.

6.   The director shouted, "Louder, faster, funnier!"

7. What an astounding performance, take a bow!

8. "That was out of bounds," the lookout shouted.

9. We'll all meet downtown around the fountain.

10. Pouting won't increase your allowance, Howard.

SOUND CHECK #1: /aŭ/ before /l/. The tip of the tongue rests down behind the lower teeth on /aŭ/, then moves to touch the gum ridge on /l/. The middle of the tongue remains relaxed and uninvolved, and the lips remain slightly rounded, to avoid inserting /ə/ (uh) before /l/. Speak 'owl' not 'owuhl'.

/aŭl/	/aŭl/	/aŭl/	/aŭl/
owl	cowl	jowl	prowl
howl	afoul	yowl	growl
befoul	peafowl	scowl	seafowl

PHRASES /aŭ/ before /l/

1. heard yowling
2. owls downtown
3. scowling mouth
4. prominent jowl
5. something afoul
6. prowling around

SENTENCES /aŭ/ before /l/

1. The owl isn't considered a seafowl, is it?

2. Now, no howling if you don't get the part.

3. We saw thousands of Southeast Asian peafowl.

4. Scowling and growling could befoul your reputation.

5. She wore a cowl-necked evening gown to the awards.

NEUTRAL AMERICAN TEXT /aŭ/ (now). *Mark the following and speak out loud.*

/aŭ/ before /l/:

       aŭ
It was the owl that shriek'd.

(Macbeth: II, ii, 3)

Howl, howl, howl! O, you are men of stones!

(King Lear: V, iii, 258)

Foul stigmatic, that's more than thou canst tell.

(2 Henry VI: V, i, 215)

O thou foul thief, where hast thou stow'd my daughter?

(Othello: I, ii, 62)

Wilt thou ever be a foul-mouth'd and ca**'lum**nious knave?

(All's Well That Ends Well: I, iii, 56)

How the knave jowls it to the ground, as if 'twere Cain's jaw-bone.

(Hamlet: V, i, 76)

Bring forth that fatal screech-owl to our house
That nothing sung but death to us and ours.

(3 Henry VI: II, vi, 56)

/aŭ/ various positions:

Now are our brows bound with victorious wreaths.

(Richard III: I, i, 5)

Methought I saw a thousand fearful wracks;
A thousand men that fishes gnaw'd upon.

(Richard III: I, iv, 24)

I wouldn't pity him; he's lived without
Concessions…free to think…and move about.

(Rostand: Cyrano de Bergerac)

But now mischance hath trod my title down,
And with dishonor laid me on the ground.

(3 Henry VI: III, iii, 8)

Until my misshap'd trunk that bears this head
Be round impaled with a glorious crown.

(3 Henry VI: III, ii, 170)

Thou wouldst be great,
Art not without ambition, but without
The illness should attend it.

(Macbeth: I, v, 18)

Thou toad, thou toad, where is thy brother Clarence?

(Richard III: IV, iv, 145)

DIPHTHONGS OF 'R'

See Overview pages 18-26

Diphthongs of 'r' all have unstressed /ɚ/ (er) as their second element. Therefore, it is the first element of the diphthongs that differentiates them from each other.

/ ɪɚ̆ / (h<u>ere</u>)

Form / ɪɚ̆ / (h<u>ere</u>) by beginning in the position and shape for the second front vowel /ɪ/ (w<u>i</u>ll), then seamlessly blending in the very short mid-vowel /ɚ/ (<u>er</u>). During the blend, the back of the tongue remains relaxed, while the tongue tip raises from its position resting down behind the lower teeth and points toward the hard palate for the 'r' coloring necessary in Neutral American. Be careful to initiate the diphthong with /ɪ/ (w<u>i</u>ll) rather than with the more closed, energized /i/ (w<u>e</u>) sound.

Stress is on the <u>first</u> element of all diphthongs. The second element is rhythmically shorter as notated by / ˘ / in the IPA symbol.

AUDIO 28► /ɪɚ̆/ (h<u>ere</u>)

      ɪɚ̆   ɪɚ̆
Pox dry their t<u>ears</u>, what should I do with t<u>ears</u>?
             (Tourneur: The Revenger's Tragedy)

            ɪɚ̆
Still he alone, since she's been cloistered h<u>ere</u>,
           ɪɚ̆
Distracts her from that sorrow so aust<u>ere</u>.
          (Rostand: Cyrano de Bergerac)

       ɪɚ̆
You had more b<u>ear</u>d when I last saw you, but your favour
  ɪɚ̆
is well ap<u>ear</u>'d by your tongue.
            (Coriolanus: IV, iii, 8)

WORDS /ɪɚ/ (h<u>ere</u>)

Initial	Medial	Final
ʔ ear	weird	tear
ʔ Erie	nearly	here
ʔ eerily	steering	clear
ʔ earring	cheerful	career
ʔ earache	appeared	revere

PHRASES /ɪɚ/ (h<u>ere</u>)

1. h<u>ear</u> cl<u>ear</u>ly
2. bl<u>eary</u> eyed
3. prem<u>iere</u>d h<u>ere</u>
4. overh<u>ears</u> an <u>ear</u>ful
5. souven<u>irs</u> app<u>eared</u>
6. insinc<u>ere</u> ch<u>eer</u>
7. exp<u>eri</u>enced f<u>ear</u>
8. p<u>eer</u>less financ<u>ier</u>
9. cl<u>ear</u>ly engin<u>eer</u>ed
10. w<u>eird</u> mountain<u>eers</u>

SENTENCES /ɪɚ/ (h<u>ere</u>)

1. How mysterious.

2. We're here to volunteer.

3. What an austere cashier.

4. Mrs. O'Leary reveres cashmere.

5. She appeared in the series premiere.

6. Will interiors or exteriors be shot first?

7. The spherical chandelier is in steerage.

8. Kirsten is her nearest and dearest friend.

9. I fear their material witness has disappeared.

10. Pioneers enjoyed ginger beer on the frontier?

11. Dear, please don't pierce your ears with shears.

12. That's a cheerful souvenir from my trip to Zaire.

13. Vera will be appearing in *Same Time Next Year*.

14. I played the racketeer who was delirious with fear.

15. Three cheers: you're here, you're here, you're here!

16.   Would your character drink Kir, beer, or Smirnoff?

17.   It appears we should steer clear of Greer; she's fierce!

18.   Seriously, Pearson played *King Lear* his entire career.

19.   It's clear he's been a sound engineer for years and years.

20.   I'm weary of being an extra, though it's good experience.

NEUTRAL AMERICAN TEXT /ɪɚ/ (h<u>ere</u>). *Mark the following and speak out loud.*

ɪɚ
Oh no! Not that! Oh, too grotesque, I f<u>ear</u>—
ɪɚ
That down this nose of mine should run one t<u>ear</u>!
                                        (Rostand: Cyrano de Bergerac)

It was the nightingale, and not the lark,
That pierced the fearful hollow of thine ear.
                                        (Romeo and Juliet: III, v, 2)

SERVANTS. Here, here, sir, here, sir.
PETRUCHIO. Here, sir! Here, sir! Here, sir! Here, sir!
                                        (The Taming of the Shrew: IV, i, 123)

See you, my princes and my noble peers,
These English monsters!
                                        (Henry V: II, ii, 84)

The skies they were ashen and sober;
        The leaves they were crisped and sere—
        The leaves they were withering and sere;
It was night in the lonesome October
        Of my most immemorial year;
It was hard by the dim lake of Auber,
        In the misty mid region of Weir—
It was down by the dank tarn of Auber,
        In the ghoul-haunted woodland of Weir.
                                        (Poe: Ulalume)

/ eɝ̆ / (the<u>ir</u>)

Form / eɝ̆ / (the<u>ir</u>) by beginning in the position and shape for the third front vowel /e/ (g<u>e</u>t), then seamlessly blending in the very short mid-vowel /ɚ/ (er). During the blend, the jaw closes slightly and the back of the tongue remains relaxed, as the tongue tip raises from its position resting down behind the lower teeth to point toward the hard palate for the 'r' coloring necessary in Neutral American.

Stress is on the first element of all diphthongs. The second element is rhythmically shorter as notated by / ˘ / in the IPA symbol.

AUDIO 29▶ /eɝ̆/ (the<u>ir</u>)

>   eɝ̆
> I d<u>are</u> do all that may become a man;
>   eɝ̆
> Who d<u>are</u>s do more is none.
>> (Macbeth: I, vii, 46)
>
>   eɝ̆   eɝ̆
> Call you me f<u>air</u>? That f<u>air</u> again unsay.
>   eɝ̆   eɝ̆
> Demetrius loves your f<u>air</u>, O happy f<u>air</u>!
>> (A Midsummer Night's Dream: I, i, 181)
>
>   eɝ̆
> We might have met them d<u>are</u>ful, beard to beard.
>> (Macbeth: V, v, 6)

WORDS /eɝ̆/ (the<u>ir</u>)

Initial	Medial	Final
ʔ air	bears	share
ʔ aerial	squared	where
ʔ Aryan	prepared	prayer
ʔ heiress	staircase	au pair
ʔ airplane	chairman	beware

PHRASES /eɚ/ (th<u>eir</u>)

1.	solit<u>ary</u> h<u>eir</u>	6.	Delaw<u>are</u> aff<u>air</u>
2.	b<u>are</u>ly th<u>ere</u>	7.	desp<u>airing</u> G<u>ary</u>
3.	gl<u>aring</u> ch<u>air</u>man	8.	ordin<u>arily</u> p<u>air</u>ed
4.	million<u>aire</u>'s m<u>are</u>	9.	sp<u>are</u> earthenw<u>are</u>
5.	rep<u>airing</u> armch<u>airs</u>	10.	decl<u>ared</u> a zillion<u>aire</u>

SENTENCES /eɚ/ (th<u>eir</u>)

1. Mary is gregarious.

2. Play fair and square.

3. Don't stare. It's scary.

4. They're very caring parents.

5. That's unfair and embarrassing.

6. Pierre's fairly happy anywhere.

7. Barry is now Department Chair.

8. Beware, malaria can cause despair.

9. Store all threadbare chairs upstairs.

10. Gary's music blared across the prairie.

11. Mary's allergic to various dairy products.

12. Can Karen's secretary type the questionnaire?

13. Who was paired with the debonair Fred Astaire?

14. Would you like to be an au pair somewhere, Sara?

15. There's no comparison between peaches and pears.

16. Name that fairy tale: "Who is the fairest of them all?"

17. Sharon's character is hilarious! What is she wearing?

18. Go through the square; then turn onto the thoroughfare.

19. That interview won't be aired; there's too much swearing.

20. Don't stare at my haircut. It's terrible, but will be repaired.

NEUTRAL AMERICAN TEXT **/eə̆/ (th<u>eir</u>).** *Mark the following and speak aloud.*

      eə̆

O, bew<u>are</u>, my lord, of jealousy!

(Othello: III, iii, 165)

Fair is foul, and foul is fair,
Hover through the fog and filthy air.

(Macbeth: I, i, 11)

Oh, it strikes, it strikes! Now body turn to air,
Or Lucifer will bear thee quick to hell.

(Marlowe: Doctor Faustus)

As waggish boys in game themselves forswear,
So the boy Love is perjur'd every where.

(A Midsummer Night's Dream: I, i, 240)

There's the promised signal! Trumpets! There—
The Marshal's men return with brazen fare!

(Rostand: Cyrano de Bergerac)

Fair sir, God save you! Where's the Princess?

(Love's Labor's Lost: V ii, 310)

Action and accent did they teach him there:
"Thus must thou speak," and "thus thy body bear".

(Love's Labor's Lost: V, ii, 99)

CAMILLO.   I dare not know, my lord.
POLIXENES. How, dare not? Do not? Do you know, and dare not?
              Be intelligent to me, 'tis thereabouts.

(The The Winter's Tale: I, ii, 376)

'Tis just like a summer bird-cage in a garden: the birds that are
without despair to get in, and the birds that are within despair and
are in a consumption for fear they shall never get out.

(Webster: The White Devil)

/ ʊ̆ɚ / (p<u>oo</u>r)

Form /ʊ̆ɚ/ (p<u>oo</u>r) by beginning in position and shape for the second back vowel sound /ʊ/ (w<u>ou</u>ld), then seamlessly blending in the very short mid-vowel /ɚ/ (er). During the blend, the lips unround and the tongue tip raises from its position resting down behind the lower teeth, to point toward the hard palate for the 'r' coloring necessary in Neutral American.

Stress is on the first element of all diphthongs. The second element is rhythmically shorter as notated by / ˘ / in the IPA symbol.

AUDIO 30▶ /ʊ̆ɚ/ (p<u>oo</u>r)

     ʊ̆ɚ
The p<u>oo</u>r Vershinins had a fright.

(Chekhov: The Three Sisters)

       ʊ̆ɚ   ʊ̆ɚ
But what would my ass<u>ur</u>ances have been worth against y<u>ours</u>?

(Ibsen: A Doll's House)

       ʊ̆ɚ
But this rough magic I here abj<u>ure</u>.

(The Tempest: V, i, 50)

WORDS /ʊ̆ɚ/ (p<u>oo</u>r)

Initial	Medial	Final
*	fury	moor
*	sure	contour
*	mural	insecure
*	during	pedicure
*	insurance	caricature

        jʊ̆ɚ
Y<u>ou're</u> a peach!

(Chekhov: The Cherry Orchard)

The strong form of 'your' is pronounced /jʊ̆ɚ/ as in the quote above. The weak form of 'your' can be /jʊ/ or /jɚ/ as in the selection at the top of the next page.

ʊɚ̆   jʊ (or jɚ)
Ass<u>u</u>rance bless y<u>our</u> thoughts!

(Timon of Athens: II, ii, 180)

The /ʊɚ̆/ (p<u>oor</u>) diphthong should be used for speakers of classic text. It is often mispronounced as /ɔɚ̆/ (sp<u>or</u>ts) or /ɝ/ (<u>ER</u>)—as in the contemporary pronunciation of 'sure' as '*sherr*'.

abjure	allure	amour	assure
boorish	bourse	brochure	bureau
bureaucrat	caesura	contour	cure
curious	demure	detour	dour
duration	during	endure	ensure
fury	gourd	gourmet	impure
insecure	insurance	injurious	inure
jury	Lourdes	lures	lurid
luxurious	mature	moor	mural
obscure	plural	poor	procure
prurient	pure	rural	secure
spoor	tour	velour	Zurich

PHRASES /ʊɚ̆/ (p<u>oor</u>)

1. sec<u>ur</u>ity lapse
2. an obsc<u>ure</u> t<u>our</u>
3. b<u>oor</u>ish for s<u>ure</u>
4. needs ins<u>ur</u>ance
5. proc<u>ure</u>s a C<u>oor</u>s
6. y<u>our</u>s for sure
7. all<u>ur</u>ing j<u>ur</u>ies
8. imp<u>ure</u> and l<u>ur</u>id
9. c<u>ur</u>ious in L<u>our</u>des
10. an obsc<u>ure</u> broch<u>ure</u>

SOUND CHECK #1: The first element of this diphthong begins with the back vowel /ʊ/ (w<u>oul</u>d), which requires lip-rounding. The rounded lips are released as the second element, the short mid-vowel /ɚ̆/ (er) is blended. *Read across.*

/ʊ/	/ʊɚ̆/	/ʊ/	/ʊɚ̆/
put	poor	look	lure
shook	sure	took	tour
book	boor	cook	Coors
sugar	insure	Sputnik	spoor
should	assure	should	brochure

PHRASES /ʊ/ and /ʊɚ/

1.	poorly put	6.	the cook's cure
2.	shook for sure	7.	looks luxurious
3.	looks alluringly	8.	furious footballer
4.	should be assured	9.	curious cookbooks
5.	took a premature tour	10.	insured sugar shipment

See /ʊɚ/ (poor) and /ɔɚ/ (sports) comparison, pages 196-197.

SENTENCES /ʊɚ/ (poor)

1. You're on the jury?

2. Surely there's a cure.

3. That's yours, isn't it?

4. He's furious, I'm sure.

5. You're an insecure, immature boor.

6. Where do you have your pedicures?

7. She's no longer poor. She's out on tour!

8. That mural has a strangely alluring contour.

9. You're sure this poor brochure's for tourists?

10. Be assured they're not stranded on the moor.

11. How do I procure a copy of that obscure play?

12. I'm curious how you worked on your character.

13. The detour took us through the rural countryside.

14. A luxurious trip to Zurich cures the 'winter blues'.

15. He's always furious about something. How immature.

16. They seem to have a prurient interest in bloody murders.

17. Your paramour is the beneficiary on your life insurance?

18. It was reassuring to have you there during the performance.

Muriel's Tour

Muriel's career took a curious detour when she played 'the Moor' in a rural bus-and-truck tour. She endured for the duration of the tour, needing to be sure her health insurance was secure.

NEUTRAL AMERICAN TEXT /ʊɚ/ (**poor**). *Mark the following and speak out loud.*

ʊɚ
I feel, so to speak, more sec<u>ure</u>.

(Ibsen: Ghosts)

Sure, Luciana, it is two a' clock.

(The Comedy of Errors: II, i, 3)

But yet I'll make assurance double sure.

(Macbeth: IV, i, 83)

Of this their purpose hither to this wood,
And I in a fury hither followed them.

(A Midsummer Night's Dream: IV, i, 161)

Your own is yours, and I am yours, and all.

(Richard II: III, iii, 197)

Proceed, Solinus, to procure my fall,
And by the doom of death end woes and all.

(The Comedy of Errors: I, i, 1)

She turns her blessed eye upon me now,
And I'll endure all storms before I part with it.

(Middleton & Rowley: The Changeling)

Saw you not yet the Moor that's come to court?

(Webster: The White Devil)

And I am faint, and cannot fly their fury;
And were I strong, I would not shun their fury.

(3 Henry VI: I, iv, 23)

She loves me sure, the cunning of her passion
Invites me in this churlish messenger.

(Twelfth Night: II, ii, 22)

/ ɔɚ̆ / (sp<u>or</u>ts)

Form /ɔɚ̆/ (sp<u>or</u>ts) by beginning in the position and shape for the fourth back vowel sound /ɔ/ (<u>a</u>ll), then seamlessly blending in the very short mid-vowel /ɚ/ (<u>er</u>). During the blend, the jaw closes slightly, the lips unround and the tongue tip raises from its position resting down behind the lower teeth, to point toward the hard palate for the 'r' coloring necessary in NAS.

Stress is on the first element of all diphthongs. The second element is rhythmically shorter as notated by / ˘ / in the IPA symbol.

AUDIO 31▶ /ɔɚ̆/ (sp<u>or</u>ts)

>   ɔɚ̆   ɔɚ̆
> The purest treasure m<u>or</u>tal times aff<u>or</u>d
>
> Is spotless reputation.
>
>   (Richard II: I, i, 177)
>
>   ɔɚ̆   ɔɚ̆
> The m<u>ore</u> I hate, the m<u>ore</u> he follows me.
>   ɔɚ̆   ɔɚ̆
> The m<u>ore</u> I love, the m<u>ore</u> he hateth me.
>   (A Midsummer Night's Dream: I, i, 198)
>
>   ɔɚ̆
> To leave my Julia—shall I be forsw<u>or</u>n?
>   ɔɚ̆
> To love fair Silvia—shall I be forsw<u>or</u>n?
>   ɔɚ̆
> To wrong my friend, I shall be much forsw<u>or</u>n.
>   (The Two Gentlemen of Verona: II, vii, i)

WORDS /ɔɚ̆/ (sp<u>or</u>ts)

Initial	Medial	Final
ʔ orbit	sword	war
ʔ order	report	shore
ʔ organic	horses	abhor
ʔ ordinary	former	adore
ʔ orchestra	toward	ignore

PHRASES /ɔɚ/ (sports)

1.	divorce court	6.	normal corks
2.	adores metaphors	7.	corporate reports
3.	troubadour of yore	8.	landlord's discord
4.	Singapore sophomore	9.	waterborne storks
5.	transforms the morgue	10.	informing discourses

SENTENCES /ɔɚ/ (sports)

1. Encore, encore!

2. *H.M.S. Pinafore* is adored.

3. Are all dinosaurs carnivores?

4. Soaring organ music fortifies.

5. Morgan's an authority on Horton Foote.

6. Who orchestrated the score for *West Side Story*?

7. The restored first floor auditorium looks gorgeous.

8. Theodore played the part of TORVALD in Singapore.

9. More and more people gathered outside the stage door.

10. Those reports distort the effect of morphine on hornets.

SOUND CHECK #1: Compare /ʊɚ/ (**poor**) and /ɔɚ/ (**sports**). The /ʊɚ/ diphthong is initiated with the jaw slightly more closed, the back tongue arch slightly higher, and the lips slightly more rounded and energized than for the /ɔɚ/ diphthong. Feel this small but important difference in shape when speaking the following words, phrases, and sentences out loud. *Read across.*

/ʊɚ/	/ɔɚ/	/ʊɚ/	/ɔɚ/
poor	pore	tour	tore
you're	yore	boor	bore
fury	fjord	lure	lore
moor	more	rural	roar
jury	George	dour	door

ʊɚ   ɔɚ   ɔɚ
Alas, poor Yorick! I knew him, Horatio.

(Hamlet: V, i, 184)

PHRASES /ʊɚ/ (po̲o̲r̲) and /ɔɚ/(sp̲o̲r̲ts)

1. surely s̲o̲re
2. t̲o̲rn velour
3. poor no m̲o̲re
4. touring Ge̲o̲rgia
5. c̲o̲u̲r̲ts prematurely

6. during c̲o̲u̲r̲t
7. alluring L̲o̲rna
8. surely not sh̲o̲rn
9. obscure, curious l̲o̲re
10. N̲o̲rm's furious C̲o̲rgi

SENTENCES /ʊɚ/ (po̲o̲r̲) and /ɔɚ/(sp̲o̲r̲ts)

1. Sure, I snore.

2. I'll be insured shortly.

3. You're from New York?

4. Unfortunately, he's furious.

5. Dorothy's character is very demure.

6. How do I procure an extension cord?

7. Be assured you're on jury duty, Norman.

8. Important: Don't drink the water; it's impure.

9. Cora's costume tore on tour, so it was made shorter.

10. Are you sure you'd like to spend more time on shore?

SOUND CHECK #2: The first element of both the /ɔɚ/ (sp̲o̲r̲ts) and /ɔɪ/ (b̲o̲y̲) diphthongs is /ɔ/ (a̲l̲l̲) not the more closed, lip-rounded /ʊ/ (wo̲u̲ld) sound. Keep this in mind when speaking the following words and phrases. *Read across.*

/ɔ/	/ɔɚ/	/ɔɚ/	/ɔɪ/
saw	sore	sort	soy
caw	core	court	coy
tall	tore	torch	toys
ball	bore	borscht	boy
fall	four	fork	foible
paw	pore	porch	poison
dog	door	dork	doily

ɔɚ   ɔ   ɔɪ
And king o̲'e̲r him and a̲l̲l̲ that he enjo̲y̲s.

(King John: II, I, 240)

CLASSICALLY SPEAKING   **NEUTRAL AMERICAN /ɔɚ/**

PHRASES /ɔ/, /ɔɚ/ and /ɔɪ/ combinations

1.	Roy's raucous roars	6.	tall toiling tornados
2.	Corey's costly coins	7.	saw the soiled shore
3.	assorted soy sausages	8.	Paul's poisoned pork
4.	Floyd's flawed floors	9.	boy drawing drawers
5.	talks of toy torpedoes	10.	applauds points scored

NEUTRAL AMERICAN TEXT /ɔɚ / (sports). *Mark the following and speak out loud.*

ɔɚ
When we have shuffled off this mortal coil.

(Hamlet: III i, 66)

As thou art forward and thy service dangerous,
Thy reward shall be precious.

(Middleton & Rowley: The Changeling)

Ah! All those things that die, yet to be born!
For fourteen years kept silent, while I mourn.

(Rostand: Cyrano de Bergerac)

O, what a noble mind is here o'erthrown!
The courtier's, soldier's, scholar's, eye, tongue, sword,
Th' expectation and rose of the fair state,
The glass of fashion and the mould of form,
Th' observ'd of all observers, quite, quite down!

(Hamlet: III, i, 150)

Once upon a midnight dreary, while I pondered, weak and weary,
Over many a quaint and curious volume of forgotten lore—
While I nodded, nearly napping, suddenly there came a tapping,
As if some one gently rapping, rapping at my chamber door.
" 'Tis some visitor," I muttered, "tapping at my chamber door—
                       Only this and nothing more."

Ah, distinctly I remember it was in the bleak December,
And each separate dying ember wrought its ghost upon the floor.
Eagerly I wished the morrow; — vainly I had sought to borrow
From my books surcease of sorrow—sorrow for the lost Lenore—
For the rare and radiant maiden whom the angels name Lenore—
                    Nameless here for evermore.

(Edgar Allan Poe: The Raven)

/ aɚ̆ / (car)

Form /aɚ̆/ (are) by beginning in the position and shape for the fifth and most open back vowel sound /a/ (car), then seamlessly blending in the very short mid-vowel /ɚ/ (er). During the blend, the jaw closes slightly, the back of the tongue remains relaxed as the tongue tip raises from its position resting down behind the lower teeth and points toward the hard palate, to form the 'r' coloring necessary in Neutral American. Lip rounding is not required for either element of this diphthong.

Stress is on the first element of all diphthongs. The second element is rhythmically shorter as notated by / ˘ / in the IPA symbol.

AUDIO 32▶ /aɚ̆/ (car)

>   aɚ̆
> How darkly and how deadly dost thou speak!
> (Richard III: I, iv, 169)
>
>   aɚ̆
> Where is the thousand marks thou hadst of me?
> (The Comedy of Errors: I ii, 81)
>
> Oh, I am gone already, the infection
>   aɚ̆   aɚ̆
> Flies to the brain and heart. O thou strong heart!
> (Webster: The White Devil)

WORDS /aɚ̆/ (car)

Initial	Medial	Final
ʔ art	heart	car
ʔ arch	farmer	star
ʔ armed	alarmed	afar
ʔ arbors	arbitrary	cigar
ʔ arduous	charming	radar

PHRASES /ɑɚ/ (car)

1.	impartial memoir	6.	unmarked cars
2.	unguarded guitars	7.	state-of-the-art
3.	charming peignoir	8.	enlarged sharks
4.	Mozart's sweetheart	9.	alarming remarks
5.	too far from Navarre	10.	surcharge for sonar

SENTENCES /ɑɚ/ (car)

1. I beg your pardon, Carla.

2. Who starred in *Lonestar*?

3. Use darker yarn when darning.

4. Is it avant-garde or just bizarre?

5. Madame Defarge was in charge.

6. That sergeant is a bit argumentative.

7. Barbara jogs daily around the reservoir.

8. I don't suppose Renoir wrote his memoirs.

9. Arthur's Martial Arts Champion of Arkansas.

10. Mark disembarked from the train at Hartford.

11. Marnie's name flashes from the largest marquee.

12. Park the car in Harvard Yard during the seminar.

13. They have a remarkably harmonious partnership.

14. Why is there a large crowd under the marble archway?

15. Snarling barnyard gargoyles look bizarre and sardonic.

16. Ms. Stark is playing Mozart's sweetheart in that new farce.

17. You look very artistic in that charming garment, Margery.

18. *Arms and the Man* can be purchased at Barnes and Noble.

19. We'll garnish the barley soup with parsley from the garden.

20. Barb is starring in *Carmen*; it's marvelous she won the part.

SOUND CHECK #1: The first element of the /ɔɚ/ (sp<u>or</u>ts) diphthong requires lip-rounding, or sinking of the cheeks, while /ɑɚ/ (c<u>ar</u>) does not. Notice this difference when speaking the following words and phrases. *Read across.*

/ɔɚ/	/ɑɚ/	/ɔɚ/	/ɑɚ/
for	far	tore	tar
pour	par	bore	bar
lord	lard	dork	dark
cored	card	horde	hard
gored	guard	stork	stark

PHRASES /ɔɚ/ and /ɑɚ/

1.	torn t<u>ar</u>ps	6.	more m<u>ar</u>velous
2.	boring b<u>ar</u>s	7.	pours in the p<u>ar</u>k
3.	rem<u>ar</u>kable encore	8.	gorgeous g<u>ar</u>dens
4.	c<u>ar</u>peted with corks	9.	no more n<u>ar</u>cotics
5.	m<u>ar</u>ching in formation	10.	h<u>ar</u>d-h<u>ear</u>ted whores

NEUTRAL AMERICAN TEXT /ɑɚ/ (c<u>ar</u>). *Mark the following and speak out loud.*

    ɑɚ   ɑɚ
P<u>ar</u>don me, p<u>ar</u>don me.

> (Troilus and Cressida: I, ii, 83)

I hate the Moor. My cause is hearted.

> (Othello: I iii, 366)

I humbly do beseech you of your pardon.

> (Othello: III, iii, 212)

And I, the mistress of your charms,
The close contriver of all harms,
Was never call'd to bear my part,
Or show the glory of our art?

> (Macbeth: III, v, 6)

Oh gentle Faustus, leave this damned art,
This magic, that will charm thy soul to hell,
And quite bereave thee of salvation.

> (Marlowe: Doctor Faustus)

Mischief, thou art afoot.

(Julius Caesar: III, ii, 260)

Gentlemen, importune me no farther,
For how I firmly am resolv'd you know.

(The Taming of the Shrew: I, i, 48)

Remember March, the ides of March remember.

(Julius Caesar: IV iii, 18)

We here discharge your Grace from being Regent
I' th' parts of France, till term of eighteen months
Be full expir'd.

(2 Henry VI: I, i, 66)

And if I were thy nurse, thy tongue to teach,
"Pardon" should be the first word of thy speech.
I never long'd to hear a word till now,
Say "pardon," King, let pity teach thee how.
The word is short, but not so short as sweet,
No word like "pardon" for kings' mouths so meet.

(Richard II: V, iii, 113)

Put on this nightcap sir, 'tis charmed—and now
I'll show you by my strong commanding art
The circumstance that breaks your duchess' heart.

(Webster: The White Devil)

K. RICHARD.   Harp not on that string, madam, that is past.
Q. ELIZABETH. Harp on it still shall I till heart-strings break.

(Richard III: IV, iv, 364)

Romeo, come forth, come forth, thou fearful man:
Affliction is enamor'd of thy parts,
And thou art wedded to calamity.

(Romeo and Juliet: III, iii, 1)

    Ah, less—less bright
    The stars of night
    Than the eyes of the radiant girl!

(Poe: Eulalie)

TRIPHTHONGS OF 'R'

See Overview pages 18-26

/ aĭɚ/ (fire)

Form the triphthong /aĭɚ/ (fire) by seamlessly blending the /aĭ/ (my) diphthong with the very short mid-vowel /ɚ/ (er) to sound as one sound. During the blend, the tongue tip raises from its position resting down behind the lower teeth and points toward the hard palate for the 'r' coloring necessary in Neutral American. Lip rounding is not required for any element of this triphthong.

Rhythmically, this sound can also be blended as a diphthong, followed immediately by the unstressed vowel /ɚ/ (er), which would be represented as /aĭ ɚ/ instead of /aĭɚ/. In any case, the first element is stressed, while the second and third elements are unstressed.

AUDIO 33▶ /aĭɚ/ or /aĭ ɚ/ (fire)

> Think'st thou that I will leave my kingly throne,
>   aĭɚ
> Wherein my grandsire and my father sat?
>
> (3 Henry VI: I, i, 124)
>
> Thou art too ugly to attend on me.
>   aĭ ɚ
> Go and return an old Franciscan friar.
>
> (Marlowe: Doctor Faustus)
>
> And love shall play the wanton on your lip,
>   aĭɚ   aĭɚ
> Meet and retire, retire and meet again.
>
> (Middleton & Rowley: The Changeling)

WORDS /aɪɚ/ or /aɪ ɚ/ (fire)

Initial	Medial	Final
? ire	fiery	pyre
? iron	friars	wire
? irony	attired	choir
? ironed	desiring	squire
? ironing	enquired	expire

ADDITIONAL WORDS /aɪɚ/ or /aɪ ɚ/ (fire)

admire	tire	hire	dire
inspire	afire	entire	mire
acquire	squire	bemire	retire
esquire	inquire	perspire	suspire
transpire	hellfire	Maguire	conspire

PHRASES /aɪɚ/ or /aɪ ɚ/ (fire)

1. enquiring minds
2. admired empires
3. conspiring to hire
4. undesired wildfires
5. requires new wiring
6. fires the buyer
7. the entire choir
8. aspires to retire
9. prior to expiring
10. desires new attire

SOUND CHECK #1: The back of the tongue should remain relaxed and uninvolved, so the /j/ (you) sound is not inserted before the /ɚ/, whatever the rhythmic pronunciation of this sound. For example, speak: 'tire' not 'tiyyre'.

---

tire	fire	hire	dire
liar	wire	spire	mire
pyre	crier	buyer	retire

PHRASES /aɪ/ and /aɪɚ/

1. fights fires
2. right to enquire
3. perspiring pipes
4. sighted the squire
5. might by inspired
6. lying liars
7. wise to hire
8. denies desires
9. high church spire
10. finding Ms. Myer

SENTENCES /aɪ̆/ and /aɪ̆ɚ/

1. The temperature climbed higher and higher.

2. The children called, "Liar, liar pants on fire!"

3. Does the party require certain attire, Ms. Meyer?

4. The entire chain of events conspired against him.

5. I admire people who can change their own flat tires.

NEUTRAL AMERICAN TEXT /aɪ̆ɚ/ or /aɪ̆ ɚ/ (fire). *Mark the following and speak out loud.*

But most miserable
    aɪ̆ɚ
Is the de<u>sire</u> that's glorious.

(Cymbeline: I, vi, 7)

I have within mine eye all my desires.

(Middleton & Rowley: The Changeling)

Ha, majesty! How high thy glory tow'rs
When the rich blood of kings is set on fire!

(King John: II i, 350)

Belike he means,
Back'd by the power of Warwick, that false peer,
To aspire unto the crown and reign as king.

(3 Henry VI: I, i, 51)

Why should a man, whose blood is warm within,
Sit like his grandsire cut in alabaster?

(The Merchant of Venice: I, i, 83)

It was your duty to bear with humility the cross which a Higher
Power had, in its wisdom, laid upon you.

(Ibsen: Ghosts)

DE FLORES. I'll set some part a-fire
        Of Diaphanta's chamber.
BEATRICE. How? Fire, sir?
        That may endanger the whole house.
DE FLORES. You talk of danger when your fame's on fire.

(Middleton & Rowley: The Changeling)

/ aŭə̆ / (power)

Form the triphthong /aŭə̆/ (power) by seamlessly blending the /aŭ/ (now) diphthong with the very short mid-vowel /ə/ (er) as one sound. During the blend, the lips unround as the tongue tip raises from its position resting down behind the lower teeth, and points toward the hard palate for the 'r' coloring required in Neutral American.

Rhythmically, this sound can also be blended as a diphthong followed immediately by the unstressed vowel /ə/ (er), which would be represented as /aŭ ə/ instead of /aŭə̆/. In any case, the first element is stressed, while the second and third elements are unstressed.

AUDIO 34► /aŭə̆/ or /aŭ ə/ (power)

> aŭə̆
> One writ with me in sour misfortune's book!
> > (Romeo and Juliet: V, iii, 82)
>
> aŭə̆
> I never can see him but I am heart-burn'd an hour after.
> > (Much Ado About Nothing: II i, 3)
>
> aŭə̆   aŭə̆
> That same cowardly, giant-like ox-beef hath devour'd many a
> aŭ
> gentleman of your house.
> > (A Midsummer Night's Dream: III, i, 192)

WORDS /aŭə̆/ or /aŭ ə/ (power)

Initial	Medial	Final
ʔ our	soured	sour
ʔ ours	powerful	scour
ʔ hour	glowered	cower
ʔ hours	flowering	devour
ʔ hourly	deflowered	shower

SOUND CHECK #1: Do not over-round or over-energize the lips when moving between the /aŭ/ and /ɚ/, or a distinct /w/ sound will be inserted. Speak the practice words on the previous page again, with this in mind.

PHRASES /aŭɚ/ or /aŭ ɚ/ (**power**)

1.	cowers for hours	4.	ours soured
2.	powerful scouring	5.	flowers in towers
3.	showers on flowers	6.	glowering (brooding) look

SENTENCES /aŭɚ/ or /aŭ ɚ/ (**power**)

1. Why do you look so sour?

2. They called every hour on the hour.

3. What a powerful scouring detergent.

4. The cowering hound devoured doggie treats.

5. We scoured the woods looking for wildflowers.

NEUTRAL AMERICAN TEXT /aŭɚ/ or /aŭ ɚ/ (**power**). *Mark the following and speak out loud.*

aŭɚ
The heavens do low'r upon you for some ill.

(Romeo and Juliet: IV, v, 94)

ALIBIUS.   What hour is't, Lollio?
LOLLIO.   Towards belly-hour sir.
ALIBIUS.   Dinner time?

(Middleton & Rowley: The Changeling)

Larded all with sweet flowers,
Which bewept to the ground did not go
With true-love showers.

(Hamlet: IV, v, 38)

Within the infant rind of this weak flower
Poison hath residence and medicine power.

(Romeo and Juliet: II, iii, 23)

CONSONANTS

WARM-UPS

Speak the speech, I pray you, as I pronounc'd it to you, trippingly on the tongue, but if you mouth it, as many of our players do, I had as lief the town-crier spoke my lines.

(Hamlet: III, ii, 1)

Tip of the Tongue

/ n /   / d /   / t /   / l /

Four consonants: /t, d, n, l/ require that the tip of the tongue make contact with the upper gum ridge, just *behind* the upper front teeth, during articulation. The tongue blade should not be involved, and the tongue tip should have no contact with the upper front teeth.

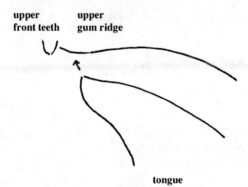

upper front teeth   upper gum ridge

tongue

There is a strong tendency for actors to speak with unnecessary tension in the jaw, throat, and tongue, especially during moments of high emotion, in order to compensate for a weak tongue tip or improper placement. The following warm-ups will help develop strength and precision of contact.

WARM-UP 1

Look in a mirror. Relax your lower jaw open with the body of the tongue relaxed and flat and the tongue tip gently touching the back of the *bottom* teeth. This is both the 'start' and 'finish' position. Breathe.

Touch the upper gum ridge directly behind your upper front teeth with your fingertip, feeling the bumpy surface of the gum ridge, also known as the alveolar ridge. This is the 'target'.

(a)   Begin in the 'start' position, looking in a mirror. Breathe in. Lift the tongue tip up to touch the 'target'. Breathe out, releasing the tongue back down to rest in the 'finish' position. Repeat 3X.

(b)   Breathe in. Touch the tongue tip up to the 'target', sound 'n', push-off on 'aahhh', and release the tongue back to 'finish'. The 'word' spoken is 'naaaaah' or **/na/**. Repeat on: '**d**aaaaah', 't**aaaaah', '**l**aaaaah', **/da, ta, la/** in IPA.

TARGET PRACTICE

(a)   Speak the 'words' in lines 1-5 below in the same manner, observing in a mirror. The tongue should be the active articulator, not the jaw, which remains relaxed. If you begin to feel tense, take a moment to massage your face, jaw, and neck. Work slowly, breathing between each word.

				IPA
nah	dah	tah	lah	/na, da, ta, la/
nuh	duh	tuh	luh	/nʌ, dʌ, tʌ, lʌ/
nae	dae	tae	lae	/næ, dæ, tæ, læ/
nie	die	tie	lie	/naĭ, daĭ, taĭ, laĭ/
nay	day	tay	lay	/neĭ, deĭ, teĭ, leĭ/

(b)   Repeat, without looking in the mirror, trying to duplicate the feel and placement of the tongue tip on the start/target/finish positions.

(c)   Pinch the tongue tip lightly between each phrase that follows in order to increase tip of the tongue awareness.

		IPA
breathe	nah dah	/na, da/
breathe	nah dah tah	/na, da, ta/
breathe	nah dah tah lah	/na, da, ta, la/

breathe	nuh duh	/nʌ, dʌ/
breathe	nuh duh tuh	/nʌ, dʌ, tʌ/
breathe	nuh duh tuh luh	/nʌ, dʌ, tʌ, lʌ/
breathe	nie die	/naɪ̆, daɪ̆/
breathe	nie die tie	/naɪ̆, daɪ̆, taɪ̆/
breathe	nie die tie lie	/naɪ̆, daɪ̆, taɪ̆, laɪ̆/

(d) Tap the tongue tip on the 'target' three times, before fully releasing the tongue tip back down to the 'finish' position on the following.

breathe	t, t, t, tah	/tʰ, tʰ, tʰ, tʰɑ/
breathe	t, t, t, tuh	/tʰ, tʰ, tʰ, tʰʌ/
breathe	t, t, t, tae	/tʰ, tʰ, tʰ, tʰæ/
breathe	t, t, t, tie	/tʰ, tʰ, tʰ, tʰaɪ̆/
breathe	t, t, t, tay	/tʰ, tʰ, tʰ, tʰeɪ̆/

(e) Repeat the previous exercise substituting /d/ for /t/.

WORDS tip of the tongue placement. The following words begin and end with the tip of the tongue consonants /n, d, t, l/. Speak these words with, then without, the aid of a mirror. Remember to breathe, keep the jaw relaxed, and stop to massage the jaw if you begin to tense. If pinching the tongue helps you to focus attention onto the tongue tip, then add that also.

none	dine	ton	nod	dean	dull	led
Tate	done	dad	den	Ned	net	lend
tied	teen	dud	dead	teed	deed	lied
Dan	gnat	Tad	tan	ten	let	tend
diet	dial	dale	lad	dill	tail	lean

(f) Consult a dictionary for practice words with initial /n, d, t, l/.

AUDIO 35▶ /n, d, t, l/ tip of tongue placement

And let us not be dainty of leave-taking.

(Macbeth: II, iii, 144)

Your wit's too hot, it speeds too fast, 'twill tire.

(Love's Labor's Lost: II, i, 119)

So full of dismal terror was the time.

(Richard III: I, iv, 7)

PHRASES tip of the tongue placement. Notice unstressed /d/ between two vowels tends to be lighter, as in the word 'de_d_icated' in phrase three.

1.	dull lead weight	11.	identifies intent
2.	tender teenagers	12.	delicate day today
3.	dedicated to dad	13.	deleted a done deal
4.	time to talk today	14.	topsy-turvy tonight
5.	tinted tomato red	15.	tend to defend Tom
6.	loved real gold	16.	toiled for oil
7.	filled ten pools	17.	loaded with pulp
8.	gulped cold milk	18.	held less holdings
9.	boiled and broiled	19.	milled around sulking
10.	told it's too moldy	20.	hulky, bulky sculpture

SENTENCES tip of the tongue placement

1. Tackle it today, Teddy.

2. Take Tina to tennis, Tad.

3. Don't talk until Act Two ends.

4. Terry decided to go to town Tuesday.

5. You can take out a tail light tailgating.

6. Did Derrick treat Dad to dinner downtown?

7. You can count on Daniel to do a good deed.

8. Day-to-day work has delicate Donna dead tired.

9. Dana delighted in cooking delicious tandoori at night.

10. Our director decided to delete a scene during rehearsal.

EXERCISE Speak the following sound combinations *slowly* first, to establish accuracy, then speak more quickly. Remember, the tongue tip contacts the gum ridge on 't', 'd', 'n', 'l'.

			IPA
Breathe	puh, tuh, kuh	*(3X fast!)*	/pʌ tʌ kʌ/
Breathe	buh, duh, guh	*(3X fast!)*	/bʌ dʌ gʌ/
Breathe	buh, nuh, guh	*(3X fast!)*	/bʌ nʌ gʌ/
Breathe	buh, luh, guh	*(3X fast!)*	/bʌ lʌ gʌ/

EXERCISE

Step 1. Stand in front of a mirror. Place the tip of your tongue down behind your lower front teeth, and drop your lower jaw open so there is at least ½ inch of space between your lips. Remember to breathe.

Step 2. Protrude your lips slightly forward. Place your index fingers vertically at the corners of your lips. Slide your fingers toward the tips of your protruding lips, catching the tips of your lips between your fingers and pulling them slightly out from your teeth.

There should be enough space to breathe easily through your mouth, and to slide the tongue out between the corner of your mouth and fingers. If not, begin again.

Step 3. Step away from the mirror and look back to your book, page 211. Read sentences 1-10 again (yes, with your lips held 'out of commission' between your fingers) emphasizing the tip of the tongue consonants and trying to be clearly understood.

Continue reading even though sounds that require lip involvement or rounding will be awkward; this exercise is not for them. Remember to breathe through your mouth whenever you need to and breathe between each sentence.

Step 4. Now, release your fingers and speak the sentences again. Hopefully, you will notice an increased clarity, dexterity, and ease on the tip of the tongue consonants.

This exercise is useful in auditioning emergencies: to wake up the tip of the tongue sounds before last minute auditions, or to supplement a warm-up done earlier on in the day.

ADDITIONAL PRACTICE *Try the previous exercise on the following lines, or on a memorized selection of text, a monologue, or a nursery rhyme.*

I do see
Danger and disobedience in thine eye.

(1 Henry IV: I, iii, 15)

All's cheerless, dark, and deadly.
Your eldest daughters have foredone themselves,
And desperately are dead.

(King Lear: V, iii, 291)

EXERCISE Speak the following. Stronger/longer utterances are indicated by the use of capital letters. Remember to breathe!

LAH lah lah—LAH lah lah—LAH lah lah—LAH   breathe
LAH lay lee LIE low loo,
LAH lay lee LIE low loo,
LAH lay lee LIE low loo loo.   breathe

TAH tah tah—TAH tah tah—TAH tah tah—TAH   breathe
TAH tay tee TIE toe too,
TAH tay tee TIE toe too,
TAH tay tee TIE toe too too.   breathe, etc.

DAH dah dah—DAH dah dah—DAH dah dah—DAH
DAH day dee DIE doe doo,
DAH day dee DIE doe doo,
DAH day dee DIE doe doo doo.

NAH nah nah—NAH nah nah—NAH nah nah—NAH
NAH nay nee NIE no noo,
NAH nay nee NIE no noo,
NAH nay nee NIE no noo noo.

PAH pah pah—PAH pah pah—PAH pah pah—PAH
PAH pay pee PIE po poo,
PAH pay pee PIE po poo,
PAH pay pee PIE po poo poo.

BAH bah bah—BAH bah bah—BAH bah bah—BAH
BAH bay bee BIE bo boo,
BAH bay bee BIE bo boo,
BAH bay bee BIE bo boo boo.

MAH mah mah—MAH mah mah—MAH mah mah—MAH
MAH may mee MIE mo moo,
MAH may mee MIE mo moo,
MAH may mee MIE mo moo moo.

also:

   KAH kah kah—KAH kah kah—KAH kah kah—KAH   (etc.)

   GAH gah gah—GAH gah gah—GAH gah gah—GAH   (etc.)

   NGAH ngah ngah—NGAH ngah ngah—NGAH ngah ngah—NGAH   (etc.)

and consonant combinations:
   SPAH—SKAH—SLAH—STAH—STRAH (etc.)

TONGUE TWISTERS

Speak the following slowly for accuracy, then three times *FAST!*

/ w l j /   Will you William?

/ l /   He is literally literary.

/ r l /   Red leather, yellow leather.

/ d j /   Did you, would you, could you?

/ s n l /   Cinnamon, aluminum, linoleum.

/ d /   Don't you dare to do damaging deeds.

/ t /   A tidy tiger tied a tie tighter to tidy her tiny tail.

/ t d n l /   What a to-do to die today at a minute or two to two;
A thing distinctly hard to say but harder still to do.
For they'll beat a tattoo at twenty-to-two
A ra-<u>t</u>a-<u>t</u>a-<u>t</u>a-<u>t</u>a-<u>t</u>a-<u>t</u>a-<u>t</u>a-<u>t</u>a-<u>t</u>oo
[A ra-<u>d</u>a-<u>d</u>a-<u>d</u>a-<u>d</u>a-<u>d</u>a-<u>d</u>a-<u>d</u>a-<u>d</u>a-<u>d</u>oo]   [bracketed text added
[A ra-<u>n</u>a-<u>n</u>a-<u>n</u>a-<u>n</u>a-<u>n</u>a-<u>n</u>a-<u>n</u>a-<u>n</u>oo]   for warm-up]
[A ra-<u>l</u>a-<u>l</u>a-<u>l</u>a-<u>l</u>a-<u>l</u>a-<u>l</u>a-<u>l</u>a-<u>l</u>oo]
And the dragon will come when he hears the drum
At a minute or two to two today,
At a minute or two to two.

                                              (Anonymous)

/ t /   Tommy and Tina were tattooed in total, but Tanny was only tattooed on her toe; so Tommy told Tina where Tanny was tattoed, but Tina said Tanny's tattoo wouldn't show.

/ t,ʃ /   Charlie is choosy when checking his cheeses, and cheese is a challenge when Charlie arrives. But Charlie is charming and chooses a cheddar, then chills it and chips it and chops in some chives.

/ t θ /   Tom threw Terrence three thumbtacks. Three thumbtacks were thrown to Terrence by Tom. Why did Tom throw Terrence three thumbtacks?

/ s θ /   Theophilus Thistle, the successful thistle-sifter, in sifting a sieve full of unsifted thistles, thrust three thousand thistles through the thick of his thumb. See that thou, in sifting a sieve full of unsifted thistles, thrust not three thousand thistles through the thick of thy thumb. Success to the successful thistle-sifter!

TONGUE TWISTERS[1]

/ t b /	Toy boat.
/ j n /	Unique New York.
/ ð θ /	That thick thatched roof.
/ r l /	Upper roller, lower roller.
/ n l /	Eleven benevolent elephants.
/ ð θ /	They thanked them thoroughly.
/ r ʃ /	Rush the washing, Russell Rusk.
/ ð l t /	The lips, the teeth, the tip of the tongue—
	The tip of the tongue, the lips, the teeth.
MULTIPLE	To sit in solemn silence in a dull, dark dock,

In a pestilential prison, with a life-long lock,
Awaiting the sensation of a short, sharp shock,
From a cheap and chippy chopper on a big black block!
A dull, dark dock,
A life-long lock,
A short, sharp shock,
A big black block!
To sit in solemn silence
In a pestilential prison,
And awaiting the sensation
From a cheap and chippy chopper on a big black block!

(W.S. Gilbert: The Mikado)

/ p / Peter Piper picked a peck of pickled peppers, a peck of pickled peppers did Peter Piper pick. If Peter Piper picked a peck of pickled peppers, where is the peck of pickled peppers that Peter Piper picked?

/ ʃ s / Sheila is selling her shop by the seashore, for shops by the seashore are so sure to lose. She's not so sure just what she should be selling; should Sheila sell shell fish or should she sell shoes?

/ w t,ʃ / How much wood would a woodchuck chuck if a woodchuck could chuck wood, Chuck?

---

[1] See Ken Parkin's *Anthology of British Tongue Twisters*: New York: Samuel French, 1969, *Mother Goose*, and the works of *Dr. Seuss* for additional fun, challenging material.

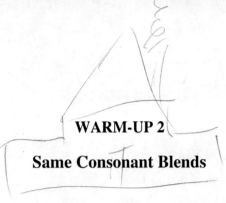

WARM-UP 2

Same Consonant Blends

The following is covered in each individual consonant chapter. Actors may choose not to incorporate well-articulated same consonant blends for all characters, but practicing provides a good warm-up, regardless.

When the same consonant sound ends a word and also begins the next word, initiate the second word with a slight rhythmic pulse of energy while maintaining the contact of the articulators.

CONSONANTS

	Voiceless		Voiced
/t$_{|}$t/	hur**t**$_{|}$ **t**oes	**/dd/**	ba**d** **d**ay
	fel**t**$_{|}$ **t**error		dare**d** **d**ad
	no**t**$_{|}$ **t**imely		hi**d** **d**ough
	tha**t**$_{|}$ **t**eenager		dea**d** **d**runk
/p$_{|}$p/	la**p**$_{|}$ **p**ool	**/bb/**	ro**b** **b**anks
	hel**p**$_{|}$ **p**eople		jo**b** **b**aking
	sho**p**$_{|}$ **p**atiently		Ro**b** **B**enson
	shi**p**$_{|}$ **p**ineapples		lo**b** **b**asketballs
/k$_{|}$k/	blac**k**$_{|}$ **c**ape	**/gg/**	be**g** **g**irls
	pic**k**$_{|}$ **c**abbage		hu**g** **G**ary
	wal**k**$_{|}$ **c**arefully		bi**g** **g**uest
	sac**k**$_{|}$ **c**rumpled		ba**g** **g**roceries
/ff/	sti**ff** **f**oam	**/vv/**	lo**ve** **v**ariety
	roo**f** **f**alling		lea**ve** **v**acant
	lea**f** **f**luttered		ha**ve** **v**isitors
	hal**f** **f**amished		revi**ve** **V**ictor
/θθ/	fif**th** **th**ief	**/ðð/**	mou**th** **th**at
	ba**th** **Th**ursday		brea**the** **th**is
	uncou**th** **th**eory		soo**the** **th**em
	mammo**th** **th**eatre		ba**the** **th**emselves

CONSONANTS

Voiceless		Voiced	
/ʃʃ/	dish shop wash shoes push sharply harsh shouts	/ʒʒ/	prestige genre camouflage Gigi massage Zsa Zsa rouge gendarmes
/ss/	hurts sales loose scarf bus station this Saturday	/zz/	is zany his zebra loves zucchini his xylophone
no voiceless partner		/mm/	gym machine hum musically gem merchants climb mountains
no voiceless partner		/nn/	seen kneeling even numbers eleven nations nine neighbors
no voiceless partner		/ll/	dull lad real lucky will linger well-leveled

The articulators do not maintain complete contact when speaking the following combinations, since there is movement within individual /tʃ/, /dʒ/, and /st/ sound combinations. A new impulse of breath and energy is required when initiating the second word of the phrase.

/tʃ tʃ/	patch chairs reach China much cheering which chocolates	/dʒ dʒ/	huge jump large jackets barge junked strange germs
/st st/	best stage cast stranded worst strategy best stationary		

WARM-UP 3

Cursing Consonants
(Courtesy of Richard II)

O villains, vipers, damn'd without redemption!
Dogs, easily won to fawn on any man!
Snakes, in my heart-blood warm'd, that sting my heart!
Three Judases, each one thrice worse than Judas!
Would they make peace? Terrible hell
Make war upon their spotted souls for this!

(Richard II: III, ii, 129)

Feed not thy sovereign's foe, my gentle earth,
Nor with thy sweets comfort his ravenous sense,
But let thy spiders, that suck up thy venom,
And heavy-gaited toads lie in their way,
Doing annoyance to the treacherous feet,
Which with usurping steps do trample thee.
Yield stinging nettles to mine enemies;
And when they from thy bosom pluck a flower,
Guard it, I pray thee, with a lurking adder,
Whose double tongue may with a mortal touch
Throw death upon thy sovereign's enemies.

(Richard II: III, ii, 12)

WARM-UP 4

THE CHORUS OF BUCKS AND BLADES   page 308.

WHEN YOU'RE LYING AWAKE (The Nightmare Song)   page 309.

THE RUDDIGORE PATTER-TRIO   page 400.
This is located in the Classical American section, but is also very good
material for a tip of the tongue warm-up.

STOP-PLOSIVES

See Overview pages 13-17

/ t d /   / p b /   / k g /
(tot did)   (pop bib)   (cap gap)

These sounds involve two steps:

(1) a complete stoppage of the outgoing air with a slight building up of air pressure, and

(2) the release or explosion of the pressurized air through the mouth. The resulting percussive rhythm on the stop, but even more on the explosion, contributes to their effectiveness in communicating anything from bubbling joy to stabbing pain. It is no accident that 'kick', 'flip', 'punch', 'push', 'hit', 'stab', 'dead' (and most swear words including '#$@%!') all contain at least one stop-plosive.

The six stop-plosives consist of three pair of voiced and voiceless partners, which are known as cognates. The 'stop' element of each pair is energized without being muscular or tense, and formed slightly differently, which distinguishes them from each other.

Form the stop element of **/t/** and **/d/** by pressing the tip of the tongue against the gum ridge, just behind the upper teeth. The blade, which is that part of the tongue directly behind the tongue tip, should not be involved, and there should be no contact with the upper teeth.

Form the stop element of **/p/** and **/b/** by an enlivened contact between the upper and lower lips.

Form the stop element of **/k/** and **/g/** by energized contact between the back of the tongue and the front of the soft palate.

Remember that all consonant sounds in NAS, except **/m, n, ŋ/**, release through the mouth as the soft palate lifts slightly, which helps direct the release.

WORDS   Remember, when 't' is spoken in an unstressed syllable between two vowel sounds, it is pronounced as a very light 'd' in NAS. This is the case for the words 'better', 'sheeting', and 'beautiful' in the Medial column, below.

	Initial	Medial	Final
/t/	time	better	flat
	toast	intone	float
	tough	pretend	right
	tennis	sheeting	sport
	tumble	beautiful	weight
/d/	diet	feeder	lied
	dead	muddy	afraid
	deed	loudest	squad
	done	reading	unsaid
	Danny	avoiding	fanned
/p/	path	caper	lip
	peace	sniper	clap
	pouch	keeper	heap
	passion	hopper	shape
	particle	skipping	elope
/b/	best	labor	cab
	beat	rabbit	tub
	baby	fibbing	glib
	bundle	clubbing	knob
	bought	snubbing	blurb
/k/	kiss	locket	hike
	kite	sticker	flake
	cone	seeking	check
	camp	packing	brook
	ketchup	thickest	smoke
/g/	glad	bigger	rag
	gosh	triangle	bug
	ghost	haggard	twig
	grape	stagnant	vague
	geese	strongest	rogue

Guidelines

Connecting Stop-Plosives with Other Sounds

Because they contain two rhythmic elements, a 'stop' and an 'explosion' or release, there are special considerations when speaking and connecting these six stop-plosives to other sounds, especially for well-pronounced characters and/or classical text.

1. When stop-plosives are followed immediately by a pause or silence, either within, or at the end of a sentence, there are two possible options for contemporary speech:

    (a) the final plosive is not released, and the 'stop' element ends the word. This is common in casual speech.

    (b) the 'stop' element is quickly released and finishes the word or phrase. This is slightly more clear and well-spoken, and should be used in classical texts.

    Try the following examples below, both ways.

    | That's i**t**. | No goo**d**. | Mess u**p**. |

Phonetic markings are used in IPA to notate whether the breath is released (aspirated) or not released (unaspirated) on voiceless plosives. The same principle of release applies to the voiced plosives, though there are no special IPA markings used for notation. The following words are marked with phonetic symbols for demonstration.

| Aspirating the voiceless plosive: | See that^h |
| Not aspirating the voiceless plosive: | See that$_1$ |

2. When followed immediately by a vowel or diphthong sound, the 'plosive' element releases into the sound that follows:

    | Step^h in. | Paint^h it. | Pick^h actors. |
    | Dub Ann. | Brad is. | Drag on. |

3. When followed immediately by another consonant sound, a clear 'stop' is required, which should be rhythmically noticeable. The plosive is not released before beginning the next consonant sound.

Stop ̗ yelling.   Don't ̗ fly.   Pick ̗ Sue.

Bob said.   Pad those.   Tag this.

SUMMARY of GUIDELINES

Well-Pronounced Neutral American:

(a) make a clear stop then release the plosive before a pause, silence, vowel or diphthong

(b) make a clear stop, but do not release the plosive before a consonant

Voiceless stop-plosives before *Read across.*

a pause	a vowel or diphthong	another consonant
p^h t^h k^h	p^h t^h k^h	p ̗ t ̗ k ̗
grip	grip it	grip lock
flop	flop over	flop down
sleep	sleep in	sleep well
hot	hot evening	hot date
pack	pack earrings	pack shoes
wait	wait a while	wait there
great	great afternoon	great meal

Voiced stop-plosives before *Read across.*

a pause	a vowel or diphthong	another consonant
dig	dig up	dig there
Bob	Bob ate	Bob left
big	big elephant	big mess
hide	hide outside	hide carefully
grab	grab apples	grab bananas
had	had everything	had nothing
child	child eating	child screaming

Additional practice exercises and sound checks follow.

> **SOUND CHECK #1a: voiceless /t^h, p^h, k^h/ before pause or silence.** Release the final plosive when playing well-pronounced characters or speaking more formal, poetic, or classical text. It can be useful to notate text with /^{h}/ as shown.

AUDIO 36 A▶ voiceless /t^h, p^h, k^h/ before a pause or silence

They have a plentiful lack of wit^h.

(Hamlet: II, ii, 199)

I shall drop this very minute^h... Ah, I shall drop^h.

(Chekhov: The Cherry Orchard)

Malcolm, awake^h!

(Macbeth: II, iii, 75)

PHRASES /t^h, p^h, k^h/ before a pause or silence

1.	just a bit^h	6.	a big slip^h
2.	heard a pop^h	7.	what a fit^h
3.	a little pack^h	8.	not shipped^h
4.	looking for Jack^h	9.	needs to pick^h
5.	searched for a hat^h	10.	puts butter on it^h

Remember: in Neutral American Speech, when 't' is spoken in an unstressed syllable between two vowel sounds, it is pronounced as a very light 'd', as in 'but̬ter (number 10, above). This is represented phonetically by a little *carat* under the symbol: /t̬/. Medial 't' remains /t/ in a stressed syllable between two vowel sounds, as in a'tt̲ached and a'tt̲ainted.

> *My father was a'ttached, not a'ttainted,*
> *Condemn'd to die for treason, but no traitor.*
> (1 Henry VI: II, iv, 96)

When 'ed' is added to the end of a verb (sometimes abbreviated 'd in classic texts, as in **dispatch'd**), the 'ed' ending is pronounced as /t/ if the sound directly preceding the 'ed' is a voiceless consonant sound, as in the following:

/ftʰ/	/ʃtʰ/	/t̞ʃtʰ/	/stʰ/
ruffed	dished	pitched	iced
doffed	cashed	coached	raced
staffed	washed	marched	passed
briefed	refreshed	thatched	rejoiced

/k̞tʰ/	/sk̞tʰ/	/p̞tʰ/	/sp̞tʰ/
licked	asked	dipped	lisped
racked	risked	rapped	rasped
packed	basked	cupped	clasped
clucked	husked	shopped	grasped

tʃtʰ
A bloody deed, and desperately dispatch'd!

(Richard III: I, iv, 271)

SENTENCES voiceless /tʰ, pʰ, kʰ/ before a pause or silence

1. Take your pick.

2. May I have a sip?

3. They were shocked.

- 4. Will you please give that back?

5. I checked; they did what you asked.

6. The music has stopped; should we clap?

7. It's fantastic; she got the part she wished!

8. It slipped and was chipped when shipped.

9. You need a vocal warm up; that note is flat.

10. The audience was in tears at the end of the first act.

SOUND CHECK #1b: Voiced /d, b, g/ are released before a pause or silence. When releasing final voiced plosives, a short /ɪ/ (w_ill) vowel sound may be heard as part of the voiced release. Do not allow the /ə/ (u_h) sound, known as an 'off-glide'. Voiced endings before a pause or silence are marked with a double underline in the audio selections and practice phrases that follow.

AUDIO 36 B▶ voiced /d, b, g/ before a pause or silence

O, thou art decei_v'd_.

(Romeo and Juliet: II, iv, 97)

It boots not to resist both wind and ti_de_.

(3 Henry VI: IV, iii, 59)

O, well be_gg'd_!

(Coriolanus: I, ix, 87)

When 'ed' is added to the end of a verb, **/d/** is spoken, unless the sound previous to the 'ed' is a voiceless consonant.

/bd/	/gd/	/ld/	/md/
ribbed	tugged	filed	filmed
fibbed	pegged	doled	steamed
robbed	bragged	felled	schemed
clubbed	mugged	mauled	thumbed

/nd/	/ðd/	/vd/	/zd/
fanned	writhed	saved	raised
chained	soothed	halved	buzzed
resigned	breathed	grieved	amazed
shunned	smoothed	resolved	quizzed

/ʒd/	/dʒd/	vowel/diph/triphthong + /d/	
garaged	lodged	faired	fired
barraged	fudged	purred	toured
massaged	engaged	cheered	poured
camouflaged	emerged	mothered	cowered

There is another element to this guideline. When 'ed' is added to the end of a verb that ends in 'd' or 't', the 'ed' ending becomes a separate syllable, as in: "They pain_ted_ the wall but the color fa_ded_." In this case, voiced **/ɪ/** is the sound that comes before the final 'd', so the ending remains voiced **/d/**.

PHRASES voiced /d, b, g/ before a pause or silence

1.	naughty chi_ld_		6.	hurt by the co_ld_
2.	politely wor_ded_		7.	brazenly snu_bbed_
3.	defending Dou_g_		8.	watching the ba_gs_
4.	incredibly relie_ved_		9.	beautifully inscri_bed_
5.	passing every gra_de_		10.	rightfully bequea_thed_

SENTENCES voiced /d, b, g/ before a pause or silence

1. Hey, that's my cab!
2. That's it; you're grounded.
3. You are exceptionally rude.
4. They should have been told.
5. Is that your answer, a shrug?
6. I've never seen such an unruly mob.
7. Do you mean my document can't be found?
8. When they were young, they were very wild.
9. Stand up, turn around, and don't make a sound.
10. Yesterday, you swore my contract was finalized!

See also SONNET 27 and SONNET 50 by William Shakespeare, pages 316 and 317, for additional practice text with voiced plosive endings.

SOUND CHECK #2: Stop-plosives are released before a vowel or diphthong sound. This is not generally a problem for native English speakers.

PHRASES stop-plosives followed by a vowel or diphthong:

1.	shipped[h] it	6.	led on
2.	slipped[h] up	7.	job over
3.	leapt[h] over it	8.	bag open
4.	caught[h] in the heat	9.	begged off
5.	packed[h] everything	10.	required a break

SOUND CHECK #3: Stop-plosives are not released before another consonant sound. A clear stop is required, which should be rhythmically noticeable, before beginning the consonant sound of the word that follows the stop-plosive, below.

AUDIO 36 C ▶ **final voiceless /t, p, k/, voiced /d, b, g/ before a consonant**

Rude, in sooth, in good sooth, very rude.

(Troilus and Cressida: III, i, 56)

Now in good time, here comes the Duke[1] of York.

(Richard III: III, i, 95)

If every trick were told that's dealt by night,

There are few here that would not blush outright.

(Tourneur: The Revenger's Tragedy)

PHRASES final voiceless /t, p, k/ before another consonant

1.	what fun	6.	hot coffee
2.	might rain	7.	not finished
3.	pick fights	8.	stop shaking
4.	peanut butter	9.	back stabbing
5.	leap tall buildings	10.	help someone

PHRASES final voiced /d, b, g/ before another consonant

1.	made supper	6.	wild thing
2.	paid the price	7.	rag sullied
3.	big promotion	8.	compiled files
4.	prime rib restaurant	9.	good riddance
5.	had second thoughts	10.	grabbed something

SOUND CHECK #4: stop-plosives before the same stop-plosive. When the same stop-plosive sound ends a word and also begins the next word, the stop between the two may be held slightly longer than usual before continuing. In any case, there should be a noticeable stop before beginning the 2nd word.

ship pens	curt talk	think kindly
rob banks	dad did	bag groceries

PHRASES voiceless /t, p, k/ before the same stop-plosive

1.	hurt toes	6.	lap pool
2.	felt terror	7.	not timely
3.	black cabbage	8.	that teenager
4.	bought tabloids	9.	sack crumpled
5.	hot tomato soup	10.	stopped talking

[1] The title 'Duke' may also be pronounced /djuk/ with a liquid ju (you).

PHRASES voiced /d, b, g/ before the same stop-plosive. Be sure to make a clear stop on the first voiced plosive and begin the second with a new impulse of energy.

1.	big guest	6.	beg Gary
2.	hid dough	7.	bad dope
3.	dead drunk	8.	dared dad
4.	Rob Benson	9.	job baking
5.	dated Daniel	10.	fed demonstrators

God match me with a good dancer!
(Much Ado About Nothing: II, i, 107)

SOUND CHECK #5: /d/, /t/ before /j/ (you). Make a clear stop using the tongue tip to contact the upper gum ridge on final /d/ and /t/ when followed directly by a word beginning with /j/ (you). If the blade or front of the tongue is used, /dʒ/ will be spoken instead of /d/, and /tʃ/ instead of /t/, resulting in: 'would jew' instead of 'would you', and 'get chure' instead of 'get your'.

---

would you	could you	did you
put your	sat your	let your

SENTENCES /d/ and /t/ before /j/

1.	Did you eat?	6.	Did you know?
2.	Would you go?	7.	Bet your brother.
3.	Should you ask?	⌐ 8.	Did your dad stay?
4.	Put your sox on.	9.	Let your hair down.
5.	We met your parents.	10.	Set your things there.

MORE SENTENCES /d/ and /t/ before /j/

1. Did you get it?

2. Could you run lines?

3. Shouldn't you audition?

4. Didn't you like the play?

5. Did you do a vocal warm-up?

6.   Would your character do that?

7.   Couldn't you produce it yourself?

8.   Didn't your agent give you the sides?

9.   Could you change our rehearsal time?

10.   Did you let your hair grow for the part?

11.   Should you take the job for that money?

12.   Did your lawyer negotiate your contract?

13.   Would you mind if we put your check in the mail?

14.   Did you want to know who was in the audience tonight?

15.   Sorry, kid. We ate your snacks while you were on stage.

SOUND CHECK #6: /d, t/ before /θ, ð/. When speaking /d, t, n, l/ before a 'th', the tip of the tongue generally moves forward onto the teeth in anticipation of the 'th' position. This is represented phonetically by placing a little 'tooth' underneath the IPA symbol, which signifies dentalization: / n̪, d̪, t̪, l̪ /.

PHRASES /d̪/ and /t̪/ before 'th'

1.	fanned the flames	6.	what thinking
2.	planted them here	7.	thought that over
3.	not the bad things	8.	had that for dinner
4.	extended the width	9.	hated the bad traffic
5.	brought those to work	10.	acted that out Thursday

NEUTRAL AMERICAN TEXT stop-plosives. *Mark the following and speak out loud.*

voiceless plosives before a pause or silence:

Is this a trap^h?

(Strindberg: The Father)

You lie in your throat!

(2 Henry IV: I, ii, 85)

230

A hit, a very palpable hit.

(Hamlet: V, ii, 281)

Don't do that! I hate when you do that.

(Strindberg: Miss Julie)

I for a Clarence weep, so doth not she;
These babes for Clarence weep, and so do I;
I for an Edward weep, so do not they.

(Richard III: II, ii, 83)

But each Saturday, he says with such conceit:
Again, this Friday, sister, I ate…meat!

(Rostand: Cyrano de Bergerac)

voiced plosives before a pause or silence:

I'll be reveng'd.

(Cymbeline: II, iii, 155)

What, you egg!

(Macbeth: IV, ii, 83)

A second time I kill my husband dead,
When second husband kisses me in bed.

(Hamlet: III, ii, 184)

He's dead, he's dead, he's dead!
We are undone, lady, we are undone!
Alack the day, he's gone, he's kill'd, he's dead!

(Romeo and Juliet: III, ii, 37)

You have never known how to endure any bond.

(Ibsen: Ghosts)

voiced/voiceless plosives before a vowel or diphthong:

Piteous predicament! Even so lies she,
Blubb'ring and weeping, weeping and blubb'ring.

(Romeo and Juliet: III, iii, 86)

Why brand they us
With base? with baseness? bastardy? base, base?

(King Lear: I, ii, 9)

KATHERINE. What is your crest? a coxcomb?
PETRUCHIO. A combless cock, so Kate will be my hen.
KATHERINE. No cock of mine, you crow too like a craven.

(The Taming of the Shrew: II, i, 225)

To die, to sleep—
To sleep, perchance to dream—ay, there's the rub,
For in that sleep of death what dreams may come,
When we have shuffled off this mortal coil,
Must give us pause.

(Hamlet: III, i, 63)

Believe me, sir, had I such venture forth,
The better part of my affections would
Be with my hopes abroad. I should be still
Plucking the grass to know where sits the wind,
Peering in maps for ports and piers and roads.

(The Merchant of Venice: I, i, 15)

DUKE.   Hath he borne himself penitently in prison? How seems
he to be touch'd?
PROVOST. A man that apprehends death no more dreadfully but as
a drunken sleep, careless, reckless, and fearless of what's
past, present, or to come; insensible of mortality, and
desperately mortal.

(Measure for Measure: IV, ii, 140)

ANTONY.   For Brutus' sake, I am beholding to you.
4 PLEBEIAN. What does he say of Brutus?
3 PLEBEIAN. He says, for Brutus' sake
He finds himself beholding to us all.
4 PLEBEIAN. 'Twere best he speak no harm of Brutus here!

(Julius Caesar: III, ii, 65)

/d/ and /t/ before /j/:

I won't allow it! I forbid you!

(Ibsen: A Doll's House)

Could you oblige me…with a loan of 240 rubles…?

(Chekhov: The Cherry Orchard)

Mend your speech a little,
Lest you may mar your fortunes.

(King Lear: I, i, 94)

CONTINUANTS

See Overview pages 13-17

Continuants hold their position through the duration of the sound, and thus are capable of 'lingering'. This elongation offers rhythmic contrast with the abruptness of the previous group, the stop-plosives.

Continuants have three sub-groups: Nasal, Lateral, and Fricative.

Nasal Continuants

/ m /   / n /   / ŋ /
(<u>m</u>o<u>m</u>)   (o<u>n</u>)   (si<u>ng</u>)

These are the only three sounds in English that are released through the nose, not the mouth. All three are voiced and do not have voiceless partners.

/ m / (<u>m</u>o<u>m</u>)

Form **/m/** by closing the lips and directing sound through the nose.

AUDIO 37► /m/ (<u>m</u>o<u>m</u>)

> But how now, Sir John Hu<u>m</u>e?
> Seal up your lips, and give no words but <u>m</u>u<u>m</u>.
>
> (2 Henry VI: I, ii, 88)
>
> It is so delicious to lie and drea<u>m</u>.
>
> (Ibsen: The Master Builder)
>
> And tell fair Hero I a<u>m</u> Claudio,
> And in her boso<u>m</u> I'll unclasp my heart.
>
> (Much Ado About Nothing: I, i, 322)

WORDS /m/ (mom)

Initial	Medial	Final
much	timer	him
magic	chemist	lamb
mercy	summer	dome
maybe	scamming	chime
money	remember	scream

PHRASES /m/ (mom)

1. muddy camp
2. seems timely
3. some sympathy
4. Monday morning
5. memorize dramas
6. my mugs
7. dumb mime
8. musical mom
9. hums melodies
10. murmuring musician

SENTENCES /m/ (mom)

1. My, oh my!
2. Those limericks rhyme.
3. Michael, don't look so glum.
4. Maybe I will, maybe I won't.
5. Condemn him, and assign blame.
6. The anthem has a mystical theme.
7. Money, money, everything costs money.
8. Who is that mysterious man from Miami?
9. What's the most majestic monument in Maine?
10. Remember, submit the manuscript sometime in March.

SOUND CHECK #1: voiced /m/ endings. Maintain contact of the articulators through the end of vocal fold vibration. The last sound of the word should be a resonant /m/, rather than /mə/ (muh), which is /m/ followed by an off-glide.

PHRASES voiced /m/ endings

1.	mid-ter<u>m</u>	6.	yu<u>mmm</u>
2.	invite hi<u>m</u>	— 7.	oh, da<u>mn</u>
3.	nice costu<u>me</u>	8.	under the el<u>m</u>
4.	meant no har<u>m</u>	9.	not the custo<u>m</u>
5.	developing stor<u>m</u>	10.	saw the phanto<u>m</u>

SOUND CHECK #2 Rhythm Highlighter: syllabic /m̩/. Eliminate the vowel
sound in the last (unstressed) syllable, allowing /m/ to resonate in its place, as in
the word 'prism'. Syllabic endings include /n̩ l̩ m̩/. Syllabic /m̩/ is the least
common, and is not usually a problem for native American English speakers.

The difference in rhythm and pitch between the stressed (first) and the
unstressed (usually last) syllable is accentuated by the total absence of a vowel
sound in the unstressed ending. This can be represented rhythmically as:

LONGshort   (*or*)   **TUM**tuh

WORDS /m̩/ words ending in

som   **'blo**ssom, **'ran**som
sm   **'a**theism, **'bap**tism, **'cri**ticism, en**'thu**siasm **'he**roism, **'pri**sm,
       'sarcasm, **'spa**sm, **'wit**ticism

SOUND CHECK #3: same consonant blends /m m/. When the same
consonant sound ends one word and also begins the next, very well-pronounced
characters can use a slight rhythmic pulse of breath and energy to connect them,
while maintaining the shape and contact of the articulators, as in the following.

1.	ski**m m**oney	4.	Ti**m m**imics
2.	gy**m m**achine	5.	ge**m m**erchants
3.	hu**m m**usically	6.	clim**b m**ountains

NEUTRAL AMERICAN TEXT /m/ (<u>m</u>o<u>m</u>). *Mark the following and speak
out loud.*

voiced /m/ endings:

Live to be the show and gaze o' th' ti<u>me</u>.

(Macbeth: V, viii, 24)

More health and happiness betide my liege
Than can my care-tun'd tongue deliver him!

(Richard II: III, ii, 91)

Sometimes it seems
In some half-life our hearts entwine in dreams.

(Rostand: Cyrano de Bergerac)

syllabic /m̩/:

Now, by this maiden blossom in my hand,
I scorn thee and thy fashion, peevish boy.

(1 Henry VI: II, iv, 75)

/m/ various positions:

He's all my exercise, my mirth, my matter;
Now my sworn friend, and then mine enemy;
My parasite, my soldier, statesman, all.

(The The Winter's Tale: I, ii, 166)

Wert thou as young as I, Juliet thy love,
An hour but married, Tybalt murdered,
Doting like me, and like me banishéd,
Then mightst thou speak, then mightst thou tear thy hair,
And fall upon the ground, as I do now,
Taking the measure of an unmade grave.

(Romeo and Juliet: III, iii, 65)

PETRUCHIO. Myself am mov'd to woo thee for my wife.
KATHERINE. Mov'd! in good time! Let him that mov'd you hither
        Remove you hence. I knew you at the first
        You were a moveable.
PETRUCHIO.   Why, what's a moveable?

(The Taming of the Shrew: II, i, 194)

Much drink may be said to be an equivocator with lechery:
it makes him, and it mars him; it sets him on, and it takes him off;
it persuades him, and disheartens him; makes him stand to, and
not stand to; in conclusion, equivocates him in a sleep, and giving
him the lie, leaves him.

(Macbeth: II, iii, 31)

Nasal Continuant

/ n / (o<u>n</u>)

Form /n/ by placing the tip of the tongue against the upper gum ridge and releasing sound through the nose.

AUDIO 38 A▶ /n/ (o<u>n</u>)

> Give me my si<u>n</u> agai<u>n</u>.
>
> (Romeo and Juliet: I, v, 109)
>
> <u>N</u>ews, lads! our wars are do<u>n</u>e.
>
> (Othello: II, i, 20)
>
> Yes, my good lord—treaso<u>n</u>! treaso<u>n</u>! treaso<u>n</u>!
>
> (Tourneur: The Revenger's Tragedy)

WORDS /n/ (o<u>n</u>)

Initial	Medial	Final
none	pencil	fun
niece	runner	rain
never	kindly	been
knock	thinnest	mine
notice	whining	phone

PHRASES /n/ (o<u>n</u>)

1.	see<u>n</u> i<u>n</u> gree<u>n</u>		6.	<u>n</u>ever do<u>n</u>e
2.	u<u>n</u>commo<u>n</u> me<u>n</u>		7.	<u>n</u>o u<u>n</u>ki<u>n</u>d<u>n</u>ess
3.	raisi<u>n</u>s a<u>n</u>d bra<u>n</u>		8.	u<u>n</u>be<u>n</u>ded k<u>n</u>ees
4.	te<u>n</u> a<u>nn</u>ou<u>n</u>ceme<u>n</u>ts		9.	<u>n</u>asal co<u>n</u>so<u>n</u>a<u>n</u>ts
5.	<u>n</u>otorious <u>N</u>apoleo<u>n</u>		10.	u<u>n</u>frie<u>n</u>dly k<u>n</u>ights

---

SOUND CHECK #1: voiced /n/ endings. Maintain contact of the articulators and vocal fold vibration until the word (and the thought) is finished, so that an off-glide or /ə/ (<u>uh</u>) vowel sound is not added after the final, resonant /n/.

PHRASES voiced /n/ endings

1.	very lea<u>n</u>	6.	what fu<u>n</u>
2.	downtow<u>n</u>	7.	how sere<u>ne</u>
3.	missed trai<u>n</u>	8.	weighs a to<u>n</u>
4.	before daw<u>n</u>	9.	Mister Lenno<u>n</u>
5.	new black va<u>n</u>	10.	rehearsing a sce<u>ne</u>

SOUND CHECK #2 Rhythm Highlighter: syllabic /n̩/. Eliminate the vowel sound in the last, unstressed syllable, allowing the /n/ sound to resonate in its place, as in the word 'wooden'. Syllabics are notated in IPA by a small line under the resonating consonant, which can be represented / n̩ ! m̩ /. Text is marked with the phonetic symbol throughout for demonstration purposes.

AUDIO 38 B▶ **syllabic /n̩/**

He hath 'eaten̩ me out of house and home.

(2 Henry IV: II, i, 74)

Contempt, farewell, and 'maiden̩ pride, adieu!

(Much Ado about Nothing: III, i, 109)

The smallest worm will turn, being 'trodden̩ on.

(3 Henry VI: II, ii, 17)

The difference in rhythm and pitch between the stressed (first) and the unstressed (usually last) syllable is accentuated by the total absence of a vowel sound in the unstressed ending. This can be represented rhythmically as:

LONG_{short}   (*or*)   **TUM**_{tuh}

WORDS syllabic /dn̩ / words ending in the spelling

den/don: 'ardent, 'bidden, 'broaden, 'burden, 'garden, 'gladden, 'golden, 'harden, 'hidden, 'maiden, 'olden, 'prudence, 'ridden, 'rodent, 'sadden, 'strident, 'student, 'sudden, 'widen, 'wooden, 'Gordon, 'pardon

dn't: 'couldn't, 'didn't, 'hadn't, 'shouldn't, 'wouldn't

EXERCISE for speaking syllabic /dn̩/ (wooden)

1. Speak the word 'wood'. Bring the tip of the tongue up to the gum ridge for the final 'd' and maintain that position. Do not release the final 'd' sound; feel the tip of the tongue making solid contact with the upper gum ridge.

2. Speak the word 'wooden'. Maintain contact between the tip of the tongue and upper gum ridge throughout the entire second, unstressed syllable, eliminating the vowel sound and speaking it as if spelled 'dn'. The entire word is spoken as if spelled: 'woodn'.

Speak the following:

> Would you know if this wood is wooden?
>
> No, I wouldn't know if it's wooden.
>
> Wouldn't it be nice if it <u>were</u> wooden!
>
> Why this obsession with things wooden?
>
> Well, wouldn't you like to know!
>
> *Tush, that's a* **'wooden** *thing!*
>
> (1 Henry VI: V, iii, 89)

3. Speak the word 'wouldn't'. Maintain contact of the tip of the tongue against the gum ridge throughout the 'dnt' ending. Release the 't' when the word is finished.

PHRASES syllabic /dn̩/ (wooden)

1.	'didn't drive	6.	ten 'students
2.	'couldn't you	7.	they 'wouldn't
3.	in the 'garden	8.	'didn't want to
4.	received a 'pardon	9.	good 'riddance
5.	'hadn't thought of it	10.	'shouldn't buy that

SENTENCES syllabic /dn̩/ (wooden)

1. Wouldn't Gordon enjoy playing that part!

2. We couldn't imagine where they found the hidden treasure.

3. Didn't anyone tell you?

4. Couldn't I play both parts?

5. I shouldn't have answered my phone.

6. It would be better to meet later, wouldn't it?

7. Didn't you get your ticket at the student rate?

8. They couldn't have been nicer at the audition.

9. He couldn't wait to widen all the wooden floors.

10. I'm an ardent admirer and was saddened by his death.

11. Prudence felt gardening every weekend was a burden.

12. That was a strident warning; couldn't you tone it down?

13. Pardon me; did he suddenly say that laughing is forbidden?

14. In olden times, young maidens were forbidden many things.

15. I didn't anticipate all the hidden charges on my phone service.

Goldens' Rodents

Rodney and Gordon Golden entered the rodent control business after discovering their overly strident voices were capable of rooting out rodents from gardens and under wooden floors. Their parents hadn't foreseen this talent, but are happy to bid good riddance to the burden of paying for college tuition.

WORDS syllabic /t̩n̩/ words ending in the spelling

ten: 'batten, 'beaten, 'bitten, 'brighten, 'eaten, en'lighten, 'flatten, 'frighten, 'heighten, 'kitten, 'lighten, 'mitten, 'smitten, 'sweeten, 'tighten, 'wheaten, 'whiten, 'written

ton: 'button, 'cotton, 'Keaton, 'mutton, 'Newton

tant: 'blatant, com'batant, im'portant, 'mutant

The tip of the tongue contacts the gum ridge for unaspirated /t̩/, which is followed immediately (without moving the tongue tip) by voiced /n̩/, which resonates and releases through the nose. The throat remains open throughout the entire word, including the syllabic ending, so no glottal is formed.

SENTENCES syllabic /tn̩/ endings

1. She dislikes mutton.

2. He's originally from Manhattan.

3. Mr. Whitney dislikes impoliteness.

4. Brighten up! Don't be disheartened.

5. Did Richard Burton ever play Satan?

6. When flattened, the rotten eggs smelled.

7. It's important to sweeten Mrs. Keaton's tea.

8. I've forgotten; do they make cotton buttons?

9. Don't be frightened; show us what you've written.

10. I was bitten by that kitten, right through my mittens.

Something is rotten in the state of Denmark.

(Hamlet: I, iv, 90)

WORDS additional syllabic /n̩/

/fn̩/	fen, fin, fon	'deafen, 'muffin, 'griffon
/vn̩/	ven	'driven, e'leven, en'liven
/sn̩/	sen, son, cen	'loosen, 'mason, 'recent, 'decent
/zn̩/	sin, sen, son, zon	'cousin, 'chosen, 'reason
/ʃn̩/	tion, sion, ian	'action, 'passion, lo'gician
/ʒn̩/	sion, sian	de'rision, sub'mersion, 'Asian

SOUND CHECK #3: same consonant blends /n n/. When the same consonant sound ends one word and also begins the next, very well-pronounced characters can use a slight rhythmic pulse of breath and energy to connect them, while maintaining the shape and contact of the articulators.

1.	one **n**ame	6.	won **n**achos
2.	te**n** **kn**ives	7.	Mai**n**e **n**ights
3.	see**n** **kn**eeling	8.	lemo**n** **n**oodles
4.	eve**n** **n**umbers	9.	ni**n**e **n**eighbors
5.	eleve**n** **n**ations	10.	fi**n**e **kn**owledge

NEUTRAL AMERICAN TEXT /n/ (o̲n̲). *Mark the following, including IPA notations on syllabic endings, if useful, and speak out loud.*

syllabic /n̩/

I didn̩'t find it dull.

(Ibsen: A Doll's House)

All I say is: prudence, my dear lady!

(Ibsen: Ghosts)

I had rather lose the battle than that sister
Should loosen him and me.

(King Lear: V, i, 18)

What, are you mad, that you do reason so?

(The Comedy of Errors: III, ii, 53)

'Tis certain he hath pass'd the river Somme.

(Henry V: III, v, 1)

Who being so heighten'd,
He watered his new plants with dews of flattery.

(Coriolanus: V, vi, 21)

I was the head footman before the emancipation came.

(Chekhov: The Cherry Orchard)

Alas! Yes, family life is certainly not always so pure as it
ought to be.

(Ibsen: Ghosts)

Our kinsman Gloucester is as innocent
From meaning treason to our royal person
As is the sucking lamb or harmless dove.

(2 Henry VI: III, i, 69)

I have been feasting with mine enemy,
Where on a sudden one hath wounded me.

(Romeo and Juliet: II, iii, 49)

Smooth runs the water where the brook is deep,
And in his simple show he harbors treason.

(2 Henry VI: III, i, 53)

And you have hidden the truth from me all these years?
Hidden it from me...

(Ibsen: Ghosts)

ALSEMERO. You seem displeased, lady, on the sudden.
BEATRICE.   Your pardon sir, 'tis my infirmity.

(Middleton & Rowley: The Changeling)

ISABEL. Must he needs die?
ANGELO.   Maiden, no remedy.
ISABEL. Yes; I do think that you might pardon him,
        And neither heaven nor man grieve at the mercy.

(Measure for Measure: II, ii, 48)

voiced /n/ endings

Yet this my comfort, when your words are done,
My woes end likewise with the evening sun.

(The Comedy of Errors: I, i, 26)

You souls of geese,
That bear the shapes of men.

(Coriolanus: I, iv, 34)

When you durst do it, then you were a man;
And to be more than what you were, you would
Be so much more the man.

(Macbeth: I, vii, 49)

They're not alone!
Two deaths must I avenge: Christian's, my own.

(Rostand: Cyrano de Bergerac)

Villain?
Nay, heaven is just, scorns are the hires of scorns:
I ne'er knew yet adulterer without horns.

(Tourneur: The Revenger's Tragedy)

Nasal Continuant

/ ŋ / (si**ng**)

Form /ŋ/ by resting the tip of the tongue down behind the lower front teeth, pressing the back of the tongue against the front of the soft palate, and releasing sound through the nose.

AUDIO 39▶ /ŋ/ (si**ng**)

ŋk
I thi**nk** it would be desirable for her in every respect.

(Ibsen Ghosts)

ŋ
My Lord Bassanio, let him have the ri**ng**.

(The Merchant of Venice: IV, i, 449)

ŋ   ŋ   ŋg
Ki**ng** John, your Ki**ng** and E**ng**land's, doth approach.

(King John: II, i, 313)

WORDS /ŋ/ (si**ng**)

Initial	Medial	Final
*	finger	fling
*	ringer	bring
*	thinker	thing
*	clinging	string
*	strongest	swing

* indicates there are no words beginning with this sound in NAS.

PHRASES /ŋ/ (si**ng**)

1.	anythi**ng** else	6.	sti**nk**ing ju**nk**
2.	swi**ng** danci**ng**	7.	do**nk**ey du**ng**
3.	wonderful si**ng**er	8.	recta**ng**ular ta**nk**
4.	rhymi**ng** in E**ng**lish	9.	ma**ng**led la**ng**uage
5.	bri**ng**ing somethi**ng**	10.	bli**nk**ing and cli**nk**ing

---

SOUND CHECK #1: use of /ŋ/ 'ng' alone or /ŋg/ 'ng + g'. If you are unsure whether to speak /ŋ/ alone or in combination with /g/, refer to the following.

Use /ŋ/ 'ng' alone:

(a)   when a word *ends* in the spellings 'ng' or 'ngue' as in:

bang	strong	saying	ring
cling	spring	crying	rung
meringue	harangue	bringing	seeing

(b)   when a suffix is added to the *root* of a word that ends in 'ng' as in:

'er'	'ster'	'ed'	'y'
singer	gangster	longed	slangy
hanger	songster	winged	clangy

Use /ŋg/ 'ng + g':

(a)   when there is a superlative (est) or comparative (er) ending added to adjectives. Most common:

'est'	'er'
longest	longer
strongest	stronger
youngest	younger

(b)   when the suffixes 'ate' and 'al' are added to the *root* of a word ending in 'ng', as in:

elon**g**ate   diphthon**g**al

(c)   when 'ng' is in the middle of the root of a word:

angle	language	finger	mingle
dangle	hungry	English	tangle

Use /ŋk/ 'ng + k': when the end of a syllable is spelled:

'nc'   zinc, franc,
'nk'   kink, pink, wink, think, spank, bank

Use /ŋks/ 'ng + ks': when spelled:

'nx'   sphinx, lynx, phalanx, Manx, minx, Bronx

PHRASES medial /ŋ/ (ng) alone

1.	winging it	6.	longed to belong
2.	slinging hash	7.	singing youngster
3.	clingy clothes	8.	catching gangsters
4.	stinging remarks	9.	ringed by strangers
5.	unstringing lights	10.	hanging up hangers

PHRASES medial /ŋg/ (ng/g) combinations

1.	bilingual class	6.	angry language
2.	mangled finger	7.	lingering anguish
3.	jingled triangles	8.	bungled strangling
4.	mingling singles	9.	longer and stronger
5.	hungry for Pringles	10.	distinguished English

PHRASES medial /ŋ/ /ŋg/ /ŋk/

1.	inky fingers	6.	single singer
2.	jingle jangle	7.	youngest uncle
3.	singing jingles	8.	stronger thinker
4.	thankful banker	9.	instinctive things
5.	meringue filling	10.	blinks when thinking

SENTENCES /ŋ/ /ŋg/ /ŋk/ various positions and combinations

1. The singer made that long song famous.

2. We're anxious to learn the English language.

3. Hank fell off the donkey and broke his ankle.

4. What's playing at Lincoln Center in the spring?

5. Think about bringing along something to drink.

6. That distinguished gentleman is from Hong Kong.

7. I'm ironing a few things before traveling to Long Island.

8. The lizard blinked, winked, and thrust out its long tongue.

9. Use the wooden hanger. It's stronger than the plastic hanger.

10. The swing hung from a long rope and banged into the house.

SOUND CHECK #2: voiced /ŋ/ endings. Maintain contact of the articulators and vocal fold vibration until the word and thought are finished. Otherwise, an off-glide or short /ə/ (uh) vowel sound may be added after the final /ŋ/.

See also pages 100-102 for 'ing' endings, and the poem on page 312.

1.	ding dong	6.	nothing doing
2.	strong gang	7.	earning a living
3.	beautiful ring	8.	developing a song
4.	charming king	9.	nothing remaining
5.	spring gardening	10.	bringing everything

NEUTRAL AMERICAN TEXT /ŋ/ (sing). *Mark the following and speak out loud.*

voiced /ŋ/ endings

You are too much mistaken in this king.

(Henry V: II, iv, 30)

How can the authorities tolerate such things!

(Ibsen: Ghosts)

The ears are senseless that should give us hearing.

(Hamlet: V, ii, 369)

If the Prince be too important, tell him there is measure
in every thing.

(Much Ado About Nothing: II, i, 70)

Whom should we match with Henry, being a king,
But Margaret, that is daughter to a king?

(1 Henry VI: V, v, 66)

Is whispering nothing?
Is leaning cheek to cheek? Is meeting noses?
Kissing with inside lip? ...
Is this nothing?
Why then the world and all that's in't is nothing,
The covering sky is nothing, Bohemia nothing,
My wife is nothing, nor nothing have these nothings,
If this be nothing.

(The The Winter's Tale: I, ii, 284)

/ŋ/ various positions

I have been feasting with mine enemy.

(Romeo and Juliet: II, iii, 49)

Ambassadors from Harry King of England.

(Henry V: II, iv, 65)

What's this but libelling against the Senate,
And blazoning our unjustice every where?

(Titus Andronicus: IV, iv, 17)

I kept a-hallowing and whooping in his ears, but all could not
wake him. I, seeing that, took him by the leg and never rested
pulling, till I had pulled me his leg quite off.

(Marlowe: Doctor Faustus)

I feel as though I had been born long, long ago; I trail my life
along like an endless train... And often I have not the slightest
desire to go on living.

(Chekhov: The Seagull)

A whoreson cold, sir, a cough, sir, which I caught with ringing
in the King's affairs upon his coronation-day, sir.

(2 Henry IV: III, ii, 181)

Some wine ho!
"And let me the canakin clink, clink;
And let me the canakin clink.
A soldier's a man;
O, man's life's but a span;
Why then let a soldier drink."

(Othello: II, iii, 68)

ROSENCRANTZ.
    My lord, you must tell us where the body is, and go with us
    to the King.
HAMLET.
    The body is with the King, but the King is not with the body.
    The King is a thing—
GUILDENSTERN.
    A thing, my lord?
HAMLET.
    Of nothing, bring me to him.

(Hamlet: IV, ii, 25)

Lateral Continuant

There is only one lateral continuant. This particular voiced sound has no voiceless partner, and is represented by the phonetic symbol:

/ l / (lily)

Form /l/ by gently touching the tip of the tongue to the gum ridge and allowing sound to release over the sides of the tongue and through the mouth. The tongue tip should not slide onto, or protrude between, the teeth. The sides of the tongue may be felt gently pressing against the insides of the upper molars.

AUDIO 40 A▶ /l/ (lily)

I love long life better than figs.

(Antony and Cleopatra: I, ii, 32)

There is not yet so ugly a fiend of hell
As thou shalt be, if thou didst kill this child.

(King John: IV, iii, 123)

You're a spoilt soft creature, Dunyasha.

(Chekhov: The Cherry Orchard)

WORDS /l/ (lily)

Initial	Medial	Final
leg	apply	tall
life	Paula	will
late	wilder	foul
lease	foolish	coal
lunch	spilling	smell

Note: Additional practice material on vowels and diphthongs before consonant /l/ is available in all of the vowel and diphthong sections.

PHRASES /l/ (lily)

1.	long laundry list	6.	bulky sculptures
2.	lingering leopards	7.	seagulls in the pool
3.	boiled and broiled	8.	lovely lemon yellow
4.	lasting love in Italy	9.	legalized lawlessness
5.	dull, clueless culprit	10.	millions and millions

SOUND CHECK #1: consonant combinations. The tip of the tongue should make contact with the gum ridge and clearly sound /l/ before finishing the consonant combination. Back of the tongue tension should be avoided. Place a thumb on the underside of the chin to feel if the tongue is overly tense during /l/.

/lt^h/	/lt^h/	/lt^h/	/lp^h/
colt	lilt	felt	help
bolt	hilt	fault	pulp
dolt	belt	guilt	gulp
holt	wilt	built	scalp
molt	vault	adult	whelp

/lk^h/	/lf/	/ls/	/lt͡ʃ/
ilk	elf	else	filch
silk	self	false	belch
bilk	shelf	pulse	gulch
milk	itself	repulse	welch
hulk	himself	impulse	squelch

PHRASES /l/ and combinations

1.	belching elf	6.	or else
2.	wilting adults	7.	halts the salt
3.	engulfed in silk	8.	repulsive cults
4.	milk on the shelf	9.	false consultants
5.	squelched impulses	10.	someone else's colts

SOUND CHECK #2: voiced /l/ endings. The tip of the tongue should make gentle contact with the gum ridge in the following consonant /l/ combinations. Avoid tensing the back of the tongue or using the tongue blade. Fully sound /l/ before continuing on to the consonant(s) that follow, voicing through the end of the last consonant without adding an off-glide, or short /ə/ (uh) vowel sound.

/lm/	/lv/	/lz/	/ld/
elm	solve	pals	field
film	valve	pills	billed
helm	delve	pails	felled
realm	twelve	miles	pulled
overwhelm	involve	squalls	polled

/ld/ [1]	/ld/	/ld/	/ldz/
cold	ruled	tiled	folds
bold	willed	failed	scalds
hold	called	soiled	builds
mold	polled	smiled	worlds
doled	spilled	compiled	beholds

PHRASES voiced /l/ endings

1. slippery eels
2. terribly cruel
3. not involved
4. brightest gold
5. gargoyle's jowls

6. hurling towels
7. saying farewell
8. impulsive child
9. alliance dissolved
10. terribly overwhelmed

SOUND CHECK #3 Rhythm Highlighter: syllabic /l̩/. Eliminate the vowel sound in the last, unstressed syllable, allowing the consonant /l/ to resonate in its place, as in the word 'little'. Syllabics are notated phonetically by a small line under the resonating consonant, which can be seen in the previous IPA symbol. Text is marked with the IPA symbol throughout for demonstration purposes.

AUDIO 40 B▶ syllabic /l̩/

A 'maiden̩ 'battl̩e then?

(Troilus and Cressida: IV, v, 87)

You 'didn̩'t call me a 'littl̩e 'devil̩ then?

(Ibsen: The Master Builder)

This 'articl̩e, my liege, yourself must break.

(Love's Labor's Lost: I, i, 133)

---

[1] 'Have' /hæv/ is usually pronounced /hæf/ before an infinitive: 'I have to see'.

The difference in rhythm and pitch between the stressed (first) and the unstressed (usually last) syllable is accentuated by the total absence of a vowel sound in the unstressed ending. This can be represented rhythmically as:

LONG short   (*or*)   **TUM** tuh

The lips are <u>un</u>rounded as the tongue tip contacts the gum ridge on final syllabic / ļ /. This allows sound to escape laterally over the sides of the tongue without producing an /o/ sound at the end of the word.

Syllabic endings spelled 'tle' and 'ttle' are usually pronounced /dļ/ in Neutral American, as in the words: bee<u>tle</u>, li<u>ttle</u>, ba<u>ttle</u>, bo<u>ttle</u>.

WORDS syllabic / ļ / common spellings and sample words

/fļ/	ful, fle	'awful, 'beautiful, 'muffle
/vļ/	vel, vil, val	'novel, un'ravel, 'evil
/pļ/	ple	'apple, 'purple, 'ripple
/bļ/	ble	'cable, 'feeble, 'rubble
/kļ/	cle, ckle, cal	'tricycle, 'buckle, 'tackle
/ŋkļ/	nkle	'sprinkle, 'twinkle, 'wrinkle
/gļ/	gle	'bugle, 'giggle, 'wriggle
/mļ/	mal, mel	'animal, 'minimal, e'namel
/ŋgļ/	ngle	'dangle, 'strangle, 'wrangle
/tļ/	tle, tile, tal	'hostile, 'vestal, 'crystal
/dļ/	dle	'middle, 'puddle, 'riddle
/nļ/	nal, nel	'tonal, 'tunnel, 'panel
/ndļ/	ndle	'bundle, 'candle, 'trundle
/sļ/	stle, sel, sal	e'pistle, 'thistle, 'whistle
/zļ/	zle, sel, sal	'frazzle, 'puzzle, 'weasel
/ʃļ/	tial, cial	'martial, 'partial, 'racial

PHRASES syllabic / ļ /

1.	'little 'weaseļ	6.	'battļe 'eviļ
2.	'primaļ urges	7.	'middļe child
3.	'dreadfuļ cold	8.	'woodeņ 'paddļe
4.	'willfuļ 'toddļer	9.	'hostiļe 'paneļists
5.	em'bezzļed money	10.	'whistļing 'damseļs

> **SOUND CHECK #4: same consonant blends / l l /.** When the same consonant sound ends one word and also begins the next word, then very well-pronounced characters can use a slight rhythmic pulse of breath and energy to connect them, while maintaining the shape and contact of the articulators.

1.	dull lad	6.	Bill left
2.	real lucky	7.	file ledgers
3.	will linger	8.	boil lettuce
4.	well leveled	9.	whole lesson
5.	howl loudly	10.	scrawl lightly

Give me my robe, put on my crown, I have
Immortal longings in me.

(Antony and Cleopatra: V, ii, 281)

> **SOUND CHECK #5: /l/ followed by /θ, ð/.** When speaking /l/ followed immediately by a 'th', the tongue tip generally moves forward onto the teeth on /l/ in anticipation of the 'th' position. This holds true for /l d t n/ before 'th', and is notated in IPA by a little 'tooth' symbol under the consonant: / l̪ d̪ t̪ n̪ /.

1.	He's real thirsty.	6.	Foil thieves.
2.	She'll think of it.	7.	Heal thumbs.
3.	Get school things.	8.	Fool thousands.
4.	They feel thankful.	9.	Reveal thoughts.
5.	That was well thundered!	10.	Tell them everything.

> **SOUND CHECK #6: /l/ followed by /j/ (you).** Be sure to make distinct contact between the tongue tip and gum ridge on /l/, before dropping the tongue tip down behind the lower front teeth for the /j/ sound that comes directly after.

1.	I'll tell you.	6.	all civilians
2.	Will you go?	7.	brilliant Italian
3.	Celia's familiar.	8.	alienated stallions
4.	rebellious William	9.	value the familiar
5.	Julia's a millionaire.	10.	trillions of billions

The King is a noble gentleman, and my familiar.

(Love's Labor's Lost: V, i, 95)

NEUTRAL AMERICAN TEXT /l/ (lily). *Mark the following, including IPA notations on syllabic endings, if useful, and speak out loud.*

syllabic / ļ /:

A pox of wrinkļes!

(Timon of Athens: IV, iii, 148)

Double, double, toil and trouble;
Fire burn, and cauldron bubble.

(Macbeth: IV, i, 10)

HAMLET.   Methinks it is like a weasel.
POLONIUS. It is back'd like a weasel.

(Hamlet: III, ii, 379)

Fair isle, that from the fairest of all flowers
　　　Thy gentlest of all gentle names dost take!
How many memories of what radiant hours
　　　At sight of thee and thine aț once awake!

(Poe: To Zante)

RAGUENEAU. Have you met with trouble?
CYRANO.   No; no trouble.
LISE.   You're telling us a lie!
CYRANO.   Did my nose double?

(Rostand: Cyrano de Bergerac)

voiced /l/ in various positions and in consonant combinations:

Two households, both aļike in dignity.

(Romeo and Juliet: Prologue)

Whereat, with blade, with bloody blameful blade,
He bravely broach'd his boiling bloody breast.

(A Midsummer Night's Dream: V, i, 146)

Thou art a bile,
A plague-sore, or embossed carbuncle,
In my corrupted blood. But I'll not chide thee,
Let shame come when it will.

(King Lear: II, iv, 223)

A heavy summons lies like lead upon me.

(Macbeth: II, i, 6)

Banners yellow, glorious, golden,
  On its roof did float and flow,
(This—all this—was in the olden
  Time long ago,)
And every gentle air that dallied,
  In that sweet day,
Along the ramparts plumed and pallid,
  A winged odor went away.

                            (Poe: The Haunted Palace)

Such an exploit have I in hand, Ligarius,
Had you a healthful ear to hear of it.

                            (Julius Caesar: II, i, 318)

There fell a silvery-silken veil of light,
With quietude, and sultriness, and slumber,
Upon the upturn'd faces of a thousand
Roses that grew in an enchanted garden.

                            (Poe: To Helen)

Villainy, villainy, villainy!
I think upon't, I think—I smell't—O villainy!
I thought so then—I'll kill myself for grief—
O villainy! villainy!

                            (Othello: V, ii, 190)

My uncle's will in this respect is mine.
If he see aught in you that makes him like,
That any thing he sees, which moves his liking,
I can with ease translate it to my will;
Or if you will, to speak more properly,
I will enforce it eas'ly to my love.

                            (King John: II, i, 510)

To-morrow night look that thou lie alone,
Let not the nurse lie with thee in thy chamber.
Take thou this vial, being then in bed,
And this distilling liquor drink thou off,
When presently through all thy veins shall run
A cold and drowsy humor; for no pulse
Shall keep his native progress, but surcease;
No warmth, no breath shall testify thou livest.

                            (Romeo and Juliet: IV, i, 91)

Fricative Continuants

Releasing air between two articulators that are close enough together to cause a friction sound produces the fricatives **f** (lea<u>f</u>), **v** (lea<u>ve</u>), **θ** (ba<u>th</u>), **ð** (ba<u>the</u>), **s** (bu<u>s</u>), **z** (bu<u>zz</u>), **ʃ** (ru<u>sh</u>), **ʒ** (rou<u>ge</u>), and **h** (<u>h</u>e).

/ f / (lea<u>f</u>)   / v / (lea<u>ve</u>)

Form **/f, v/** by resting the tip of the tongue down behind the lower front teeth, gently placing the bottom edge of the upper teeth on the lower lip, and releasing air (or air and sound) through the mouth between these two articulators.

AUDIO 41▶ /f/ (lea<u>f</u>) and /v/ (lea<u>ve</u>)

A <u>f</u>ool, a <u>f</u>ool! I met a <u>f</u>ool i' th' <u>f</u>orest.

(As You Like It: II, vii, 12)

<u>F</u>orgi<u>v</u>e me, Alsemero, all <u>f</u>orgi<u>v</u>e:
'Tis time to die, when 'tis a shame to li<u>v</u>e.

(Middleton & Rowley: The Changeling)

Gi<u>v</u>e me thy <u>f</u>ist, thy <u>f</u>ore-<u>f</u>oot to me gi<u>v</u>e.

(Henry V: II, i, 67)

WORDS /f/ (lea<u>f</u>) and /v/ (lea<u>ve</u>)

	Initial	**Medial**	**Final**
/f/	fee	prefer	leaf
	find	defiled	half
	form	refined	wife
	finish	roofing	strife
	fashion	stuffiest	cough

/v/		
vow	travels	save
very	starved	have
vote	heaven	leave
verse	hovering	nerve
vixen	revealing	prove

SOUND CHECK #1: consonant combinations containing voiceless /f/. Be sure to include all of the sounds in the consonant combinations that follow.

/sf/	/fs/	/ftʰ/	/ft͵s/
sphere	briefs	craft	lifts
sphenoid	muffs	cuffed	lofts
sphincter	proofs	roughed	thefts

SENTENCES consonant /f/ and combinations

1. Draft Jeff.
2. They left no proof.
3. Be rough and tough.
4. Sift through the gifts.
5. She's bereft of beliefs.
6. The chiefs laughed.
7. Mr. Wolf triumphed.
8. That's the thief's stuff.
9. Leaf through the drafts.
10. Kids sniffed cream puffs.

SOUND CHECK #2: final consonant combinations containing voiced /v/[1]. Speak all of the sounds in the following combinations. Voice through the end of the last consonant without adding an off-glide, or short /ə/ (uh) vowel sound.

/lv/	/vz/	/vd/	/vlz/
delve	lives	loved	revels
solve	halves	moved	novels
valve	perceives	grieved	travels

PHRASES voiced /v/ endings

1. can't save
2. ten loaves
3. freed captives
4. vigorously loved
5. vacations dissolved
6. big graves
7. well loved
8. not behaved
9. badly received
10. worried executives

---

[1] 'Have' /hæv/ is usually pronounced /hæf/ before an infinitive: 'I have to see'.

SOUND CHECK #3: same consonant / f f /, / v v / blends. When the same consonant sound ends one word and also begins the next word, then very well-pronounced characters can use a slight rhythmic pulse of breath and energy to connect them, while maintaining the shape and contact of the articulators.

1.	stiff foam	6.	Save voices.
2.	roof falling	7.	Love Venice.
3.	wife famous	8.	Revive Victor.
4.	leaf fluttering	9.	Leave Virginia.
5.	half-famished	10.	Have vacations.

NEUTRAL AMERICAN TEXT /f/ (leaf) and /v/ (leave). *Mark the following and speak out loud.*

voiced /v/ endings:

Scurvy knave!

(Romeo and Juliet: II, iv, 162)

Neither can be enjoy'd
If both remain alive.

(King Lear: V, i, 58)

Have you ever been in love?

(Strindberg: Miss Julie)

Pray you, who does the wolf love?

(Coriolanus: II, i, 7)

And my large kingdom for a little grave,
A little little grave, an obscure grave.

(Richard II: III, iii, 153)

Awake! what ho, Brabantio! thieves, thieves!
Look to your house, your daughter, and your bags!
Thieves, thieves!

(Othello: I, i, 79)

Most sweet voices!
Better it is to die, better to starve,
Than crave the hire which first we do deserve.

(Coriolanus: II, iii, 112)

/f/ and /v/ various positions:

O viper vile!

(Henry V: II, i, 46)

Fair Margaret knows
That Suffolk doth not flatter, face, or feign.

(1 Henry VI: V, iii, 141)

For France, for France, for it is more than need.

(King John: I, i, 179)

With witchcraft of his wits, with traitorous gifts—
O wicked wit and gifts that have the power
So to seduce!

(Hamlet: I, v, 43)

I wonder men dare trust themselves with men.
Methinks they should invite them without knives:
Good for their meat, and safer for their lives.

(Timon of Athens: I, ii, 43)

France is a bawd to Fortune and King John,
That strumpet Fortune, that usurping John!
Tell me, thou fellow, is not France forsworn?
Envenom him with words, or get thee gone.

(King John: III, i, 60)

In you, I came to know a friend, if never...wife...
And in your grace, a woman has crossed my life.

(Rostand: Cyrano de Bergerac)

Let floods o'erswell, and fiends for food howl on!

(Henry V: II, i, 93)

False face must hide what the false heart doth know.

(Macbeth: I, vii, 82)

Away, the foul fiend follows me!... The foul fiend hath led through
fire and through flame, through ford and whirlpool.

(King Lear: III, iv, 46)

Fricative Continuants

/ θ / (ba<u>th</u>) / ð / (ba<u>the</u>)

Form /θ/ and /ð/ by touching the underside of the upper front teeth with the flattened tip of the tongue and releasing breath, or breath and sound, between the upper teeth and flattened tongue.

AUDIO 42▶ /θ/ (ba<u>th</u>) and /ð/ (ba<u>the</u>)

    θ   θ   θ   θ

<u>Th</u>ree <u>th</u>ousand ducats for <u>th</u>ree mon<u>th</u>s, and Antonio bound.

(The Merchant of Venice: I, iii, 9)

        ð   θ θ   θ

Shame serves <u>th</u>y life and do<u>th</u> <u>th</u>y dea<u>th</u> attend.

(Richard III: IV, iv, 196)

   θ ð   ð ð   ð

I <u>th</u>ink <u>th</u>ou wast created for men to brea<u>the</u> <u>th</u>emselves upon thee.

(All's Well That Ends Well: II, iii, 255)

WORDS /θ/ (ba<u>th</u>) and /ð/ (ba<u>the</u>)

	Initial	**Medial**	**Final**
/θ/	thin	faithful	path
	think	nothing	faith
	thumb	birthday	death
	thanks	breathless	mouth
	thermos	mathematics	wealth
/ð/	that	rather	bathe
	them	brother	teethe
	there	another	soothe
	these	loathing	smooth
	those	seething	breathe

PHRASES cognate pairs /θ/ (ba<u>th</u>) and /ð/ (ba<u>the</u>)

1.	<u>th</u>inks of <u>th</u>em	6.	ano<u>th</u>er mou<u>th</u>
2.	any<u>th</u>ing <u>th</u>erein	7.	heal<u>th</u>y wea<u>th</u>er
3.	soo<u>th</u>ing O<u>th</u>ello	8.	dear<u>th</u> of clo<u>th</u>ing
4.	<u>th</u>rough bla<u>th</u>ering	9.	<u>th</u>ankful for <u>th</u>ose
5.	au<u>th</u>ored by Hea<u>th</u>er	10.	<u>th</u>ree for <u>th</u>emselves

SENTENCES /θ, ð/

1. That youth has great rhythm.

2. The author is wearing a very thin tie.

3. I think that Mr. Smithy is from the South.

4. Beth, tell little Ethan it's time for his bath.

5. Ruth is known for always telling the truth.

6. I know of an Elizabethan youth named Othello.

7. They drove through Ithaca last Thursday evening.

8. The thieves left a thermos at the scene of the crime.

9. Say 'Martha McCarthy' three times fast. It's a mouthful!

10. Ask Mother and Father if they plan to attend the gathering.

SOUND CHECK #1: /θ, ð/ *vs.* /t, d/. 'Th' sounds are continuants, have some length, and should not be 'exploded' like stop-plosives. Notice the contrast in rhythm and placement of the tongue tip on the following words. *Read across.*

Initial		Final	
/θ/	/t/	/θ/	/t/
thin	tin	hath	hat
thirst	terse	bath	bat
thought	taught	quoth	quote
/ð/	/d/	/ð/	/d/
than	Dan	loathe	load
then	den	smooth	sued
those	doze	breathe	breed

PHRASES /θ, ð/ *vs.* /t, d/

1.	no<u>th</u>ing doing	6.	hotter <u>th</u>an <u>th</u>at
2.	wi<u>th</u>out telling	7.	<u>th</u>rongs downtown
3.	two dry <u>th</u>roats	8.	good whe<u>th</u>er today
4.	dandy bir<u>th</u>day	9.	smattering of <u>th</u>under
5.	dead Elizabe<u>th</u>an	10.	determined to brea<u>the</u>

SOUND CHECK #2: consonant combinations. Include all of the consonant sounds in the following combinations. Remember, / ṇ, ḍ, ṭ, ḷ / are usually dentalized when they occur directly before 'th'. *Read down the columns.*

/θs/	/ḷθ/	/d̪θ *and* t̪θ/	/ðd/	/ðz/
baths	health	width	teethed	bathes
births	wealth	eighth	breathed	loathes
heaths	stealth	breadth	mouthed	soothes

PHRASES consonant combinations

1.	too<u>th's</u> root	6.	stea<u>lth</u> sleu<u>ths</u>
2.	Ru<u>th's</u> breath	7.	ba<u>thes</u> ano<u>th</u>er
3.	the ear<u>th's</u> my<u>ths</u>	8.	tee<u>th</u>ing py<u>th</u>ons
4.	the you<u>th's</u> weal<u>th</u>	9.	wi<u>dth</u> and brea<u>dth</u>
5.	hea<u>lth</u>y sou<u>th</u>erners	10.	Elizabe<u>th</u> brea<u>thed</u>

SOUND CHECK #3: Compare /f/ with /θ/ *and* /v/ with /ð/. The flattened tip of the tongue should be placed against the underside of the upper teeth when speaking /θ *or* ð/, otherwise /f *or* v/ will be spoken instead. This is evident in Cockney pronunciation of 'think' as 'fink' and 'breathing' as 'breaving'.

PHRASES voiceless /f/ *vs.* /θ/

1.	fif<u>th</u> floor lifts	6.	finally <u>th</u>inking
2.	twelf<u>th</u> triumph	7.	brea<u>th</u>less sphinx
3.	half <u>th</u>eir weal<u>th</u>	8.	spiffy Elizabe<u>th</u>an
4.	left in the dep<u>ths</u>	9.	deciphers an<u>th</u>ems
5.	engulfed by warm<u>th</u>	10.	mon<u>th</u>ly certificates

PHRASES voiced /v/ vs. /ð/

1.	nor<u>th</u>ern revels	6.	leveled altoge<u>th</u>er
2.	eleven hea<u>th</u>ens	7.	five others ba<u>th</u>ing
3.	smoo<u>th</u>ed graves	8.	disheveled clo<u>th</u>ing
4.	you<u>th</u>s disapprove	9.	relieved of wri<u>th</u>ing
5.	believed unwor<u>th</u>y	10.	grieving and soo<u>th</u>ing

SOUND CHECK #4: same consonant blends / θ θ / and / ð ð /. When the same consonant sound ends one word and also begins the next word, then very well-pronounced characters can use a slight rhythmic pulse of breath and energy to connect them, while maintaining the shape and contact of the articulators.

1.	fif**th th**ief	6.	mou**th th**at
2.	mou**th th**irsty	7.	brea**the th**is
3.	ba**th Th**ursday	8.	smoo**th th**em
4.	uncou**th th**eory	9.	wri**the th**ereafter
5.	mammo**th th**eatre	10.	ba**the th**emselves

NEUTRAL AMERICAN TEXT /θ/ (ba**th**) and /ð/ (ba**the**). *Mark the following and speak out loud.*

θ   θ
Forsoo**th**, a great ari**th**metician.

(Othello: I, i, 19)

Our thunder from the south
Shall rain their drift of bullets on this town.

(King John: II, i, 411)

His health was never better worth than now.

(1 Henry IV: IV, i, 27)

He's awfully clever, and he plays the violin!

(Chekhov: Three Sisters)

Hast thou not spoke like thunder on my side?

(King John: III, i, 124)

A man so breathed, that certain he would fight.

(Love's Labours Lost: V, ii, 653)

Grim death, how foul and loathsome is thine image!

(The Taming of the Shrew: Ind. i. 35)

I do defy
The tongues of soothers, but a braver place
In my heart's love hath no man than yourself.

(1 Henry IV: IV, i, 6)

What shall I say to thee, Lord Scroop, thou cruel,
Ingrateful, savage, and inhuman creature?
Thou that didst bear the key of all my counsels,
That knew'st the very bottom of my soul,
That almost mightst have coin'd me into gold,
Wouldst thou have practic'd on me, for thy use?

(Henry V: II, ii, 94)

AUSTRIA.   O, that a man should speak those words to me!
BASTARD.   And hang a calve's-skin on those recreant limbs.
AUSTRIA.   Thou dar'st not say so, villain, for thy life.
BASTARD.   And hang a calve's-skin on those recreant limbs.
K. JOHN.   We like not this, thou dost forget thyself.

(King John: III, i, 130)

ZANCHE.   You remember your oaths?
FLAMINEO. Lovers' oaths are like mariners' prayers, uttered
                    In extremity.

(Webster: The White Devil)

SAMUEL.   I will bite my thumb at them, which is disgrace to them
                    if they bear it.
ABRAHAM. Do you bite your thumb at us, sir?
SAMUEL.   I do bite my thumb, sir.
ABRAHAM. Do you bite your thumb at us, sir?

(Romeo and Juliet: I, i, 42)

Death, that hath suck'd the honey of thy breath,
Hath had no power yet upon thy beauty:
Thou art not conquer'd, beauty's ensign yet
Is crimson in thy lips and in thy cheeks,
And death's pale flag is not advanced there.
Tybalt, liest thou there in thy bloody sheet?
O, what more favor can I do to thee,
Than with that hand that cut thy youth in twain
To sunder his that was thine enemy?

(Romeo and Juliet: V, iii, 92)

CLASSICALLY SPEAKING   **NEUTRAL AMERICAN /θ, ð/**

Fricative Continuants

/ ʃ / (ru<u>sh</u>) / ʒ / (rou<u>ge</u>)

Form /ʃ/ and /ʒ/ by raising the blade of the tongue up toward the back of the gum ridge, anchoring the sides of the tongue against the insides of the upper molars, and releasing air over the tongue blade and through the mouth.

The tongue is pulled slightly further back in the mouth than for /s/ and /z/, and the blade is involved rather than the tip, which makes the groove of the tongue wider for /ʃ/ and /ʒ/. Lip rounding is unnecessary.

AUDIO 43▶ /ʃ/ (ru<u>sh</u>) and /ʒ/ (rou<u>ge</u>)

>   ʃ   ʒ
> Leave <u>sh</u>all you have to court her at your plea<u>s</u>ure.
>
>   (The Taming of the Shrew: I, i, 54)
>
>   ʃ
> He was not born to <u>sh</u>ame:
>   ʃ   ʃ
> Upon his brow <u>sh</u>ame is a<u>sh</u>am'd to sit.
>
>   (Romeo and Juliet: III, ii, 91)
>
>   ʃ
> But why speak you in this strange halting fa<u>sh</u>ion?
>   ʃ   ʃ
> Has your wit grown <u>sh</u>ort of breath? or pa<u>ss</u>ion?
>
>   (Rostand: Cyrano de Bergerac)

WORDS /ʃ/ (ru<u>sh</u>) and /ʒ/ (rou<u>ge</u>)

	Initial	Medial	Final
/ʃ/	shun	special	dish
	shop	passion	bash
	shine	anxious	mesh
	sheep	wishing	relish
	shame	machine	marsh

	Initial[1].	Medial	Final
/ʒ/	*	usual	loge
	*	Asian	rouge
	*	lesion	garage
	*	vision	prestige
	*	measure	massage

PHRASES /ʃ/ and /ʒ/

1.	shiny beige shift	6.	unconscious wish
2.	precious freshness	7.	Russian vacations
3.	ensures succession	8.	treasured pleasures
4.	rushes to conclusions	9.	occasionally shaky
5.	spacious shoe shelves	10.	diminished seizures

SENTENCES /ʃ/ and /ʒ/

1. Shrill shrieks shocked the gendarmes.

2. Who's the most gracious shellfish chef?

3. We occasionally treasure hunt in Persia.

4. She envisions planting unusual rosebushes.

5. Sheila unleashed her vicious dog on Frazier.

6. Sharon expressed her displeasure in the garage.

7. The camouflaged espionage team remains cautious.

8. Gigi is on vacation, so her fashionable shoe shop is closed.

A little lip-rounding on these sounds is fine. But, many people use excessive lip-rounding to overcompensate for inaccurate alignment and coordination of the tongue and breath release on /ʃ/ and /ʒ/.

SOUND CHECK #1: same consonant blends / ʃ ʃ / and / ʒ ʒ /. When the same consonant sound ends one word and also begins the next word, very well-pronounced characters can use a slight rhythmic pulse of breath and energy to connect them, while maintaining the shape and contact of the articulators.

---

[1] 'Have' /hæv/ is usually pronounced /hæf/ before an infinitive: 'I have to see'.

1.	dish shop	6.	flesh shook
2.	wish shyly	7.	wash shoes
3.	posh shawls	8.	harsh shouts
4.	push sharply	9.	massage **Zs**a Zsa
5.	fresh showers	10.	camouflage gendarmes

NEUTRAL AMERICAN TEXT /ʃ/ (ru**sh**), /ʒ/ (rou**ge**). *Mark the following and speak out loud.*

ʃ   ʃ
S̲hallow, s̲hallow.

(As You Like It: III, ii, 57)

Have leave and leisure to make love to her.

(The Taming of the Shrew: I, ii, 136)

Petruchio, shall I then come roundly to thee,
And wish thee to a shrewd ill-favor'd wife?

(The Taming of the Shrew: I, ii, 59)

You owe me no subscription. Then let fall
Your horrible pleasure.

(King Lear: III, ii, 18)

There's but three furies found in spacious hell,
But in a great man's breast three thousand dwell.

(Webster: The White Devil)

First, mighty liege, tell my your Highness' pleasure.

(Richard III: IV, iv, 447)

Urge neither charity nor shame to me.
Uncharitably with me have you dealt,
And shamefully my hopes, by you, are butcher'd.
My charity is outrage, life my shame,
And in that shame still live my sorrow's rage!

(Richard III: I, iii, 273)

GLO'STER. She should have stay'd in France, and starv'd in France,
     Before—
CARDINAL.   My Lord of Gloucester, now ye grow too hot:
     It was the pleasure of my lord the King.

(2 Henry VI: I, i, 136)

Fricative Continuant

/ h / (h<u>e</u>)

Form **/h/** by releasing air through the glottis, or space between the vocal folds, through a relaxed throat, and out the mouth.

AUDIO 44▶ **/h/** (h<u>e</u>)

> But <u>h</u>e! why, <u>h</u>e <u>h</u>ath a <u>h</u>orse better than the Neapolitan's.
> $\qquad$ (The Merchant of Venice: I, ii, 58)
>
> I wonder at this <u>h</u>aste, that I must wed
> Ere <u>h</u>e that should be <u>h</u>usband comes to woo.
> $\qquad$ (Romeo and Juliet: III, v, 118)
>
> <u>H</u>old, take my sword. There's <u>h</u>usbandry in <u>h</u>eaven.
> $\qquad$ (Macbeth: II, i, 4)

WORDS /h/ (h<u>e</u>)

Initial	Medial	Final
he	ahoy	*
how	yahoo	*
who	inherit	*
heave	behind	*
whore	inhabit	*

Several common words contain **/hju/** sounds including <u>hu</u>man, <u>hu</u>mid, <u>hu</u>miliation, <u>hu</u>mor, <u>hu</u>ge. Do not drop the **/h/** from these words in Neutral American. There are also a few words with 'h' in the spelling that have no **/h/** in American pronunciation, for example: herb, heiress and honor.

PHRASES /h/ (h<u>e</u>)

1.	<u>h</u>appy <u>h</u>oliday		6.	<u>h</u>as <u>h</u>igh <u>h</u>opes
2.	<u>h</u>alf way <u>h</u>ome		7.	<u>h</u>and <u>h</u>eld <u>h</u>ammer
3.	<u>h</u>ardly <u>h</u>abitual		8.	<u>h</u>ypothermic Henry
4.	<u>wh</u>olly <u>h</u>elpless		9.	<u>h</u>ow <u>h</u>ot and <u>h</u>umid
5.	<u>h</u>ospitalized <u>h</u>ere		10.	<u>h</u>armonious and <u>h</u>oly

SENTENCES /h/ (h̲e̲)

1. Holly is happiest when rehearsing.

2. Henry is humorless when it's humid.

3. The humanitarian hails from Houston.

4. Hurry up. Hospitalize him for hypothermia.

5. Have you heard if the hurricane is headed here?

NEUTRAL AMERICAN TEXT /h/ (h̲e̲). *Mark the following and speak out loud.*

H̲e comes to you so h̲elplessly, accusing h̲imself and confessing
h̲is own weakness.

(Ibsen: Ghosts)

Because he hath a half-face like my father!
With half that face would he have all my land—
A half-fac'd groat five hundred pound a year!

(King John: I, i, 92)

Hast thou, according to thy oath and band,
Brought hither Henry Herford thy bold son,
Here to make good the boist'rous late appeal,
Which then our leisure would not let us hear?

(Richard II: I, i, 2)

Go, horse these traitors on your fiery backs,
And mount aloft with them as high as heaven;
Thence pitch them headlong to the lowest hell.

(Marlowe: Doctor Faustus)

SALISBURY. What other harm have I, good lady, done,
But spoke the harm that is by others done?
CONSTANCE. Which harm within itself so heinous is
As it makes harmful all that speak of it.

(King John: III, i, 38)

MARIA. Sir, I have not you by th' hand.
AGUECHEEK. Marry, but you shall have—and here's my hand.

(Twelfth Night: I, iii, 65)

Fricative Continuants

/ s / (<u>s</u>ue)   / z / (<u>z</u>oo)

To form the fricative continuants /s/ and /z/:

the jaw   should be relaxed closed, the teeth almost touching

the tongue tip   points toward the gum ridge without actually touching
   the sides press against the inner edges of the upper teeth, and
   the back is raised

the lips   remain un-rounded, except when combined with other sounds
   that require lip rounding

A stream of air is then released down the thin groove in the tongue, over the tongue tip, and through the mouth. The sound /s/ (or /z/, if voiced) is formed as air passes between the enlivened tip of the tongue and the front of the upper gum ridge.

It is also possible to speak /s/ and /z/ with the tip of the tongue resting down behind the lower teeth. This will sometimes produce an overly thick or lisping sound, however, and can interfere with clear pronunciation of consonant combinations.

AUDIO 45▶ **/s/ and /z/**

        s   str   z   z   z
Courteou<u>s</u> de<u>str</u>oyer<u>s</u>, affable wolve<u>s</u>, meek bear<u>s</u>.

(Timon of Athens: III, vi, 95)

           sts
Unbidden gue<u>sts</u>
             st
Are often welcome<u>st</u> when they are gone.

(1 Henry VI: II, ii, 55)

           st   siz
My hair doth <u>st</u>and on end to hear her cur<u>ses</u>.

(Richard III: I, iii, 303)

If an actor is not articulating clearly using his/her current positioning on /s/ and /z/, a change might be beneficial. A coordinated effort is required for /s/ and /z/, and any deviation can result in a distortion, from a lisp to a whistle.

Some common deviations result from:

(a)   the tongue tip slipping forward onto or between the teeth

(b)   overly tensing the tongue or pulling the tongue too far back

(c)   allowing air to escape over the sides of the tongue rather than sealing the sides and releasing air over the tongue tip

(d)   opening the jaw too much or too little

(e)   rounding the lips while allowing the tongue tip to drop

(f)   over-extending the duration of the final 's'

All in all, /s/ and /z/ can be very tricky to correct or fine tune. If one has difficulties, it is best to work with an experienced speech teacher or speech pathologist.

Of the 49 sounds in well-spoken Neutral American, only 12 require some lip rounding. These include:

/u/ (wh<u>o</u>)   /ʊ/ (w<u>ou</u>ld)   /o/ (<u>o</u>'mit)   /ɔ/ (<u>a</u>ll)   /ɔɪ̆/ (b<u>oy</u>)   /oʊ̆/ (g<u>o</u>)

/aʊ̆/ (n<u>ow</u>)   /ʊɚ̆/ (p<u>oor</u>)   /ɔɚ̆/ (sp<u>or</u>ts)   /aʊ̆ɚ̆/ (p<u>ower</u>)

The consonant sound /w/ (<u>we</u>) and, to some extent, /r/ (<u>r</u>ed), also round before releasing into the vowel sound that follows. Some people round the lips on the long and short vowels /ɝ/ (<u>ER</u>) and /ə/ (<u>er</u>), but these are mid-vowels and lip rounding is not required.

It is also unnecessary to round on the six sibilant (hissing) sounds listed below, though many people do. Over-rounding of the lips can cause these sounds to be more sibilant, intrusive, and difficult to record than necessary.

/s/ (<u>s</u>ue)   /z/ (<u>z</u>oo)

/ʃ/ (<u>sh</u>e)   /ʒ/ (mea<u>s</u>ure)

/t͜ʃ/ (<u>ch</u>ur<u>ch</u>)   /dʒ/ (<u>j</u>u<u>dge</u>)

Try feeling the effect of rounded lips on the six sibilant sounds listed above, and on the amount and direction of breath released, by speaking them first with, and then without, lip rounding.

WORDS /s/ and /z/ with other sounds not requiring lip rounding

No whistle!
Put ath. to the vowel

	Initial	Medial	Final
/s/	see	lesser	nice
	sack	inside	niece
	save	lasting	chase
	same	leasing	rocks
	sense	enticing	checks
/z/	zap	isn't	his
	zeal	hazy	glaze
	zinc	dizzy	please
	zany	diseased	figures
	zither	wheezing	despise

SOUND CHECK #1: tongue tip placement for /s, z/. Feel the tongue tip contact the gum ridge on /n, d, t, l/ in the consonant combinations that follow. Then release the tip from touching the ridge, ever so slightly, so it is pointing toward the upper gum ridge for the /s/ or /z/ that comes immediately after.

Pay special attention to the presence of an enlivened stream of breath originating from the middle of the torso and releasing over the tongue tip when speaking /s/ or /z/. *Read across.*

t,s	t,s	t,s	t,s	heats, hits, hats
dz	dz	dz	dz	heeds, kids, dads
ns	ns	ns	ns	tense, dunce, lance
nz	nz	nz	nz	means, lens, dean's
ndz	ndz	ndz	ndz	fiends, hands, lends
ls	ls	ls	ls	else, pulse, impulse
lz	lz	lz	lz	heels, bells, mills

Correct tip-of-the-tongue placement on /n, d, t, l/ is crucial for correct placement on /s, z/ in the following exercises, so warm up with tip-of-the-tongue exercises on pages 208-218 before continuing any further with /s, z/.

Make a complete stop which can be rhythmically noticed, and feel the tongue tip contact the upper gum ridge for final /t/ or /d/ of the first word. Then, release a tiny stream of air over the tongue tip for the /s/ that immediately follows. Correct positioning on the 'stop' will help set up the tongue tip for correct positioning on the /s/.

PHRASES final /t̗/ into initial /s/

hot̗ seat	can't̗ see	cut̗ silk	get̗ Sam
paint̗ sign	can't̗ save	hot̗ sand	light̗ side
heat̗ some	cat̗ sitting	not̗ signed	not̗ sunny

The following 'tasty' exercise increases tip-of-the-tongue strength and awareness:

Hold a dime-sized paper mint up against the gum ridge just behind the upper teeth with the tip of the tongue. Maintain the tip-of-the-tongue position (even when swallowing) until the mint has dissolved – and enjoy!

PHRASES tip-of-the-tongue placement and awareness

1. heat̗ so hot̗
2. hat̗ sent to him
3. cat̗ sitting there
4. neat̗ stuff to buy
5. hat̗ someone forgot

6. hot̗ soda
7. hot̗ savage sun
8. can't̗ stand still
9. hot̗ summer's day
10. can't̗ stay for dinner

The following exercises continue to develop awareness of correct tip-of-the-tongue placement for /s/ and /z/, by working off the tip-of-the-tongue positioning for consonants: /n, d, t, l/.

Give the 'tippity tip' of the tongue an occasional 'pinch' to increase awareness of the tongue tip when practicing.

PHRASES final /t̗/ into initial /st^h/

hat̗ stand	did sting	did stay	led stunt
hut̗ stunk	lid̗ stuck	dead stop	had steak
hot̗ steam	cat̗ stopped	neat̗ stuff	bad station

PHRASES tip-of-the-tongue placement and awareness

1.	hat₁ stayed still	6.	lid still stuck
2.	made Stacy stay	7.	had stuff stuffed
3.	band still standing	8.	did sting Stanley
4.	hot₁ steaming steam	9.	bad stock statements
5.	debt₁ stays stationary	10.	bet₁ stagehand stayed

PHRASES tip-of-the-tongue placement and awareness

had zinc	hid zeal	need Zen	mad zap
bad zipper	need zing	feed zealots	sad Zane
dead zebra	did zigzag	spied zenith	paid zilch
ten seats	can see	mean zit	fun still
tan zebra	fan sitting	man says	non-stick
tin zipper	nine sides	mean sun	pin some
yell zinc!	he'll sell	file says	bill Sam
feel sorry	tell zealots	dull stuff	fill seats
till Sunday	deal zapped	mail Sandy	chill some

SOUND CHECK #2: side edges of the tongue—placement and awareness. The sides of the tongue can press or anchor against the inner edges of the upper teeth, offering stability when forming /s/ and /z/. This pressing can often be felt more acutely when forming 'sh' /ʃ/ and 'ch' /t,ʃ/. Therefore, the following exercise compares /ʃ/ /t,ʃ/ and /s/ words to help identify the pressing feeling.

Speak the first two words in the row below with an awareness of the positioning and feeling of the side edges of the tongue. Try to maintain some contact of the sides of the tongue with the inside of the upper teeth during the initial /s/ of the third word in the row. The tongue may flatten and move slightly forward as air shoots out over the tip on 's'. *Read across.*

/ʃ/	/t,ʃ/	/s/		/ʃ/	/t,ʃ/	/s/
shin	chin	sin		shine	china	sign
shill	chill	sill		ship	chip	sip
shy	chai	sigh		Shea	change	say
Shane	chain	sane		sheep	cheap	seep

SENTENCES side edges of the tongue placement and awareness

1.	Shine china signs.	6.	Shift Chuck's status.
2.	Shake cheap stilts.	7.	Shake chicken soup.
3.	She'll change seats.	8.	Shane, change seats.
4.	Ship chipped statues.	9.	Share Chan's sneaks.
5.	Shock Chuck on stage.	10.	Shun cheese Sunday.

> **SOUND CHECK #3:. back of tongue placement and awareness.** The back of the tongue should be raised toward the soft palate when forming **/s/** and **/z/**. When speaking **/g/** and **/k/**, the back of the tongue raises to touch the front of the soft palate. Therefore, back of tongue awareness when speaking **/g/** and **/k/** may help the speaker's awareness of back of tongue positioning on **/s/** and **/z/**.

Raise the back of the tongue to touch the soft palate on final **/g/** and **/k/** of the first word of the pair, below. Keep the back of the tongue raised toward the soft palate while positioning the tip for initial **/s/** that begins the second word of the pair. *Read down the columns.*

Column 1	Column 2	Column 3
pack, some	pick, some	big state
pack, steak	pick, Steve	big stake
pack, steel	pick, sage	big stain
pack, snakes	pick, season	big stein
pack, staples	pick, Simon	big snap
pack, samples	pick, singer	big sneak

SENTENCES back of the tongue placement and awareness

1.	Pick, Stan.	6.	Hug Stan.
2.	Pick, Stacey.	7.	Hug Stacey.
3.	Pick, Steven.	8.	Hug Steven.
4.	Pick, starlets.	9.	Hug starlets.
5.	Pick, somebody.	10.	Hug somebody.

> **SOUND CHECK #4: /s, z/ in combination with sounds that require lip rounding.** Round only for the sounds that require it, and do not allow this rounding to draw the tongue tip forward onto the teeth on **/s/** and **/z/**.

	Initial	Medial	Final
/s/	sue	assume	juice
	soil	forcing	horse
	soap	assorted	sauce
	sawing	roasting	across
	soothe	resource	choice
/z/	zoo	frozen	rose
	zone	noises	doze
	zoom	pauses	pews
	zodiac	abused	poise
	zounds	choosing	views

PHRASES /s, z/ with rounded vowels

1.	Zorro's horses	6.	Zodiac zone
2.	soothing snoring	7.	zucchini soup
3.	roasted soy sauce	8.	owns used suits
4.	soaring forcefully	9.	confused closing
5.	Susan's sore voice	10.	zooms through zoos

WORD PAIRS unrounded/rounded vowels *Read across.*

see	sue	seep	soup	sit	soot
zebra	zoo	zip	zone	say	soy
sigh	saw	sick	soak	sire	sore

PHRASES /s, z/ with unrounded and rounded vowels

1.	sitting in soot	6.	soiled snails
2.	sawing outside	7.	so, so sea sick
3.	snoring sleeper	8.	soon to see him
4.	seen with Susan	9.	storks stay soaked
5.	saving soy sauce	10.	store forks at Stella's

Softly, silently, the scythe
Slithered through the thick sweet sward;
Seething, sweating, sad serfs writhe,
Slicing swaths so straight and broad.

(Anonymous)

SOUND CHECK #5: consonant combinations and clusters (three back-to-back consonants) beginning with /s/. Pronounce all of the sounds listed.
Note: /str/ instruction and practice appears on pages 297-299 with /r/.

/sf/	/sk^h/	/sl/	/sm/
sphinx	scold	sled	smug
sphere	skimp	slime	smile
sphincter	scamp	slope	smooth

/sn/	/sp^h/	/st^h/	/sw/
snuff	spat	stay	sway
snows	speed	stoke	sweat
snakes	spool	stoned	swoon

/sp₁r/	/st₁r/	/sk₁r/	/sk₁w/
sprain	street	scraps	squid
spring	strive	scrawl	squall
spruce	strokes	scream	squire

PHRASES consonant combinations with initial /s/

1. snaking streets
2. sneak previews
3. strategic squeeze
4. slanderous scandal
5. spoonful of sweets
6. smug speakers
7. six suave swindlers
8. inexplicable spying
9. scrambled switches
10. sleek smelly sneakers

PHRASES initial /st/ (aspirating the 't' depends on what comes after the 't')

1. steamy stairs
2. standing still
3. stainless steel
4. stepping stones
5. stimulating style
6. stiff stitching
7. still stigmatized
8. stammering stars
9. staying in steerage
10. starched stationary

PHRASES initial /sk/ (aspirating the 'k' depends on what comes after the 'k')

1. skipper's skiff
2. skates and skis
3. skillful sketches
4. skin-tight ski masks
5. squashed mosquitoes
6. skidding skiers
7. skinny skinflint
8. sketch skeletons
9. squarely miscast
10. skin care skeptic

PHRASES final /st/ (aspirating the 't' depends on what comes after the 't')

1.	best dressed	6.	held in trust
2.	worst colorist	7.	kindest finalist
3.	deceased ghost	8.	cheeriest contest
4.	lost in Budapest	9.	unsurpassed cast
5.	feminist journalist	10.	outclassed in the past

PHRASES final /sk/ (aspirating the 'k' depends on what comes after the 'k')

1.	risky to ask	6.	a flashy flask
2.	musk bisque	7.	statuesque desk
3.	grotesque mask	8.	masked asterisk
4.	flask in Basque	9.	tusk in a mosque
5.	burlesque at dusk	10.	picturesque kiosk

SOUND CHECK #6: consonant combinations and clusters ending with /s/.
Pronounce all of the sounds listed. Be careful in the following instances.

(a)   When a voiceless stop-plosive is followed directly by another consonant, a definite unaspirated 'stop' is required prior to the second consonant, notated in IPA: **/ k̗s   p̗s   t̗s /**.

(b)   When a voiceless stop-plosive is between two continuants in the same syllable, speak the first consonant, make the definite 'stop' of the second, followed by the last consonant sound, as in: **/ lp̗s   mp̗s   ft̗s   sk̗s   sp̗s   st̗s /**.

/fs/	/k̗s/	/p̗s/	/t̗s/
cuffs	fix	leaps	hats
beefs	packs	ships	fights
whiffs	hawks	soups	shoots

/lfs/	/lp̗s/	/mfs/	/mp̗s/
elf's	gulps	lymph's	lumps
gulfs	scalps	nymphs	skimps
wolfs	whelps	harrumphs	mumps

/ft̗s/	/sk̗s/	/sp̗s/	/st̗s/
lifts	asks	lisps	tests
tufts	husks	gasps	fasts
crafts	whisks	wasps	rusts

WORDS final /skʰ/ and /kˌs/ comparison *Read across.*

/skʰ/	/kˌs/	/skʰ/	/kˌs/
risk	Rick's	Fisk	fix
ask	ax	bask	backs
flask	flax	task	tacks
desk	decks	disk	Dick's
brisk	bricks	dusk	ducks

When speaking /skˌt/ combinations, remember to make a definite 'stop' on the 'k' before continuing on to the 't'. Aspirating the final 't' or not depends on the sound that comes immediately after it.

SENTENCES final /sk/ and /skˌt/ in the words 'ask' / 'asked'

1.	Ask about it.	6.	I asked you.
2.	Don't ask me.	7.	Ask him again.
3.	Ask Mr. Rusk.	8.	Ask me anything.
4.	Ask a question.	9.	What did you ask?
5.	Who asked you?	10.	I've asked you before.

PHRASES final /stˌs/ /spˌs/ /skˌs/ /lfs/ /lpˌs/ /mfs/ /mpˌs/ /ftˌs/

1.	past reque*sts*	6.	takes ri*sks*
2.	li*sps* the least	7.	worst pe*sts*
3.	cla*sps* his fi*sts*	8.	cla*sps* for ma*sks*
4.	he*lps* the ca*sts*	9.	thu*mps* on de*sks*
5.	ski*mps* on cra*fts*	10.	el*f's* loud harru*mphs*

Amidst the mists and coldest frosts,
With stoutest wrists and loudest boasts,
He thrusts his fists against the posts,
And still insists he sees the ghosts.

(Anonymous)

SENTENCES final /stˌs/ /spˌs/ /skˌs/ /lfs/ /lpˌs/ /mfs/ /mpˌs/ /ftˌs/

1. Are egoists realists?

2. Pianists need strong wrists.

3. Will the essayists be missed?

4. Chris resists chips and crisps.

5. *The Duellists* was not to be missed.

6. The book's antagonists slit their wrists.

7. Wasps were seen eating crusts at dusk.

8. Bicyclists, stay to the right of motorists.

9. He asks that you finish your tasks, at last.

10. The scientist insists the cysts pose no risks.

11. The elephant thrusts, then adjusts his tusks.

12. Violinists playing for the vocalists are pacifists.

13. When pissed, the linguist lisps and twists his fists.

14. Perhaps mystics think ghosts float over the coasts.

15. The accompanists pressed their wrinkled costumes.

16. When they flashed, the powder flasks were trashed.

17. He hoists the posts to his chest, but it exhausts him.

18. Priests were distressed by the results of the contests.

19. Guests detest pests performing arabesques on desks.

20. Journalists are at risk of losing their computer disks.

21. The stout anthropologist was stuck amidst the stones.

22. They gasped when the mask's clasps came unclasped.

23. Statistics state stardom can elude even the best actors.

24. When asked, beasts stop in their tracks, or so he attests.

25. Little nymphs and elves gave the accompanists the mumps.

SOUND CHECK #7: same consonant blends /s s/. When the same consonant sound ends one word and also begins the next, very well-pronounced characters can use a slight rhythmic pulse of breath and energy to connect them, while maintaining the shape and contact of the articulators.

PHRASES same consonant blends /s s/

1.	hurts sales	6.	bus station
2.	loose scarf	7.	cents saved
3.	nice students	8.	peace sought
4.	niece singing	9.	this Saturday
5.	sauce spilling	10.	nurse sighing

PHRASES same consonant blends /st, st/

1.	best stage	6.	dust storm
2.	cast stranded	7.	must sting
3.	protest stories	8.	inquest started
4.	worst strategy	9.	decreased stench
5.	best stationary	10.	least stifling state

SOUND CHECK #8: /θ, s/ combinations. Feel the movement of the tip of the tongue from between the teeth on /θ/, up to point toward the gum ridge on /s/.

1.	bath Sunday	6.	both singing
2.	path seekers	7.	wealth secured
3.	Beth staying	8.	stealth security
4.	math solutions	9.	breath spraying
5.	growth stabilized	10.	mouth screaming

SOUND CHECK #9: plural, possessive, third-person /z/ endings. When an 's' is added to the end of a noun making it plural or possessive, or to the end of a third-person singular verb, the 's' is pronounced /z/ when the sound directly preceding it is voiced, as in: dogs, ribs, cows, Phil's, Brad's, Sue's, runs, plays.

/bz/	/dz/	/gz/	/lz/
curbs	lads	kegs	piles
babes	buds	bags	Bill's
Rob's	Jude's	Meg's	pencils

/mz/	/nz/	/vz/	/dʒɪz/
teams	fins	caves	cages
dimes	pines	leaves	ridges
Kim's	Ken's	Dave's	judge's

Since vowels, diphthongs and triphthongs are <u>voiced</u>:

bees	furs	laws	rows
eyes	brother's	Fay's	Roy's
fleas	Martha's	glues	dramas

PHRASES voiced /z/ endings

1. Hazel's things
2. bathes squirrels
3. loves bold films
4. the wolves' howls
5. eggs with cheeses
6. Paul's pizzas
7. has ten tables
8. those zany cousins
9. thousands of grizzlies
10. appetizing vegetables

SOUND CHECK #10: When a word ends in /s, z, t∫, *or* dʒ/ and 'es' is added to make the word plural or possessive, a separate syllable ending in /ɪz/ is formed. For example: 'batch' becomes 'batches' and 'quiz' becomes 'quizzes'.

PHRASES voiced /ɪz/ endings   /ɪz/

1. urges marches
2. races to places
3. Marge's revenges
4. fizzes and whizzes
5. pitches and catches
6. Liz's curses
7. poses with roses
8. bunches of riches
9. presses and passes
10. smudges on judges

Three little ghostesses,
Sitting on postesses,
Eating buttered toastesses,
Greasing their fistesses,
Up to their wristesses.
Oh, what beastesses
To make such feastesses!

(Mother Goose: Three Ghostesses)

See also THE TIDE RISES, THE TIDE FALLS by Henry Wadsworth Longfellow, page 318, for additional practice text with voiced /z/ endings.

SOUND CHECK #11: /ð, z/ combinations. Feel the tip of the tongue moving from the position for forming /ð/, with the flattened tip of the tongue between the teeth, to /z/, with the tip of the tongue pointing up toward the gum ridge.

1.	bathes	6.	soothe **Z**oe
2.	teethes	7.	breathe **Z**en
3.	sheathes	8.	loathes zoos
4.	loathe zinc	9.	mouths zilch
5.	sunbathe zestfully	10.	bathe zombies

SOUND CHECK #12: same consonant blends /z z/. When the same consonant sound ends one word and also begins the next, very well-pronounced characters can use a slight rhythmic pulse of breath and energy to connect them, while maintaining the shape and contact of the articulators.

1.	his zebra	6.	is zany
2.	raise Zoe	7.	has zero
3.	praise Zen	8.	ooze zeal
4.	people's zoo	9.	his xylophone
5.	curses Czars	10.	loves zucchini

NEUTRAL AMERICAN TEXT /s/ (sue) and /z/ (zoo). *Mark the following and speak out loud.*

voiced /z/ endings and consonant combinations:

> Ay, in the catalogue ye go for men,
> As hounds and greyhounds, mongrels, spaniels, curs,
> Shoughs, water-rugs, and demi-wolves are clept
> All by the name of dogs.
>
> (Macbeth: III, i, 91)

> Hath not a Jew eyes? Hath not a Jew hands, organs, dimensions, senses, affections, passions...
>
> (The Merchant of Venice: III, i, 59)

> NORTHUMBERLAND. Think not that Henry shall be so depos'd.
> WARWICK.　　　　Depos'd he shall be, in despite of all.
>
> (3 Henry VI: I, i, 153)

voiceless /s/ consonant combinations:

> Skipper, stand back.
>
> (The Taming of the Shrew: II, i, 339)

> Let the offender stand forth.
>
> (Tourneur: The Revenger's Tragedy)

O Cassius, I am sick of many griefs.

(Julius Caesar: IV, iii, 144)

O, 'twas the foulest deed to slay that babe.

(Richard III: I, iii, 182)

Thou toldst me thou didst hold him in thy hate.

(Othello: I, i, 6)

Recounts most horrid sights seen by the watch.

(Julius Caesar: II, ii, 16)

Be bright and jovial among your guests to-night.

(Macbeth: III, ii, 28)

What says my sweet queen, my very very sweet queen?

(Troilus and Cressida: III, i, 80)

Ask for me to-morrow, and you shall find me a grave man.

(Romeo and Juliet: III, i, 97)

At the dance tonight, she snapped the gamekeeper away from
Anna—no waiting to be asked.

(Strindberg: Miss Julie)

And he requires your haste-post-haste appearance,
Even on the instant.

(Othello: I, ii, 37)

Madam, the guests are come, supper serv'd up, you call'd, my
young lady ask'd for.

(Romeo and Juliet: I, iii, 100)

My lips, two blushing pilgrims, ready stand
To smooth that rough touch with a tender kiss.

(Romeo and Juliet: I, v, 95)

I am not sick, if Brutus have in hand
Any exploit worthy the name of honor.

(Julius Caesar: II, i, 316)

Strike as thou didst at Caesar; for I know,
When thou didst hate him worst, thou lovedst him better
Than ever thou lovedst Cassius.

(Julius Caesar: IV, iii, 105)

They are as sick that surfeit with too much as they that starve
with nothing.

(The Merchant of Venice: I, ii, 5)

O, it came o'er my ear like the sweet sound
That breathes upon a bank of violets,
Stealing and giving odor.

(Twelfth Night: I, i, 5)

Oh mighty Caesar! dost thou lie so low?
Are all thy conquests, glories, triumphs, spoils,
Shrunk to this little measure? Fare thee well!

(Julius Caesar: III, i, 148)

Doubly divorc'd! Bad men, you violate
A twofold marriage—'twixt my crown and me,
And then betwixt me and my married wife.—
Let me unkiss the oath 'twixt thee and me;
And yet not so, for with a kiss 'twas made.

(Richard II: V, i, 71)

VITTORIA. O, ye dissembling men!
FLAMINEO.   We sucked that, sister,
       From women's breasts, in our first infancy.

(Webster: The White Devil)

Rebellious subjects, enemies to peace,
Profaners of this neighbor-stainéd steel—
Will they not hear?— What ho, you men, you beasts!
That quench the fire of your pernicious rage
With purple fountains issuing from your veins—
On pain of torture, from those bloody hands
Throw your mistempered weapons to the ground.

(Romeo and Juliet: I, i, 81)

Thou orb aloft full-dazzling! thou hot October noon!
Flooding with sheeny light the gray beach sand,
The sibilant near sea with vistas far and foam,
And tawny streaks and shades and spreading blue;
O sun of noon refulgent! my special word to thee.

(Walt Whitman: Thou Orb Aloft Full-Dazzling)

AFFRICATES

See Overview pages 13-17

There is only one affricate cognate pair, which consists of a stop-plosive and fricative sound seamlessly blended to sound as one.

/ t͜ʃ / (ri<u>ch</u>)   / dʒ / (ri<u>dge</u>)

Form voiceless /t͜ʃ/ by putting the tongue tip against the upper gum ridge, making firm contact for the initial stop element /t/, then quickly releasing into /ʃ/. No lip rounding is necessary.

Form voiced /dʒ/ by putting the tongue tip against the upper gum ridge, making firm contact for the initial stop element /d/, then quickly releasing into the /ʒ/ sound. No lip rounding is necessary.

AUDIO 46▶ /t͜ʃ/ (ri<u>ch</u>) /dʒ/ (ri<u>dge</u>)

                         t͜ʃ
The air hath starv'd the roses in her <u>ch</u>eeks,
     t͜ʃt   t͜ʃ
And pin<u>ch</u>'d the lily-tin<u>ct</u>ure of her face.
                 (The Two Gentlemen of Verona: IV, iv, 154)

                            dʒ
Bravo! Now my boot, kiss it — and pay me homa<u>ge</u>!
                         (Strindberg: Miss Julie)

        t͜ʃ
Tremble, thou wre<u>tch</u>
                dʒ
That hast within thee undivulged[1] crimes
     dʒ
Unwhipt of <u>j</u>ustice!

                                 (King Lear: III, ii, 51)

---

1 The word 'undivulged' may be pronounced with four syllables, especially if written: undivulgéd.

WORDS /t͡ʃ/ (ri<u>ch</u>) /dʒ/ (ri<u>dge</u>)

	Initial	Medial	Final
/t͡ʃ/	chin	inched	rich
	cheap	ratchet	patch
	chimes	culture	hutch
	chance	watching	coach
	chapter	miniature	bunch

	Initial	Medial	Final
/dʒ/	gym	rejoice	rage
	Jack	bridged	edge
	joke	merging	lodge
	joint	graduated	judge
	juggle	degenerate	visage

PHRASES /t͡ʃ/ and /dʒ/

1. whi<u>ch</u> <u>ch</u>eap wat<u>ch</u>
2. <u>j</u>agged e<u>dge</u>d gor<u>ge</u>
3. ri<u>ch</u> <u>ch</u>ocolate <u>ch</u>ips
4. <u>ch</u>unky <u>ch</u>erry fu<u>dge</u>
5. <u>ch</u>ecking ea<u>ch</u> ba<u>dge</u>
6. ma<u>t</u>ure fea<u>t</u>ures
7. gigantic <u>ch</u>ickens
8. <u>ch</u>ecking messages
9. dis<u>ch</u>ar<u>g</u>ing <u>G</u>eor<u>ge</u>
10. stran<u>ge</u> <u>J</u>une journey

SENTENCES /t͡ʃ/ (ri<u>ch</u>) /dʒ/ (ri<u>dge</u>)

1. Chet sketched with chalk.

2. That's wretched cheesecake.

3. Marge chose to change agents.

4. What strange and tempestuous weather.

5. The roads merge after the bridge, Jason.

6. The judge convicted Jonathan of perjury.

7. Jill switched her jury duty to July from June.

8. If I stay on a rigid budget maybe I'll become rich.

9. Which chapter challenges your imagination, Jackie?

10. Our coach has us jumping rope. We actually enjoy it.

SOUND CHECK #1: tip-of-the-tongue placement on /t t͡ʃ/ and /d d͡ʒ/. The tongue tip contacts the gum ridge when initiating these sounds. *Read across.*

tin	chin	din	gin
Tad	Chad	dad	Jack
tug	chug	dug	jug
two	chew	dew	juice
talk	chalk	dawn	Jaw

SOUND CHECK #2: connecting final stop-plosives and initial affricates. Stop the final plosive of the first word completely, before initiating the second.

	/t͵ t͵ʃ/		/d d͡ʒ/
1.	hat͵ check	6.	bad jump
2.	cut͵ cheese	7.	fired John
3.	not͵ chosen	8.	plaid jersey
4.	what͵ children	9.	glad journey
5.	great͵ chocolate	10.	read journals

SOUND CHECK #3: voiced /d͡ʒ/ endings. Maintain vocal fold vibration through the end of the last word without adding an off-glide, or /ə/ (uh) sound.

1.	no ju__dge__	6.	over indu__lge__
2.	great on sta__ge__	7.	off the bri__dge__
3.	had him pa__ged__	8.	need for reve__nge__
4.	became enra__ged__	9.	everything cha__nged__
5.	shouldn't be ca__ged__	10.	must not be divu__lged__

SOUND CHECK #4: same consonant blends /t͡ʃ t͡ʃ/ and /d͡ʒ d͡ʒ/. When the same consonant sound ends one word and also begins the word that follows, a slight rhythmic pulse of breath (and energy) is used to connect them. The articulators do move slightly within the formation of these sound combinations.

1.	pat**ch ch**airs	6.	hu**ge j**ump
2.	rea**ch Ch**ina	7.	Jud**ge J**ason
3.	sear**ch Ch**uck	8.	lar**ge j**ackets
4.	mu**ch ch**eering	9.	bar**ge j**unked
5.	whi**ch ch**ocolates	10.	stran**ge g**erms

NEUTRAL AMERICAN TEXT /tʃ/ (ri<u>ch</u>) /dʒ/ (ri<u>dge</u>). *Mark the following and speak out loud.*

voiced /dʒ/ endings:

dʒ

What is your parenta<u>ge</u>?

(Twelfth Night: I, v, 277)

The King is in high rage.

(King Lear: II, iv, 296)

You're like to have a swift and pleasant passage.

(Middleton & Rowley: The Changeling)

Gentle Lucetta, fit me with such weeds
As may beseem some well-reputed page.

(The Two Gentlemen of Verona: II, vii, 42)

Oh! So simple, really, how I managed!
I continued where I saw the country ravaged,
Torn, with horrors—ah! such wasteful siege!
Messieurs, if this be service to your liege,
I believe a woman could do better!

(Rostand: Cyrano de Bergerac)

/tʃ/ and /dʒ/ in various positions

No, no, they do but jest, poison in jest.

(Hamlet: III, ii, 234)

O me, the word choose! I may neither choose who I would, nor refuse who I dislike.

(The Merchant of Venice: I, ii, 22)

Then take him up, and manage well the jest.
Carry him gently to my fairest chamber,
And hang it round with all my wanton pictures.

(The Taming of the Shrew: Ind. i, 45)

ELEANOR.   Come to thy grandame, child.
CONSTANCE. Do, child, go to it grandame, child,
             Give grandame kingdom, and it grandame will
             Give it a plum, a cherry, and a fig.

(King John: II, i, 159)

GLIDES

See Overview pages 13-17

There are three voiced 'glide' sounds in Neutral American Speech, none of which have voiceless partners:

/ w / (we)   / j / (you)   / r / (red)

Glides all begin by forming the shape for a vowel sound, but rather than holding that shape and producing the vowel sound, the articulators are released from this shape and flow or 'glide' into the vowel sound that always follows. The three glides do not fit neatly into the definition of consonants, and are sometimes referred to as 'semi-vowels'.

/ w / (we)

Form /w/ by resting the tip of the tongue down behind the lower teeth and rounding the lips, as if speaking the back vowel /u/ (who). While voicing sound, immediately release this shape into the vowel sound that always comes after, or /u/ might be spoken instead of /w/.

AUDIO 47▶ /w/ (we)

And in a word, but even now worth this,
And now worth nothing?

(The Merchant of Venice: I, i, 35)

A will! A wicked will,
A woman's will, a cank'red grandam's will!

(King John: II, i, 193)

Why should I war without the walls of Troy,
That find such cruel battle here within?

(Troilus and Cressida: I, i, 2)

WORDS /w/ (<u>w</u>e)

Initial	Medial	Final
we	away	*
went	equal	*
wild	bewail	*
watch	rewind	*
wonder	language	*

PHRASES /w/ (<u>w</u>e)

1. <u>w</u>ire s<u>w</u>ing set
2. <u>w</u>ild <u>w</u>ilderness
3. <u>w</u>orse and <u>w</u>orse
4. <u>w</u>hispering <u>w</u>illows
5. some<u>wh</u>ere s<u>w</u>anky
6. <u>wh</u>at questions
7. <u>w</u>ell, <u>w</u>ell, <u>w</u>ell
8. <u>w</u>orsening <u>w</u>eather
9. <u>w</u>hen <u>W</u>illiam s<u>w</u>ore
10. s<u>w</u>eaty ac<u>qu</u>aintances

SENTENCES /w/ (<u>w</u>e)

1. Why not wear it?

2. Twyla is always misquoted.

3. Which one do you want, Wanda?

4. Wow, you're wearing a Swiss watch.

5. We love winter walks in white snow.

6. Do squirrels squeak or are they quiet?

7. William was sworn in, then questioned.

8. Will you water the flowers on Wednesday?

9. Wacky Wendell wants whiskey with wine.

10. I'm not sure whether the weather will worsen or not.

The voiceless partner /hw/ is *not* spoken in Neutral American, though it is used in Classical American and, occasionally, in Standard British (RP). It is covered with these dialects.

NEUTRAL AMERICAN TEXT /w/ (we). *Mark the following and speak out loud.*

But will you woo this wild-cat?
(The Taming of the Shrew: I, ii, 196)

If I be waspish, best beware my sting.
(The Taming of the Shrew: II, i, 210)

Why, what wouldst thou do there before I go?
(Richard III: IV, iv, 454)

Some word there was, worser than Tybalt's death.
(Romeo and Juliet: III, ii, 108)

Women, being the weaker vessels, are ever thrust to the wall;
therefore I will push Montague's men from the wall, and thrust
his maids to the wall.
(Romeo and Juliet: I, i, 15)

We were so sorry we couldn't give you a seat in the carriage.
(Ibsen: Hedda Gabler)

DUKE. Why, you are nothing then: neither maid, widow, nor wife?
LUCIO. My lord, she may be a punk; for many of them are neither
maid, widow, nor wife.
(Measure for Measure: V, i, 177)

Read the will, we'll hear it, Antony.
You shall read us the will, Caesar's will.
(Julius Caesar: III, ii, 147)

JULIET. "Romeo is banished"!
There is no end, no limit, measure, bound,
In that word's death, no words can that woe sound.
Where is my father and my mother, nurse?
NURSE. Weeping and wailing over Tybalt's corse.
Will you go to them? I will bring you thither.
JULET. Wash they his wounds with tears? Mine shall be spent,
When theirs are dry, for Romeo's banishment.
(Romeo and Juliet: III, ii, 124)

Glide

/ j / (you)

Form /j/ by beginning in almost the same shape as for the front vowel /i/ (we), with the lower jaw nearly closed, the tip of the tongue down behind the lower teeth, and the front and middle[1] of the tongue arched high and forward toward the hard palate.

Immediately release this shape into the vowel sound that always comes after, or /i/ might be spoken instead of /j/.

AUDIO 48▶ /j/ (you)

    j   j   j
O Cupid, Cupid, Cupid!

                         (Troilus and Cressida: III, i, 111)

    j   j   j   j
Be you his eunuch, and your mute I'll be.

                         (Twelfth Night: I, ii, 62)

                  j
They that have the yellow jaundice think all objects they
           j
look on to be yellow.

                       (Webster: The White Devil)

WORDS /j/ (you)

Initial	Medial	Final
yes	fuse	*
use	cute	*
yell	beyond	*
yawn	opinion	*
yesterday	reunion	*

---

[1] The vowel /i/ (we) requires *front* tongue arching only.

PHRASES /j/ (<u>y</u>ou)

1.	musical revue	6.	yellow onions
2.	yammer at you	7.	miniscule feuds
3.	young and beautiful	8.	yogurt for youth
4.	yelling your excuses	9.	yearly arguments
5.	yearning for Yankees	10.	yoo-hoo, yourself

NEUTRAL AMERICAN TEXT /j/ (<u>y</u>ou). *Mark the following and speak out loud.*

j   j
<u>Y</u>onder comes my master, <u>y</u>our brother.

(As You Like It: I, i, 26)

To yourself; why, she woos you by a figure.

(The Two Gentlemen of Verona: II, i, 148)

Oh you abuse me, you abuse me, you abuse me!

(Webster: The White Devil)

Farewell to you, and you, and you, Voluminus.

(Julius Caesar: V, v, 31)

Yet he's gentle, never school'd and yet learned.

(As You Like It: I, i, 166)

See you yond coign a' th' Capitol, yond cornerstone?

(Coriolanus: V, iv, 1)

Off with his head, and set it on York gates,
So York may overlook the town of York.

(3 Henry VI: I, iv, 179)

"Will you walk a little faster?" said a whiting to a snail,
"There's a porpoise close behind us, and he's treading on my tail.
See how eagerly the lobsters and the turtles all advance!
They are waiting on the shingle—will you come and join the dance?
Will you, won't you, will you, won't you, will you join the dance?
Will you, won't you, will you, won't you, won't you join the dance?"

(Lewis Carroll: Alice in Wonderland)

Glide

/ r / (<u>r</u>ed)

Form /r/ by relaxing the jaw half open, arching the middle of the tongue high near the hard palate, and pointing the tip of the tongue up behind the alveolar ridge. While voicing sound, immediately release this shape into the vowel sound that always comes after, dropping the tongue tip down behind the lower teeth.

The back of the tongue and throat remain relaxed throughout, or /ɝ/ (ER) may be spoken instead of /r/. More or less lip rounding is involved, depending on the shape of the vowel sound that follows. Compare: '<u>r</u>ed' to '<u>r</u>oom'.

Some friction is involved during the production of consonant /r/ (<u>r</u>ed), which is why it can be classified as both a glide *and* a fricative sound.

AUDIO 49 A▶ /r/ (<u>r</u>ed)

I <u>pr</u>ay come and <u>cr</u>ush a cup of wine.

(Romeo and Juliet: I, ii, 80)

Sir, spare your <u>thr</u>eats.
The bug which you would <u>fr</u>ight me with, I seek.

(The The Winter's Tale: III, ii, 91)

I will here <u>shr</u>oud till the <u>dr</u>egs of the storm be past.

(The Tempest: II, ii, 40)

WORDS /r/ (<u>r</u>ed)

Initial	Medial	Final
red	bereft	*
raft	erased	*
rust	drafted	*
rival	derelict	*
rescue	strained	*

PHRASES consonant /r/

1.	racing Ryan	6.	raging roosters
2.	rough and ready	7.	removing risks
3.	ruffles and ridges	8.	wrinkled rabbits
4.	rowdy roughhousing	9.	ridiculous reasons
5.	reasonable restaurant	10.	really, really right

Consonant and vowel sounds spelled with 'r'. An 'r' in the spelling of a word can represent a vowel *or* a consonant. If you are uncertain which is which, look at the sound that comes *after* the 'r', and remember the following:

A vowel spelled with 'r' is always followed by a consonant sound, as in 'bird' and 'hurt', or by nothing—when it is the last sound of a word—as in 'mother' and 'sister'. Five diphthongs and two triphthongs contain the vowel of 'r'.

A consonant spelled with 'r' is always followed by a vowel sound, as in 'around' and 'arrest', and is often the first sound of a word, as in 'red' and 'right'. It is often preceded by other consonant sounds in consonant combinations, as in the words tree, drive, three, street, prime, scream.

SOUND CHECK #1: consonant /r/ and combinations. Make sure the back of the tongue remains relaxed and uninvolved when forming the consonant, so /ɜ/ (ER) is not inserted before, or spoken instead of, consonant /r/. This is what happens when Tony the Tiger says: "It's GERRRRATE!". Transcribed: gɜ‑reĭt.

WORDS consonant /r/ and combinations

read	rap	room	riot
rip	run	rookie	ride
rash	rush	raw	rage
prim	prime	practice	press
brash	brief	breath	bride
crash	crave	create	crunch
grave	grumpy	grime	grunt
freed	fraction	frenetic	fresh
thread	three	through	throw
shriek	shrill	shrank	shrew
sprayed	spry	sprung	spruce
scream	scratch	scramble	scrim
stray	street	strangle	strip
strength	striated	structure	straws

PHRASES consonant /r/ and combinations

1.	pricey promotions	6.	scraped screens
2.	brings bright brass	7.	springy sprinters
3.	crooning crocodiles	8.	shrieking shrapnel
4.	great green groceries	9.	Fred framing Frank
5.	radical remembrance	10.	throws three thrones

SOUND CHECK #2: /dr/ and /tr/ combinations. Feel the tip of the tongue contact the gum ridge before releasing into the consonant /r/. If the blade of the tongue is used, 'tr' will sound like 'chr' /t͜ʃr/ and 'dr' will sound like 'jr' /dʒr/.

See the tip of the tongue warm-ups on pages 209-218.

AUDIO 49 B▶ /dr/ and /tr/ combinations

I have had a dream, past the wit of man to say what dream it was.
(A Midsummer Night's Dream: IV, i, 205)

I'll prove more true
Than those that have more cunning to be strange.
(Romeo and Juliet: II, ii, 100)

Truly, the tree yields bad fruit.
(As You Like It: III, ii, 116)

WORDS /dr/ and /tr/ combinations

drill	drastic	treble	drape
dread	dredge	drifter	trigger
tripped	trimmed	treason	transfer

PHRASES /dr/ and /tr/ combinations

1.	trades tractors	6.	dried droplets
2.	tranquil trance	7.	dreadful dress
3.	trampled trails	8.	dripping drain
4.	treasonous trap	9.	drunken drivel
5.	trouble trusting	10.	droning druggist

SENTENCES /dr/ and /tr/ combinations

1. What's in the truck's trunk?

2. Drinking and driving don't mix.

3. Drew dreaded the drudgery of the draft.

4. Tracy's playing the trendsetting stock trader.

5. The trio rode the tricycle in the drizzling rain.

— 6. The translation is tremendous—very dramatic.

7. Trampolines were transported via tractor trailer.

8. Tracy, trim the trees before they droop into traffic.

9. Clever Trevor Trump was cast as COUNT DRACULA.

10. Try trick-or-treating on the train tracks; trust me, trouble!

SOUND CHECK #3: /str/. Make certain to begin this combination of consonants with 'st' **/st/**, which requires that air release over the tip of the tongue, not 'sh' **/ʃ/**, which requires that air release over the sides of the tongue.

AUDIO 49 C▶ /str/ combinations

Destruction straight shall dog them at the heels.

(Richard II: V, iii, 139)

How strange it is to see a famous actress cry.

(Chekhov: The Seagull)

But must my sons be slaughtered in the streets
For valiant doings in their country's cause?

(Titus Andronicus: I, i, 112)

WORDS comparing /st/ and /str/ combinations. Maintain the initial **/st/** in the following word pairs **/st str/** *Read across.*

stay/stray	stack/strap	sty/stride	sty/stripe
steep/street	sting/string	stick/strict	step/strep
stuck/struck	stung/strung	stay/straight	sty/astride

EXERCISES   (1) Elongate initial /s/ in the previous word pairs. Make sure to say 's' and not 'sh'. Then, repeat without elongating.

(2) Pulse initial /st/ twice in the previous word pairs, then finish the word (for example: 'st'..'st'..'stay' / 'st'..'st'..'stray'). Repeat without pulsing.

If the above exercises were helpful, use them with the following:

WORDS /str/

strict	stray	strut	strobe
street	stride	strip	straws
strum	strode	stroll	strikes
strong	stretch	stroke	stringy
strewn	strudel	distract	struggle

When /s/ is followed by a sound that requires lip-rounding, initiate the /s/ before rounding the lips for the sound that comes after. This pertains to several words in the columns above.

PHRASES /str/

1.	strategic strokes	6.	straight-faced
2.	astride a stroller	7.	strained straps
3.	strapping strangers	8.	obstructed street
4.	strenuous stretches	9.	strutting strumpet
5.	strident red streamers	10.	structured strategy

ADDITIONAL PHRASES /str/

1.	stringy straps	6.	stricken strikers
2.	strange stripes	7.	strategic stretches
3.	strong structure	8.	strengthened streets
4.	stressed strippers	9.	struggling strummers
5.	strained strawberries	10.	straightened streamers

SENTENCES /str/

1.   I'm a straphanger.

2.   Comedy is her strong suit.

3.   Three strikes — you struck out!

4.   They were stressed out when stranded.

5.   Strenuous workouts can strain muscles.

6.   Could you straighten that; it's not straight.

7.   Still typecast as the strutting strong-man?

8.   The strained strawberries are in the strainer.

9.   Unstring my straitjacket; it's a bit restrictive.

10.   We strive to yawn and stretch when stressed.

11.   Strange screams rang out from Screech Street.

12.   What a unique strain of streptococcus bacteria.

13.   Drew's offspring adore fresh strawberry strudel.

14.   She looks straight-laced in that strange costume.

15.   Astral sightings distressed the strong astronomer.

16.   Her straight shiny shift with the red stripes shrank.

17.   Last spring, strikers threatened to halt construction.

18.   Three structures were constructed in a straight line.

19.   You're strong; could you string up the strobe lights?

20.   A strolling string quartet at a street fair? What a treat!

21.   They strove to streamline production of the astringent.

22.   She kept a straight face with a straight flush in her hand.

23.   That stray streaked straight into the street and was struck.

24.   That's strange. Why wasn't it structured in a straight line?

25.   Here come the Stratford triplets: Trevor, Tracy and Trina.

Stratford Triplets

Trevor, Tracy, and Trina, the strapping little Stratford triplets, adore freshly strained strawberries. Their parents' strenuous struggle to produce a continuous stream of freshly strained strawberry compote saps all their strength. The stricken parents are determined to streamline production, stretch out current supplies, and drastically restrict their offspring's consumption.

> **SOUND CHECK #4: 'linking' consonant /r/.** When vowel or diphthong of 'r' is followed directly by another vowel or diphthong sound, consonant /r/ can be inserted between the two to insure that they are smoothly linked, and to prevent the second sound from being initiated with a glottal attack.

The addition of a linking consonant /r/ is often automatic, for example:

Mother is here in the dining room.

Taken word by word, there is only one consonant /r/ in the sentence above: 'room'. But when smoothly speaking the sentence, linking consonant /r/ is added after the vowel of 'r' in moth<u>er</u>, and after the diphthong of 'r' in h<u>ere</u>.

Words are not usually linked with the consonant /r/ if linking results in the formation of another word, as in:

Do you know 'A Flea In Her Ear' by Feydeau?

Words are never linked with consonant /r/ in Neutral American Speech if there is no 'r' in the spelling of the word.

PHRASES linking consonant /r/

1.	for a while	6.	paying for it
2.	fear of flying	7.	sneer at them
3.	no particular area	8.	whether or not
4.	bear in the woods	9.	gather everything
5.	hear everyone else	10.	brother advised him

O for a horse with wings!

(Cymbeline: III, ii, 48)

Note. Intrusive *vowel* of 'r': Speaking an 'er' sound when there is no 'r' in the spelling is called adding an intrusive 'r'. This can be heard, for example, in the pronunciation of sofa as 'sofer' and saw as 'sawr'.

Intrusive 'r' correction is addressed on pages 129-130 and 153-154.

NEUTRAL AMERICAN TEXT /r/ (<u>red</u>). *Mark the following and speak out loud.*

/r/ alone and in various combinations:

Holy <u>Fr</u>anciscan <u>fr</u>iar! <u>br</u>other, ho!

(Romeo and Juliet: V, ii, 1)

The sea's more rough and raging than calm rivers.

(Webster: The White Devil)

By all the gods that Romans bow before,
I here discard my sickness! Soul of Rome!
Brave son, deriv'd from honorable loins!

(Julius Caesar: II, i, 320)

I will not do them wrong; I rather choose
To wrong the dead, to wrong myself and you,
Than I will wrong such honorable men.

(Julius Caesar: III, ii, 125)

Arthur, that great forerunner of thy blood,
Richard, that robb'd the lion of his heart,
And fought the holy wars in Palestine,
By this brave duke came early to his grave;
And for amends to his posterity,
At our importance hither is he come
To spread his colors, boy, in thy behalf,
And to rebuke the usurpation
Of thy unnatural uncle, English John.
Embrace him, love him, give him welcome hither.

(King John: II, i, 2)

/dr/ and /tr/ combinations:

The drink, the drink! I am pois'ned.

(Hamlet: V, ii, 310)

Give me my bed by stealth, there's true delight
What breeds a loathing in't, but night by night?

(Tourneur: The Revenger's Tragedy)

Of fantasy, of dreams, and ceremonies.

(Julius Caesar: II, i, 197)

There's no more faith in thee than in a stew'd prune, nor no
more truth in thee than in a drawn fox.

(1 Henry IV: III, iii, 112)

I used to have fine dreams and great thoughts, and the present
and the future were bright with hope.

(Chekhov: Three Sisters)

/str/ combinations:

Is it not strange? and strange?

(Measure for Measure: V, i, 42)

I cannot strike, I see his brother's wounds.

(Middleton & Rowley: The Changeling)

He that strikes the first stroke, I'll run him up to the hilts. ·

(Henry V: II, i, 63

I see you stand like greyhounds in the slips,
Straining upon the start.

(Henry V: III, i, 31)

If ever you disturb our streets again
Your lives shall pay the forfeit of the peace.

(Romeo and Juliet: I, i, 96)

She swore, in faith 'twas strange, 'twas passing strange;
'Twas pitiful, 'twas wondrous pitiful.

(Othello: I, iii, 160)

linking consonant /r/:

Horatio — or I do forget myself.

(Hamlet: I, ii, 161)

Only most people don't formulate it to themselves, or else keep
quiet about it.

(Ibsen: Ghosts)

You will not do't for all the world, I hope.

(Pericles: IV, i, 84)

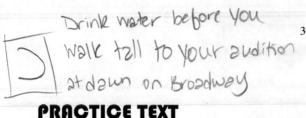

PRACTICE TEXT

Fill in the blank lines with the appropriate IPA marking for well-pronounced Neutral American. Voiced endings before a (possible) pause have been double-underlined, syllabic endings have been marked, and consonant /r/ and consonant combinations have been underlined. See the key on page 320 and the Shakespeare monologues on pages 321-325 for samples of other marked text. Speak the selections aloud.

Example:

The swiftest traveler is he that goes afoot.

(Thoreau: Walden, 1, Economy)

---

1. Beware of all enterprises that require new clothes.

(Thoreau: Walden, 1, Economy)

2. I love a broad margin to my life.

(Thoreau: Walden, 4, Sounds)

3. The gentleman has not seen how to reply to this.

(Webster: Second Speech on Foote's Resolution)

4. She was a phantom of delight

When first she gleamed upon my sight.

(Wordsworth: She Was a Phantom of Delight)

5. Belike some noble gentleman that means

Traveling some journey to repose him here.

(The Taming of the Shrew: Ind. i, 75)

6. She might lie by an emperor's side and command him tasks.

(Othello: IV, i, 184)

7.   She dwelt among the untrodden ways

Beside the springs of Dove.

              (Wordsworth: She Dwelt Among the Untrodden Ways)

8.   Sweet childish days, that were as long

As twenty days are now.

              (Wordsworth: To a Butterfly)

9.   Be not as extreme in submission as in offense.

              (The Merry Wives of Windsor: IV, iv, 11)

10.   The deep of night is crept upon our talk.

              (Julius Caesar: IV, iii, 226)

11.   O, let me stay, befall what may befall!

              (2 Henry VI: III, ii, 402)

12.   As Tammie glowered, amazed and curious,

The mirth and fun grew fast and furious.

              (Robert Burns: Tam O'Shanter)

13.   He said fever...the brain...if I heard right...

If you could see him! Ah! his head bound tight!

              (Rostand: Cyrano de Bergerac)

14.   Death is my son-in-law, Death is my heir,

My daughter he hath wedded. I will die,

And leave him all; life, living, all is Death's.

              (Romeo and Juliet: IV, v, 38)

PRACTICE TEXT

Mark Neutral American sound changes, then speak out loud.

1.   God pardon sin!

(Romeo and Juliet: II, iii, 44)

2.   True service merits mercy.

(Middleton & Rowley: The Changeling)

3.   Come let's away to prison.

(King Lear: V, iii, 8)

4.   I tell thee ere thou ask it me again.

(Romeo and Juliet: II, iii, 48)

5.   Silence is the perfectest herald of joy.

(Much Ado About Nothing: II, i, 306)

6.   There's matter in't indeed, if he be angry.

(Othello: III, iv, 139)

7.   Adieu, brave Moor, use Desdemona well.

(Othello: I, iii, 291)

8.   'Twere good methinks to steal our marriage.

(The Taming of the Shrew: III, ii, 140)

9.   I'll not be tied to hours, nor 'pointed times.

(The Taming of the Shrew: III, i, 19)

10.   To the contrary I have express commandment.

(The The Winter's Tale: II, ii, 8)

11.   Away with him to prison! Lay bolts enough upon him.

(Measure for Measure: V, i, 346)

12.   I see in all bouts, both of sport and wit,
Always a woman strives for the last hit.

(Middleton & Rowley: The Changeling)

306

13. Her voice was ever soft,
Gentle, and low, an excellent thing in woman.

(King Lear: V, iii, 273)

14. Some twenty of them fought in this black strife,
And all those twenty could but kill one life.

(Romeo and Juliet: III, i,178)

15. When you are weary, you may leave the school,
For all this while you have but played the fool.

(Middleton & Rowley: The Changeling)

16. And for these fourteen years, he's played the role
Of my old friend who comes to amuse, cajole...

(Rostand: Cyrano de Bergerac)

17. He requires someone near him whom he cares for, and whose
judgement he respects.

(Ibsen: Ghosts)

18. For my voice, I have lost it with hallowing and singing of anthems.

(2 Henry IV: I, ii, 189)

19. Last week, two snufflers were themselves snuffed out,
Because they dared address him through the...snout!

(Rostand: Cyrano de Bergerac)

20. I never spake with her in all my life.

(The Comedy of Errors: II, ii, 165)

21. You knew, none so well, none so well as you, of my daughter's flight.

(The Merchant of Venice: III, i, 25)

22. Repair me with thy presence, Silvia;
Thou gentle nymph, cherish thy forlorn swain.

(The Two Gentlemen of Verona: V, iv, 11)

23. I'll ne'er put my finger in the fire, and need not.

(Merry Wives of Windsor: I, iv, 85)

24.   If thou but frown on me, or stir thy foot,
Or teach thy hasty spleen to do me shame,
I'll strike thee dead. Put up thy sword betime,
Or I'll so maul you and your toasting-iron
That you shall think the devil is come from hell.

(King John: IV, iii, 96)

25.   Then call our captains and our colors forth,
And, madam, at your father's castle walls
We'll crave a parley, to confer with him.

(1 Henry VI: V, iii, 128)

26.   IAGO.   You were best go in.
OHELLO.   Not I; I must be found.

(Othello: I, ii, 30)

27.   Your plainness and your shortness please me well.

(The Taming of the Shrew: IV, iv, 39)

28.   The urging of that word "judgment" hath bred a kind of
remorse in me.

(Richard III: I, iv, 107)

29.   Be not afeard, the isle is full of noises,
Sounds, and sweet airs, that give delight and hurt not.

(The Tempest: III, ii, 135)

30.   If thou dost love, my kindness shall incite thee
To bind our loves up in a holy band.

(Much Ado About Nothing: III, i, 113)

31.   Arrogant Winchester, that haughty prelate.

(1 Henry VI: I, iii, 23)

32.   Let it be lawful that law bar no wrong.

(King John: III, i, 186)

33.   All right—all right.—There now, Hedda, now you have both
shade and fresh air.

(Ibsen: Hedda Gabler)

From **RUDDIGORE**

Gilbert and Sullivan

CHORUS of Bucks and Blades

When thoroughly tired
Of being admired
By ladies of gentle degree—degree,
With flattery sated,
High-flown and inflated,
Away from the city we flee—we flee!
From charms intramural
To prettiness rural
The sudden transition
Is simply Elysian,
So come, Amaryllis,
Come, Chloe and Phyllis,
Your slaves, for the moment, are we!

CHORUS of Bridesmaids

The sons of the tillage
Who dwell in this village
Are people of lowly degree—degree.
Though honest and active,
They're most unattractive,
And awkward as awkward can be—can be.
They're clumsy clodhoppers
With axes and choppers,
And shepherds and ploughmen,
And drovers and cowmen,
And hedgers and reapers,
And carters and keepers,
But never a lover for me!

From **IOLANTHE**

WHEN YOU'RE LYING AWAKE
(The Nightmare Song)

Gilbert and Sullivan

When you're lying awake with a dismal headache,
    and repose is taboo'd by anxiety,

I conceive you may use any language you choose
    to indulge in, without impropriety;

For your brain is on fire — the bedclothes conspire
    of usual slumber to plunder you:

First your counterpane goes, and uncovers your toes,
    and your sheet slips demurely from under you;

Then the blanketing tickles — you feel like mixed pickles —
    so terribly sharp is the pricking,

And you're hot, and you're cross, and you tumble and toss
    till there's nothing 'twixt you and the ticking.

Then the bedclothes all creep to the ground in a heap,
    and you pick 'em all up in a tangle;

Next your pillow resigns and politely declines
    to remain at its usual angle!

Well, you get some repose in the form of a doze,
    with hot eye-balls and head ever aching,

But your slumbering teems with such horrible dreams
    that you'd very much better by waking!

From **THE TELL-TALE HEART**

Edgar Allan Poe

True!—nervous—very, very dreadfully nervous I had been and am; but why *will* you say that I am mad? The disease had sharpened my senses—not destroyed—not dulled them. Above all was the sense of hearing acute. I heard all things in the heaven and in the earth. I heard many things in hell. How, then, am I mad? Hearken! And observe how healthily—how calmly I can tell you the whole story.

It is impossible to say how first the idea entered my brain; but once conceived, it haunted me day and night. Object there was none. Passion there was none. I loved the old man. He had never wronged me. He had never given me insult. For his gold I had no desire. I think it was his eye! Yes, it was this! One of his eyes resembled that of a vulture—a pale blue eye, with a film over it. Whenever it fell upon me, my blood ran cold; and so by degrees—very gradually—I made up my mind to take the life of the old man, and thus rid myself of the eye forever.

Now this is the point. You fancy me mad. Madmen know nothing. But you should have seen *me*. You should have seen how wisely I proceeded—with what dissimulation I went to work! I was never kinder to the old man than during the whole week before I killed him. And every night, about midnight, I turned the latch of his door and opened it—oh, so gently! And then, when I had made an opening sufficient for my head, I put in a dark lantern, all closed, closed, so that no light shone out, and then I thrust in my head. Oh, you would have laughed to see how cunningly I thrust it in! I moved it slowly—very, very slowly, so that I might not disturb the old man's sleep.

A FRAGMENT

H. W. Longfellow

Awake! arise! the hour is late!
  Angels are knocking at thy door!
They are in haste and cannot wait,
  And once departed come no more.

Awake! arise! the athlete's arm
  Loses its strength by too much rest;
The fallow land, the untilled farm
  Produces only weeds at best.

From **THE SPHINX**

Edgar Allan Poe

During the dread reign of the Cholera in New York, I had accepted the invitation of a relative to spend a fortnight with him in the retirement of his *cottage ornée* on the banks of the Hudson. We had here around us all the ordinary means of summer amusement; and what with rambling in the woods, sketching, boating, fishing, bathing, music, and books, we should have passed the time pleasantly enough, but for the fearful intelligence which reached us every morning from the populous city. Not a day elapsed which did not bring us news of the decease of some acquaintance. Then, as the fatality increased, we learned to expect daily the loss of some friend. At length we trembled at the approach of every messenger. The very air from the South seemed to us redolent with death. That palsying thought, indeed, took entire possession of my soul. I could neither speak, think, nor dream of any thing else. My host was of a less excitable temperament, and, although greatly depressed in spirits, exerted himself to sustain my own. His richly philosophical intellect was not at any time affected by unrealities. To the substances of terror he was sufficiently alive, but of its shadows he had no apprehension.

312

/ðə/ /kætəækt/ /əv/ /lədɔːr/

/luh-door/

/kætəækt/

From THE CATARACT OF LODORE

Robert Southey

How does the water come down at Lodore?

Rising and leaping,
Sinking and creeping,
Eddying and whisking,
Spouting and frisking,
Turning and twisting,
Around and around
With endless rebound!
Dividing and gliding and sliding,
And falling and brawling and sprawling,
And driving and riving and striving,
And sprinkling and twinkling and wrinkling,
And sounding and bounding and rounding,
And bubbling and troubling and doubling,
And grumbling and rumbling and tumbling,
And clattering and battering and shattering;
Retreating and beating and meeting and sheeting,
Delaying and straying and playing and spraying,
Advancing and prancing and glancing and dancing,
Recoiling, turmoiling and toiling and boiling,
And gleaming and streaming and steaming and beaming,
And rushing and flushing and brushing and gushing,
And flapping and rapping and clapping and slapping,
And curling and whirling and purling and twirling,
And thumping and plumping and bumping and jumping,
And dashing and flashing and splashing and clashing;
And so never ending, but always descending,
Sounds and motions for ever and ever are blending
All at once, and all o'er, with a mighty uproar,—
And this way, the water comes down at Lodore.

. The ʌ

~ ~ the. ð

HOPE

Emily Dickinson

XXXII

HOPE is the thing with feathers
That perches in the soul,
And sings the tune without the words,
And never stops at all,

And sweetest in the gale is heard;
And sore must be the storm
That could abash the little bird
That kept so many warm.

I've heard it in the chillest land,
And on the strangest sea;
Yet, never, in extremity,
It asked a crumb of me.

From **MOBY-DICK**

Herman Melville

Call me Ishmael. Some years ago—never mind how long precisely—having little or no money in my purse, and nothing particular to interest me on shore, I thought I would sail about a little and see the watery part of the world. It is a way I have of driving off the spleen, and regulating the circulation. Whenever I find myself growing grim about the mouth; whenever it is a damp, drizzly November in my soul; whenever I find myself involuntarily pausing before coffin warehouses, and bringing up the rear of every funeral I meet; and especially whenever my hypos get such an upper hand of me, that it requires a strong moral principle to prevent me from deliberately stepping into the street, and methodically knocking people's hats off— then, I account it high time to get to sea as soon as I can.

From **CYRANO DE BERGERAC**

Edmond Rostand

CHRISTIAN
Get me that kiss!

CYRANO   No!

CHRISTIAN   Now, or later...

CYRANO   True!
That heady moment comes, when both of you —
Your lips inevitably touching, close!
Yours, the lion's whiskers...hers, the rose!

THE SHUTTERS OPEN. CHRISTIAN HIDES UNDER THE BALCONY.

Would that it were otherwise...

ROXANE (ABOVE)   Is it you?
We spoke of a...

CYRANO   ...a kiss, and sweet word, too!
You shy from forming it upon your lips.
If that word burn, how you must fear eclipse
Of mine, on yours, in one consuming fire!
And yet, tonight, you recklessly conspire,
And gracefully slip, almost denying fears,
From mockery, to smiles, from sighs, to tears...
You need only slip once more from tears to this
One word, one trembling word away...a kiss!

ROXANE
Be still —!

CYRANO A kiss, and what is that? A contract
Signed and sealed, a promise more exact...
A desire that longs to be confirmed...the blush of
The embracing 'o' within the verb "to love"...
A secret whisper drawing lips as ears...
Infinity...the music of the spheres...
As bees hum in communion with the flower...
A way to touch a heartbeat...and the power,
As you taste one lingering instant of the soul!

ROXANE
Be still—!

CYRANO   A kiss, madame, a noble toll,
So noble that the Queen of France decreed
The English Buckingham to steal!

ROXANE   Indeed!

CYRANO (IMPASSIONED)
Like this her lord, an ocean lies between
This melancholy lord and you, his queen—
Your subject, I, and to the death!

ROXANE   And you—
As handsome...!

CYRANO (ASIDE, SOBERED)
                  Handsome—I forgot! That's true!

ROXANE
Well then! Mount...and taste the flower in me...

CYRANO (URGING CHRISTIAN)
Mount!

ROXANE
        This heart beating...

CYRANO   Mount!

ROXANE   This humming bee...

CYRANO
Mount, mount!

CHRISTIAN (HESITATES)
              The moment must be right, at least...

ROXANE
An instant of forever...!

CYRANO (PUSHING)   Mount, you beast!

(English version: Christopher Martin)

SONNET 23

William Shakespeare

As an unperfect actor on the stage,
Who with his fear is put besides his part,
Or some fierce thing replete with too much rage,
Whose strength's abundance weakens his own heart,
So I, for fear of trust, forget to say
The perfect ceremony of love's rite,
And in mine own love's strength seem to decay,
O'ercharg'd with burden of mine own love's might.
O, let my books be then the eloquence
And dumb presagers of my speaking breast,
Who plead for love, and look for recompense,
More than that tongue that more hath more express'd.
  O, learn to read what silent love hath writ:
  To hear with eyes belongs to love's fine wit.

SONNET 27

William Shakespeare

Weary with toil, I haste me to my bed,
The dear repose for limbs with travel tired,
But then begins a journey in my head
To work my mind, when body's work's expired;
For then my thoughts (from far where I abide)
Intend a zealous pilgrimage to thee,
And keep my drooping eyelids open wide,
Looking on darkness which the blind do see;
Save that my soul's imaginary sight
Presents thy shadow to my sightless view,
Which like a jewel hung in ghastly night,
Makes black night beauteous, and her old face new.
  Lo thus by day my limbs, by night my mind,
  For thee, and for myself, no quiet find.

SONNET 40

William Shakespeare

Take all my loves, my love, yea, take them all,
What hast thou then more than thou hadst before?
No love, my love, that thou mayst true love call,
All mine was thine, before thou hadst this more.
Then if for my love thou my love receivest,
I cannot blame thee for my love thou usest,
But yet be blam'd if thou this self deceivest
By willful taste of what thy self refusest.
I do forgive thy robb'ry, gentle thief,
Although thou steal thee all my poverty;
And yet love knows it is a greater grief
To bear love's wrong than hate's known injury.
     Lascivious grace, in whom all ill well shows,
     Kill me with spites, yet we must not be foes.

SONNET 50

William Shakespeare

How heavy do I journey on the way,
When what I seek (my weary travel's end)
Doth teach that ease and that repose to say,
"Thus far the miles are measured from thy friend."
The beast that bears me, tired with my woe,
Plods dully on, to bear that weight in me,
As if by some instinct the wretch did know
His rider lov'd not speed, being made from thee.
The bloody spur cannot provoke him on,
That sometimes anger thrusts into his hide,
Which heavily he answers with a groan,
More sharp to me than spurring to his side,
     For that same groan doth put this in my mind:
     My grief lies onward and my joy behind.

THE TIDE RISES, THE TIDE FALLS

Henry Wadsworth Longfellow

The tide rises, the tide falls,
The twilight darkens, the curlew calls;
Along the sea-sands damp and brown
The traveler hastens toward the town,
       And the tide rises, the tide falls.

Darkness settles on the roofs and walls,
But the sea, the sea in the darkness calls;
The little waves, with their soft, white hands,
Efface the footprints in the sands,
       And the tide rises, the tide falls,

The morning breaks; the steeds in their stalls
Stamp and neigh, as the hostler calls;
The day returns, but nevermore
Returns the traveler to the shore,
       And the tide rises, the tide falls.

632

Emily Dickinson

The Brain—is wider than the Sky—
For—put them side by side—
The one the other will contain
With ease—and You—beside—

The Brain is deeper than the sea—
For—hold them—Blue to Blue—
The one the other will absorb—
As Sponges—Buckets—do—

The Brain is just the weight of God—
For—Heft them—Pound for Pound—
And they will differ—if they do—
As Syllable from Sound.

HENRY V: Prologue

William Shakespeare

O for a Muse of fire, that would ascend
The brightest heaven of invention!
A kingdom for a stage, princes to act,
And monarchs to behold the swelling scene!
Then should the warlike Harry, like himself,
Assume the port of Mars, and at his heels
(Leash'd in, like hounds) should famine, sword, and fire
Crouch for employment. But pardon, gentles all,
The flat unraised spirits that hath dar'd
On this unworthy scaffold to bring forth
So great an object. Can this cockpit hold
The vasty fields of France? Or may we cram
Within this wooden O the very casques
That did affright the air at Agincourt?
O, pardon! since a crooked figure may
Attest in little place a million,
And let us, ciphers to this great accompt,
On your imaginary forces work.
Suppose within the girdle of these walls
Are now confin'd two mighty monarchies,
Whose high, upreared, and abutting fronts
The perilous narrow ocean parts asunder.
Piece out our imperfections with your thoughts;
Into a thousand parts divide one man,
And make imaginary puissance;
Think, when we talk of horses, that you see them
Printing their proud hoofs i' th' receiving earth;
For 'tis your thoughts that now must deck our kings,
Carry them here and there, jumping o'er times,
Turning th' accomplishment of many years
Into an hour-glass: for the which supply,
Admit me Chorus to this history;
Who, Prologue-like, your humble patience pray,
Gently to hear, kindly to judge, our play.

wouldn't, you = no (chew)

KEY TO MARKING NEUTRAL AMERICAN MONOLOGUES

Rhythm Highlighters	Marking
Stressed syllables (all marked for awareness)	ˈpurchase
Noun verb variations (stressed syllable marked)	ˈdiscourse
Weak forms (marked sparingly, actor's choice)	ə ə i a, the (vs.) the
/ɪ/ (wi̱ll) prefixes and suffixes	ɪ ɪ reˈpeat, ˈcloset
/ə/ (u̱h) schwa suffixes	ə ˈstatement
Syllabic endings marked: /n̩ l̩ m̩/	ˈwooden̩, ˈlittl̩e, ˈprism̩,
Vowel Sound Considerations	**Marking**
Linking words (marked sparingly, actor's choice)	here‿it‿is
/e/ (ge̱t) before 'm', 'n' (in a stressed syllable)	e e e them, when, sent
/æ/ (tha̱t) vowel (relaxed vowel, not a nasal diphthong)	æ æ æ cast, sand, man
/ɔ/ (a̱ll) (marked to distinguish from fa̱ther sound)	ɔ ɔ ɔ fall, often, song
/ʊɚ/ (poo̱r) diphthong (not /ɝ/ E̱R or /ɔɚ/ spo̱rts)	ʊɚ ʊɚ aˈssure, tour
/aɪ̆/ (my̱) diphthong (marked before a voiceless consonants in the same word)	aɪ̆ aɪ̆ aɪ̆ white, pipe, wife
Consonant Sound Considerations	**Marking**
Voiceless stop-plosive endings (aspirated before a pause or silence)	hit^h, pack^h, lip^h
Voiced consonant ends (clearly voiced—especially before a pause or silence)	dead̲, foun̲d̲, kin̲g̲
Consonant /r/ and combinations (clear—especially tr, dr, and str combinations)	t̲r̲ap, d̲r̲ead, s̲t̲r̲eet

The /æ/ (tha̱t) sound is generally u̱nmarked in ALL monologues in words that can be spoken with either a weak OR strong form, as in the words: and, that, an, than, shall, etc.

NEUTRAL AMERICAN MONOLOGUES

(with sound changes marked)

AUDIO 50▶ **spoken by Jonathan Fielding**

ROMEO

But soft^h, what light <u>through</u> 'yonder 'window <u>breaks</u>?

It is the east^h, and 'Juliet is the su<u>n</u>.

A'<u>rise</u>, fair su<u>n</u>, and kill the 'envious moo<u>n</u>,

Who is al'<u>rea</u>dy sick and pale with <u>g</u>rief

That thou, her maid, art far more fair than she.

Be not her mai<u>d</u>, since she is 'envious;

Her 'vestal 'livery is but sick and <u>g</u>ree<u>n</u>,

And none but fools do wear it^h; cast it off.

It is my 'lady, O it is my lo<u>ve</u>!

O that she knew¹ she were!

---

1   Try speaking liquid **/ju/** (<u>you</u>) on this word for a slightly more formal sound.
    See pages 345-348 in Classical American.

CLASSICALLY SPEAKING   **NEUTRAL AMERICAN text & monologues**

She speaks, yet she says 'noth<u>ing</u>; what‿of that[h]?   [ɪ] [æ]

Her[1] eye dis'**cour**s<u>e</u>s, I will‿'**answer**‿it[h].   [ɪ] [ɪ] [æ]

I‿am too bo<u>ld</u>, 'tis not to me she speaks.

Two‿of the '**fai**<u>r</u>est stars in‿all the '**heaven**[2],   [ɪ] [ɔ] [ə]

'**Ha**ving some '**business**, do en'**treat** her eye<u>s</u>   [æ] [ɪ] [ɪ] [ɪ] [hɚ]

To '**twinkl<u>e</u>**‿in their spheres till they <u>r</u>e'**tur<u>n</u>**.   [ɪ]

What‿if her eyes were there, they‿in her hea<u>d</u>?   [hɚ] [hɚ]

The '**bright**ness‿of her cheek would shame those star<u>s</u>,   [aɪ] [ɪ] [hɚ]

As '**day**light doth‿a lamp[h]; her eyes‿in '**heaven**   [aɪ] [ʌ] [ə] [æ] [hɚ]

Would <u>th</u>rough the‿'**ai**<u>r</u>y '**region** <u>s</u>tream so bri<u>gh</u>t[h]   [i] [aɪ]

That birds would sing and think‿it were not nigh<u>t</u>[h].   [ɪ] [ɪ] [aɪ]

See how she leans her cheek up'**on** her ha<u>nd</u>!   [hɚ] [hɚ] [æ]

O that‿I were‿a glo<u>ve</u>‿up'**on** that ha<u>nd</u>,   [ə] [æ]

That‿I might touch that cheek[h]!

(Romeo and Juliet: II, ii, 2)

---

[1] Linking is optional. If a new word is formed by hitting the 'r' so heavily that it sounds like 'her <u>r</u>ye', then do not link.
[2] The last syllable can be spoken with a syllabic ending or with a schwa.

AUDIO 51▶ **spoken by Rebecca Dumaine**

EMILIA

But I do think it is their 'husbands' faults

If wives do fall. Say that they slack their 'duties,[1]

And pour our 'treasures into 'foreign laps;

Or else break out in 'peevish 'jealousies,

'Throwing re'straint up'on us; or say they strike us,

Or scant our 'former 'having in de'spite[h]:

Why, we have galls; and though we have some grace,

Yet have we some re'venge. Let 'husbands know

Their wives have sense like them; they see and smell,

And have their 'palates both for sweet and sour,

As 'husbands have. What is it that they do

When they change us for 'others? Is it sport[h]?

I think it is. And doth a'ffection breed it[h]?

I think it doth. Is't 'frailty that thus errs?

It is so too. And have not we a'ffections,

---

[1] Liquid /ju/ (you) could be spoken, if preferred. (See Classical American page 345.)

    ɪ   e   æ

De'**sires** for sport[h], and '**frailty**, as men ha<u>ve</u>?

    e   e   e   e   e   e

Then let them‿use‿us we<u>ll</u>; else let them know,

      i

The‿ills we do, their‿ills‿in'**struct**‿us so.

                                                (Othello: IV, iii, 86)

AUDIO 52 ▶   **spoken by Walton Wilson**

ANGELO

          ɪ

Who will be'**lieve** thee, '**Isabe**<u>l</u>?

                    ɔ   ɪ ə   aɪ

My‿un'**soil'd** na<u>me</u>, th'‿au'**stere**ness‿of my life,

               e   ə

My vouch‿a'**gainst** you, and my place‿i'‿the state[h],

         jʊə̆ æ

Will so your‿accu'**sation**‿over'**weigh**,

               aɪ   jʊə̆   ɪ

That you shall '**stifle**‿in your‿own re'**port**[h],

               æ   ɪ

And smell‿of '**ca**lumny. I have be'**gu**<u>n</u>,

               e   ə

And now‿I give my '**sen**sual <u>r</u>ace the <u>rein</u>.

             e   æ   aɪ

Fit thy con'**sent** to my sharp‿'**appetit**[h]e,

          ɔ   aɪ   ə   ɪz

Lay by‿all '**nicety**‿and <u>pro</u>'**lixious** '**blushe**<u>s</u>

That 'banish what they sue for. Re'deem thy 'brother

By 'yielding up thy 'body to my will,

Or else he must not 'only die the death,

But thy un'kindness shall his death draw out^h

To 'ling'ring 'sufferance. 'Answer me to-'morrow,

Or by the a'ffection that now guides me most^h,

I'll prove a 'tyrant to him. As for you,

Say what you can: my false o'er'weighs your true.

(Measure for Measure: II, iv, 154)

CLASSICAL AMERICAN DIALECT

AUDIO SELECTIONS▶
Patricia Fletcher

SUMMARY CHECKLIST

It may be useful to read the Introduction, pages 1-4, for an overview and comparison with Neutral American and Standard British, before continuing.

When switching from Neutral American to Classical American dialect, the following adjustments and sound changes are necessary.

CONSONANTS

Aspirated medial / tʰ /

In Neutral American, when /t/ occurs in an unstressed syllable between two vowel sounds, it is actually said as a very light 'd', represented phonetically by /t̮/, for example:

butter = / 'bʌt̮ɚ / or budder

In Classical American, the light 'd' sound is not spoken, a lightly aspirated /tʰ/ is used instead. This is sometimes called a 'flutter t'. The tip of the tongue touches the gum ridge and voiceless 't' is released on a puff of breath.

The small phonetic marking / ʰ / written in one's script can provide a useful reminder to speak a flutter 't'.

AUDIO 53▶ **lightly aspirated medial /tʰ/**

Methinks nobody should be sad butʰ I.

(King John: IV, i, 13)

Itʰ is the law, notʰ I, condemn your brother.

(Measure for Measure: II, ii, 80)

Yes, I hear people talk of thatʰ; butʰ itʰ is uttʰerly impossible.

(Ibsen: The Master Builder)

Highlight the vowel in the stressed syllable, and pronounce the 'flutter t' as part of the unstressed syllable. If the /t/ seems too sharp or intrusive, try releasing it on a little more breath.

butter: →'bʌtʰɚ	litter: →'lɪtʰɚ
batter: →'bætʰɚ	bitter: →'bɪtʰɚ
better: →'betʰɚ	bit of: →'bɪtʰ əv

WORDS with lightly aspirated medial /t^h/

'witt^{h}y	'pit^{h}y	'kitt^{h}y	'cit^{h}y
'fatt^{h}er	'ditt^{h}y	a'bilit^{h}y	'snott^{h}y
'sanit^{h}y	'litt^{h}er	'might^{h}y	'writ^{h}er
'prett^{h}y	'vanit^{h}y	'cheat^{h}er	'fitt^{h}ing
'light^{h}ing	'seat^{h}ing	ad'mitt^{h}ing	'sweet^{h}est

PHRASES with lightly aspirated medial /t^h/

1. hitt^{h}ing the lott^{h}ery
2. that^h everyone did
3. what^h Alan thought
4. what^{h}ever you want
5. vot^{h}ing his conscience
6. what^h it^h is
7. stop hat^{h}ing
8. whit^{h}e as snow
9. wait^{h}ing outside
10. a little[1] fight^{h}ing

SENTENCES with lightly aspirated medial /t^h/

1. Your shirt is dirty.

2. Where are you sitting?

3. She's my favorite aunt.

4. Katie isn't permitted to go.

5. We'll meet in the waiting room.

6. You danced a fine minuet on stage.

7. She's waiting until there's available seating.

8. My flashlight isn't working, it needs batteries.

9. The bitter chocolate cookies need a sugar coating.

10. People with no sense of gratitude have bad attitudes.

11. I bet everyone will wait in line to get into the audition.

12. I'll have a little bit of butter on my lettuce and tomatoes.

13. How can you think of fighting on a beautiful autumn day?

---

[1] Syllabic endings spelled with a 't' as in bee<u>tle</u>, li<u>ttle</u>, bo<u>ttle</u>, are pronounced /tl̩/ in Classical American, not /dl̩/ as in Neutral American.

14.   He tried to get out of it without[1] hurting anyone's feelings.

15.   The meeting was cancelled when the heating system broke.

Eat^{h}ing Keat^{h}ing's

Sweet^{h}ie, it^h is bett^{h}er to butt^{h}er your biscuit^h and toast^h
With the very best butt^{h}er from Keat^{h}ing's.
If you cheat^h and use butt^{h}er from Kat^{h}ie's or Kroft's,
You will never be sure what you're eat^{h}ing.

Betty Botta bought some butter.
"But," said she, "this butter's bitter.
If I put it in my batter,
It will make my batter bitter.
But a bit of better butter
Will make my bitter batter better."
So she bought a bit of butter
Better than the bitter butter
And it made her bitter batter better.
So, 'twas better Betty Botta
Bought a bit of better butter.

(Anonymous)

See the patter trio by Gilbert and Sullivan on page 400 for additional 'flutter t' practice.

CLASSICAL AMERICAN TEXT lightly aspirated medial /t^h/. *Mark the following for 'flutter t' and speak out loud.*

It^h isn't money that matt^{h}ers.

(Chekhov: The Seagull)

Arm me audacity from head to foot.

(Cymbeline: I, vi, 19)

That is very nice and dutiful of him.

(Ibsen: Ghosts)

---

[1] Use voiced 'th' /ð/ when speaking 'with' in all forms (without, within, etc.).

Lay breath so bitter on your bitter foe.

(A Midsummer Night's Dream: III, ii, 44)

When we are both accoutered like young men,
I'll prove the prettier fellow of the two.

(The Merchant of Venice: III, iv, 63)

She was brought up in a milieu of equality and women's rights,
and all that.

(Strindberg: Miss Julie)

I'm through with ghosted letters, borrowed wit,
And acting roles I know I just don't fit!

(Rostand: Cyrano de Bergerac)

It's carnival week, and the servants are so excited about it.

(Chekhov: Three Sisters)

I am so used to frequent flattery,
That, being alone, I now flatter myself.

(Webster: The White Devil)

I pray you let us satisfy our eyes
With the memorials and the things of fame.

(Twelfth Night: III, iii, 22)

She better would have fitted me or Clarence;
But in your bride you bury brotherhood.

(3 Henry VI: IV, i, 54)

Saturday, the twenty-sixth—while supper waited—
M'sieur de Bergerac died. Assassinated.

(Rostand: Cyrano de Bergerac)

Well, wait a moment, Mrs. Alving. Let us look into the matter
a little more closely.

(Ibsen: Ghosts)

Leave it all behind! Tell me you love me, or else—what am I, what?

(Strindberg: Miss Julie)

But you know someone ought to write a play on how we poor
teachers live, and get it acted.

(Chekhov: The Seagull)

Voiceless / hw / (<u>wh</u>y)

spelled 'wh'

When the /w/ sound is represented by 'wh' in the spelling, voiceless or whispered /hw/ is spoken instead of voiced /w/. An exception to the spelling guideline occurs when the 'wh' spelling represents /h/ as in 'who' and 'whore'.

Voiceless /hw/ should not involve friction or tension in the throat. Release a little puff of breath through gently rounded lips and continue on to the vowel sound that always follows.

AUDIO 54▶ voiceless /hw/ (<u>wh</u>y)

                      hw
Let's sit down here for a <u>wh</u>ile.

(Chekhov: Three Sisters)

           hw   hw
Go to bed <u>wh</u>en I was dressed—damnation! <u>Wh</u>at have you

done to me?

(Strindberg: The Father)

           hw   hw   hw
Aye, sir, and <u>wh</u>ere'fore; for they say, every <u>wh</u>y hath a <u>wh</u>ere'fore.

(The Comedy of Errors: II, ii, 43)

WORDS /w/ (<u>we</u>) *vs.* /hw/ (<u>wh</u>y) *Read across.*

/w/	/hw/	/w/	/hw/
wet	whet	we'll	wheel
wig	Whig	wail	whale
witch	which	wear	where
wacky	whack	well	whelp
weather	whether	wine	whine

PHRASES using voiceless /hw/ (<u>wh</u>y)

1.	<u>wh</u>at I know	6.	<u>wh</u>ich one
2.	any<u>wh</u>ere else	7.	well, <u>wh</u>y not
3.	heard <u>wh</u>irring	8.	<u>wh</u>ittling away
4.	<u>wh</u>imsical note	9.	asking Mr. <u>Wh</u>ite
5.	<u>wh</u>enever you wish	10.	going every<u>wh</u>ere

Let there be no honor
hw   hw
<u>Wh</u>ere there is beauty; truth, <u>wh</u>ere semblance; love,
hw
<u>Wh</u>ere there's another man.

(Cymbeline: II, iv, 108)

SENTENCES using voiceless /hw/ (<u>wh</u>y)

1. Where's Mr. White?

2. What's that whirring noise?

3. Which witch was with you?

4. Is whiskey made from wheat?

5. Wait awhile for Mr. Whatling.

6. Why are you doing cartwheels?

7. I don't know whether or not he went.

8. Stop whining about spilling the wine.

9. What's that whinnying and wheezing?

10. When whipped, the wild beast whinnied.

11. Why, oh why, can't I whistle when I want?

12. Do white whales swim off the coast of Wales?

13. The whitecaps overwhelmed those in the waves.

14. Why, she heard whispering and whimpering everywhere.

15. Where are you going, when are you going, and with whom?

Whirling Wheat

  hw   hw   hw   hw

Why not lay awhile amidst the whirling wheat,

  hw   hw   hw   hw

Whirring, whistling, whispering while we sleep?

Whether the weather be fine
Or whether the weather be not
Whether the weather be cold
Or whether the weather be hot
We'll weather the weather
Whatever the weather
Whether we like it or not.

(Anonymous)

CLASSICAL AMERICAN TEXT voiceless /hw/ (why). *Mark the following and speak out loud.*

 hw hw

Why whisper you, my lords, and answer not?

(3 Henry VI: I, i, 149)

What amorous whirlwind hurried you to Rome?

(Webster: The White Devil)

Here burns my candle out; ay, here it dies,
Which whiles it lasted, gave King Henry light.

(3 Henry VI: II, vi, 1)

What plagues and what portents, what mutiny!
What raging of the sea, shaking of earth!

(Troilus and Cressida: I, iii, 96)

Theses are but wild and whirling words, my lord.

(Hamlet: I, v, 133)

We mourn in black, why mourn we not in blood?

(1 Henry VI: I, i, 17)

What noise is this? What traitors have we here?

(1 Henry VI: I, iii, 15)

336

What, are my deeds forgot?

(Troilus and Cressida: III, iii, 144)

Tend to th' master's whistle.

(The Tempest: I, i, 6)

My salad days,
When I was green in judgment.

(Antony and Cleopatra: I, iv, 73)

Be frank! where did I fall?
Hold nothing back! what place, and on what site
Have I come tumbling like an asterite?

(Rostand: Cyrano de Bergerac)

In sooth, I know not why I am so sad;
It wearies me, you say it wearies you;
But how I caught it, found it, or came by it,
What stuff 'tis made of, whereof it is born,
I am to learn;
And such a want-wit sadness makes of me,
That I have much ado to know myself.

(The Merchant of Venice: I, i, 1)

Had women navigable rivers in their eyes,
They would dispend them all. Surely I wonder
Why we should wish more rivers to the city,
When they sell water so good cheap.

(Webster: The White Devil)

And yet, to me, what is this quintessence of dust?

(Hamlet: II, ii, 308)

When didst thou sleep when such a deed was done?

(Richard III: IV, iv, 24)

Then may I set the world on wheels, when she can spin for
her living.

(Two Gentlemen of Verona: III, i, 315)

VOWELS & DIPHTHONGS

The short, slightly lip-rounded back vowel /ɒ/, often referred to as the 'honest' sound, is added in Classical American dialect. The symbol can be found in the right column of the vowel chart that follows, between /ɔ/ (all) and /ɑ/ (father). Also added is the use of liquid /ju/ (you) in certain circumstances.

In addition, several adjustments are made to vowel and diphthong sounds previously covered in Neutral American.

Front	Mid or Central	Back
Lips slightly spread **Lower jaw most closed**	**Lips neutral** **Lower jaw most closed**	**Lips most rounded** **Lower jaw most closed**
High i we		u who **High**
↓ ɪ will		ʊ would ↓
	ɝ **ER**	
Mid e get	ɚ er	o o'mit **Mid**
↓	ə uh	↓
	ʌ **UH**	
↓		ɔ all ↓
æ that		ɒ honest
Low (a* laugh[1])		ɑ fathers **Low**
Lips neutral **Lower jaw most open**	**Lips neutral** **Lower jaw most open**	**Lips unrounded on /ɑ/** **Lower jaw most open**

---

[1] The most open front vowel sound represented by the symbol /a/, which is the most low, open front vowel on the chart, is spoken on certain words in the Mid-Atlantic dialect. This and other sound changes and adjustments that need to be made to *Classical American* in order to speak the more formal *Mid-Atlantic* dialect are covered briefly on pages 417-433.

CLASSICALLY SPEAKING   **CLASSICAL AMERICAN** vowel chart

/ ɒ / (h<u>o</u>nest)

In certain words, this short, slightly lip-rounded back vowel sound is spoken instead of /ɔ/ (<u>a</u>ll) *or* /ɑ/ (f<u>a</u>ther). It is also used occasionally instead of /ʌ/ (<u>UH</u>), which adds additional rhythmic variation to Classical American.

The same sound, slightly more rounded, energized, and clipped, is spoken in Standard British in words such as 'top' and 'stop', which may sound familiar.

AUDIO 55▶ /ɒ/ (h<u>o</u>nest)

           ɒ   ɒ

Who's that kn<u>o</u>cking <u>o</u>n the floor?

(Chekhov: Three Sisters)

           ɒ   ae

For Brutus is an h<u>o</u>nor<u>a</u>ble man.

(Julius Caesar: III, ii, 82)

           ɒ

Why, wh<u>a</u>t a candy deal of courtesy

                   ɒ

This fawning greyhound then did pr<u>o</u>ffer me!

(1 Henry IV: I, iii, 251)

The /ɒ/ (h<u>o</u>nest) sound is used:

(a)   in words spelled with 'o' and pronounced with the /ɑ/ (f<u>a</u>ther) sound in Neutral American, as in:

not, hot, on, box, top, stop, job, shopping, probably, Tom

(b)   in words spelled with 'qua' or 'wa' and pronounced with the /ɑ/ (f<u>a</u>ther) sound in Neutral American including:

kumquat, quad, quaff, squab, squad, squalid, squalor, squash, squat, swaddling, swallow, swamp, wad, wallet, wallow, Wally, wan, wand, wander, want, wash, wasp, wast, wassail, watch, watt, yacht

(c)   in words spelled with 'o' and pronounced with the /ɔ/ (a̱ll) sound in Neutral American, as in:

cloth, moth, cross, boss, dog, office, often, song, belong

Exception: words spelled 'ought' as in bought, fought, and sought, are spoken with /ɔ/ in both Neutral and Classical.

(d)   in strong forms of a few words pronounced with the /ʌ/ (U̱H) sound in Neutral American, including:

from, of, 'twas, was, wasn't, what, whatnot, whereof

This alteration should be subtle to avoid sounding like the Standard British dialect. The jaw and back of the tongue are relaxed and the sinking of the cheeks is slight, as is the corresponding rounding of the lips.

WORDS /ɒ/ (ho̱nest)

on	tot	dot	job
God	mob	slob	Tom
jolly	bond	from	what
body	knob	office	soften
jostle	strong	model	follow
fondle	doctor	sobbing	robbery
holiday	Robert	monster	modern
popular	promise	Holland	contents
obvious	voluntary	response	stomped
comment	chocolate	nominate	common

The swine wa̱sn't worth the love I squa̱ndered o̱n him.

(Strindberg: Miss Julie)

If it is difficult to find the right shape for /ɒ/, begin by relaxing the jaw open for the long /ɑ/ (fa̱ther) sound. Then, slightly sink in the cheeks and corners of the lips, which makes the small alteration in shape needed for the open, slightly rounded /ɒ/ (ho̱nest) sound. The back of the tongue arch may lift slightly, but placing too much focus on this element can result in the more tense, clipped sound associated with Standard British pronunciation.

Follow this procedure while reading the samples below. *Read across.*

/hɑ/	/hɒ/	hot, hospital, hop, hockey, hollow
/tɑ/	/tɒ/	top, Tom, tock, toss, Todd, tolerant
/dɑ/	/dɒ/	Don, dot, dock, docile, doctor
/bɑ/	/bɒ/	box, bottle, bond, boss, Bob, body
/pɑ/	/pɒ/	possible, posture, posh, pop, pomp
/stɑ/	/stɒ/	stop, stock, stodgy, stocking
/ʃɑ/	/ʃɒ/	shot, shop, shock, shoddy, shopping

$$\overset{\textit{ɒ}}{} \qquad \overset{\textit{ɒ}}{}$$

In truth, fair Montague, I am too fond.

(Romeo and Juliet: II, ii, 98)

It may help to think of /ɒ/ (honest) as a shorter, more relaxed /ɔ/ (all) sound. With this in mind, try speaking the previous words and the phrases that follow.

PHRASES /ɒ/ (honest)

1.	wasn't honest		6.	lost her wallet
2.	costly donkey		7.	wants tolerance
3.	not the opposite		8.	speaks too softly
4.	the longest song		9.	spotted ten dollars
5.	slobbering stopped		10.	hears the clock tock

SENTENCES /ɒ/ (honest)

1. Rob cannot[1] stop sobbing.

2. The actors want hot coffee.

3. Todd's office is off the lobby.

4. Was he in Washington or wasn't he?

5. Are you positive she played ROSALIND?

6. Robin, your posh collar needs washing.

---

[1] Stress falls on the first syllable of the word 'cannot' /ˈkænɒtʰ/ in classic texts.

7.   Oliver spoke so softly, we lost his lines.

8.   The clock is on top of the closet, Robert.

9.   John will probably go to college in Boston.

10.   The shocked mobster was throttled by a toddler.

11.   What star is speaking the donkey's jolly dialogue?

12.   Empty the contents of your pockets onto the table.

13.   Doctor, stop drinking all the hospital's hot chocolate.

14.   Bob stopped swallowing scotch after spotting a Hobbit.

15.   What popular jockey is famous for his coffee commercial?

Honest Bob's Coffee Shop

If possible, I always stop by Honest Bob's Coffee Shop when on holiday in Boston. A constantly evolving menu offers a positively intoxicating array of entrees, like hot Macintosh omelets served in crock-pots, and roasted peacock simmered in a light butterscotch broth.

Grip Top Sock

Give me the gift of a grip-top-sock;
A clip-drape, ship-shape, tip-top sock.
Not your spiv-slick, slap-stick, slip-shod stock,
But a plastic, elastic grip-top sock.
None of your fantastic slack swap-slop
From a slapdash flash cash haberdasher shop!
Not a knick-knack, knock-kneed knickerbocker's sock
With a mock-shot, blob-mottled ticker-tocker clock.
Not a rucked-up puckered up flip-flop sock,
Not a super-sheer seersucker ruck-sack sock,
Not a spot-speckled, frog-freckled, cheap sheik's sock
Off a hodgepodge, moss-blotched botched Scotch block.
Nothing slip-slop, drip-drop,
Flip-flop or clip-clop:
Tip me to a tip-top grip-top sock.

(Anonymous)

WORDS comparing back vowels /ɔ/ /ɒ/ /ɑ/

Note: /ɔ/ and /ɑ/ are generally long, while /ɒ/ is short. The lips are relaxed and unrounded for /ɑ/. *Read across.*

	/ɔ/	/ɒ/	/ɑ/		/ɔ/	/ɒ/	/ɑ/
1.	awe	opt	ah	11.	hall	hot	hah
2.	saw	sop	saga	12.	Paul	pot	pa
3.	ball	box	Bach	13.	Shaw	shock	shah
4.	call	cost	calm	14.	draw	drop	drama
5.	fall	fog	father	15.	jaw	jot	java
6.	Saul	sot	saga	16.	slaw	slot	Slavic
7.	caw	cot	koala	17.	stall	stock	Stalin
8.	cause	cough	Kafka	18.	dawn	don	Dante
9.	paw	pop	papa	19.	talk	tock	taco
10.	mall	mop	macho	20.	call	cop	Kahn

ɒ   ɒ ɒ ɔ   ɒ   ɒ ɒ   ɔ

If a Hottentot tot taught a Hottentot tot to talk,

ɒ   ɒ

Ere the tot could totter;

ɔ   ɒ   ɒ ɒ ɔ   ɔ

Ought the Hottentot tot be taught to say aught,

ɒ ɔ   ɔ

Or what ought to be taught her?

(Edward Lear: Nonsense Rhymes)

SENTENCES comparing back vowels /ɔ/ /ɒ/ /ɑ/

/ɔ/   /ɒ/   /ɑ/

Call Tom at the spa.
Talk to honest father.
Water Molly's corsage.
Salt the rotten avocados.
Authors were honored in Tahoe.

/ɔ/   /ɒ/   /ɑ/

Saul wants hot tacos.
Authors promise drama.
We bought Florida palms.
Australians wanted guava.
They sought dogs and koalas.

/ɒ/   /ɔ/   /ɑ/

Stop calling father.
Watch Paul samba.
Officers are taught to be calm.
The tots fought in Palm Springs.
Holly's daughter is in the armada.

/ɒ/   /ɑ/   /ɔ/

Honestly, Bali's bawdy.
It's probably Sinatra calling.
The cost of pasta is awesome.
We got the hibachi in August.
An impossible scenario was drawn.

/ɑ/	/ɔ/	/ɒ/

/ɑ/	/ɒ/	/ɔ/

The suave caller is a mobster.

IAGO is auditioning tomorrow.

Picasso's drawings are popular.

These debutants are a saucy lot.

The sonata's thought to be modern.

The Mafia shot Paul.

Tanya shops at the mall.

Calamari with hot sauce.

Gandhi's moral thoughts.

That aria is often withdrawn.

CLASSICAL AMERICAN TEXT /ɒ/ (honest). *Mark the following and speak out loud.*

        ɒ   ɒ   ɒ   ɒ

Nay, mock not, mock not.

(Much Ado About Nothing: I, i, 285)

I speak French shockingly.

(Chekhov: The Cherry Orchard)

Now blessed be the great Apollo!

(The The Winter's Tale: III, ii, 137)

I love thee not; therefore pursue me not.

(A Midsummer Night's Dream: II, i, 188)

Mine honor is my life, both grow in one;

Take honor from me, and my life is done.

(Richard II: I, i, 182)

No; let him die, in that he is a fox,

By nature prov'd an enemy to the flock.

(2 Henry VI: III, i, 257)

And ah! what dialogue!

My prince, I do believe you've turned the frog!

(Rostand: Cyrano de Bergerac)

I am so fond of coffee, I drink it day and night.

(Chekhov: The Cherry Orchard)

What do you want? Stop where you are. You're positively dripping.

(Ibsen: Ghosts)

Come lead me, officers, to the block of shame;

Wrong hath but wrong, and blame the due of blame.

(Richard III: IV, v, 28)

Nay, then he is a conjurer.

(2 Henry VI: IV, ii, 92)

Plead what I will be, not what I have been;
Not my deserts, but what I will deserve.

(Richard III: IV, iv, 414)

Mars laid waste to the sweets of poor Apollo—
Wife, shop, and all in a single swallow!

(Rostand: Cyrano de Bergerac)

No, Titus, no, the Emperor needs her not,
Nor her, nor thee, nor any of thy stock.

(Titus Andronicus: I, I, 299)

Cancel his bond of life, dear God, I pray,
That I may live and say, "The dog is dead."

(Richard III: IV, iv, 77)

What shall be done with him? What is your plot?

(The Merry Wives of Windsor: IV, iv, 46)

You are not really happy—that is at the bottom of it.

(Ibsen: Hedda Gabler)

You have taken your hat off. Put it on or you will catch cold.

(Chekhov: The Sea Gull)

Loves me, loves me not; loves me, loves me not; loves me, loves
me not.

(Chekhov: The Seagull)

He is six-or seven-and-twenty, and has never had the opportunity
of learning what a well-ordered home really is.

(Ibsen: Ghosts)

Well, 'tis no matter, honor pricks me on. Yea, but how if honor
prick me off when I come on? How then? Can honor set to a leg?
No. Or an arm? No. Or take away the grief of a wound? No.
Honor hath no skill in surgery then? No. What is honor? A word.
What is in that word honor? What is that honor? Air. A trim
reckoning! Who hath it? He that died a' Wednesday.

(1 Henry IV: V, i, 129)

'Liquid' / ju / (you)

When the /u/ sound occurs after 't', 'd' or 'n' in the spelling, /j/ is added before /u/ so that **'liquid'** /ju/ (you) is spoken. This is optional after 's' or 'l'.

AUDIO 56▶ **'liquid'** /ju/ (you)

                                                                         dju

Women, you see—in certain matters, they have a <u>deu</u>cedly

    tju

keen in<u>tui</u>tion.

(Ibsen: The Master Builder)

                              tju

Like sweet bells jangled out of <u>tu</u>ne, and harsh.

(Hamlet: III, i, 158)

                dju

The old fantastical <u>Du</u>ke of dark corners.

(Measure for Measure: IV, iii, 156)

WORDS with liquid /ju/ (you)

after 't'   astute, attitude, beatitude, constitution, costume, destitute, gratitude, institute, institution, latitude, obtuse, opportunity, platitudes, servitude, stew, steward, Stewart, Stuart, student, studious, stupendous, stupid, tuba, tube, tuber, tuberculosis, tubular, Tudor, Tuesday, tufa, tuition, tulip, tumescence, tumor, tumult, tuna, tune, tunic, Tunisia, Turin, tutelage, tutor

after 'd'   adieu, conducive, dude, deduce, deuce, dew, duality, dubiety, dubious, dubitation, duel, duenna, dues, duet, duke, dukedom, duly, dune, duo, duped, duplex, duplicate, duplicity, dutiful, duty, indubitably, induce, introduce, reproduce, residue

after 'n'   annuity, avenue, enumerate, ingenuity, knew, minute (*adj.*), minutiae, mononucleosis, neume, neuter, neutral, neutralize, neutron, Newark, newborn, newcomer, newel, news, newspaper, newt, nuance, nuclear, nucleus, nude, nuisance, numerous, nutriments, nutrition, renewal, retinue, revenue

after 's' **(optional)**	assume, consume, ensue, presume, pursuit, pursue, sucrose, sue, suet, suicide, suit, suitor, super, superficiality, superfluous, superintendent, superior, superlative, supine
after 'l' **(optional)**	absolute, allude, allusions, aluminum, delude, dissolute, eluded, elusive, evolution, illuminate, illusory, lewd, lieu, lieutenant, lubricate, lucency, lucerne, lucid, Lucifer, lucrative, lucubrate, ludicrous, lugubrious, lukewarm, luminous, lunacy, lunar, lunatic, lute, resolution, salubrious, salute, solution

Note: There are also a few words that add the 'liquid' /ju/ (you) after 'z' and voiceless 'th', including:

> enthused, enthusiasm, enthusiastic, exhume, exude, exuberant, exuviate, presume, resume, Zeus

The 'liquid' /ju/ (you) is not used:

(a) when the /u/ sound is represented by 'o' in the spelling, as in:

> to, too, two, toot, do, noose, soup, Lou, loom, balloon

(b) when consonant combinations of /l/ are involved, as in:

> flew, slew, blue, fluent, and plume

PHRASES with liquid /ju/ (you)

1.	great stew		6.	singing duo
2.	happy news		7.	overdue dues
3.	salutes stupidity		8.	brand new suit
4.	stupendous tune		9.	another new student
5.	introducing the duke		10.	passed the resolution

SENTENCES with liquid /ju/ (you)

1. Is tuna nutritious?

2. The news was amusing.

3. What a stupendous duet.

4. Don't assume he's destitute.

5. Was Hugo's contract renewed?

6.   Students resume classes Tuesday.

7.   The scene was played in the nude.

8.   The price of costumes is ludicrous.

9.   Mr. Nugent felt the apology gratuitous.

10.   What's the intersecting longitude and latitude?

11.   The newscaster remains enthusiastically neutral.

12.   The lute of unpolluted silver was sold on Tuesday.

13.   Don't presume your positive new attitude is lunacy.

14.   The news that there are no new tumors is stupendous.

15.   Cigarette smoke left a thin residue on all the new tables.

Studious Stewart Dumaine

You could argue that the studious humanitarian, Stewart Dumaine, is quite a suitable suitor for the enthusiastic beauty from Tulane. Presumably, the opportunity to introduce the duo will ensue on Tuesday at the Numerological Institute.

> A tutor who tooted the flute,
> Tried to tutor two tooters to toot.
> Said the two to the tutor:
> "Is it harder to toot,
> Or to tutor two tooters to toot?"
>
> (Anonymous)

CLASSICAL AMERICAN TEXT 'liquid' /ju/ (you). *Mark the following and speak out loud.*

tju
I seem likely to be a perpetual student.

(Chekhov: The Cherry Orchard)

I do perceive here a divided duty.

(Othello: I, iii, 181)

Ah, tutor, look where bloody Clifford comes!

(3 Henry VI: I, iii, 2)

If opportunity and humblest suit
Cannot attain it, why then hark you hither!

(The Merry Wives of Windsor: III, iv, 20)

That she was never yet that ever knew
Love got so sweet as when desire did sue.

(Troilus and Cressida: I, ii, 290)

A goodly lady, trust me, of the hue
That I would choose were I to choose anew.

(Titus Andronicus: I, i, 261)

Were I a man, a duke, and next of blood,
I would remove these tedious stumbling-blocks.

(2 Henry VI: I, ii, 63)

Come now, which one of you will head the list?
You m'sieur? No? You? Or you? First duellist
Will meet with all grave honor can command.

(Rostand: Cyrano de Bergerac)

Never dropped mildew on a flower here till now.

(Webster: The White Devil)

Your honour, I stand ready for any duteous employment.

(Tourneur: The Revenger's Tragedy)

For strokes receiv'd and many blows repaid
Have robb'd my strong-knit sinews of their strength.

(3 Henry VI: II, iii, 3)

Tomorrow I shall have to speak to the whole assembled multitude.

(Ibsen: Ghosts)

This news is old enough, yet it is every day's news.

(Measure for Measure: III, ii, 229)

These clever fellows are all so stupid; there's not a creature for me
to speak to.

(Chekhov: The Cherry Orchard)

What difference is between the duke and I? No more than between
two bricks, all made of one clay: only't may be one is placed on the
top of a turret, the other in the bottom of a well, by mere chance.

(Webster: The White Devil)

/ æ / (th<u>a</u>t)

before 'm' 'n' 'g' 'ng' 'nk' spellings

In heightened[1] speech, the pure non-nasal vowel /æ/ is spoken before / m n g ŋ ŋk /. The back of the tongue remains relaxed and uninvolved.

AUDIO 57▶ /æ/ (th<u>a</u>t)

　　　　　ae　　　　ae　　　　　ae　ae　(or use weak forms)
But I c<u>an</u>'t underst<u>an</u>d how you c<u>an</u> h<u>a</u>ve made it go far

enough for two.

(Ibsen: Hedda Gabler)

　　　　　　　æ　　　　　　　　　　　æ　ə
By heaven, I r<u>a</u>ther would have been his h<u>ang</u>man.

(Othello: I, i, 34)

　　　　　　æ　　　　ae (or ə)　　æ
You speak a l<u>ang</u>uage th<u>a</u>t I underst<u>an</u>d not.

(The The Winter's Tale: III, ii, 80)

Tension, nasality, or variation in pronunciation of /æ/ sounds can be identified through the following exercise.

WORDS /æ/ sounds in the following should 'rhyme' *Read across.*

/æ/	apple	/æ/	am, amber, ambulance
/kæ/	cat	/kæ/	camp, camphor, camera
/dæ/	dash	/dæ/	damn, damp, damsel
/gæ/	gas	/gæ/	gamma, gamble, gamut
/hæ/	has	/hæ/	Hamlet, hammer, hamster

---

[1] The need for a slight relaxation of /æ/ before /m n g ŋ ŋk/ was addressed in NAS, since it is a tense sound in many North American dialects—but pure /æ/ is not required in NAS.

/hæ/	hat	/hæ/	hamper, hammock, hamstring
/stæ/	stack	/stæ/	stamp, stammer, stamina
/fæ/	fat	/fæ/	famished, family, famine
/læ/	lack	/læ/	land, landscape, landward
/hæ/	hat	/hæ/	hand, handsome, handbag

Assure that the vowel sound is releasing through the mouth by pinching the nose shut on the vowel. Be sure to release the pinching before the three consonant sounds that exit through the nose: / m n ŋ /.

/stæ/	stack	/stæ/	stand, standard, stand-in
/fæ/	fat	/fæ/	fan, fancy, fantasy, fantastic
/dæ/	dad	/dæ/	dang, dank, dangle, dangling
/ræ/	rack	/ræ/	rang, rank, rankle, ranked
/ʃæ/	shack	/ʃæ/	shank, Shanghai, Shangri-La

/ræ/	rack	/ræ/	rancor, rancorous, rancorously
/hæ/	hack	/hæ/	hang, Hank, hanker, hanger
/jæ/	yak	/jæ/	yang, yank, Yankee, Yangtze
/væ/	vat	/væ/	van, vanished, vanity, vantage
/æ/	at	/æ/	angry, angle, angular, anguished

/dʒæ/	Jack	/dʒæ/	jangle, jangly, jangling
/wæ/	wax	/wæ/	Wang, wangle, wangling
/stræ/	distract	/stræ/	strangle, strangler, strangling
/læ/	lack	/læ/	Lang, lank, languish, langley
/læ/	lap	/læ/	language, languid, languor

       ae   *ae ae (or weak form) ae*   *ae*
I daresay you fancy that I am an extremely happy man.
(Ibsen: The Master Builder)

PHRASES /æ/ (that)

1.	pulling rank	6.	grand oat bran
2.	back to the bank	7.	Jackie, not Jan
3.	languidly fanned	8.	hamming it up
4.	trampled fantasies	9.	stacks of stamps
5.	not monogrammed	10.	thanks, but no thanks

SENTENCES /æ/ (th<u>a</u>t)

1. Yes, Lady Anne?

2. Thanks, but no thanks.

3. Who starred in *Champ*?

4. Terrific back-hand, Frank.

5. Nancy sent us a candygram.

6. That stage-gun shoots blanks.

7. What's the brand of champions?

8. Pam sang the Thanksgiving anthem.

9. Turn on a fan; it's so hot I can't stand it!

10. What's wrong, Francis? You look angry.

11. He sang his name, rank and serial number.

12. There's Hank, the family's favorite spaniel.

13. Mandy, you can't drink brandy on the left bank.

14. The jogger is stamping to stop muscle cramping.

15. I need a bigger tank for my brand new angle fish.

Lanky Frankie

L<u>a</u>nky Fr<u>a</u>nkie, P<u>a</u>mela's p<u>a</u>mpered sp<u>a</u>niel, r<u>a</u>n <u>a</u>fter a t<u>a</u>n <u>a</u>fgh<u>a</u>n r<u>a</u>mbling down Gr<u>a</u>nd <u>A</u>venue. Th<u>a</u>nkfully, Fr<u>a</u>nkie is b<u>a</u>ck with his f<u>a</u>mily, b<u>a</u>nqueting on h<u>a</u>m s<u>a</u>ndwiches. They are not <u>a</u>ngry, and Fr<u>a</u>nkie will h<u>a</u>ve no reprim<u>a</u>nd.

CLASSICAL AMERICAN TEXT /æ/ (th<u>a</u>t). *Mark the following and speak out loud.*

<pre>
 ae   ae   ae
</pre>
D<u>a</u>mn her, lewd minx! O, d<u>a</u>mn her, d<u>a</u>mn her!

(Othello: III, iii, 475)

Come, Hamlet, come, and take this hand from me.

(Hamlet: V, ii, 224)

Fate's a spaniel,
We cannot beat it from us.

(Webster: The White Devil)

I am your sorrow's nurse,
And I will pamper it with lamentation.

(Richard III: II, ii, 87)

The words would add more anguish than the wounds.

(3 Henry VI: II, i, 99)

You see me, Lord Bassanio, where I stand,
Such as I am. Though for myself alone
I would not be ambitious in my wish.

(The Merchant of Venice: III, ii, 149)

Look at me, my friend, and say what chance,
What hope have I, with this...protuberance?

(Rostand: Cyrano de Bergerac)

ROSALINE. Thou canst not hit it, hit it, hit it,
        Thou canst not hit it, my good man.
BOYET.   And I cannot, cannot, cannot[1],
        And I cannot, another can.

(Love's Labor's Lost: IV, i, 125)

BENEDICK. Fair Beatrice, I thank you for your pains.
BEATRICE. I took no more pains for those thanks than you take pains
           to thank me.

(Much Ado About Nothing: II, iii, 249)

Why, if thou never wast at court, thou never saw'st good manners;
if thou never saw'st good manners, then thy manners must be wicked,
and wickedness is sin, and sin is damnation.

(As You Like It: III, ii, 40)

        The ring is on my hand,
        And the wreath is on my brow;
        Satins and jewels grand
        Are all at my command,
        And I am happy now.

(Poe: Bridal Ballad)

---

[1] Remember, stress usually falls on the first syllable of the word 'cannot' **/'kænɒtʰ/** in classic texts.

/ aʊ̆ / (n<u>ow</u>)

/ aʊ̆ɚ/ (p<u>ower</u>)

This is an *optional,* subtle adjustment to the above sounds, which may be useful if they seem overly nasal or bright within the dialect. It is based on an older, more traditional Standard British pronunciation, which initiates these sounds with the relaxed back vowel /ɑ/ (f<u>a</u>ther) rather than the brighter /a/ sound. The tongue arch gently flattens, dropping to the floor of the mouth for the first element, while the lips, cheeks, tongue, and throat muscles remain relaxed.

AUDIO 58▶ /aʊ̆/ (n<u>ow</u>) and /aʊ̆ɚ/ (p<u>ower</u>)

> aʊ̆
> It s<u>ou</u>nded like harps in the air.
>
> (Ibsen: The Master Builder)
>
> aʊ̆ aʊ̆
> H<u>ow</u> n<u>ow</u>, you sec<u>r</u>et, black, and midnight hags?
>
> (Macbeth: IV, i, 48)
>
> aʊ̆   aʊ̆   aʊ̆   aʊ̆
> Fl<u>out</u> 'em and sc<u>out</u> 'em and sc<u>out</u> 'em and fl<u>out</u> 'em!
>
> Thought is free.
>
> (The Tempest: III, ii, 121)

WORDS /aʊ/→/aʊ̆/

ouch	chow	vow	proud
allow	crowd	growl	prowl
down	count	mount	drown
flounce	astound	bounce	around
compound	paramount	surround	befouled

EXERCISE relationship between /ɑ/, /aʊ̆/, and /aʊ̆ɚ /. Relax the lips, cheeks, tongue, and throat, and flatten the tongue arch when initiating the following words, all of which begin with the most open back vowel /ɑ/ (f<u>a</u>ther).

Read across.

/ɑ/	/aʊ/	/aʊ/	/aʊɚ/[1]
Saga	sound	souse	sour
papa	pounce	pound	power
father	found	fountain	flower
tra-la-la	louse	loud	lower
bah	boughs	bounced	bower

PHRASES /aʊ/ (n<u>ow</u>)

1.	not all<u>ow</u>ed	6.	l<u>ou</u>d sh<u>ou</u>ting
2.	b<u>ou</u>nced ar<u>ou</u>nd	7.	t<u>ow</u>n due s<u>ou</u>th
3.	ch<u>ow</u> d<u>ow</u>n n<u>ow</u>	8.	<u>ou</u>nces and p<u>ou</u>nds
4.	s<u>ou</u>ndless h<u>ou</u>nd	9.	pr<u>ou</u>d <u>ow</u>ls p<u>ou</u>ncing
5.	ast<u>ou</u>nding h<u>ou</u>se	10.	acc<u>ou</u>ntant fl<u>ou</u>ndered

aʊ   aʊ   aʊ
Th<u>ou</u> thing of no b<u>ow</u>els, th<u>ou</u>!

(Troilus and Cressida: II, i, 49)

SENTENCES /aʊ/ (n<u>ow</u>) and /aʊɚ/ (p<u>ow</u>er)

1. No kowtowing allowed.

2. Start the countdown now.

3. Sound all vowels out loud.

4. Do Girl Scouts sell sauerkraut?

5. Ever heard of 'surround sound'?

6. That sounded like a putdown, Howard.

7. The scoundrel impounded both houses.

8. What a well-pronounced announcement.

9. The guests caught trout and hunted grouse.

10. They found him cowering in the flowerbed.

11. I'm not so fond of that brown evening gown.

---

[1] Remember, the triphthong may also be rhythmically separated into a diphthong followed by the short, unstressed vowel of 'r' as in /aʊ ɚ/.

12.   Mr. Powell ran the endowment into the ground.

13.   He was found of wandering around down town.

14.   *Encounters* is playing at the Roundabout Theatre.

15.   After shopping for hours, she rested by the fountain.

CLASSICAL AMERICAN TEXT /aʊ/ (n<u>ow</u>) and /aʊɚ/ (p<u>ower</u>). *Mark the following and speak out loud.*

                aʊ

For courage m<u>ou</u>nteth with occasion.

                            (King John: II, i, 82)

Or perhaps a wart adorns one jowl…?

                      (Rostand: Cyrano de Bergerac)

For God's sake let us sit upon the ground
And tell sad stories of the death of kings.

                        (Richard II: III, ii, 155)

Set down, set down your honorable load,
If honor may be shrouded in a hearse.

                        (Richard III: I, ii, 1)

How now, my pretty knave, how dost thou?

                        (King Lear: I, iv, 96)

Where art thou, proud Demetrius? Speak thou now.

              (A Midsummer Night's Dream: III, ii, 401)

Even now we hous'd him in the abbey here.

                    (The Comedy of Errors: V, i, 188)

Enter Cyrano! saves the dangling grouse…
And I wake…as steward in his cousin's house!

                    (Rostand: Cyrano de Bergerac)

Drown thyself? drown cats and blind puppies!

                      (Othello: I, iii, 335)

I was afraid, partly on my own account. I was such a coward.

                      (Ibsen: Ghosts)

How now, thou core of envy?

(Troilus and Cressida: V i, 4)

A thousand crowns, or else lay down your head.

(2 Henry VI: IV, i, 16)

Beauford's red sparkling eyes blab his heart's malice,
And Suffolk's cloudy brow his stormy hate.

(2 Henry VI: III, i, 154)

I won't find peace till I'm down, won't rest till I'm down, down on
the ground! And once I'm down, I want to keep on going down
and down...

(Strindberg: Miss Julie)

Stay we no longer, dreaming of renown,
But sound the trumpets, and about our task.

(3 Henry VI: II, i, 199)

No one has any grounds to separate spirit from matter, seeing
that spirit itself may be a combination of material atoms.

(Chekhov: The Seagull)

Oh 'tis a brave thing for a man to sit by himself; he may stretch
himself in the stirrups, look about, and see the whole compass of
the hemisphere. You're now, my lord, i' th' saddle.

(Webster: The White Devil)

I would thou couldst stammer, that thou mightst pour this conceal'd
man out of thy mouth, as wine comes out of a narrow-mouth'd bottle,
either too much at once, or none at all.

(As You Like It: III, ii, 198)

As the bee hums communion with the flower...
A way to touch a heartbeat...and the power
As you taste a lingering instant of the soul!

(Rostand: Cyrano de Bergerac)

PURE VOWELS
before consonant / r /

When the consonant /r/ (red) occurs in the middle of a word, it is preceded by a pure vowel sound, not by a diphthong of 'r'.

This element of Classical American is taken from Standard British pronunciation and can serve several purposes. This usage:

(a) affords a formality and an authenticity to the pronunciation of British-English proper names and places, especially in Shakespeare

(b) diminishes the amount of 'r' coloring, which helps encourage a release of the voice and speech forward through the mouth

(c) provides differentiation between words that would otherwise be pronounced the same, for example 'hairy' and 'Harry'

(d) helps to establish a time and place other than present-day America—as do the rest of the Classical American changes

This is an important body of work for students interested in studying other dialects. People with English as a second language often learn from British-English speakers. Therefore, the adjustments that follow are often required for speaking other dialects as well.

The vowel sounds and consonant /r/ that follow are separated by a dash (–) throughout.

/ ɪ / (wɪll)

before consonant / r /

Use pure /ɪ/ (wɪll), rather than the /ɪɚ / (here) diphthong, before consonant /r/ within a word. Words requiring this adjustment can often be recognized by an /ɪ/ prefix (see page 97) and/or by the initial spellings: 'ir', 'irr'.

AUDIO 59▶ /ɪ/ (w<u>i</u>ll) before consonant /r/

I
You seem a bit low-sp<u>i</u>-rited to-day, aren't you?

(Chekhov: Three Sisters)

I
The m<u>i</u>-rror of all courtesy.

(Henry VIII: II, i, 53)

I
O cruel, <u>i</u>-rreligious piety!

(Titus Andronicus: I, i, 130)

NAMES & PLACES /ɪ/ (w<u>i</u>ll) before consonant /r/

Be-rowne	Hispe-ria	I-ran	I-raq
I-roquois	Pi-randello	Sy-ria	Ty-rrel

WORDS /ɪ/ (w<u>i</u>ll) before consonant /r/

be-rate	be-reaved	be-reft	de-rision
de-rive	empi-rical	e-radicate	e-rase
e-rect	e-rogenous	e-rosion	e-rotic
e-rratic	e-rroneous	e-ruption	he-reditary
he-roic	i-rrational	i-rritable	i-rregular
i-rrelevant	i-rrespective	ly-rical	mi-racle
mi-rror	pre-rogative	py-ramid	se-rene
spi-rit	sy-rup	ty-ranny	vi-rile[1]

PHRASES /ɪ/ (w<u>i</u>ll) before consonant /r/

1.	i-rregular day	6.	clear mi-rror
2.	feeling be-reft	7.	tall py-ramid
3.	se-rene vacation	8.	trip to Sy-ria
4.	lovely pi-rouette	9.	e-rased pages
5.	floating di-rigible	10.	i-rreparable break

SENTENCES /ɪ/ (w<u>i</u>ll) before /r/

1. Change direction.

2. Who played BEROWNE?

---

[1] Standard British pronunciation of 'ile' endings is usually /aɪl/ (<u>aisle</u>) i.e., sterile, futile.

3. What remarkable lyrics.

4. The disease was hereditary.

5. How many lira for that mirror?

6. Do I see stirrups on that giraffe?

7. The tyrannical ruler was replaced.

8. They were bereaved and dispirited.

9. What spirited material he's written.

10. Rinaldo remains an imperious individual.

11. It was a pyrrhic victory, costing too much.

12. Imagine berating the delinquent instructor.

13. The irascible director erupted during rehearsal.

14. Challenge the satirical bully to a debate, sirrah!

15. Confidence in the relationship eventually eroded.

16. That was a heroic portrayal of the Iroquois Indians.

17. How miraculous: a serene vacation in a secluded spot.

18. We were explicitly advised to rely on empirical evidence.

19. We desire an innovative production, not a derivative one.

20. Two short, unstressed syllables? That's a pyrrhic rhythm.

Moose Mirage

Was it a mi̱-rage?

No, it was the largest stack of pancakes I had ever seen a gi̱-raffe eat.

Pouring on the sy̱-rup, the se̱-rene chewing of each little bite, it was both ly̱-rical

and he-roic. This tho-roughly e-rased the time I saw a moose preparing a

soufflé.

Exception: when /ɪɚ/ (h<u>ere</u>) diphthong ends the root of a word that is followed by a suffix, the diphthong is maintained and linking consonant /r/ is used to connect the suffix, including: 'age', 'ance', 'ence', 'eth', 'er', 'est', 'ing', 'y'. Therefore, 'hearing' is pronounced: /ˈhɪɚ-rɪŋ/.

ɪɚ-r   *ɪɚ-r*

My nea-rest and dea-rest enemy.

(1 Henry IV: III, ii, 123)

SOME EXCEPTION WORDS that keep /ɪɚ/ (h<u>ere</u>) before /r/

reareth	bleary	leery	wearier
fearing	gearing	cheery	peerage
appearance	smearing	queerer	clearance

CLASSICAL AMERICAN TEXT /ɪ/ (w<u>i</u>ll) before /r/. *Mark the following and speak out loud.*

        ɪ

Tell me, s<u>i</u>rrah, what's my name?

(2 Henry VI: II, i, 115)

Now my spirit is going.

(Antony and Cleopatra: IV, xv, 58)

Poor rogue hereditary.

(Timon of Athens: IV, iii, 274)

The tyrannous and bloody act is done.

(Richard III: IV, iii,1)

Lord Bassianus lies beray'd in blood.

(Titus Andronicus: II, iii, 222)

Confirmed; this be the doom irrevocable.

(Tourneur: The Revenger's Tragedy)

Hast thou not spirit to curse thine enemy?

(2 Henry VI: III, ii, 308)

I have perhaps some shallow spirit of judgment.

(1 Henry VI: II, iv, 16)

In them I trust, for they are soldiers,
Witty, courteous, liberal, full of spirit.

(3 Henry VI:, I ii, 42)

Erroneous, mutinous, and unnatural,
This deadly quarrel daily doth beget!

(3 Henry VI: II, v, 90)

That all your interest in those territories
Is utterly bereft you: all is lost.

(2 Henry VI:, III i, 84)

And I, who at his hands receiv'd my life,
Have by my hands of life bereaved him.
Pardon me, God, I knew not what I did!

(3 Henry VI: II, v, 67)

Upon thy eyeballs murderous tyranny
Sits in grim majesty, to fright the world.

(2 Henry VI: III, ii, 49)

Lend your romantic looks, heroic stance –
And between us we'll make one *par excellence*!

(Rostand: Cyrano de Bergerac)

GLOUCESTER. Fellow, what miracle dost thou proclaim?
ONE.   A miracle, a miracle!
SUFFOLK.   Come to the King and tell him what miracle.

(2 Henry VI: II, i, 58)

The last is Berowne, the merry madcap lord. Not a word with
him but a jest.

(Love's Labor's Lost: II, i, 215)

Sirrah, your lord and master's married, there's news for you.
You have a new mistress.

(All's Well That Ends Well: II, iii, 242)

The girl with the irritating hair, that she was always showing off.

(Ibsen: Hedda Gabler)

/ e / (g<u>e</u>t)

before consonant / r /

Use pure /e/ (g<u>e</u>t) before the consonant /r/ rather than the /e<u>ə</u>/ (th<u>ei</u>r) diphthong. Use of pure /e/ is often indicated by the spellings: 'er', 'err'.

AUDIO 60▶ /e/ (g<u>e</u>t) before consonant /r/

>   e
> I often feel ready to sink under this t<u>e</u>-rrible burden of debt.
> > (Ibsen: The Master Builder)
>
>   e
> Pleas'd you to do't at p<u>e</u>-ril of your soul.
> > (Measure for Measure: II, iv, 67)
>
>   e
> I am never m<u>e</u>-rry when I hear sweet music.
> > (The Merchant of Venice: V, i, 69)

NAMES & PLACES /e/ (g<u>e</u>t) before consonant /r/

Ame-rica	Be-resford	Be-ring	Che-ryl
De-rek	De-rry	E-rebus	E-ric
Fe-rris	Ge-rald	Ge-raldine	He-reford
He-rod	He-ron	He-rrick	Hespe-rides
Je-rry	Ke-rry	Me-rrill	Pe-rry
She-ridan	She-rry	Spe-rry	Te-rence

WORDS /e/ (g<u>e</u>t) before consonant /r/

auste-rity	bu-ry	cele-rity	ce-remony
che-rish	che-rub	de-relect	de-rivation
de-rogate	e-rror	e-rrant	e-rrand
e-remite	fe-rry	fe-rrous	gene-ric
he-rald	he-resy	he-retic	he-roine

he-rring	hyste-rical	inhe-rit	ke-rosene
me-rit	me-rry	pe-ril	pe-rish
prospe-rity	she-riff	ste-rile	te-rrace
te-rrible	te-rrify	ve-ry	ve-ritable

PHRASES /e/ (g**e**t) before consonant /r/

1.	yes, Je-rry	6.	ve-ry me-rry
2.	te-rribly angry	7.	E-ric's he-ritage
3.	e-rrant Te-rence	8.	playing He-rod
4.	pe-rilous e-rrors	9.	te-rrible she-rry
5.	He-rrick's entrance	10.	pe-rilous walkway

SENTENCES /e/ (g**e**t) before consonant /r/

1. Verify everything, Jerry.

2. Buy strawberries, Gerald.

3. Sheridan, what's a gerund?

4. Serenade the heroine, Merrill.

5. Terrence is a veritable cherub.

6. Heroism is cherished in Derry.

7. What is the derivation of 'serif'?

8. The secretary committed an error.

9. I wish you the merriest of holidays.

10. Eric cherishes *The Cherry Orchard*.

11. Geraldine played the erudite heroine.

12. Sherry experienced great peril on the job.

13. Serried together, they were terribly crowded.

14. They took the wherry, not the ferry, to Derry.

15. Which is merrier: winged seraphs or cherubs?

16. Hesperides and dragons guard the golden apples.

17. The broken glass of sherry was just a red herring.

18. The steel, spherical room is very sterile in appearance.

19.   Well managed austerity can be followed by prosperity.

20.   The American General merited a special burial ceremony.

Exception: when **/eə̆ /** (th<u>eir</u>) diphthong ends the root of a word that is followed by a suffix, the diphthong is maintained and linking consonant **/r/** is used to connect the suffix, including: 'age', 'ance', 'er', 'est', 'ious', 'ing', 'y'. Therefore, 'pairing' is pronounced: **/'peə̆-rɪŋ/.**

SOME EXCEPTION WORDS keeping /eə̆/ (th<u>eir</u>) before /r/

airy	bearer	caring	despairing
forbearance	hairy	parentage	rarely
scary	therein	vicarious	wary

feə̆-rə eə̆ͮr aĭ
You shall look fairer ere I give or hazard.

(The Merchant of Venice: II, ix, 22)

CLASSICAL AMERICAN TEXT /e/ (g<u>e</u>t) before consonant /r/. *Mark the following and speak out loud.*

                    e
Blood! He speaks t<u>e</u>rribly!

(Marlowe: Doctor Faustus)

And to be talk'd with in sincerity,
As with a saint.

(Measure for Measure: I, iv, 36)

Their dwarfish pages were
As cherubins, all gilt.

(Henry VIII: I, i, 22)

I would rather do it myself, very, very gently.

(Strindberg: The Father)

It is the very error of the moon.

(Othello: V, ii, 109)

You have, I know, petition'd all the gods
For my prosperity!

(Coriolanus: II, i, 170)

The net has fall'n upon me! I shall perish.

(Henry VIII: I, i, 203)

Father, you cannot disinherit me.
If you be king, why should not I succeed?

(3 Henry VI: I, i, 226)

Her funeral shall be wealthy, for her name
Merits a tomb of pearl.

(Tourneur: The Revenger's Tragedy)

Come go along and see the truth hereof,
For our first merriment hath made thee jealous.

(The Taming of the Shrew: IV, v, 75)

Who sent thee? What's thy errand? Leave my sight.

(Middleton & Rowley: The Changeling)

Whilst I at home starve for a merry look.

(The Comedy of Errors: II, i, 88)

It needs not, nor it boots thee not, proud queen,
Unless the adage must be verified,
That beggars mounted run their horse to death.

(3 Henry VI: I, iv, 125)

But now I come to the next great error in your life.

(Ibsen: Ghosts)

I come to bury Caesar, not to praise him.

(Julius Caesar: III, ii, 74)

Be merry? Hang merry, draw and quarter merry!

(Tourneur: The Revenger's Tragedy)

I needn't tell you your cherry orchard is to be sold to pay
your debts.

(Chekhov: The Cherry Orchard)

Being sheriff, you know, he has to travel about a good deal
in his district.

(Ibsen: Hedda Gabler)

CLASSICALLY SPEAKING   **CLASSICAL AMERICAN /e-r/**

/ æ / (th<u>a</u>t)

before consonant / r /

Use pure /æ/ (th<u>a</u>t) before consonant /r/, rather than the /eə/ (th<u>ei</u>r) diphthong in proper names, places, and words (some of which follow). The use of /æ/ (th<u>a</u>t) is often indicated by the spellings: 'ar', 'arr'.

AUDIO 61▶ /æ/ (th<u>a</u>t) before consonant /r/

>   æ   æ   æ
> The B<u>a</u>-ron is drunk, the B<u>a</u>-ron is drunk, the B<u>a</u>-ron is drunk.
>   (Chekhov: Three Sisters)
>
>   æ
> This punk is one of Cupid's c<u>a</u>-rriers.
>   (Merry Wives of Windsor: II, ii, 135)
>
>   æ
> You're a strange ch<u>a</u>-racter, no doubt about it.
>   (Chekhov: Three Sisters)

NAMES & PLACES /æ/ (th<u>a</u>t) before consonant /r/

A-rab	A-ragon	A-riadne	Ba-rry
Ca-ribbean	Ca-rrol	Cha-ring	Cla-rence
Da-rrow	Da-rryl	Fa-rrell	Fa-rrow
Fa-rragut	Ga-rrick	Ga-rry	Ha-rold
Ha-rriet	Ha-rris	Ha-rrod	Ha-rry
Ja-rrett	La-rry	Pha-ramond	Sa-racen

WORDS /æ/ (th<u>a</u>t) before consonant /r/

ala-rum	a-rid	a-rras	a-rrogant
a-rrow	a-ristocracy	ba-ritone	ba-ron
ba-rrel	ba-rrier	ba-rricade	ca-ravan
ca-ricature	ca-rriage	ca-rrion	ca-rry
cha-racter	cha-riot	cha-rity	cla-ret

compa-rison	emba-rrass	ga-rish	ga-rret
gua-rantee	ga-rrison	ha-rass[1]	ha-rrowing
hila-rity	la-rynx	ma-rigold	ma-rry
ma-rriage	ma-rrow	ma-rathon	ma-riner
na-rrate	na-rrative	na-rrow	pa-rable
pa-rachute	pa-ragon	pa-ragraph	pa-rallel
pa-rasite	pa-rry	pa-rish	pa-rody
pa-rrot	pha-risee	singula-rity	spa-rrow
ta-rantella	ta-rragon	ta-rry	transpa-rent

PHRASES /æ/ (th<u>a</u>t) before consonant /r/

1.	such a cha-racter	6.	ca-rried on
2.	not emba-rrassed	7.	yes, Ha-rry
3.	decided to ma-rry	8.	overly a-rrogant
4.	sexual ha-rassment	9.	thinking na-rrowly
5.	straight as an a-rrow	10.	getting ca-rried away

MORE PHRASES /æ/ (th<u>a</u>t) before consonant /r/

1.	too emba-rrassing	6.	a-rid weather
2.	cha-racter building	7.	lovely pa-rrot
3.	na-rrating the book	8.	ta-rries awhile
4.	makes compa-risons	9.	especially ba-rren
5.	prepared a ga-rrison	10.	recounted pa-rables

SENTENCES /æ/ (th<u>a</u>t) before consonant /r/

1. They'll marry.

2. Carry it, Harriet.

3. Barry, tarry awhile.

4. Who's in the garrison, Garry?

5. I love playing arrogant characters.

6. She was harassed on Arrow Street.

7. I characterize him as a working barracuda.

---

[1] Accent the first syllable: **'ha-<u>r</u>ass** /**'hæres**/.

8. *The Marriage Proposal* is playing in Paris.

9. Darryl is playing the character of the Baron.

10. Arid weather contributes to her harried look.

11. The parish priest is a paragon of good health.

12. Apparently, the garrison refused to eat carrion.

13. The passage is too narrow for Harold's carriage.

14. Harry and Larry were cast as the arrogant twins.

15. The thought of running the marathon is hilarious.

16. Mr. Farrell, the Barrister, disparaged the Saracens.

17. Jarret proved a paragon in navigating the labyrinth.

18. What garrulous baritone gets laryngitis with regularity?

19. Harold Harris narrated the harrowing maritime parable.

20. Barry Darrow is unparalleled in his charitable activities.

21. Aragon was once its own Kingdom in Northeastern Spain.

22. Ariadne guided Theseus through the maze without alarum.

23. Ms. Farrow is known for her garish, claret-colored apparel.

24. The Pharisee was carried through the barricade in a chariot.

25. Harold wrote a comparative narrative from a garret in Paris.

Verily, Harry's Married

eə̆   æ   æ   e   e   eə̆   æ
When hairy Ha-rry ma-rried ve-ry me-rry Mary in a ca-rriage,

e   e   e
it was a pe-rilous and te-rrible e-rror.

CLASSICAL AMERICAN TEXT /æ/ (tha̱t) before consonant /r/. *Mark the following and speak out loud.*

æ
Ma̱rry, God forbid!

(Richard II: IV, i, 114)

Search the market narrowly.

(Pericles: IV, ii, 3)

I have a triple-barreled name.

(Chekhov: Three Sisters)

It is no sin at all, but charity.

(Measure for Measure: II, iv, 66)

That's a telegram from Paris.

(Chekhov: The Cherry Orchard)

How am I then a villain,
To counsel Cassio to this parallel course.

(Othello: II, iii, 348)

Sound, trumpets, alarum to the combatants!

(2 Henry VI: II, iii, 92)

Do you not follow the young Lord Paris?

(Troilus and Cressida: III, i, 1)

Fie! charity, for shame! speak not in spite,
For you shall sup with Jesu Christ to-night.

(2 Henry VI: V, i, 213)

But match to match I have encount'red him,
And made a prey for carrion kites and crows.

(2 Henry VI: V, ii, 10)

And after summer evermore succeeds
Barren winter, with his wrathful nipping cold.

(2 Henry VI: II, iv, 2)

That was not my most arrant cowardice—that evening.

(Ibsen: Hedda Gabler)

This was sometime a paradox, but now the time gives it proof.

(Hamlet: III, i, 113)

Call me Julie—there are no barriers between us now.

(Strindberg: Miss Julie)

Harry to Harry shall, hot horse to horse,
Meet and ne'er part till one drop down a corse.

(1 Henry IV: IV, i, 122)

She's not well married that lives married long,
But she's best married that dies married young.

(Romeo and Juliet: IV, v, 77)

Heat me these irons hot, and look thou stand
Within the arras.

(King John: IV, i, 1)

The fashion wears out more apparel than the man.

(Much Ado About Nothing: III, iii, 139)

Why, this is an arrant counterfeit rascal, I remember him now;
a bawd, a cutpurse.

(Henry V: III, vi, 61)

They circle round that thoughtful perch, seduced—
At last, you bring the sparrows home to roost!

(Rostand: Cyrano de Bergerac)

I learn in this letter that Don Pedro of Arragon comes this night
to Messina.

(Much Ado About Nothing: I, i, 1)

O peers of England, shameful is this league,
Fatal this marriage, cancelling your fame,
Blotting your names from books of memory,
Raising the characters of your renown,
Defacing monuments of conquer'd France.

(2 Henry VI: I, i, 98)

Not so, not so; his life is parallel'd
Even with the stroke and line of his great justice.

(Measure for Measure: IV, ii, 79)

Come, come, you paraquito, answer me
Directly unto this question that I ask.
In faith, I'll break thy little finger, Harry,
And if thou wilt not tell me all things true.

(I Henry IV: II, iii, 85)

Your father is not a man of strong character, Miss Engstrand.
He stands terribly in need of a guiding hand.

(Ibsen: Ghosts)

/ ʌ / (UH)

before consonant / r /

There are many words spoken with /ʌ/ (UH) before consonant /r/ rather than /ɜ/ (ER) in Classical American, which is derived from Standard British.

AUDIO 62▶ /ʌ/ (UH) before consonant /r/

ʌ
Why do you keep wo̲-rrying me?

(Chekhov: Three Sisters)

ʌ   o
I should like your conscience to be — to be tho̲-roughly ro'bust.

(Ibsen: The Master Builder)

ʌ
And men sit down to that no̲u-rishment which is called supper.

(Love's Labor's Lost: I, i, 236)

NAMES & PLACES /ʌ/ (UH) before consonant /r/

Cu-rrier	Cu-rran	Du-rham	Cu-rrer
Cu-rrie	Mu-rray	Mu-rrow	Su-rrey

WORDS /ʌ/ (UH) before consonant /r/

bo-rough	bu-rrow	cou-rage	cu-rrant
cu-rrency	cu-rrent	cu-rricle	cu-rry
discou-rage	encou-rage	discou-raged	flou-rish
flu-rry	fu-rrier	fu-rrow	hu-rricane
hu-rry	hu-rrying	mu-rrain	nou-rish
nou-rishment	occu-rrence	scu-rrilous	scu-rry
su-rrogate	tu-rret	tho-roughly	wo-rry

ʌ
Lend me the flo̲u-rish of all gentle tongues.

(Love's Labor's Lost: IV, iii, 234)

PHRASES /ʌ/ (<u>UH</u>) before consonant /r/

1.	hot cu-rry	6.	snow flu-rries
2.	too tho-rough	7.	not nou-rishing
3.	large fu-rrows	8.	fu-rrowed brow
4.	always hu-rrying	9.	changed cu-rrency
5.	very discou-raged	10.	needs encou-raging

SENTENCES /ʌ/ (<u>UH</u>) before consonant /r/

1. He has luck and courage!

2. Are there currants in curry?

3. Check the currency exchange.

4. Mother loved Currier and Ives.

5. No scurrilous language, please.

6. Can furriers flourish in summer?

7. Dudley needs a nourishing lunch.

8. They worried about murrains in Surrey.

9. The bulky gunner was stuck in the turret.

10. Your current assets are in what currency?

11. Murray was suddenly in no hurry to leave.

12. Children come running to see snow flurries.

13. Are there surrogate mothers in this borough?

14. You musn't furrow your brow so much, honey.

15. Murray is thoroughly discouraged by injustice.

16. The judge invoked the Durham Rule in sentencing.

17. Uncle Chuck worries compulsively about hurricanes.

18. He took his pulse before plunging into the swift current.

19. Humphrey was in a hurry to purchase *dhurries* from India.

20. Young Doug burrowed a tunnel under Durham just for fun.

CLASSICAL AMERICAN TEXT /ʌ/ (UH) before /r/. *Mark the following and speak out loud.*

ʌ

Met him in boroughs, cities, villages,
Attended him on bridges, stood in lanes.

(1 Henry IV: IV, iii, 69)

There is no answer, thou unfeeling man,
To excuse the current of thy cruelty.

(The Merchant of Venice: IV, i, 63)

A red murrion a' thy jade's tricks!

(Troilus and Cressida: II, i, 19)

You put sharp weapons in a madman's hands,
Whiles I in Ireland nourish a mighty band.

(2 Henry VI: III, i, 347)

A flourish, trumpets! strike alarum, drums!

(Richard III: IV, iv, 149)

Why do the Emperor's trumpets flourish thus?

(Titus Andronicus: IV, ii, 49)

Thanks, thanks, there is no hurry, my dear child.

(Ibsen: Ghosts)

Three times did Richard make a lane to me,
And thrice cried, "Courage, father! fight it out!"

(3 Henry VI: I, iv, 9)

No more, no more! worse than the sun in March,
This praise doth nourish agues. Let them come!

(1 Henry IV: IV, i, 111)

That island of England breeds very valiant creatures;
their mastiffs are of unmatchable courage.

(Henry V: III, vii, 140)

But Jean—give me courage—tell me that you love me!

(Strindberg: Miss Julie)

Now, if it were in a thoroughly nice house, with a real gentleman...

(Ibsen: Ghosts)

/ ɔ / (all)

before consonant / r /

Use pure /ɔ/ (all) before consonant /r/ rather than the /ɔɚ/ diphthong. Use of /ɔ/ (all) is often indicated by the spellings: 'or', 'aur'.

AUDIO 63▶ /ɔ/ (all) before consonant /r/

          ɔ

A frightful sto-ry. What am I to believe?

                (Strindberg: Crimes and Crimes)

               ɔ

Now are our brows bound with victo-rious wreaths.

                (Richard III: I, i, 5)

          ɔ

You may my glo-ries and my state depose,

But not my griefs; still am I king of those.

                (Richard II: IV, i, 192)

NAMES & PLACES /ɔ/ (all) before consonant /r/

Au-ro-ra	Isado-ra	Lau-ra	Mau-reen
O-rient	Tau-rus	To-ry	Victo-ria

WORDS /ɔ/ (all) before consonant /r/

au-ra	au-ral	au-ricle	au-riferous
cho-rus	cho-ral	deco-rum	eupho-ria
flo-ra	fo-rum	glo-ry	glo-rious
glo-rify	histo-rian[1]	labo-rious	lau-reate
memo-rial	merito-rious	mo-ron	noto-rious
o-ral	sto-ry	quo-rum	victo-rious

---

[1] histo̱ric, -al, -ally: pronounced with /ɒ/ (honest) rather than /ɔ/.

PHRASES /ɔ/ (all) before consonant /r/

1.	saw the To-ry	6.	Lau-ra's place
2.	quite an au-ra	7.	eupho-ric cho-rus
3.	a glo-rious day	8.	not quite a quo-rum
4.	mo-ronic sto-ry	9.	buying o-riental rugs
5.	noto-rious events	10.	cho-ral arrangements

SENTENCES /ɔ/ (all) before consonant /r/

1. Hello, Laura.

2. We're victorious!

3. What's the quorum?

4. Where is Laurel Canyon?

5. See you on Memorial Day.

6. That's a lovely Oriental rug.

7. What a glorious performance!

8. Victoria is a notorious Taurus.

9. Write the definition of 'moron'.

10. Saul's oral report was laborious.

11. Who is England's Poet Laureate?

12. He's sitting with the other Tories.

13. We saw you at the mall, Maureen.

14. What's the famous story of Aurora?

15. Paul, did you just call him a moron?

16. They thought he'd talk about the Orient.

17. There is a lack of decorum at Shoreham.

18. Maybe you'll be cast as QUEEN VICTORIA.

19. In our forum, a quorum isn't necessary for a vote.

20. The Orient is notorious for its floral arrangements.

Exception: When /ɔɚ/ (sp<u>or</u>ts) diphthong ends the root of a word that is followed by a suffix, the diphthong is maintained and linking consonant /r/ is used to connect the suffix, including: 'age', 'eth', 'ic', 'ing', 'ous', 'y'. Therefore, 'pouring' and 'caloric' are pronounced /ˈpɔɚ-rɪŋ/ and /kəˈlɔɚ-rɪk/.

ˈpɔɚ-rɪŋ
When creeping murmur and the po<u>r</u>ing dark
Fills the wide vessel of the universe.

(Henry V: IV Chorus, 2)

SOME EXCEPTION WORDS that keep /ɔɚ/ (sp<u>or</u>ts) before consonant /r/

abhorreth	adoring	allegoric	boring
coring	exploring	gory	hoary
porous	soaring	storage	warring

CLASSICAL AMERICAN TEXT /ɔ/ (<u>al</u>l) before /r/. *Mark the following and speak out loud.*

ɔ
Sir, make me not your st<u>o</u>ry.

(Measure for Measure: I, iv, 30)

Devils! Sharpen up your memory!
Here's that glorious opportunity —

(Rostand: Cyrano de Bergerac)

You are as good as a chorus, my lord.

(Hamlet: III, ii, 245)

O, bless me here with thy victorious hand,
Whose fortunes Rome's best citizens applaud!

(Titus Andronicus: I, i, 163)

But thinkst thou heaven is such a glorious thing?

(Marlowe: Doctor Faustus)

And by an auricular assurance have your satisfaction.

(King Lear: I, ii, 92)

That's the story I was loathe to tell you a moment ago.

(Strindberg: Miss Julie)

/ ɒ / (h<u>o</u>nest)

before consonant / r /

Use the pure /ɒ/ (h<u>o</u>nest) sound, rather than the /ɔ<u>ə̆</u> / (sp<u>or</u>ts) diphthong, before consonant /r/. The use of /ɒ/ (h<u>o</u>nest) is often indicated by the spellings: 'or', 'ar', 'aur'.

AUDIO 64▶ /ɒ/ (h<u>o</u>nest) before consonant /r/

        ɒ
But that's h<u>o</u>-rrible! And you did not suffer?

(Strindberg: Crimes and Crimes)

        ɒ
We started qu<u>a</u>-rreling at seven o'clock.

(Chekhov: Three Sisters)

        ɒ
I will instruct my s<u>o</u>-rrows to be proud,

For grief is proud and makes his owner stoop.

(King John: III, i, 68)

NAMES & PLACES /ɒ/ (h<u>o</u>nest) before consonant /r/

Bo-ris	Co-rin	Do-ris	Do-rothy
Flo-rida	Flo-rence	Flo-rizel	Go-rell
Ho-race	Ho-rowitz	Lau-rence	Mo-rris
No-rris	Wa-rwick	Yo-rick	Zo-rro

WORDS /ɒ/ (h<u>o</u>nest) before consonant /r/

abho-rrence	autho-rity	bo-rrow	co-ral
co-ronation	co-rrespond	flo-rid	flo-rist
fo-rage	fo-reign	fo-rest	histo-rical
ho-roscope	ho-rrible	ho-rrid	ho-rror
inco-rrigible	lau-rel	lo-rry	majo-rity

mino-rity	mo-ral	o-range	o-racle
o-rator	o-rigin	o-risons	o-rotund
po-rridge	qua-rantine	qua-rrel	qua-rry
rheto-rical	so-rry	tomo-rrow	to-rrent
to-rrid	wa-rrant	wa-rren	wa-rrior

PHRASES /ɒ/ (h<u>o</u>nest) before consonant /r/

1.	docile o-racle	6.	so so-rry
2.	reluctant wa-rrior	7.	a to-rrid affair
3.	so-rry for Mo-rris	8.	point of o-rigin
4.	very hot fo-rehead[1]	9.	not the mino-rity
5.	not another qua-rrel	10.	resist bo-rrowing

SENTENCES /ɒ/ (h<u>o</u>nest) before consonant /r/

1. What a horrible holiday!

2. Orangeade is popular in Potsdam.

3. It's too hot to play golf in Florida.

4. Gosh, Dorothy eats lots of porridge.

5. The forest filled with torrential rain.

6. Historical dramas are Oliver's favorite.

7. Robin, look at John and say you're sorry.

8. Norris, what's on the bottom of the lorry?

9. Laurence lives in a posh lodge in Oregon.

10. Florian was in the foreign release of *Zorro*.

11. Rob felt it immoral to pollute the coral reefs.

12. I'm fond of Laurence; he's my favorite florist.

13. Is it immoral to quarantine quarrelling warriors?

14. Doris found the orator's style horribly annoying.

15. The majority of Horace's employees have seniority.

---

[1] forehead: /ˈfɒ-rɪd/

16.   Boris borrowed from Corin to attend the coronation.

17.   Authorities presented a warrant to the somber mobster.

18.   Morris, Horowitz must remain quarantined in the forest.

19.   Is it possible the oracle's oratory will restore confidence?

20.   Sorry, but this correspondence won't go out until tomorrow.

CLASSICAL AMERICAN TEXT /ɒ/ (honest) before consonant /r/. *Mark the following and speak out loud.*

ɒ

What's the quarrel?

(Troilus and Cressida: II, i, 89)

No, I can better play the orator.

(3 Henry VI: I, ii, 2)

A sorry war—
We lay the siege, and starve ourselves!

(Rostand: Cyrano de Bergerac)

He receives comfort like cold porridge.

(The Tempest: II, i, 10)

On Wednesday next we solemnly proclaim
Our coronation. Lords, be ready all.

(Richard II: IV, i, 319)

I felt sorry, oh! So sorry for mamma all at once.

(Chekhov: The Cherry Orchard)

And have you changed your orisons?

(Middleton & Rowley: The Changeling)

Unlike young men, whom Aristotle thought
Unfit to hear moral philosophy.

(Troilus and Cressida: II, ii, 166)

Some foreign university has made him a doctor.

(Ibsen: Hedda Gabler)

I really must borrow of you just 180 roubles, only 180 roubles.

(Chekhov: The Cherry Orchard)

Present fears
Are less than horrible imaginings.

(Macbeth: I, iii, 137)

Sir, let me borrow of you but one kiss.

(Webster: The White Devil)

My brothers to bring a warrant for my death?

(Tourneur: The Revenger's Tragedy)

He'll be as full of quarrel and offense
As my young mistress' dog.

(Othello: II, iii, 50)

And when the hardiest warriors did retire,
Richard cried, "Charge! And give no foot of ground!"

(3 Henry VI: I, iv, 14)

Her hair is sprinkled with orris powder,
That makes her look as if she had sinned in the pastry.

(Webster: The White Devil)

Ah, you're naturally in great spirits to-day — what with to-morrow's
festival and Oswald's return.

(Ibsen: Ghosts)

1 MURDERER. What? art thou afraid?
2 MURDERER. Not to kill him, having a warrant, but to be damn'd for
               killing him, from the which no warrant can defend me.

(Richard III I, iv, 109)

There's horror in my service, blood and danger.

(Middleton & Rowley: The Changeling)

My niece is horribly in love with a thing you have, sweet queen.

(Troilus and Cressida: III, i, 97)

'ary' 'berry' 'ory'

pure vowels before consonant / r /

Polysyllabic words are words of three or more syllables. Use a pure vowel sound before the consonant /r/ in the second to the last syllable of polysyllabic words ending spelled: 'ory', 'ary', and 'berry'. This adds formality without necessarily sounding British.

(a) Words ending in 'ary' and 'berry' use pure **/e/** before the consonant **/r/**

(b) Words ending in 'ory' use pure **/ɔ/** before the consonant **/r/**

AUDIO 65▶ **polysyllabic word endings pure vowel before /r/**

> This goodly frame, the earth, seems to me a sterile promonto-ry.
>
> (Hamlet: II, ii, 298)

> If it should ever be necessa-ry. But it will never be necessa-ry.
>
> (Ibsen: Ghosts)

> If reasons were as plentiful as blackbe-rries, I would give no man
>
> a reason on compulsion.
>
> (1 Henry IV: II, iv, 239)

WORDS 'ary' endings pronounced /e-ri/

'actua-ry	'capilla-ry	'ordina-ry	'arbitra-ry
fi'ducia-ry	'necessa-ry	'legenda-ry	'Februa-ry
'customa-ry	'adversa-ry	a'potheca-ry	'mercena-ry
bene'ficia-ry	'dictiona-ry	'commenta-ry	re'actiona-ry
'momenta-ry	he'redita-ry	evo'lutiona-ry	con'fectiona-ry

WORDS 'berry' endings pronounced /e-ri/

'barbe-rry	'baybe-rry	'dogbe-rry	'chinabe-rry
'cranbe-rry	'dewbe-rry	'blackbe-rry	'goosebe-rry
'hackbe-rry	'mulbe-rry	'snowbe-rry	'winterbe-rry

WORDS 'ory' endings pronounced /ɔ-ri/

'orato-ry	'audito-ry	'mandato-ry	'purgato-ry
'minato-ry	'laudato-ry	de'rogato-ry	a'ccusato-ry
'predato-ry	de'posito-ry	'circulato-ry	con'ciliato-ry
con'tributo-ry	o'bligato-ry	'promisso-ry	ex'clamato-ry
inter'rogato-ry	pre'parato-ry	ob'servato-ry	ma'nipulato-ry

PHRASES polysyllabic word endings, pure vowel before /r/

1. small invento-ry
2. difficult reperto-ry
3. conservato-ry class
4. elocutiona-ry expert
5. derogato-ry message
6. great libra-ry
7. not necessa-ry
8. hucklebe-rry bush
9. tempora-ry position
10. unsanita-ry conditions

SENTENCES polysyllabic word endings, pure vowel before /r/

1. They requested sanctuary.

2. What a transitory itinerary.

3. That was forbidden territory.

4. Hallucinatory drugs were forbidden.

5. Improvisatory training is mandatory.

6. Oh, my favorite: brambleberry stew.

7. Not all migratory beasts are predatory.

8. There's no need for derogatory remarks.

9. She had coronary and auditory weakness.

10. Is it necessary to have a literary manager?

11. Actors need improved elocutionary skills.

12. The circus offered funambulatory training.

13.   What an extraordinary vocabulary you have.

14.   Monetary problems affected their inventory.

15.   Intermediaries decide the compensatory amount.

16.   She'll begin at the acting conservatory in January.

17.   After secondary school he began veterinary training.

18.   Boysenberry pie is made with special confectionaries.

19.   He's in a quandary and will take a temporary position.

20.   The missionary found sanctuary in religious ceremony.

CLASSICAL AMERICAN TEXT polysyllabic word endings, pure vowel before /r/. *Mark the following and speak out loud.*

e-ri
That was most extraordin<u>a</u>ry.

(Ibsen: Ghosts)

It were but necessary you were wak'd.

(2 Henry VI: III, ii, 261)

My mind was never yet more mercenary.

(The Merchant of Venice: IV, i, 418)

Like one that stands upon a promontory
And spies a far-off shore where he would tread.

(3 Henry VI: III, ii, 135)

Come, come, my boy, we will to sanctuary.

(Richard III, II, iv, 66)

And now again the same; what omen yet
Follows of that? None but imaginary.

(Middleton & Rowley: The Changeling)

I know him for a man divine and holy,
Not scurvy, nor a temporary meddler.

(Measure for Measure: V, i, 144)

Feed him with apricocks and dewberries;
With purple grapes, green figs, and mulberries.

(A Midsummer Night's Dream: III, i, 166)

But myself,
Who had the world as my confectionary.

(Timon of Athens: IV, iii, 259)

Made you my guardians, my depositaries.

(King Lear: II, iv, 251)

But nor the time nor place
Will serve our long interrogatories.

(Cymbeline: V, v, 392)

Oh, those horrible, revolutionary, free-thinking books!

(Ibsen: Ghosts)

You are full of heavenly stuff, and bear the inventory
Of your best graces in your mind.

(Henry VIII: III, ii, 137)

I'll prove the contrary, if you'll hear me speak.

(3 Henry VI: I, ii, 20)

The strawberry grows underneath the nettle,
And wholesome berries thrive and ripen best
Neighbor'd by fruit of baser quality.

(Henry V: I, i, 60)

Forgive the comment that my passion made
Upon thy feature, for my rage was blind,
And foul imaginary eyes of blood
Presented thee more hideous than thou art.

(King John: IV, ii, 263)

Whatsoever you may hear to the contrary, let Claudio be executed
by four of the clock, and in the afternoon Barnardine.

(Measure for Measure: IV, ii, 120)

PRACTICE TEXT: Front vowels before consonant /r/

Cheryl's Peril

e   I   eǝ̃-r Iǝ̃-r
Che-ryl can't seem to e-rase the scary experience of being

e   e   e   ae (or eǝ̃-r) ae
te-rrorized by E-ric the te-rrier from her mind. Appa-rently, Ba-rry,

e   e   ae   ae   eǝ   eǝ
E-ric's e-rrant owner, constructed a na-rrow ba-rrier on their shared

e   ae   e
te-rrace that was supposed to gua-rantee that E-ric would remain on

ae   e   ɔǝ   ae   e
Ba-rry's side of the te-rrace. Unfortunately, Ba-rry, being de-relict in

dju   e   eǝ̃-r
his duties, made an e-rror and constructed the precarious obstruction

Iǝ̃-r   Iǝ̃-r   eǝ ɔǝ   e
from inferior materials. Therefore, when Che-ryl, whose balcony looks

ae   ae   eǝ̃-r e
like pa-radise, came out to water her ma-rigolds, hairy E-ric (looking

ɝ(or ʌ) ae   aǝ   ae
like quite the fu-rry cha-racter) came charging toward her ca-rrying on

I   ae   e   eǝ̃-r   eǝ
in a sati-rical manner. Ba-rry, with his ste-reo blaring, was unaware of

e   e   e   e
Che-ryl's pe-ril. Thinking she would pe-rish, Che-ryl, who was never

e   e   e   ʌ
one to be te-rribly me-rry, got hyste-rical. She's cu-rrently living with

eǝ̃-r   e   Iǝ   e
her parents while she's getting the-rapy at a nearby sanita-rium.

        eǝ̃-r   eǝ̃-r   ae or eǝ̃-r
Note: parent, precarious, appa-rent.

PRACTICE TEXT: Back vowels before consonant /r/

Isadora's Story

      ɑɚ-r   ɒ   ɒ   ɒ
Cesa<u>r</u>io, in his c<u>o</u>-rresp<u>o</u>ndence, requested my next c<u>o</u>mposition be

ɑ   ɒ   ɒ
an <u>a</u>-ria of hist<u>o</u>-rical significance: something with a m<u>o</u>-ral, but nothing too

ɒ   ɒ
h<u>o</u>-rrible. (He's inc<u>o</u>-rrigible!)

                                ɔ   ɔ   ɔ
Finally, I came up with something <u>au</u>thentic, mem<u>o</u>-rializing Isad<u>o</u>-ra

      ɔ   ɒ   ɒ   ɑɚ-r   ɒ
the not<u>o</u>-rious f<u>o</u>-reign w<u>a</u>-rrior from some f<u>a</u>raway place like Fl<u>o</u>-rence or the

ɔ   ɒ
<u>O</u>-rient. (No one is really certain of her <u>o</u>-rigin.)

                  ɔ   ɔ   ɒ   ɔɚ   ɔɚ   ɑ
This s<u>au</u>cy T<u>au</u>-rus l<u>o</u>st her f<u>or</u>tune while at w<u>ar</u> in the Sah<u>a</u>-ra, and

ɔ   ɒ   ɔ   ɔ   ɔ
fl<u>au</u>nted her t<u>o</u>-rrid affairs; <u>a</u>ll of which makes for an enthr<u>a</u>lling st<u>o</u>-ry. It's

                     ɔ   ɒ
finished, except the ch<u>o</u>-rus, which should be completed by tom<u>o</u>-rrow, and—

ɑɚ-r   ɒ   ɔ   ɒ   ɔ
b<u>ar</u>ring any qu<u>a</u>-rrel with the <u>au</u>th<u>o</u>-rities'—it will be playing in <u>Au</u>stralia to

ɒ   ɔ   ɔ   ɔɚ-r
an <u>o</u>nsl<u>au</u>ght of appl<u>au</u>se. . . f<u>o</u>rever!

          ɔɚ   ɒ
Note: w<u>ar</u>, w<u>a</u>-rrior

RHYTHM HIGHLIGHTER ADJUSTMENTS

Two more adjustments to NAS may be incorporated, if slightly more formality is desired. The rhythm of certain words is modified by speaking:

(a) slightly shorter /i/ (w<u>e</u>) sound in unstressed word endings

(b) slightly less 'r' coloring in vowels, diphthongs and triphthongs of 'r'

Unstressed / i / (w<u>e</u>) endings

The /i/ (w<u>e</u>) sound can be slightly shorter in length when in an unstressed position at or near the end of a word. These endings are usually spelled with a 'y', and occasionally with an 'i', as in 'marr<u>ie</u>d'. This is a subtle rhythmic adjustment, not a sound adjustment, and can be facilitated by emphasizing the vowel in the stressed syllable.

AUDIO 66▶ **slightly shorter /i/ (w<u>e</u>) endings**

The air bites **'shrewd**l<u>y</u>.

(Hamlet: I, iv, 1)

Why do we get **'lazy**, indifferent, useless, un**'ha**pp<u>y</u>?

(Chekhov: Three Sisters)

Ad**'ver**sit<u>y</u>'s sweet milk, phi**'lo**soph<u>y</u>.

(Romeo and Juliet: III, iii, 55)

WORDS slightly shorter /i/ (w<u>e</u>) endings

'an<u>y</u>	**'**witt<u>y</u>	**'**eleg<u>y</u>	**'**ratt<u>y</u>
'Ital<u>y</u>	**'**prett<u>y</u>	**'**reall<u>y</u>	**'**amit<u>y</u>
'parit<u>y</u>	**'**rand<u>y</u>	**'**salar<u>y</u>	**'**man<u>y</u>
'vanit<u>y</u>	**'**sanit<u>y</u>	**'**fairl<u>y</u>	**'**hone<u>y</u>
'water<u>y</u>	**'**notar<u>y</u>	**'**cavit<u>y</u>	**'**chatt<u>y</u>

'pantry	'felony	'battery	'eighty
'faculty	'sweaty	'nightly	a'cidity
'regency	'brevity	di'vinity	'charity
'amnesty	a'trocity	curi'osity	a'ffinity
'certainly	'carefully	ca'lamity	bru'tality

PHRASES slightly shorter /i/ (we) endings. These can be notated with an underline or strikethrough, whichever marking works as a better reminder.

1.	some money	6.	just barely
2.	out of brandy	7.	real artistry
3.	the understudy	8.	has elasticity
4.	shines brightly	9.	a bit too drafty
5.	very very tricky	10.	fond domesticity

Days of the week can also be spoken with a short /i/ (we) ending rather than the Neutral American /eĭ/ (hey).

SENTENCES slightly shorter /i/ (we) ending:

1. See you Tuesday.

2. Bradley loves old movies.

3. The baby is due in January.

4. I saw her at a party on Friday.

5. Can I borrow a twenty, Mary?

6. Cathy's character is very fussy.

7. Actually, he's wary of investing.

8. Sorry I missed the charity event.

9. Gary visited Sally in the infirmary.

10. He's happily and hopelessly in love.

11. It can be especially cold in February.

12. I thought there would be reciprocity.

13.   There has been no scarcity of publicity.

14.   The celebrity gave a wishy-washy response.

15.   Harry is understudying in *The Cherry Orchard*.

CLASSICAL AMERICAN TEXT slightly shorter /i/ (w<u>e</u>) endings.   *If marking text with an underline or strikethrough helps you to adjust this sound slightly, do so. Then practice out loud.*

Farewell, fair cruelty.

(Twelfth Night: I, v, 288)

O, beware, my lord, of jealousy!

(Othello: III, iii, 165)

Ye say honestly, rest you merry!

(Romeo and Juliet: I, ii, 62)

O, yet I do repent me of my fury,
That I did kill them.

(Macbeth: II, iii, 106)

False prelates, for this hateful treachery,
Cursed be your souls to hellish misery.

(Marlowe: Doctor Faustus)

That reverend Vice, that grey Iniquity, that father ruffian,
that vanity in years.

(1 Henry IV: II, iv, 453)

Fine Villain! Troth, I like him wondrously.

(Tourneur: The Revenger's Tragedy)

But this! To have thrown away so shamefully, thoughtlessly,
recklessly, one's own happiness.

(Ibsen: Ghosts)

He has been here a week already. Just fancy—a whole week!

(Ibsen: Hedda Gabler)

But that should have been said 'differently, so 'differently.

(Chekhov: The Cherry Orchard)

Bleed, bleed, poor country!

(Macbeth: IV, iii, 31)

Sister, farewell, I must to Coventry.

(Richard II: I, ii, 56)

All unavoided is the doom of destiny.

(Richard III: IV, iv, 218)

Who would e'er suppose
They had such courage and audacity?

(1 Henry VI: I, ii, 35)

Who says this is improvident jealousy?

(The Merry Wives of Windsor: II, ii, 289)

But are you sure
That Benedick loves Beatrice so entirely?

(Much Ado About Nothing: III, i, 36)

Our scouts have found the adventure very easy.

(3 Henry VI: IV, ii, 18)

The lords are all come back,
And brought Prince Henry in their company,
At whose request the King hath pardon'd them,
And they are all about his Majesty.

(King John: V, vi, 33)

Now thou and I are new in amity,
And will to-morrow midnight solemnly
Dance in Duke Theseus' house triumphantly,
And bless it to all fair prosperity.
There shall the pairs of faithful lovers be
Wedded, with Theseus, all in jollity.

(A Midsummer Night's Dream: IV, i, 87)

How sweetly she looks! Oh, but there's a wrinkle in her brow
as deep as philosophy.

(Middleton & Rowley: The Changeling)

'r' Coloring

vowels, diphthongs, triphthongs

Slightly less 'r' coloring (or slightly less 'er') can be spoken, especially when it occurs in unstressed syllables. Remember, the first element is stressed in all diphthongs and triphthongs; the unstressed element contains the weak vowel of 'r'.

A strikethrough (/) is placed over the letter(s) that represent(s) the vowel, diphthong or triphthong of **'r'**, as a reminder to make that sound slightly shorter and more relaxed. If you are using this section to practice the Mid-Atlantic dialect covered on pages 417-433, then completely *eliminate* 'r' coloring.

If you are unsure how to tell whether an **'r'** in the spelling reflects a vowel or a consonant, see the guidelines on page 295.

AUDIO 67▶ **slightly less 'r' coloring**

> You're working at your school, and I'm working at home.
>> (Chekhov: Three Sisters)
>
> I curse the day I was born in my mother's womb!
>> (Strindberg: Miss Julie)
>
> Fiddler, forbear. You grow too forward, sir.
>> (The Taming of the Shrew: III, i, 1)

WORDS less 'r' coloring

'racer	'actor	'favor	'later
'paper	'placer	'writer	'lever
'clover	'arbiter	'clipper	'tenor
'slipper	'bastard	'shirker	'easier
'master	'wonder	'happier	'plaster

'skipp<u>er</u>	'whisp<u>er</u>	'travel<u>er</u>	'Jupit<u>er</u>
'vineg<u>ar</u>	'plea<u>sure</u>	'voy<u>ag</u>er	'funni<u>er</u>
'Lucif<u>er</u>	'man<u>ag</u>er	'lavend<u>er</u>	'canist<u>er</u>
'pris<u>on</u>er	'gard<u>en</u>er	'alabast<u>er</u>	'drows<u>ier</u>
'harb<u>ing</u>er	'me<u>ss</u>eng<u>er</u>	'common<u>er</u>	'passeng<u>er</u>

PHRASES slightly less 'r' coloring. These can be notated with an underline or strikethrough, whichever marking works as a better reminder.

1.	had a seizu<u>re</u>	6.	doesn't figu~~r~~e
2.	must be ti<u>red</u>	7.	too much ga~~r~~lic
3.	playing the lead<u>er</u>	8.	hanging pictu~~r~~es
4	makes it disapp<u>ear</u>	9.	wants to conspi~~r~~e
5.	some mo<u>re</u> cho<u>res</u>	10.	living nea~~r~~ Vassa~~r~~

SENTENCES slightly less 'r' coloring

1. Yes, dear.

2. Don't you dare!

3. What's the score?

4. Your publisher is over there.

5. I hear you worked as an au-pair.

6. Bernie plays the 'computer nerd'.

7. He's been an actor for many years.

8. She's a collector of old typewriters.

9. Are you sure your slippers are lost?

10. He is the most charming writer, by far.

11. They were tired and filled with despair.

12. She was honored by a jury of her peers.

13. How much ginger beer do you drink yearly?

14. He was unaware of her martial arts training.

15. Bertha attended the Academy Awards in 2004.

CLASSICAL AMERICAN slightly less 'r' coloring. *If marking text with an underline or strikethrough helps you to adjust this sound slightly, do so. Then practice out loud.*

Infirm of purpose!

(Macbeth: II, ii, 49)

Words, words, words.

(Hamlet: II, ii, 192)

I have no further with you.

(Coriolanus: II, iii, 173)

Surrender, musketeers!

(Rostand: Cyrano de Bergerac)

Where's my serpent of old Nile?

(Antony and Cleopatra: I, v, 25)

I do not much dislike the matter, but
The manner of his speech.

(Antony and Cleopatra: II, ii, 111)

Good Doctor Pinch, you are a conjurer.

(The Comedy of Errors: IV, iv, 47)

And therefore by His majesty I swear,
Whose far-unworthy deputy I am,
He shall not breathe infection in this air
But three days longer, on the pain of death.

(2 Henry VI: III, ii, 285)

Bring him his confessor, let him be prepar'd.

(Measure for Measure: II, i, 35)

And like an eagle o'er his aery tow'rs,
To souse annoyance that comes near his nest.

(King John: V, ii, 149)

Zounds, I was never so bethump'd with words
Since I first call'd my brother's father dad.

(King John: II, i, 466)

A woman would run through fire and water for such a kind heart.

(The Merry Wives of Winsor: III, iv, 102)

Against my heart, his letter, paled with years —
And still the faintest trace of blood, his tears.

(Rostand: Cyrano de Bergerac)

Look you how his sword is bloodied, and his helm more hack'd
than Hector's.

(Troilus and Cressida: I, ii, 232)

Ah, wretched man, would I had died a maid
And never seen thee, never borne thee son,
Seeing thou hast prov'd so unnatural a father!
Hath he deserv'd to lose his birthright thus?

(3 Henry VI: I, i, 216)

O, pardon me, thou bleeding piece of earth,
That I am meek and gentle with these butchers!

(Julius Caesar: III, i, 254)

Fetch hither the swain, he must carry me a letter.

(Love's Labor's Lost: III, I, 49)

I'll cull thee out the fairest courtesans
And bring them every morning to thy bed.

(Marlowe: Doctor Faustus)

We have no right whatever to give offence to the weaker brethren.

(Ibsen: Ghosts)

What glory our Achilles shares from Hector,
Were he not proud, we all should share with him.

(Troilus and Cressida: I, iii, 366)

A bloody deed! Almost as bad, good mother,
As kill a king, and marry with his brother.

(Hamlet: III, iv, 28)

To be a well-favor'd man is the gift of fortune, but to write and
read comes by nature.

(Much Ado About Nothing: III, iii, 14)

PRACTICE TEXT

IPA TRANSCRIPTION WORDS

Transcribe the following for Classical American.

1. cough	_____		21. story	_____
2. whining	_____		22. arrows	_____
3. cannot	_____		23. hurry	_____
4. duke	_____		24. dubious	_____
5. belong	_____		25. spirited	_____
6. student	_____		26. horrible	_____
7. within	_____		27. mirage	_____
8. whinny	_____		28. current	_____
9. renew	_____		29. terrible	_____
10. ominous	_____		30. voluntary	_____
11. anywhere	_____		31. glorious	_____
12. tomorrow	_____		32. secretary	_____
13. nuclear	_____		33. ludicrous	_____
14. monstrous	_____		34. minority	_____
15. detective	_____		35. character	_____
16. lieutenant	_____		36. promissory	_____
17. knowledge	_____		37. ceremony	_____
18. institute	_____		38. perilously	_____
19. tentative	_____		39. strawberry	_____
20. Washington	_____		40. supervision	_____

PRACTICE TEXT

Fill in the blank lines with the appropriate phonetic marking for Classical American pronunciation, then speak aloud. If slightly less 'r' coloring or shorter 'y' endings are being used, mark those with a strikethrough, too. Voiced endings before a (possible) pause have been double-underlined, syllabics and consonant combinations have been marked. See key page 410.

1.   I saw but I never let on I saw.

(Strindberg: Miss Julie)

2.   I beg the law, the law, upon his head.

(A Midsummer Night's Dream: IV, i, 155)

3.   Alack, thou dost usurp authority.

(King John: II, i, 118)

4.   It strook mine ear most terribly.

(The Tempest: II, i, 313)

5.   I have a king's oath to the contrary.

(King John: III, i, 10)

6.   Who dares not stir by day must walk by night.

(King John: I, i, 172)

7.   Oh! An endless summer of oranges, evergreens...

(Strindberg: Miss Julie)

8.   But I will remedy this gear ere long,

Or sell my title for a glorious grave.

(2 Henry VI: III, i, 91)

9.   The King is not himself, but basely led

By flatterers, and what they will inform.

(Richard II: II, i, 241)

10.   In wrongful quarrel you have slain your son.

(Titus Andronicus: I, i, 293)

11.   There's law and warrant, lady, for my curse.

(King John: III, i, 184)

12.   "Three merry men be we."

(Twelfth Night: II, iii, 76)

13.   O, give ye good ev'n! here's a million of manners.

(The Two Gentlemen of Verona: II, i, 99)

14.   Come on, my boy. How dost, my boy? Art cold?

(King Lear: III, ii, 68)

15.   And what's more—if I'm not mistaken—the mob's out hunting

for me—and if they find us here together, we're lost!

(Strindberg: Miss Julie)

16.   Have I not forbid her my house? She comes of errands,
        does she?

(The Merry Wives of Windsor: IV, ii, 173)

17.   Seems he a dove? his feathers are but borrow'd,

For he's disposed as the hateful raven.

(2 Henry VI: III, i, 75)

18.   Well, follow me, my masters, you shall have your money
        presently.

(Pericles: IV, ii, 53)

19.   Then I would go off by myself on a pilgrimage to Kiev,

to Moscow[1].

(Chekhov: The Cherry Orchard)

20.   I should think he must be altogether too old for you. There is

at least twenty years' difference between you, is there not?

(Ibsen: Hedda Gabler)

---

[1] Classical pronunciation of 'Moscow' is usually: /ˈmɒskʰoŭ (or) ˈmɒskʰaŭ/

PRACTICE TEXT

Mark the following for Classical American and speak out loud. Also mark changes that are carried over from NAS, if this is useful.

1. Nymph, in thy orisons
   Be all my sins rememb'red.

   (Hamlet: III, i, 88)

2. I have given a mortgage on our annuity.

   (Ibsen: Hedda Gabler)

3. Lord help the woman who marries you!

   (Strindberg: Miss Julie)

4. This is the fairy land. O spite of spites!
   We talk with goblins, owls, and sprites.

   (Comedy of Errors: II, ii, 189)

5. Then it is illicit relations you are talking of!
   Irregular marriages, as people call them!

   (Ibsen: Ghosts)

6. Thou knowest the mask of night is on my face,
   Else would a maiden blush bepaint my cheek
   For that which thou hast heard me speak to-night.

   (Romeo and Juliet: II, ii, 85)

7. Ransomless here we set our prisoners free.

   (Titus Andronicus: I, i, 274)

8. A friendly fearless warrior—so he tells my wife.

   (Rostand: Cyrano de Bergerac)

9. These griefs, these woes, these sorrows make me old.

   (Romeo and Juliet: III, ii, 89)

10. My quarrel and this English queen's are one.

    (3 Henry VI: III, iii, 216)

11. Here I am, as brisk as a bird. I could take the part of a
    girl of fifteen.

    (Chekhov: The Seagull)

12.   That lie shall lie so heavy on my sword,
That it shall render vengeance and revenge
Till thou the lie-giver and that lie do lie
In earth as quiet as thy father's skull.

                      (Richard II: IV, i, 65)

13.   Forgive me, miss, but this dance is promised Kristin.

                      (Strindberg: Miss Julie)

14.   This is a sorry sight.

                      (Macbeth: II, ii, 18)

15.   Is there no pity sitting in the clouds,
That sees into the bottom of my grief?

                      (Romeo and Juliet: III, v, 196)

16.   He commands us to provide, and give great gifts,
And all out of an empty coffer.

                      (Timon of Athens: I, ii, 192)

17.   And here you have the Bank Account of the capital lying at
interest to cover the current expenses of the Orphanage.

                      (Ibsen: Ghosts)

18.   There's ne'er a villain dwelling in all Denmark
But he's an arrant knave.

                      (Hamlet: I, v, 123)

19.   Why, that's not your handwriting!

                      (Ibsen: Hedda Gabler)

20.   If I have lost it,
I should have lost the worth of it in gold.

                      (Cymbeline: II, iv, 41)

21.   What a lack-brain is this! By the Lord, our plot is a good
plot as ever was laid.

                      (1 Henry IV: II, iii, 16)

22.   Young man, thou couldst not die more honorable.

                      (Julius Caesar: V, i, 60)

From RUDDIGORE

PATTER TRIO

Gilbert and Sullivan

ROBIN.
My eyes are fully open to my awful situation—
I shall go at once to Roderic and make him an oration.
I shall tell him I've recovered my forgotten moral senses,
And I don't care twopence-halfpenny for any consequences.
Now I do not want to perish by the sword or by the dagger,
But a martyr may indulge a little pardonable swagger,
And a word or two of compliment my vanity would flatter,
But I've got to die to-morrow, so it really doesn't matter!

DESPARD.
So it really doesn't matter—

MARGARET.
So it really doesn't matter—

ALL.
So it really doesn't matter, matter, matter, matter, matter!

MARGARET.
If I were not a little mad and generally silly
I should give you my advice upon the subject, willy-nilly;
I should show you in a moment how to grapple with the question,
And you'd really be astonished at the force of my suggestion.
On the subject I shall write you a most valuable letter,
Full of excellent suggestions when I feel a little better,
But at present I'm afraid I am as mad as any hatter,
So I'll keep 'em to myself, for my opinion doesn't matter!

DESPARD.
Her opinion doesn't matter—

ROBIN.
Her opinion doesn't matter—

ALL.
Her opinion doesn't matter, matter, matter, matter, matter!

DESPARD.
If I had been so lucky as to have a steady brother
Who could talk to me as we are talking now to one another—
Who could give me good advice when he discovered I was erring
(Which is just the very favour which on you I am conferring),
My story would have made a rather interesting idyll,
And I might have lived and died a very decent indiwiddle.
This particularly rapid, unintelligible patter
Isn't generally heard, and if it is it doesn't matter!

ROBIN.
If it is it doesn't matter—

MARGARET.
If it ain't it doesn't matter—

ALL.
If it is it doesn't matter, matter, matter, matter, matter!

From **LEAVES OF GRASS**
SONG OF THE OPEN ROAD

Walt Whitman

Afoot and light-hearted I take to the open road,
Healthy, free, the world before me,
The long brown path before me leading wherever I choose.

Henceforth I ask not good-fortune, I myself am good-fortune,
Henceforth I whimper no more, postpone no more, need
     nothing,
Done with indoor complaints, libraries, querulous criticisms,
Strong and content I travel the open road.

The earth, that is sufficient,
I do not want the constellations any nearer,
I know they are very well where they are,
I know they suffice for those who belong to them.

From **PIRATES OF PENZANCE:**

THE VERY MODEL OF A MODERN MAJOR GENERAL

Gilbert and Sullivan

I am the very model of a modern Major-General,   /'genərəl/
I've information vegetable, animal, and mineral,   /hɪ'stʰɒrɪkˌl̩/
I know the kings of England, and I quote the fights historical, /'mærəθɒn/[1]
From Marathon to Waterloo, in order categorical;   /kʰætʰə'gɒrɪkˌl̩/

I'm very well acquainted, too, with matters mathematical,
I understand equations, both the simple and quadratical,
About binomial theorem I'm teeming with a lot o' news —   /'θɪərəm/
With many cheerful facts about the square of the hypotenuse. /haɪ'pʰɒtʰənjuz/

With many cheerful facts about the square of the hypotenuse,
With many cheerful facts about the square of the hypotenuse,
With many cheerful facts about the square of the hypotepotenuse.

I'm very good at integral and differential calculus,
I know the scientific names of beings animalculous;
In short, in matters vegetable, animal, and mineral,
I am the very model of a modern Major-General.

In short, in matters vegetable, animal, and mineral,
He is the very model of a modern Major-General.

I know our mythic history, King Arthur's and Sir Caradoc's,   /'kʰærədɒkˌs/
I answer hard acrostics, I've a pretty taste for paradox,   /ɪ'lidʒɪækˌs/
I quote in elegiacs all the crimes of Heliogabalus,   /hɪlɪə'gæbələs/
In conics I can floor peculiarities parabolous.   /pʰə'ræbələs/

I can tell undoubted Raphaels from Gerard Dows and Zoffanies,   /'dʒerɑə̆d/
I know the croaking chorus from the *Frogs* of Aristophanes,   /ærɪ'stʰɒfəniz/
Then I can hum a fugue of which I've heard the music's din afore,
And whistle all the airs from that infernal nonsense *Pinafore*.

---

[1] additional spoken pronunciations: /'mærəθɳ̩/, /kʰə'rædəkˌs/, /haɪ'pʰɒtˌnjuz/

And whistle all the airs from that infernal nonsense *Pinafore,*
And whistle all the airs from that infernal nonsense *Pinafore,*
And whistle all the airs from that infernal nonsense, *Pinapinafore.*

Then I can write a washing bill in Babylonic cuneiform,   /bæbɪˈlɒnɪkˌ/
And tell you ev'ry detail of Caractacus's uniform;   /kʰəˈræktʰəkʰəsɪz/
In short, in matters vegetable, animal, and mineral,
I am the very model of a modern Major-General.

In short, in matters vegetable, animal, and mineral,
He is the very model of a modern Major-General.

In fact, when I know what is meant by "mamelon" and "ravelin,"   /ˈmæmələn/
When I can tell at sight a Mauser rifle from a javelin,   /ˈrævəlɪn/
When such affairs as sorties and surprises I'm more wary at,   /ˈmaʊzə/
And when I know precisely what is meant by "commissariat,"

When I have learnt what progress has been made in modern gunnery,
When I know more of tactics than a novice in a nunnery:
In short, when I've a smattering of elemental strategy,
You'll say a better Major-General had never *sat* a gee—   /dʒi/

You'll say a better Major-General had never *sat* a gee,
You'll say a better Major-General had never *sat* a gee,
You'll say a better Major-General had never *sat* a, *sat* a gee.

For my military knowledge, tho' I'm plucky and adventury,
Has only been brought down to the beginning of the century;
But still, in matters vegetable, animal, and mineral,
I am the very model of a modern Major-General.

But still, in matters vegetable, animal, and mineral,
He is the very model of a modern Major-General.

Note: *If you are having trouble with the rhythm or lyrics, listen to a recording of the song. It is also fun to see if you can keep up with the pace of the singer, and still be understood, while speaking or singing the lyrics.*

From **THE PIT AND THE PENDULUM**

Edgar Allan Poe

A slight noise attracted my notice, and, looking to the floor, I saw several enormous rats traversing it. They had issued from the well which lay just within view to my right. Even then, while I gazed, they came up in troops, hurriedly, with ravenous eyes, allured by the scent of the meat. From this it required much effort and attention to scare them away.

It might have been half an hour, perhaps even an hour (for I could take but imperfect note of time), before I again cast my eyes upward. What I then saw confounded and amazed me. The sweep of the pendulum had increased in extent by nearly a yard. As a natural consequence its velocity was also much greater. But what mainly disturbed me was the idea that it had perceptibly descended.

From **THE ASSIGNATION**

Edgar Allan Poe

It was a night of unusual gloom. The great clock of the Piazza had sounded the fifth hour of the Italian evening. The square of the Campanile lay silent and deserted, and the lights of the old Ducal Palace were dying fast away. I was returning home from the Piazetta, by way of the Grand Canal. But as my gondola arrived opposite the mouth of the canal San Marco, a female voice from its recesses broke suddenly upon the night, in one wild, hysterical, and long-continued shriek. . .

A child, slipping from the arms of its own mother, had fallen from an upper window of the lofty structure into the deep and dim canal. The quiet waters had closed placidly over their victim; and, although my own gondola was the only one in sight, many a stout swimmer, already in the stream, was seeking in vain upon the surface, the treasure which was to be found, alas! Only within the abyss.

MY CATHEDRAL
Henry Wadsworth Longfellow

Like two cathedral towers these stately pines
  Uplift their fretted summits tipped with cones;
  The arch beneath them is not built with stones,
  Not Art but Nature traced these lovely lines,
And carved this graceful arabesque of vines;
  No organ but the wind here sighs and moans,
  No sepulcher conceals a martyr's bones,
  No marble bishop on his tomb reclines.
Enter! the pavement, carpeted with leaves,
  Gives back a softened echo to thy tread!
  Listen! the choir is singing; all the birds,
In leafy galleries beneath the eaves,
  Are singing! listen, ere the sound be fled,
  And learn there may be worship without words.

From **MOBY-DICK**
Herman Melville

There is, one knows not what sweet mystery about this sea, whose gently awful stirrings seem to speak of some hidden soul beneath; like those fabled undulations of the Ephesian sod over the buried Evangelist St. John. And meet it is, that over the sea-pastures, wide-rolling watery prairies and Potters' Fields of all four continents, the waves should rise and fall, and ebb and flow unceasingly; for here, millions of mixed shades and shadows, drowned dreams, somnambulisms, reveries, all that we call lives and souls, lie dreaming, dreaming, still; tossing like slumberers in their beds; the ever-rolling waves but made so by their restlessness.

To any meditative Magian rover, this serene Pacific, once beheld, must ever after be the sea of his adoption.

From **CYRANO DE BERGERAC**

Edmond Rostand

CYRANO.

No, no, no, my friend—too short!
Why, one could have, in the end, *mon Dieu!* such sport
By variation on the theme—suppose:
Aggressive: If I, m'sieur, had such a nose,
I'd amputate at once, without a thought!
Friendly: A nuisance when you drink? You ought
To have a special tankard fit to shape!
Descriptive: Why, 'tis a rock, a bluff...a cape!
Did I say cape? Nay! a peninsula!
Curious: What <u>is</u> that oblong capsule? a...
What? An ink-stand, hm...? A scissors-box?
Gracious: Ah, your love of birds—in flocks
They circle round that thoughtful perch, seduced—
At last, you bring the sparrows home to roost!
Truculent: When you light up to smoke,
Do the clouds, m'sieur, come billowing out to choke
Those near, who cry: "your chimney is on fire"?
Prudent: I'd take care—such a weight could tire,
And send you headlong, in a nasty fall!
Effete: It wants a tiny parasol—
To shield its fragile colors from the sun!
Pedantic: Aristophanes writes of <u>one</u>
Such Hippo-camp-elephanto-camelos—
The extent of flesh and bone, so...grandiose!
Cavalier: A-la-mode, my friend, eh, what?
Why, all the rage, this hook to hang one's hat!
Absolute: No wind, I say, but *le Mistral*
Could blow catarrh so cold through that canal!

Dramatic: When it bleeds, the Red Sea looms!
Admiring: What a clever sign—! Perfumes!
Lyric: A conch? Hark thee to Neptune's roar!
Naïve: That monument, now…what is it for?
Respectful: Oh! the envious elite!
Now this—what I'd call 'fronting on the street'!
Rustic: Eh? what say? a nose—? No tellin'!
Could be a turnip—or a Spanish melon!
Military: Train it on the Cavalry!
Practical: Why not a lottery—
With this, m'sieur, you're sure to win first prize!
And, last—the tragic *Pyramus* gives rise
To travesty: "O nose! O night so black!
O nose! O nose—! Alack! alack! alack!"
Voila—!

    These, but a sampling of the quips,
That, with wit or letters, might have graced your lips—
But of wit, alas, my cretin, have you not
One single atom! And of letters, what—?
You need but three to write you down an ass!
Yet, had you the inventiveness to pass
For quick, before these galleries that stay
Your serving me in clever repartée—
Be sure, that you would not have held the floor
One demi-quarter of a syllable, for…
I serve these up myself, m'sieur, with flair,
But allow none else to even venture there.

                (English version: Christopher Martin)

SONNET 18

William Shakespeare

Shall I compare thee to a summer's day?
Thou art more lovely and more temperate:
Rough winds do shake the darling buds of May,
And summer's lease hath all too short a date;
Sometime too hot the eye of heaven shines,
And often is his gold complexion dimm'd,
And every fair from fair sometime declines,
By chance or Nature's changing course, untrimm'd:
But thy eternal summer shall not fade,
Nor lose possession of that fair thou ow'st,
Nor shall Death brag thou wand'rest in his shade,
When in eternal lines to time thou grow'st.
    So long as men can breathe or eyes can see,
    So long lives this, and this give life to thee.

SONNET 74

William Shakespeare

But be contented when that fell arrest
Without all bail shall carry me away,
My life hath in this line some interest,
Which for memorial still with thee shall stay.
When thou reviewest this, thou dost review
The very part was consecrate to thee:
The earth can have but earth, which is his due,
My spirit is thine, the better part of me.
So then thou hast but lost the dregs of life,
The prey of worms, my body being dead,
The coward conquest of a wretch's knife,
Too base of thee to be remembered.
    The worth of that is that which it contains,
    And that is this, and this with thee remains.

SONNET 91

William Shakespeare

Some glory in their birth, some in their skill,
Some in their wealth, some in their body's force,
Some in their garments, though new-fangled ill,
Some in their hawks and hounds, some in their horse;
And every humor hath his adjunct pleasure,
Wherein it finds a joy above the rest,
But these particulars are not my measure,
All these I better in one general best.
Thy love is better than high birth to me,
Richer than wealth, prouder than garments' cost,
Of more delight than hawks or horses be;
And having thee, of all men's pride I boast:
       Wretched in this alone, that thou mayst take
       All this away, and me most wretched make.

SONNET 116

William Shakespeare

Let me not to the marriage of true minds
Admit impediments; love is not love
Which alters when it alteration finds,
Or bends with the remover to remove.
O, no, it is an ever-fixed mark
That looks on tempests and is never shaken;
It is the star to every wand'ring bark,
Whose worth's unknown, although his height be taken.
Love's not Time's fool, though rosy lips and cheeks
Within his bending sickle's compass come,
Love alters not with his brief hours and weeks,
But bears it out even to the edge of doom.
       If this be error and upon me proved,
       I never writ, nor no man ever loved.

KEY TO MARKING CLASSICAL MONOLOGUES
(adjustments or changes from <u>Neutral</u> American are shaded)

Rhythm Highlighters	Marking
Stressed syllables (all marked for awareness)	'puṟchase
Noun verb variations (stressed syllable marked)	'discourse
Weak forms (marked sparingly, actor's choice)	ə ə i a, the (vs.) the
/ɪ/ (w<u>i</u>ll) prefixes and suffixes	ɪ ɪ re'peat, 'closet
/ə/ (<u>uh</u>) schwa suffixes	ə ə 'statement, 'statesman
Syllabic endings marked /n̩ | m̩/	'wooden̩, 'little̩, 'prism̩
/i/ unstressed endings spelled: 'y' and occasionally 'i' as in marr<u>y</u>, happ<u>y</u>, happin<u>e</u>ss (can be slightly shorter than Neutral)	not marked: actors add strikethrough, if useful
'r' coloring (can be slightly less than in Neutral American)	not marked: actors add strikethrough, if useful
Vowel Sound Considerations	**Marking**
Linking words (marked sparingly, actor's choice)	here‿it‿is
/e/ (g<u>e</u>t) before 'm', 'n' (in a stressed syllable)	e e e them, when, 'sentence
/æ/ (th<u>a</u>t) before 'n', 'm', 'ng', 'nk' (pure, non-nasal vowel)	æ æ æ land, Hamlet, thank
/ɔ/ (<u>a</u>ll) (distinguish from 'h<u>o</u>nest' and 'f<u>a</u>ther' sounds)	ɔ ɔ ɔ fall, sauce, walk
/ʊɚ/ (p<u>oor</u>) diphthong (not /ɝ/ ER or /ɔɚ/ sp<u>or</u>ts)	ʊɚ ʊɚ ʊɚ a'ssure, tour, poor
/aɪ̆/ (m<u>y</u>) diphthong (before a voiceless consonant in the same word)	aɪ̆ aɪ̆ aɪ̆ white, pipe, wife
/ɒ/ (h<u>o</u>nest) sound (distinguish from 'all' and 'father' sounds)	ɒ ɒ ɒ on, what, stop
Liquid /ju/ (y<u>ou</u>) (after 't', 'd', 'n', optional after 's', 'l')	tju dju nju tune, duke, news
/aʊ̆/ /aʊ̆ɚ/ (initial element changes)	aʊ̆ aʊ̆ aʊ̆ɚ now, found, sour
Pure vowels before consonant /r/, also in polysyllabics	æ e ca̱-rry, stationa̱-ry, etc.
Consonant Sound Considerations	**Marking**
Voiceless stop-plosive endings (aspirated before a pause or silence)	hitʰ, packʰ, lipʰ
Voiced consonant endings (especially before a pause or silence)	dea̱d, fouṉd, kiṉg
Consonant /r/ combinations (dr, tr, str)	ṯred, s̱treet, ḏrain
Aspirated medial /t/ (replaces flutter 'd')	'bettʰer, a'bilitʰy
Voiceless /hw/ (wh<u>y</u>) spelled 'wh'	hw hw hw when, why, which

CLASSICAL AMERICAN
MONOLOGUES

(with sound changes marked)

Vowels, diphthongs and triphthongs of 'r' are not marked with the strikethrough symbol in the following monologues; many actors overreact and eliminate all 'r' coloring. But, if that marking is helpful, feel free to add it.

AUDIO 68▶ **spoken by Evan Muller**

PETRUCHIO

I will a'**ttend** her[1] here

And woo her with some '**spi**-rit when she comes.

Say that she rail, why then I'll tell her plain

She sings as '**sweet**ly as a '**nigh**tingale;

Say that she frown, I'll say she looks as clear

As '**mor**ning '**ro**ses '**new**ly wash'd with dew;

Say she be mute and will not speak a word,

Then I'll co'**mmend** her volu'**bili**thy,

And say she utthereth '**pier**cing '**elo**quence;

---

[1] Though the weak form of 'her' does not technically require the 'h' be spoken, characters tend to sound very casual and contemporary if the 'h' is eliminated.

θæŋk$_i$s
If she do bid me pack^h, I'll give her thanks,

ə
As though she bid me stay by her‿a week^h;

I
If she de'ny to we<u>d</u>, I'll crave the day

hwen   æ   hwen   æ
When I shall‿ask the banns‿and when be 'ma-rrie<u>d</u>.

aʊ
But here she co<u>mes</u>; and now, Pe'<u>tru</u>chio, speak^h.

(The Taming of the Shrew: II, i, 169)

AUDIO 69▶ **spoken by Nancy Mayans**

PORTIA

æ   ɔ   ə
I pray you 'ta-rry, pause‿a day‿or two

I   I   ɒ
Be'fore you 'hazar<u>d</u>, for‿in 'choosing wro<u>ng</u>

ə   ə hw
I lose your[1] 'company; there'fore for'bear‿a whi<u>le</u>.

ɒ
There's 'something tells me (but^h‿it^h‿is not lo<u>ve</u>)

ɒ   juə
I would not lose you, and you know your'self,

aʊ   ɒ   ə
Hate 'counse<u>l</u>s not^h‿in such‿a 'qualit^{h}y.

ɒ   æ
But lest you should not^h‿under'stand me we<u>ll</u>—

---

[1] The strong form of 'your' is **/juɚ/**. The weak form is **/jə/** or **/ju/** not **/jɜ/** or **/joɚ/**.

And yet^h a 'maiden hath no tongue but thought^h—

I would de'tain you here some month or two

Be'fore you 'venture for me. I could teach you

How to choose right^h, but^h I am then for'sworn.

So will I 'never be, so may you miss me,

But^h if you do, you'll make me wish a sin,

That^h I had been for'sworn. Be'shrew your eyes,

They have o'er'look'd me and di'vided me:

One half of me is yours, the 'other half yours—

Mine own, I would say; but^h if mine, then yours,

And so all yours. O, these 'naught^hy times

Put bars be'tween the 'owners and their rights!

And so though yours, not yours. Prove it so,

Let 'fortune go to hell for it^h, not^h I.

I speak too long, but 'tis to pieze the time,

To eche it^h, and to draw it^h out^h in length,

To stay you from e'lection.

(The Merchant of Venice: III, ii, 1)

414

CASSIUS

    hw   æ   ʌ   ɪ   æ
Why, man, he doth be'**stride** the '**na**-rrow wor<u>ld</u>

    aɪ ə ɒ   e
Like‿a Co'**lo**ssus, and we '**pett**ʰy me<u>n</u>

    ɔ   e   aʊ
Walk‿'**un**der his huge legs and peep‿a'**bout**ʰ

                    ɒ
To find our'**selves** dis'**ho**no<u>r</u>ab<u>l</u>e gra<u>ves</u>.

    e
Men at some time are '**ma**sters‿of their fates;

    ɔ   ɒ
The fault ʰ, dear '**Brut**ʰus, is notʰ in‿our star<u>s</u>,

      aʊɚ̆   ɪ
Butʰ in‿our'**sel**<u>ves</u>, that we‿are '**un**derli<u>ngs</u>.

                 hwɒt,
'**Bru**ʰ tus and '**Cae**sar: what should be in that '"**Cae**sar"?

    hw   aʊ ɪ   ʊɚ̆
Why should that name be '**soun**ded more than your<u>s</u>?

    aɪ   ʊɚ̆
Write them to'**ge**ther, yours‿is‿as fair‿a na<u>me</u>;

    aʊ   e   ʌ   ɪ   aʊ
Sound the<u>m</u>, it doth be'**come** the mouth‿as we<u>ll</u>;

        e   ð e
Weigh the<u>m</u>, itʰ is‿as '**hea**v<u>y</u>; '**con**jure with '**em**,

                ə ɪ
'"**Brut**ʰus" will startʰ‿a '**spi**-ritʰ‿as soon‿as '"**Cae**sar".

    aʊ   ɔ   ɒ
Now in the names‿of‿all the gods‿at once,

     ɒ hwɒt,   ʌ
Up'**on** what meat doth this‿our '**Cae**sar fee<u>d</u>

That he‿is grown so greatʰ? A<u>ge</u>, thou‿art sha<u>m'd</u>!

ɒ
Ro<u>me</u>, thou hast lost the breed‿of ˈnobl̩e bloo<u>ds</u>!

hwen e
When went there by‿an‿age since the great floo<u>d</u>

ð   ð   æ
Butʰ it was famˈd with more than with one ma<u>n</u>?

hwen   ɑʊ   ɔ   tʰ
When could they say, till now, that talkˈd‿of Ro<u>me</u>,

ɔ   ɪ ʌ   æ
That her wide walks enˈcompassˈd but one ma<u>n</u>?

ɑʊ   ɪ
Now is‿it Rome‿inˈdeed and room‿eˈnough,

hwen   æ
When there‿is‿in‿it but one ˈonly ma<u>n</u>.

O! you‿and‿I have heard‿our ˈfathers say

ɒ ə
There was‿a ˈBrutʰus once that would have brookˈd

ɪ
Thˈ eˈternal̩ ˈdevil̩ to keep his stat021eʰ in Ro<u>me</u>

ə
As ˈeasily as‿a ki<u>ng</u>.

(Julius Caesar: I, ii, 135)

MID-ATLANTIC DIALECT

OVERVIEW

AUDIO SELECTIONS▶
Patricia Fletcher

418

SUMMARY CHECKLIST

There is another, even more formal speech for the classics referred to as Mid-Atlantic or Eastern Standard. This dialect was especially popular during the mid-20th Century, and is often taught in acting schools and universities.

An overview of additional sound adjustments necessary for this more formal dialect follows.[1] It is almost indistinguishable from Standard British to most American audiences, but might be appropriate if a more British-English sound is desired, if historical characters are being portrayed, or if British and American actors are appearing together in the same production.

Additional adjustments required for Mid-Atlantic:

Note: the first three adjustments strongly affect rhythm

Note: Standard British pronunciation is also common on many words

---

[1] For a detailed rendering of Mid-Atlantic or Eastern Standard, see Edith Skinner's *Speak With Distinction*, edited by Lilene Mansell, revised by Timothy Monich.

Unstressed / ɪ / (wᵢll) endings

Mid-Atlantic dialect uses a short /ɪ/ (wᵢll) sound, rather than the longer /i/ (wẹ) sound in unstressed word endings and suffixes spelled with 'y' or, occasionally, 'i'.

Days of the week are spoken with the /ɪ/ suffix.

AUDIO 71▶ **unstressed / ɪ / (wᵢll) endings**

And so, pa'ternitᵧ 'cannot be proven.

(Strindberg: The Father)

Good mo-rrow and God save your 'Majestᵧ!

(2 Henry IV: V, ii, 43)

'Mon_day_! ha, ha! Well, 'Wednes_day_ is too soon,
O' 'Thurs_day_ let it be—o' 'Thurs_day_, tell her.

(Romeo and Juliet: III, iv, 19)

PRACTICE see Standard British section, pages 440-443.

MID-ATLANTIC TEXT /ɪ/ (wᵢll) unstressed word endings. *Mark the following and speak out loud.*

If it were done, when 'tis done, then 'twere well
It were done quickly.

(Macbeth: I, vii, 1)

And let the foes quietly cut their throats
Without repugnancy?

(Timon of Athens, III, v, 44)

He cannot choose but take this service I have done fatherly.

(Cymbeline: II, iii, 34)

'r' Coloring

vowels, diphthongs, triphthongs

Eliminate **'r'** coloring from vowels, diphthongs and triphthongs of 'r' by allowing the tip of the tongue to gently rest touching the back of the lower teeth for the duration of the vowel, diphthong, or triphthong.

AUDIO 72▶ **eliminate 'r' coloring**

> eə̆   3
> Where's my serpent of old Nile?
>
> (Antony and Cleopatra: I, v, 25)
>
>   ɑə̆
> It was the nightingale, and not the lark,
>   ɪə̆   ɪə̆   ɪə̆
> That pierc'd the fearful hollow of thine ear.
>
> (Romeo and Juliet: III, v, 2)
>
>   e   aɪə̆
> It is a he-retic that makes the fire,
>   3
> Not she which burns in't.
>
> (The Winter's Tale: II, iii, 115)

PRACTICE see Standard British pages 444-448.

MID-ATLANTIC TEXT eliminate 'r' coloring. *Mark the following and speak out loud.*

Hail, most royal sir!

(The Winter's Tale: I, ii, 366)

The worthy Leonatus is in safety
And greets your Highness dearly.

(Cymbeline: I, vi, 12)

Noble heroes! my sword and yours are kin.

(All's Well That Ends Well: II, i, 40)

Polysyllabic[1] word endings

The short schwa sound with no 'r' coloring, /ə/ (uh), is used in the second to the last syllable of polysyllabic words ending in 'ary', 'ory', 'ony', and 'berry'. The final 'y' is spoken with the short /ɪ/ (wi̱ll) suffix, so the word endings are pronounced: /ə-rɪ/

AUDIO 73► **polysyllabic word endings**

           ə-rɪ
I ran like the devil, plunging through the 'raspbe-rry canes,
  ə-rɪ
across the 'strawbe-rry beds, and came up on the rose garden.

(Strindberg: Miss Julie)

pə'pa   ə-rɪ
Papa was a 'milita-ry man.

(Chekhov: Three Sisters)

    ə-rɪ
O true a'potheca-ry! Thy drugs are quick.

(Romeo and Juliet: V, iii, 119)

PRACTICE see Standard British section, pages 464-467.

MID-ATLANTIC TEXT polysyllabic word endings. *Mark the following and speak out loud.*

LAFEW.   You have it from his own deliverance.
BERTRAM. And by other warranted testimony.

(All's Well That Ends Well: II, v, 4)

Shall we desire to raze the sanctuary
And pitch our evils there?

(Measure for Measure: II, ii, 170)

But (heav'n be thank'd!) it is but voluntary.

(King John: V, i, 29)

---

[1] Polysyllabic words are words of three or more syllables.

'Ask' List

The 'ask' list of words is spoken with the intermediate /a/ sound in Mid-Atlantic, not /æ/ (that) as in Neutral and Classical American, or /ɑ/ (father) as in Standard British.

AUDIO 74► **ask list words spoken with /a/**

>   a
> To which boarding school, might I a<u>sk</u>?
>
>   (Strindberg: The Father)
>
>   a
> I am not fit for the ta<u>sk</u>.
>
>   (Ibsen: A Doll's House)
>
>   a   a
> For you and I are p<u>a</u>st our d<u>a</u>ncing days.
>
>   (Romeo and Juliet: I, v, 31)

Which words are included in the 'ask' list? There is no distinct rule for inclusion, but spellings can offer a fairly reliable indication.

aft	abaft, aft, after, aftermath, afternoon, afterward, behalf, craft, daft, draft, graft, raft, shaft, Shaftesbury, Taft, waft, witchcraft
ampl	ample, example, sample
ance /**ans**	advance, answer, chance, chancellor, chancery, dance, enhance, France, freelance, glance, lance, prance, trance
anch	avalanche, blanch(e), branch, ranch, stanch
and	Chandler, command(o), countermand, demand, reprimand, slander
ant[1] /**aunt**	advantage, aunt, can't, chant, chantry, enchant, grant, implant, plant, shan't, slant, supplant, transpl<u>a</u>nt, vantage

---

[1] Though 'ant' spelling can indicate inclusion on the 'ask' list of words, the word 'ant' (the insect) is pronounced /ænt/.

as(s)	alas, brass, class, Glasgow, glass, grass, pass, Passover, trespass
ask	ask, bask, basket, cask, flask, mask, task, rascal, vast
asp	clasp, gasp, grasp, hasp, rasp, raspberry
ast	aghast, alabaster, avast, blast, broadcast, cast, caste, castle, contrast, disaster, fast, ghastly, last, mast, master, nasty, past, pastor, pasture, plaster, repast, telecast, vast, vasty
ath	bath, lath, lather, path, rather, wrath
aff /affe	chaff, distaff, Falstaff, gaff, giraffe, quaff, staff
alf /aph	autograph, behalf, calf, half, epitaph, graph, telegraph
augh	laugh, laughter, draught

In the previous three lines above, all the consonant spellings listed are pronounced **/f/** (af, aff, affe, alf, aph, augh).

Finding the Mid-Atlantic /a/ sound: This vowel sound is not used on its own in Neutral American speech, but is spoken as the first element of the /aĭ/ (my) diphthong.[1] Begin as if saying the pronoun "I", but do not pronounce the second element, so that only the first element /a/ is spoken.

a

For 'twas your heaven she should be advanc'd,

a

And weep ye now, seeing she is advanc'd

Above the clouds, as high as heaven itself?

(Romeo and Juliet IV: v, 72)

The American Southern dialect often uses the vowel sound /a/ rather than the diphthong /aĭ/. It may help you to just think of pronouncing the word 'hi' using the Southern dialect, written phonetically: **/ha/**. Pronounce this same vowel sound in the word 'half' for the Mid-Atlantic pronunciation of that word.

---

[1] The /a/ sound, is also an important sound in many other dialects, including Northern England, Ireland and Boston.

In the exercise that follows, isolate the /a/ sound on the word listed in the first column by using a slightly exaggerated Southern pronunciation. Then apply this vowel sound to words listed in the second column. *Read across.*

WORDS /a/ (l<u>au</u>gh) in Mid-Atlantic

'I'	/a/ in southern	/ask/	ask, after
'bye'	/ba/ in southern	/bask/	bask, bath
'die'	/da/ in southern	/daft/	daft, dance
'pie'	/pa/ in southern	/past/	past, path
'lie'	/la/ in southern	/laf/	laugh, lather
'my'	/ma/ in southern	/mask/	mask, master
'rye'	/ra/ in southern	/raft/	raft, rascal
'tie'	/ta/ in southern	/taft/	Taft, task
'sigh'	/sa/ in southern	/sav/	salve, sample
'dry'	/dra/ in southern	/draft/	draft, drafted
'fie'	/fa/ in southern	/fast/	fast, fasting, faster
'guy'	/ga/ in southern	/gasp/	gasp, ghastly
'sly'	/sla/ in southern	/slant/	slant, slander

If you are familiar with the Boston dialect, think of the phrase: "Park the car in Harvard Yard"—'r' coloring is dropped, and the remaining vowel sound is the shorter, brighter /a/, as in:

"Pahk the cah in Hahvahd yahd."

PHRASES /a/ (l<u>au</u>gh)

1. on his beh<u>alf</u>
2. good r<u>asp</u>berries
3. holds steadf<u>astly</u>
4. cutting the gr<u>ass</u>
5. a p<u>ath</u> in Fl<u>anders</u>
6. N<u>asty</u> Fr<u>ances</u>
7. just h<u>alf</u> a gl<u>ass</u>
8. adv<u>anced</u> at l<u>ast</u>
9. filling empty fl<u>asks</u>
10. entr<u>ancing</u> s<u>amp</u>ling

WORDS comparing the three vowel sounds /æ/ /a/ /ɑ/ *Read across.*

/æ/	/a/	/ɑ/		/æ/	/a/	/ɑ/
apt	ask	ah		has	hasp	hah
Sam	sample	Samba		patch	past	papa
back	bask	Bach		shank	shan't	shah
catch	casket	calm		dram	draft	drama
factor	faster	father		pad	path	palm
savage	salve	saga		slack	slant	Slavic
clap	class	koala		stack	staff	Stalin
cafe	calf	Kafka		Dan	dance	Dante
pack	pass	papa		tack	task	taco
mass	mask	macho		and	aunt	almond
gnash	nasty	nachos		can	can't	Kahn
brats	brass	bras		lamb	laugh	lama

> *I want to have it a bit lively-like in the evenings, with*
> *a*
> *singing and dan̲c̲ing, and so on.*

(Ibsen: Ghosts)

PRACTICE comparing the three vowels /æ/ /a/ /ɑ/

/æ/	/a/	/ɑ/
Cathy sampled tacos.		
Dad ate half the pasta.		
Hand Francis the corsage.		
Chad was cast in the drama.		
Marigolds are planted in Tahoe.		

/æ/	/ɑ/	/a/
That koala is trespassing.		
Vampires calmly advanced.		
Thank Sinatra for the dance.		
Slather on the avocado lather.		
Ann's sonata is a masterpiece.		

/a/	/ɑ/	/æ/
Ask if father is angry.		
Cast the drama in Athens.		
The staff at the spa is athletic.		
A disastrous scenario is planned.		
Any chance the armada has landed?		

/a/	/æ/	/ɑ/
Fast on apples and guava.		
Demand fantastic dramas.		
Dance the tango or samba.		
My glasses shattered in Bali.		
Auntie examined the hibachi.		

/ɑ/	/æ/	/a/
Tanya's cat is nasty.		
Gandhi's classical chants.		
Iago sang from the rafters.		
The suave man is enchanting.		
Mama's the family commander.		

/ɑ/	/a/	/æ/
Massages can't be bad.		
Palm branches crashed.		
Debutants laughed in Paris.		
Picasso's epitaph is romantic.		
The calamari is rather rancid.		

MID ATLANTIC TEXT ask list words spoken with /a/. *Mark the following and speak out loud.*

a
Get me a gla̲ss!

(Strindberg: Miss Julie)

The gold of France did not seduce,
Although I did admit it as a motive.

(Henry V: II, ii, 155)

You said that idle weeds are fast in growth.

(Richard III: III, i, 103)

With mirth and laughter let old wrinkles come,
And let my liver rather heat with wine
Than my heart cool with mortifying groans.

(The Merchant of Venice: I, i, 80)

Mean time but ask
What you would have reform'd that is not well,
And well shall you perceive how willingly
I will both hear and grant you your requests.

(King John: IV, ii, 43)

We cannot all be masters, nor all masters
Cannot be truly follow'd.

(Othello: I, i, 43)

But more in Troilus thousandfold I see
Than in the glass of Pandar's praise may be;
Yet hold I off.

(Troilus and Cressida: I, ii, 284)

No, no, my dream was lengthen'd after life.

(Richard III, I, iv, 43)

My legs like loaden branches bow to th' earth.

(Henry VIII: IV, ii, 2)

I almost believe your Aunt Rina's death affects you more than
it does your Aunt Julia.

(Ibsen: Hedda Gabler)

PRACTICE TEXT

Mark the following for Mid-Atlantic and speak out loud.

1. Good Master Vernon, it is well objected.
(1 Henry V: II, iv,43)

2. Fellows, stand fast; I see a passenger.
(The Two Gentlemen of Verona: IV, i, 1)

3. O heinous, strong, and bold conspiracy!
(Richard II: V, iii, 59)

4. Then you must undertake to slander him.
(The Two Gentlemen of Verona: III, ii, 38)

5. Dear daughter, I confess that I am old;
Age is unnecessary. On my knees I beg
That you'll vouchsafe me raiment, bed, and food.
(King Lear: II, iv, 154)

6. His prayers are full of false hypocrisy,
Ours of true zeal and deep integrity.
(Richard II: V, iii, 107)

7. You have sinned greatly against your husband; that you
recognize by raising yonder memorial to him.
(Ibsen: Ghosts)

8. I swear to you, I think Helen loves him better than Paris.
(Troilus and Cressida: I, ii, 107)

9. And what have kings, that privates have not too,
Save ceremony, save general ceremony?
(Henry V: IV, i, 238)

10. Say that some lady, as perhaps there is,
Hath for your love as great a pang of heart
As you have for Olivia. You cannot love her;
You tell her so. Must she not then be answer'd?
(Twelfth Night: II, iv, 89)

KEY TO MARKING MID-ATLANTIC MONOLOGUES
(adjustments or changes from <u>Classical</u> American are shaded)

Rhythm Highlighters	Marking
Stressed syllables *(not marked)*	
Weak forms *(not marked)*	
/ɪ/ (w<u>i</u>ll) prefixes and suffixes	ɪ ɪ ɪ repeat, closet, passionate
/ə/ (<u>uh</u>) schwa suffixes	ə ə statement, doorman
Syllabic endings marked /n̩ l̩ m̩/	wooden̩, littl̩e, prism̩
/i/→/ɪ/ unstressed endings spelled 'y' or 'i'	ɪ ɪ ɪ pretty, tally, happiness
Eliminate 'r' coloring	working, father, here
Vowel Sound Considerations	**Marking**
Linking words *(not marked)*	
/e/ (g<u>e</u>t) before 'm', 'n' *(in stressed syllables)*	e e e them, when, sent
/æ/ (th<u>a</u>t) before 'n', 'm', 'ng', 'nk' *(pure, non-nasal vowel)*	æ æ æ land, Hamlet, man
/ɔ/ (<u>a</u>ll) and /ɒ/ (h<u>o</u>nest) *(as in Classical American)*	ɔ ɒ ɒ fall, often, wanting
/ʊə̆/ (p<u>oor</u>) diphthong *(no 'r' coloring)*	ʊə̆ ʊə̆ ʊə̆ assure, tour, sure
/aɪ̆/ (m<u>y</u>) diphthong *(before a voiceless consonant in the same word)*	aɪ̆ aɪ̆ aɪ̆ bright, night, wife
Liquid /ju/ (<u>you</u>) *(after t, d, n, optional after s, l)*	tju dju nju tune, duke, news
/aʊ̆/ (n<u>ow</u>), /aʊ̆ə̆/ (p<u>ower</u>) *(initial element changes)*	aʊ̆ aʊ̆ə̆ mountain, sour
'Ask' list of words spoken with /a/ sound	a a a ask, pass, dance
Vowels before consonant /r/ *(complete observation)* (new change: the schwa with no 'r' coloring)	ə ə mutte-<u>r</u>er, flatte-<u>r</u>er, etc.
Polysyllabic endings: ary, ory, ony, berry spellings	trɪ (or) tə-rɪ secretary, secreta-ry
Consonant Sound Considerations	**Marking**
Voiceless stop-plosive endings *(aspirated before a pause/silence)*	hit[h], pack[h], lip[h]
Voiced consonant endings *(especially before a pause/silence)*	dea<u>d</u>, fou<u>nd</u>, ki<u>ng</u>
Consonant /r/ combinations *(dr, tr, str)*	<u>tr</u>ead, <u>str</u>eet, <u>dr</u>ain
Aspirated medial /t/ *(replaces flutter 'd')*	bett[h]er, abilit[h]y
Voiceless /hw/ spelled 'wh'	<u>wh</u>en, <u>wh</u>y, <u>wh</u>ich

MID-ATLANTIC
MONOLOGUES

(with sound changes marked)

AUDIO 75▶ **spoken by Susan Cameron**

CRESSIDA

      ɪ   aʊ̆   aə̆
Boldness comes to me now, and brings me heart[h].

                     aɪ̆
Prince <u>Tr</u>oilus, I have lov'd you night[h] and day

   ɪ 'wɪə̆-rɪ   ɔə̆
For man<u>y</u> wear<u>y</u> months. I was won, my lo<u>rd</u>,

    ð   a   aə̆
With the fi<u>r</u>st glance that[h] ever—pa<u>r</u>doṇ me,

                                 ə
If I confess much, you will play the tyrant[h].

           aʊ̆   aʊ̆ ɒ
I love you now, but till now not so much

            aɪ̆   a
But[h] I might maste<u>r</u> it[h]. In faith I lie,

           ɔ   aɪ̆
My thoughts we<u>r</u>e like unbridḷed childre<u>n</u> grow<u>n</u>

        ɒ
Too head<u>str</u>ong fo<u>r</u> their mothe<u>r</u>. See, we foo<u>ls</u>!

  hw
Why have I blabb'<u>d</u>? Who shall be <u>tr</u>ue to us,

  hwen   ɪ   aʊ̆ə̆
When we a<u>r</u>e so unsec<u>r</u>et to ou<u>r</u>sel<u>ves</u>?

But though I lov'd you we<u>ll</u>, I woo'd you not^h,
  <small>ɒ</small>

And yet^h, good faith, I wish'd myself a ma<u>n</u>,
  <small>æ</small>

Or that we women had men's privile<u>ge</u>
  <small>ɪ ɪ   e   ə ɪ</small>

Of speak^hing first^h. Sweet^h, bid me hold my to<u>ngue</u>,
  <small>ɪ</small>

For in this raptur<u>e</u> I shall su<u>r</u>ely speak^h
  <small>ʃʊəlɪ</small>

The thing I shall repent^h. See, see, you<u>r</u> silence,
  <small>ɪ e   ʊə̃ ə</small>

Cunning in dumbness, from my weakness <u>draws</u>
  <small>ɪ   ɪ ɒ   ɪ ɔ</small>

My very soul of counse<u>l</u>! Stop my mouth.
  <small>ve-rɪ   aʊ   ɒ   aʊ</small>

(Troilus and Cressida: III, ii, 113)

AUDIO 76 ▶ spoken by Eric Loscheider

PROTEUS

My gracious lo<u>rd</u>, that which I would discove<u>r</u>
  <small>ə ɔə̃   hw   ɪ</small>

The law of friendship bids me to concea<u>l</u>,
  <small>ɔ   e</small>

But when I call to mind you<u>r</u> gracious favo<u>rs</u>
  <small>hwen ɔ   jʊə̃/or weak form</small>

      ɪ   ɪ   æ
Done to me (undeserving as I am),

 'djutʰɪ   ɒ
My duty pricks me on to uttʰer thatʰ

hw   ɪ   ɔ   ɒ (or ə)
Which else no worldly good should draw from me.

      ɪ   'væləntʰaɪn   e
Know, worthy Prince, Sir Valentine, my friend,

      aĭ   e   ɔ
This nightʰ intends to steal away your daughtʰer;

           ɪ   ɒ
Myself am one made privy to the plotʰ.

         ɪ   ɪ
I know you have determin'd to bestow her

ɒ 'θjurɪoŭ   e   ɔ
On Thurio, whom your gentḷe daughtʰer hates,

And should she thus be stol'n away from you,

It would be much vexatioṇ to your age.

        'djutʰɪz   a
Thus, for my duty's sakʰe, I rather chose

ə ɒ   e   ɪn'tʰendɪd
To cross my friend in his intended driftʰ,

       ɪ   ɒ
Thaṇ, by concealing itʰ, heapʰ on your head

     ɒ   hw   ɑu
A packʰ of so-rrows which would press you dowṇ,

'biːŋ ʌnpˌɪ'ventʰɪd   ɪ
Being unprevented, to your timeless grave.

(The Two Gentlemen of Verona: III, i, 4)

AUDIO 77▶ **spoken by Leigh Dillon**

LADY PERCY

             ɒ   ɒ   ɔə̆

O yet[h] for God's sake[h], go not to these wa**rs**!

            ɒ   ʊə̆ (or weak form)

The time was, fath**er**, that you broke you**r** wo**rd**

hwen   ɔə̆ ɪ ɪə̆   aʊ

When you we**re** mo**re** endea**r**'d to it than now,

hwen   ɪ hwen   ɑə̆   æ ɪ

When you**r** own Pe**rc**y, when my hea**r**t's dea**r** Ha-rr**y**,

         e ɪ   ɔə̆

Threw man**y** a no**r**thwa**r**d look to see his fath**er**

                aʊ̆ə̆   ɒ

Bring up his powe**rs**; but he did long in vai**n**.

         e   ɪ

Who then pe**r**suaded you to stay at ho**me**?

       eə̆   ɒ   ɒ   ʊə̆   ʊə̆

The**re** we**re** two hono**rs** lost, you**rs** and you**r** so**n's**:

             ʊə̆   ɒ (ə or syllabic) aɪ̆

For you**rs**, the God of Heave**n** brighte**n** it[h]!

                ɒ

For hi**s**, it stuck upon him as the su**n**

          ɔ   aɪ̆

In the grey vault of heave**n**, and by his light[h]

      ɔ   ɪ   ɪ   ə

Did all the chivalry of England mo**ve**

                    ɒ   a

To do brave acts. He was indeed the glass

hw   e

Whe**r**ein the nob**l**e youth did <u>dress</u> themse**lves**:

                    ɒ

He had no legs that practiced not his gai**t**[h];

    ɪ   hw   e ɪ

And speaking thick^h (which nature made his blemish)

  ɪ   e (ə or syllabic) ə

Became the accents of the valiant^h;

                            ɑə ɪ

For those that could speak low and tardily

          eə̆

Would turn their own perfection to abuse

       aɪ̆

To seem like him; so that^h in speech, in gait^h,

               ɪ aɪ̆

In diet^h, in affections of delight^h,

      ə-ɾɪ

In military rules, humors of blood,

      ɒ   ɑə̆   a   ˈkɒpɪ

He was the mark^h and glass, copy and book^h,

That fashion'd others.

                                      (2 Henry IV: II, iii, 9)

STANDARD BRITISH DIALECT (RP)

AUDIO SELECTIONS▶
James Anderson

SUMMARY CHECKLIST

When switching from Classical American to Standard British,[1] the following adjustments and sound changes are necessary:

The jaw is slightly more closed, the point of resonance is more forward on the upper gum ridge, consonants are spoken with increased vocal energy, and there is increased vocal range and variation in pitch and inflection.

---

[1] The *English Pronouncing Dictionary* by Daniel Jones, Cambridge University Press, is a valuable resource for Standard British pronunciation, expecially the older fourteenth edition.

CONSONANT ADJUSTMENTS

The consonant sounds in Standard British are crisper, cleaner, and generally more energized than in American speech.

Vibrant, energized consonants and aspirated plosives

Plosives are more defined and explosive, especially aspirated /p^h t^h k^h/, which give the dialect a slightly more enlivened, staccato rhythm. Energizing the consonant /l/ will endow it with the slightly darker quality required of Standard British. This enlivened delivery also contributes to an increase in pitch variation and vocal range associated with Standard British.

Although consonant adjustment can be difficult to notate in a useful manner for other speakers, aspiration markings may be helpful, and are used on the words and phrases listed.

AUDIO 78▶ **energized consonants/plosives**

About this trip^h, Strak^{h}er.

(Shaw: Man and Superman)

The good ended hap^{h}pily, and the bad unhapp^{h}ily.

(Wilde: The Importance of Being Earnest)

Ay, you're such an amorous p^{h}upp^{h}y, that^h I'm afraid you'll

sp^{h}oil our sp^{h}ort^h.

(Farquhar: The Beaux Stratagem)

WORDS energized consonants / aspirated plosives

bik^{h}ing	diap^{h}er	lep^{h}er	sup^{h}er
supp^{h}er	p^{h}ap^{h}er	bak^{h}er	beep^{h}ers
talk^{h}ing	k^{h}ick^{h}er	chipp^{h}er	st^{h}ick^{h}er
track^{h}ing	p^{h}ick^{h}ing	ignit^{h}ing	forgett^{h}ing
p^{h}ack^{h}ing	pluck^{h}ing	upsett^{h}ing	distract^{h}ed

PHRASES energized consonants / aspirated plosives

1.	not^h a work^{h}er	6.	sp^{h}iteful vip^{h}ers
2.	st^{h}ock^{h}ing feet^h	7.	bread and butt^{h}er
3.	bett^{h}er fight^{h}ers	8.	st^{h}omp^{h}ing around
4.	dock^{h}ing the ship^h	9.	st^{h}alk^{h}ing leop^{h}ards
5.	comp^{h}act^{h}ed fractures	10.	look^{h}ing for slipp^{h}ers

SENTENCES energized consonants / aspirated plosives

1. What is it?

2. The pilot arrived.

3. Is Peter locking up?

4. This skirt is dirty and torn.

5. My aunt is in the waiting room.

6. They're not permitted backstage.

7. Have you perfected your technique?

8. Did everyone put money into the pot?

9. Patty plays the clarinet in the orchestra.

10. Put on a shirt and tie for opening night.

11. She's waiting until there's available seating.

12. Terrence likes hot peppers and greasy chips.

13. It is impossible to make a booking this week.

14. Did it occur to you to audit every single account?

15. I thought the light would be brighter in here; it's not.

STANDARD BRITISH TEXT energized consonants/plosives. *Speak the following out loud with vibrant, energized consonants.*

At the present moment I am eating muffins because I am unhappy.
(Wilde: The Importance of Being Earnest)

I shall know better in the future than to take any woman's part.
(Shaw: Man and Superman)

If you kept a little more distance, friend, it would become
you much better.

(Farquhar: The Beaux Stratagem)

MEDLEY.   There is a great critic, I hear, in these matters lately
               arrived piping hot from Paris.
BELLAIR.   Sir Fopling Flutter, you mean.

(Etherege: The Man of Mode)

Do tell her I want to talk to her particularly. I have been waiting
here all the morning to see either her or Robert.

(Wilde: An Ideal Husband)

Why, don't you know, good Captain, that telling truth is a quality
as prejudicial to a man that would thrive in the world, as square
play to a cheat, or true love to a whore?

(Wycherley: The Plain Dealer)

I shouldn't enjoy trotting around the park to advertise my
dressmaker and carriage builder, or being bored at the opera
to show off a shop windowful of diamonds.

(Shaw: Mrs. Warren's Profession)

When company comes, you are not to pop out and stare, and
then run in again, like frighted rabbits in a warren.

(Goldsmith: She Stoops to Conquer)

Pray, father, don't put me up on getting anything out of a man;
I don't understand wheedling.

(Farquhar: The Beaux Stratagem)

It's a damned long, dark, boggy, dirty, dangerous way.
(Goldsmith: She Stoops to Conquer)

Death! does he know I'm married, too?
(Wycherley: The Country Wife)

A pox! Why should anyone, because he has nothing to do, go and
disturb another man's business?

(Wycherley: The Plain Dealer)

RHYTHM HIGHLIGHTER ADJUSTMENTS

unstressed /ɪ/ (wi̲ll) endings

/i/ (we̲) suffix and unstressed word endings spelled 'y' or 'i' shorten noticeably in length or are replaced by the very short /ɪ/ (wi̲ll) sound.

This adjustment accentuates the difference in rhythm between stressed and unstressed syllables. The 'arrow' in IPA (below) represents 'adjusts to', so the sound adjustment from Classical American to Standard British is represented by: / i → ɪ /.

AUDIO 79▶ /i→ɪ/ endings

>   ɪ   ɪ   ɪ
> They were mere childish 'gree̲di̲nesses and 'crue̲lti̲es, curi'osi̲ti̲es
>
>   ɪ
> and 'fanci̲es.
>
>   (Shaw: Man and Superman)
>
>   ɪ   ɪ
> Oh, I am not 'rea̲lly̲ wicked at all, cousin 'Ceci̲ly̲.
>
>   (Wilde: The Importance of Being Earnest)
>
>   ɪ   ɪ   ɪ
> Madam, would your 'la̲dy̲ship be as 'rea̲dy̲ to apply the 'reme̲dy̲
>
> as to give the wound.
>
>   (Farquhar: The Beaux Stratagem)

Note: Days of the week are spoken with the /ɪ/ suffix.

An overall increase in vocal energy and a wider range in intonation and inflection accompany Standard British changes. Generally, the shorter and more clipped the ending, the higher the status of the character.

>   ɪ   ɪ   ɪ
> *Your ladyship looks very ill, truly.*
>
>   (Vanbrugh: The Provok'd Wife)

WORDS /i→ɪ/ endings

'early	'honey	'secrecy	'barely
'itchy	'wintery	'brutally	fu'tility
'sunny	'intimacy	ve'locity	'Tuesday
'sanity	'shadowy	versa'tility	'definitely
vul'garity	su'premacy	a'ppealingly	ma'liciously

PHRASES /i→ɪ / endings These can be notated with a phonetic symbol, underline, or strikethrough, whichever marking works as a better reminder.

1.	very weary		6.	such a bully
2.	lacks unity		7.	weekly party
3.	reading daily		8.	terribly funny
4.	rainy and snowy		9.	going on Friday
5.	amazingly angry		10.	especially fancy

SENTENCES /i→ɪ/ endings

1. Mr. Whitney's tipsy.

2. Let's watch *The Mummy*.

3. Someone committed perjury.

4. Luckily, they saved the tapestry.

5. Actually, he's wary of investing.

6. The producer's policy: no nudity.

7. He's happily and hopelessly in love.

8. It can be especially cold in February.

9. There has been no scarcity of publicity.

10. I really thought there would be reciprocity.

11. After winning the lottery they lived in luxury.

12. She spoke loathingly of their cowardly behavior.

13. It was clearly amusingly and alluringly performed.

14. Gary reviewed *The Caine Mutiny* for *The Daily News*.

15. *Merrily We Roll Along* was carefully and lavishly staged.

STANDARD BRITISH TEXT / i→ɪ / **endings.** *Mark the following and speak out loud.*

        ɪ   ɪ
How frightfully, horribly true!

                    (Shaw: Man and Superman)

Surely it's not customary.

                    (Shaw: Man and Superman)

The man is perfectly a pretty fellow.

                    (Farquhar: The Beaux Stratagem)

The old man will be here immediately.

                    (Etherege: The Man of Mode)

Its sympathies are with misery, with poverty, with starvation
of the body, and of the heart.

                    (Shaw: Man and Superman)

So my vanity has deceiv'd me, and my ambition has made me uneasy.

                    (Vanbrugh: The Provok'd Wife)

I have dared to love you wildly, passionately, devotedly, hopelessly.

                    (Wilde: The Importance of Being Earnest)

I thank you heartily, heartily.

                    (Congreve: The Way of the World)

Yes, I think the good lady would marry anything that resembled
a man.

                    (Congreve: The Way of the World)

Come, sir, we don't mind ceremonies in the country.

                    (Farquhar: The Beaux Stratagem)

Pray, out of pity to ourselves, let us find a better subject, for I am
weary of this. Do you think your husband inclin'd to jealousy?

                    (Vanbrugh: The Provok'd Wife)

Master Horner, will you never keep civil company?

                    (Wycherley: The Country Wife)

My dear Lady Sneerwell, how have you been this century?

                    (Sheridan: The School for Scandal)

How strong is fancy!

(Vanbrugh: The Provok'd Wife)

I am in love with her already.

(Farquhar: The Beaux Stratagem)

Come, for my part, I will have only those glorious manly pleasures
of being very drunk and very slovenly.

(Wycherley: The Country Wife)

Authority! No, to be sure! If you wanted authority over me, you
should have adopted me and not married me.

(Sheridan: The School for Scandal)

To think of a whirlwind, though 'twere in a whirlwind, were a case
of more steady contemplation; a very tranquility of mind and mansion.

(Congreve: Way of the World)

Happy, happy sister! your angel has been watchful for your happiness,
whilst mine hast slept.

(Farquhar: Beaux Stratagem)

Thy peace being made with heaven, death's already vanquished;
bear a little longer the pains that attend this transitory life.

(Lillo: The London Merchant)

I'll say he died in Paris of apoplexy. Lots of people die of apoplexy,
quite suddenly, don't they?

(Wilde: The Importance of Being Earnest)

I suppose you really think you're getting on famously with me.

(Shaw: Mrs. Warren's Profession)

Charity, dear Miss Prism, charity! None of us is perfect.

(Wilde: The Importance of Being Earnest)

So, carry him off, carry him off; we shall have him prate himself
into a fever by and by; carry him off.

(Vanbrugh: The Relapse)

'r' Coloring

vowels, diphthongs, triphthongs

Completely eliminate **'r'** coloring from vowels, diphthongs and triphthongs of 'r', by allowing the tip of the tongue to gently rest touching the back of the lower teeth for the duration of the vowel, diphthong, or triphthong.

AUDIO 80► no 'r' coloring

> ǫ   ɑ
> Good morning, fellow guardian.
>
> (Shaw: Man and Superman)
>
> ǫ ə   ɑ ǫ
> He's gone to order the dog cart for me.
>
> (Wilde: The Importance of Being Earnest)
>
> juə   ɑ   ə faɪəɑmz juə   ə
> Your eyes are better firearms than your pistol; they never miss.
>
> (Farquhar: The Beaux Stratagem)

WORDS stressed vowel of 'r' /ɝ → ɜ/

her	girl	pert	curt
fern	turn	bird	first
burnt	curse	blurt	burst
worth	turnip	dearth	churn
church	Gertrude	hernia	hermit

When speaking key words of more than one syllable, highlight the vowel in the stressed syllable, making the rhythmic difference between stressed and unstressed syllables noticeable. This attention to rhythm will facilitate eliminating 'r' coloring in the unstressed syllable of the word.

Also, remember to rest the tip of the tongue down behind the lower front teeth for the duration of the final vowel when eliminating 'r' coloring.

WORDS unstressed vowel of 'r' /ɚ→ə/

'litt<u>er</u>	'Pet<u>er</u>	'fath<u>er</u>	'sitt<u>er</u>
'sift<u>er</u>	'bitt<u>er</u>	'beep<u>er</u>	'fatt<u>er</u>
'tatt<u>ers</u>	'flav<u>or</u>	'feat<u>ure</u>	'mist<u>er</u>
'splint<u>er</u>	'leath<u>er</u>	'flims<u>ier</u>	dis'hon<u>or</u>
'cheap<u>er</u>	dis'ord<u>er</u>	'squand<u>er</u>	'magnif<u>ier</u>

If you are having difficulty eliminating **'r'** coloring, try rhyming with the last sound in 'sof<u>a</u>' or 'ide<u>a</u>', which is a schwa. *Read across.*

/ə/	/ə/	/ə/	/ə/
'sof<u>a</u>	'curl<u>er</u>	'sof<u>a</u>	'ang<u>er</u>
'sof<u>a</u>	'lead<u>er</u>	'sof<u>a</u>	'suff<u>er</u>
'sof<u>a</u>	'theat<u>re</u>	'sof<u>a</u>	'senat<u>or</u>
'sof<u>a</u>	'murd<u>er</u>	'sof<u>a</u>	'mann<u>er</u>
'sof<u>a</u>	par'ticul<u>ar</u>	'sof<u>a</u>	'murm<u>ur</u>

                     ə   ə

And, pray, who married my lady Manslaught<u>er</u> t'oth<u>er</u> day?

(Farquhar: The Beaux Stratagem)

When eliminating **'r'** coloring in the following, do not eliminate the short schwa.

DIPHTHONGS /ɪɚ→ɪə/

peer	dear	fear	hear
gears	veer	beard	we're
sheer	adhere	veneer	appear

DIPHTHONGS /eɚ→eə/

pair	dare	bear	hair
tear	snare	share	careful
where	aware	impaired	chairman

DIPHTHONGS /ʊɚ→ʊə/

sure	tour	you're	lure
poor	Coors	surely	Moor
curious	insurance	worsted	furious

The 'c<u>ar</u>' and 'sp<u>or</u>ts' diphthongs undergo a slightly different change. The second element, the schwa with 'r' coloring, is eliminated and the remaining vowel is lengthened: /aɚ̆→ ɑ/ and /ɔɚ̆→ ɔ̩/.

Notice the addition of a diacritical marker under[1] the IPA symbol /ɔ̩/. The direction of the short vertical line indicates that this vowel is spoken with the jaw slightly more closed and the tongue arch slightly higher in Standard British than in Neutral or Classical American.

DIPHTHONGS /ɔɚ̆→ ɔ̩/

four	tore	force	bore
core	door	wore	chore
store	snore	more	abhor

DIPHTHONGS /aɚ̆→ ɑ/

part	far	star	bar
partial	charge	darling	startle
tarnished	sergeant	alarming	farther

Note: A strikethrough (/) is placed over the letter(s) that represent(s) the vowel, diphthong or triphthong of **'r'** from this point forward, as a reminder to eliminate the 'r' coloring.

> *Perhaps a good pa̸rt of what I suffe̸r from my husband*
> *may be a judgment upon me fo̸r my cruelty to my love̸r.*
>
> (Vanbrugh: The Provok'd Wife)

PHRASES no 'r' coloring

1.	a small fo̸rtune	6.	raging sto̸rms
2.	flowe̸rs appea̸r	7.	last Septembe̸r
3.	growing a bea̸rd	8.	the British Empi̸re
4.	pictu̸re ove̸r there	9.	fractu̸red shoulde̸r
5.	majo̸r contributo̸rs	10.	many sna̸rling dogs

---

[1] The font used for *Classically Speaking* always positions the diacritical marker as a subscript, appearing under the IPA symbol. Other fonts can vary the position of the diacritical marker.

SENTENCES no 'r' coloring

1.   Is the review in the paper?

2.   The term ends in December.

3.   Her brother's a singer, a tenor.

4.   Obscure herbs curled Herb's hair.

5.   Walk no further than Mercer Street.

6.   Do actors perform at the Player's Club?

7.   Father would rather see *The Producers*.

8.   Wealthier investors attended the premiere.

9.   The sunnier the weather, the thirstier the birds.

10.   Bernice volunteered to have her ears pierced first.

11.   My character is a slanderer who banters and swears.

12.   That diaper commercial paid for her master's degree.

13.   They need to rewire the store or they may have a fire.

14.   What well-known guitar player is writing his memoirs?

15.   The director worked for free; he owed the producer a favor.

STANDARD BRITISH TEXT no 'r' coloring. *Mark a strikethrough on the vowel, diphthong and triphthong of 'r', as shown, and speak out loud. If marking with the IPA symbol increases accuracy, mark that also.*

Brother, brother, a word with you!

(Sheridan: The School for Scandal)

What sort of livery has the footman?

(Farquhar: The Beaux Stratagem)

Oh, never, never! Madam, dry up your tears.

(Lillo: The London Merchant)

In a word, never was poor creature so spurr'd on by desire and so rein'd in with fear.

(Vanbrugh: The Provok'd Wife)

CLASSICALLY SPEAKING   STANDARD BRITISH 'r' coloring

Well, my dear doctor, hast thou done what I desired?

(Wycherley: The Country Wife)

DON JUAN.   I was a murderer.
OLD WOMAN.   A murderer! Oh! how dare they send me to herd with
             murderers!

(Shaw: Man and Superman)

Dissembler, damned dissembler!

(Etherege: The Man of Mode)

I'll leave you together and lock the door.

(Congreve: The Way of the World)

My curse upon yon caller, whoe'er he be!

(Shaw: Mrs. Warren's Profession)

We shall be careful not to disturb you, sir.

(Vanbrugh: The Provok'd Wife)

Rapture, rapture, Mr. Treble, I'm all rapture! O wit and art,
what power you have when join'd!

(Vanbrugh: The Provok'd Wife)

My lady and sister, sir. –Wife, this is Master Horner.

(Wycherley: The Country Wife)

BUSY.   Dear Madam! Let me see that curl in order.
HARRIET.   Let me alone, I will shake 'em all out of order.

(Etherege: The Man of Mode)

You seem so much concerned, my dear, I fear I have told you
unawares what I had better have concealed for your quiet.

(Etherege: The Man of Mode)

I stand in need of anybody's assistance that will help me to cut
my elder brother's throat.

(Vanbrugh: The Relapse)

Men like that always live in comfortable bachelor lodgings with
broken hearts, and are adored by their landladies, and never
get married.

(Shaw: Man and Superman)

VOWEL ADJUSTMENTS

/ əŭ / (go)

Use the diphthong sound represented by the symbol /əŭ/ rather than the Neutral and Classical American /oŭ/. Begin with the short, neutral schwa sound /ə/ (uh), then blend into a rounded /u/ (who).

AUDIO 81▶ /oŭ→əŭ/ (go)

   əŭ   əŭ
So you are Hamlet, I suppose.

(Shaw: Man and Superman)

     əŭ   əŭ   ʊ əŭ
I really don't see anything romantic in proposing.

(Wilde: The Importance of Being Earnest)

       əŭ   əŭ   əŭ
A young widow, a handsome widow and would be again a widow.

(Congreve: The Way of the World)

WORDS /oŭ→əŭ/ (go)

oboe	slope	ocean	phony
home	elbow	Roman	loaning
loaves	stroked	moment	bloated
throated	disrobe	rainbow	devoted
probation	enclosure	foreshadow	overdraw

If producing this sound change is troublesome, it may be helpful to think of the first element as a bit brighter. The sound change is sometimes notated /oŭ→eŭ/, though I prefer /oŭ→əŭ/.

     ə əŭ   əŭ
Drown husbands! For yours is a provoking fellow.

(Vanbrugh: The Provok'd Wife)

CLASSICALLY SPEAKING   **STANDARD BRITISH** /əŭ/

PHRASES /oŭ→əŭ/ (g<u>o</u>)

1.	<u>o</u>ld s<u>o</u>ldiers	6.	g<u>o</u>lden h<u>o</u>lder
2.	<u>o</u>z<u>o</u>ne layer	7.	always st<u>o</u>ne c<u>o</u>ld
3.	<u>o</u>wns t<u>o</u>asters	8.	another st<u>o</u>w away
4.	large expl<u>o</u>sion	9.	getting a sore thr<u>oa</u>t
5.	newly betr<u>o</u>thed	10.	waiting to be n<u>o</u>ticed

SENTENCES /oŭ→əŭ/ (g<u>o</u>)

1. Go vote.

2. He loathes boasting.

3. Did you see *Frozen*?

4. Jonas was misquoted.

5. They filed in row by row.

6. Who is composing the music?

7. Everyone noticed his devotion.

8. I'd like a cozy evening at home.

9. Stop your moaning and groaning.

10. Don't sign a non-disclosure agreement.

11. She's playing in *The Marriage Proposal*.

12. He's chosen not to move to the west coast.

13. Lois, won't you show me your new photos?

14. She lost her composure when she won the Tony.

15. His home was in foreclosure, and then he got the part!

STANDARD BRITISH TEXT /oŭ→əŭ/ (g<u>o</u>). *Mark the following and speak out loud.*

əŭ   əŭ
A l<u>ow</u> paltry set of fell<u>ow</u>s.

(Goldsmith: She Stoops to Conquer)

No, no, hang him, the rogue has no manners at all.

(Congreve: The Way of the World)

I'll go into the army.

(Vanbrugh: The Relapse)

Oh no! I hope you do not know him!

(Etherege: The Man of Mode)

Oh, that stupid old joke of yours about me!

(Shaw: Man and Superman)

What, leave us with a filthy man alone in his lodgings?

(Wycherley: The Country Wife)

Go, go! You are a couple of provoking toads.

(Sheridan: The School for Scandal)

I won't, won't, won't, won't, WON'T marry you.

(Shaw: Man and Superman)

I have a perfect passion for listening through keyholes.

(Wilde: An Ideal Husband)

Disclose it to your wife; own what has past between us.

(Congreve: The Way of the World)

I suppose a man may eat his own muffins in his own garden.

(Wilde: The Importance of Being Earnest)

Excuse me; but I am so lonely; and this place is so awful.

(Shaw: Man and Superman)

What conceited ass has been impertinent enough to dare to propose
to you before I had proposed to you?

(Wilde: An Ideal Husband)

Oh, you can pronounce the word, then; I thought it would have
choked you.

(Vanbrugh: The Relapse)

Well, the only small satisfaction I have in the whole of this wretched
business is that your friend Bunbury is quite exploded.

(Wilde: The Importance of Being Earnest)

So, gentlemen, I hope you have all taken pains to show yourselves
masters in your professions.

(Vanbrugh: The Relapse)

Oh, to be sure—the most whimsical circumstance.

(Sheridan: School for Scandal)

If she cannot make her husband a cuckold, she'll make him jealous and pass for one.

(Wycherley: The Country Wife)

You have no right to say such things, Jack.

(Shaw: Man and Superman)

But first bring me a pipe; I'll smoke.

(Vanbrugh: The Provok'd Wife)

You said his secretaries open his letters.

(Wilde: An Ideal Husband)

My life has been mostly spent in the service of the ladies.

(Farquhar: The Beaux Stratagem)

But she's cold, my friend, still cold as the northern star.

(Vanbrugh: The Provok'd Wife)

I find high birth and titles don't recommend the man who owns them, to my affections.

(Lillo: The London Merchant)

You wrote to me as one of your oldest friends, one of your husband's oldest friends. Mrs. Cheveley stole that letter from my rooms.

(Wilde: An Ideal Husband)

When an old bachelor takes a young wife, what is he to expect?

(Sheridan: School for Scandal)

No, no, hang him, the rogue has no manners at all, that I must own— no more breeding than a bum-baily.

(Congreve: The Way of the World)

DON JUAN. I was of noble birth and rich; and when my person did not please, my conversation flattered, though I generally found myself fortunate in both.
STATUE.   Coxcomb!
DON JUAN. Yes, but even my coxcombry pleased.

(Shaw: Man and Superman)

/ ǫ / (all)

This back vowel sound is made with the jaw slightly more closed, the lips more rounded, and the back of the tongue arched slightly higher in the mouth than in Neutral or Classical. This is represented in the IPA symbol by the vertical line underneath: /ǫ/. This sound tends to be energized and long.

AUDIO 82 ▶ /ɔ → ǫ/ (**all**)

ǫ   ǫ   ǫ
This sort of talk is not kind to me, Jack.

(Shaw: Man and Superman)

ǫ   i   ǫ   ǫ
I have not been called back to town at all.

(Wilde: The Importance of Being Earnest)

ǫ   ǫ   ǫ
Nobody observes the law for the law's sake.

(Farquhar: The Beaux Stratagem)

Remember: common /ǫ/ spellings include: au, aw, alk, all, ought.

WORDS /ɔ → ǫ/ (**all**)

law	tall	chalk	fall
wall	saw	bawd	stalk
walk	balk	small	dawn
ought	sauce	sought	fought
flaunt	bought	audition	daughter

PRACTICE /ɔ → ǫ/ (**all**)

1.	bought chalk	6.	small talk
2.	tall daughters	7.	lawn party
3.	Dawn's cause	8.	doing laundry
4.	thoughtful Paula	9.	walking in autumn
5.	because it's the law	10.	altogether exhausting

SENTENCES /ɔ → ǫ/ (**all**)

1.   Loosen your jaw.

2.   Well, that was awkward.

3.   The production was awful.

4.   Return that horse to its stall.

5.   They taught class on the lawn.

6.   Is anyone in the drawing room?

7.   Let's walk towards the waterfall.

8.   Layer the sausages in the saucepan.

9.   They called out, but Saul didn't hear.

10.   The children are drawing with chalk.

11.   We haven't met your daughter-in-law.

12.   I understand the auditorium is haunted.

13.   What did Shaun order? He's inaudible.

14.   She auditioned to an onslaught of applause.

15.   The exhausted author called off his scheduled talk.

STANDARD BRITISH TEXT /ɔ → ǫ/ (**all**). *Mark the following and speak out loud.*

ǫ
I am more than usually tall for my age.

(Wilde: The Importance of Being Earnest)

How, you saucy fellow!

(Wycherley: The Country Wife)

I mean, he never speaks truth at all—that's all.

(Congreve: The Way of the World)

Run, I say; call him again. I will have him called.

(Etherege: The Man of Mode)

He talks Latin—it does me good to hear him talk Latin.

(Farquhar: The Beaux Stratagem)

Audacious villain!

(Congreve: The Way of the World)

Thought does not become a young woman.

(Sheridan: The Rivals)

Because I always had an aversion to being us'd like a dog.

(Vanbrugh: The Provok'd Wife)

Not to detain you then with longer pause
In short; my heart to this conclusion draws,
I yield it to the hand, that's loudest in applause.

(Sheridan: The School for Scandal, Epilogue)

I have brought over not so much as a bawdy picture.

(Wycherley: The Country Wife)

A cup, save thee, and what a cup hast thou brought!

(Congreve: The Way of the World)

CECILY.   Uncle Jack is sending you to Australia.
ALGERNON. Australia! I'd sooner die.

(Wilde: The Importance of Being Earnest)

Nothing but love could make me capable of so much falsehood.

(Etherege: The Man of Mode)

But who would have thought a woman could have been false to me?
I could not have thought it.

(Wycherley: The Country Wife)

You must not be so talkative, Diggory. You must be all attention
to the guests. You must hear us talk, and not think of talking.

(Goldsmith: She Stoops to Conquer)

If he has fallen from his altar, do not thrust him into the mire.

(Wilde: An Ideal Husband)

I was more than once nearly choked with gall during the honeymoon.

(Sheridan: The School for Scandal, Epilogue)

/ ɒ̩ / (ho̲nest)

This back vowel sound is similar to that spoken in Classical American, except that it is formed with the jaw slightly more closed, the lips more energized, and the back of the tongue arched slightly higher in the mouth. This is represented in the IPA symbol by the vertical line underneath: /ɒ̩/.

In addition, the sound can be expressed in a slightly more clipped manner in Standard British than in Classical American.

AUDIO 83▶ /ɒ → ɒ̩/ (ho̲nest)

>   ɒ̩   ɒ̩
> Life is no̲t all plays and poems, O̲ctavius.
>
> > (Shaw: Man and Superman)
>
>   ɒ̩   ɒ̩   ɒ̩   ɒ̩   ɒ̩
> Wha̲t? Wha̲t is it no̲t? Wha̲t is it no̲t yet? Is it no̲t yet too late.
>
> > (Congreve: The Way of the World)
>
>   ɒ̩
> A po̲x! They are come too soon!
>
> > (Wycherley: The Country Wife)

Remember: the /ɒ̩/ (ho̲nest) sound is used:

(a)   in words spelled with 'o' and pronounced with the /ɑ/ (fa̲ther) sound in Neutral American, as in:

          not, hot, on, box, top, stop, job, shopping, probably, Tom

(b)   in words spelled with 'qua' or 'wa' and pronounced with the /ɑ/ (fa̲ther) sound in Neutral American including:

          kumquat, quad, quaff, squab, squad, squalid, squalor, squash, squat, swaddling, swallow, swamp, wad, wallet, wallow, Wally, wan, wand, wander, want, wash, wasp, wast, wassail, watch, watt, yacht

(c) in words spelled with 'o' and pronounced with the /ɔ/ (a̲ll) sound in Neutral American, as in:

cloth, moth, cross, boss, dog, office, often, song, belong

Exception: words spelled 'ought' as in bought, fought, and sought, are spoken with /ɔ/ in Standard British.

(d) in strong forms of a few words pronounced with the /ʌ/ (U̲H) sound in Neutral American, including:

from, of, 'twas, was, wasn't, what, whatnot, whereof

WORDS /ɒ → ọ/ (ho̲nest)

topic	dogs	moth	boss
coffee	slosh	across	shop
strong	prompt	belong	Robin

PHRASES /ɒ → ọ/ (ho̲nest)

1.	lo̲st pro̲perty	6.	ho̲t co̲ffee
2.	wha̲t scho̲lars	7.	Bo̲xing Day
3.	no̲t pro̲blematic	8.	Jo̲hn's co̲ttage
4.	Robert's do̲ssier	9.	lo̲ts of mo̲nolo̲gues
5.	wa̲sn't wa̲tching	10.	interesting sho̲pping

SENTENCES /ɒ → ọ/ (ho̲nest)

1. It's not abolished.

2. Is peroxide toxic?

3. Economics can be problematic.

4. Robin's fond of Moroccan food.

5. Disc jockeys can be terribly cocky.

6. Who's playing PROSPERO? I'm not!

7. Stop looking at your watch, Thomas.

8. Donald handed out copies of the play.

9. It was shot in Hong Kong last October.

10.   John has such wonderful comic timing.

11.   The actor spoke of his 'process' over coffee.

12.   Doris is very cosmopolitan and knowledgeable.

13.   I need a summer cottage in the tropics, that's obvious.

14.   Who dropped his wallet in Washington, Joshua or Joffrey?

STANDARD BRITISH TEXT /ɒ → ǫ/ (h<u>o</u>nest). *Mark the following and speak out loud.*

$$\overset{\text{ǫ}}{}$$
Their malice is int<u>o</u>lerable!

> (Sheridan: The School for Scandal)

Eternal blockhead! Hey, sot.

> (Vanbrugh: The Provok'd Wife)

That's my dear little scholar, kiss me again.

> (Farquhar: The Beaux Stratagem)

Lord Foppington! I know him not.

> (Vanbrugh: The Relapse)

Here, sirrah, reach me the strong-box.

> (Farquhar: The Beaux Stratagem)

Cannot repentance wipe out an act of folly?

> (Wilde: The Importance of Being Earnest)

She's gone, but she has left a pleasing image of herself behind that wanders in my soul.

> (Etherege: The Man of Mode)

Succeed or no, still victory's my lot;
If I subdue his heart, 'tis well; if not,
I shall subdue my conscience to my plot.

> (Vanbrugh: The Relapse)

What, invite your wife to kiss men? Monstrous!

> (Wycherley: The Country Wife)

Stop a bit. I want to take you into my confidence.

> (Shaw: Mrs. Warren's Profession)

A pox on him and his smile!

(Wycherley: The Country Wife)

See who that is. Set down the bottle first.

(Congreve: The Way of the World)

The strongest vessels, if they put to sea,
May possibly be lost.

(Vanbrugh: The Relapse)

'Tis for the honour of England, that all Europe should know we
have blockheads of all ages.

(Congreve: The Way of the World)

You astonish me! I thought you did not expect him this month.

(Sheridan: School for Scandal)

I do know your wife, sir; she's a woman, sir, and consequently
a monster, sir, a greater monster than a husband, sir.

(Wycherley: The Country Wife)

I have been the miserablest dog ever since that ever committed
wedlock!

(Sheridan: The School for Scandal)

'Tis the best plot in the world: your mother, you know, will be
gone to church.

(Farquhar: The Beaux Stratagem)

Odds whips and wheels! I've traveled like a comet, with a tail
of dust all the way as long as the Mall.

(Sheridan: The Rivals)

Yes, Juan, we know the libertine's philosophy. Always ignore
the consequences to the woman.

(Shaw: Man and Superman)

What would those modern psychological novelists, of whom we
hear so much, say to such a theory as that?

(Wilde: An Ideal Husband)

'Ask' List

This is a list of words that have alternate pronunciations depending on the dialect being spoken: Neutral American, Classical American, Mid-Atlantic[1] or Standard British.

Neutral American and Classical American: there is no change, the /æ/ (th<u>a</u>t) sound is maintained on the 'ask' list of words.

Standard British: the 'ask' list of words is spoken with the /ɑ/ (f<u>a</u>ther) sound.

AUDIO 84▶ /ɑ/ (f<u>a</u>ther) on 'ask' list words

>   ɑ
> There is a r<u>as</u>cal in our midst.
>
>   (Shaw: Man and Superman)
>
>   ɑ
> Don't play that gh<u>as</u>tly tune, Algy!
>
>   (Wilde: The Importance of Being Earnest)
>
>   ɑ   ɑ
> My <u>aunt</u>, sir, yes, my <u>aunt</u>, sir, and your lady, sir; your lady
>
>   ɑ
> is my <u>aunt</u>.
>
>   (Congreve: The Way of the World)

Which words are included in the 'ask' list?

There is not a distinct rule for inclusion, but spellings can offer a fairly reliable indication. For example:

<u>aft</u>   abaft, aft, after, aftermath, afternoon, afterward, behalf, craft, daft, draft, graft, raft, shaft, Shaftesbury, Taft, waft, witchcraft

<u>ampl</u>   ample, example, sample

---

[1] Mid-Atlantic dialect uses /a/ on ask list words. See pages 422-426.

ance /ans   advance, answer, chance, chancellor, chancery, dance, enhance, France, freelance, glance, lance, prance, trance

anch   avalanche, blanch(e), branch, ranch, stanch

and   Chandler, command(o), countermand, demand, reprimand, slander

ant[1] /aunt   advantage, aunt, can't, chant, chantry, enchant, grant, implant, plant, shan't, slant, supplant, transplant, vantage

as(s)   alas, brass, class, Glasgow, glass, grass, pass, Passover, trespass

ask   ask, bask, basket, cask, flask, mask, task, rascal, vast

asp   clasp, gasp, grasp, hasp, rasp, raspberry

ast   aghast, alabaster, avast, blast, broadcast, cast, caste, castle, contrast, disaster, fast, ghastly, last, mast, master, nasty, past, pastor, pasture, plaster, repast, telecast, vast, vasty

ath   bath, lath, lather, path, rather, wrath

aff /affe   chaff, distaff, Falstaff, gaff, giraffe, quaff, staff

alf /aph   autograph, behalf, calf, half, epitaph, graph, telegraph

augh   laugh, laughter, draught

In the previous three lines above, all the consonant spellings listed are pronounced /f/ (af, aff, affe, alf, aph, augh).

There are a few words one might expect to find on the 'ask' list, which are actually pronounced with /æ/, for example: can, classicist, gather, crass. If you question pronunciation, consult a *British-English* pronouncing dictionary.

PHRASES /ɑ/ (father) on 'ask' list words

1.	on his behalf	6	Nasty Frances
2.	hold steadfastly	7.	just half a glass
3.	cutting the grass	8.	advancing at last
4.	good raspberries	9.	filling empty flasks
5.	a path in Flanders	10.	entrancing sampling

---

[1] Though 'ant' spelling can indicate inclusion on the 'ask' list of words, the word 'ant' (the insect) is pronounced /ænt/.

SENTENCES /ɑ/ (f**a**ther) on 'ask' list words

1. It's very drafty.

2. Ask me after class.

3. Fasten your seatbelts.

4. Mr. Branch is a taskmaster.

5. Chandler demanded an answer.

6. That casting call was a disaster.

7. My aunt chants every afternoon.

8. They looked aghast at the avalanche.

9. There was no answer from the bathroom.

10. The paragraph was engraved in alabaster.

11. A ghastly smell wafted through the room.

12. They're casting *Dancin'* in the next classroom.

13. Give me an example of an artistic masterpiece.

14. Look how fast the glass-blowers made that sample.

15. The school master made him write, "I shan't slander."

STANDARD BRITISH TEXT /ɑ/ (f**a**ther) on 'ask' list words. *Mark the following and speak out loud.*

ɑ
She made me l**au**gh yesterday.

(Vanbrugh: The Provok'd Wife)

I am more advanced than ever I was. I grow more advanced every day.

(Shaw: Man and Superman)

I think wit as necessary at dinner as a glass of good wine.

(Wycherley: The Country Wife)

I can't abide you; go, I can't abide you.

(Etherege: The Man of Mode)

Why, first she's an heiress, vastly rich.

(Vanbrugh: The Provok'd Wife)

Ay, ay, let that pass — there are other throats to be cut.

(Congreve: The Way of the World)

'Tis, let me see, a quarter and half quarter of a minute past eleven.

(Wycherley: The Country Wife)

They seem as a class, to have absolutely no sense of moral
responsibility.

(Wilde: The Importance of Being Earnest)

Half the pretty women in London smoke cigarettes. Personally I
prefer the other half.

(Wilde: An Ideal Husband)

When her folly makes 'em laugh, she thinks they are pleas'd with
her wit.

(Vanbrugh: The Provok'd Wife)

There's something in that which may turn to advantage.

(Farquhar: The Beaux Stratagem)

The paragraphs, you say, Mr. Snake, were all inserted?

(Sheridan: The School for Scandal)

May I ask if you are engaged to be married to this young lady?

(Wilde: The Importance of Being Earnest)

And men, I suppose, never throw off the mask when their bird is
in the net.

(Shaw: Man and Superman)

I'gad, if thou canst bring this about, I'll have thy statue cast in brass.

(Vanbrugh: The Relapse)

I take care never to come into a married family! The commands
of the master and mistress are always so contrary, that 'tis impossible
to please both.

(Farquhar: The Beaux Stratagem)

Polysyllabic word endings

There are two options for polysyllabic words (words of three or more syllables) ending in 'ary', 'ory', or 'berry' spellings:

(a)   The short schwa sound with no 'r' coloring /ə/ (uh) is used in the second to the last syllable. The final 'y' takes an /ɪ/ (wɪll) suffix, so the word endings are pronounced: /ə-rɪ/

(b)   The schwa that was in the second to the last syllable is dropped, making the word ending shorter and more clipped. So, 'purgatory' could be spoken: /ˈpɜgətə-rɪ/ or /ˈpɜgətrɪ/

Polysyllabic words ending in 'ony' are pronounced /ə-nɪ/.

AUDIO 85▶ polysyllabic word endings

(drop the schwa altogether, or speak: ə-rɪ)

Your caution may be ˈnecessa̲-ry.

(Farquhar: The Beaux Stratagem)

(drop the schwa altogether, or speak: ə-rɪ)

That is satisˈfacto̲-ry.

(Wilde: The Importance of Being Earnest)

(drop the schwa altogether, or speak: ə-rɪ)

He promises to be an exˈtraordina̲-ry person.

(Congreve: The Way of the World)

WORDS 'ony' endings pronounced /ənɪ/

ˈacrimony	ˈagrimony	ˈalimony	ˈantimony
ˈceremony	cereˈmonious	ˈmatrimony	ˈpatrimony
ˈparsimony	parsiˈmonious	ˈsanctimony	ˈtestimony

mənɪ

At what hour would you wish the cere̲mo̲ny̲ performed?

(Wilde: The Importance of Being Earnest)

WORDS 'ory' endings

'minatory	'auditory	'mandatory	'oratory
'predatory	'laudatory	'circulatory	'purgatory
a'ccusatory	o'bligatory	de'rogatory	con'ciliatory
con'tributory	de'pository	'promissory	ex'clamatory
inter'rogatory	pre'paratory	ob'servatory	ma'nipulatory

WORDS 'ary' endings

'actuary	'capillary	'ordinary	'arbitrary
fi'duciary	'necessary	'legendary	'February
'customary	'dictionary	a'pothecary	'mercenary
bene'ficiary	'adversary	'commentary	re'actionary
'momentary	he'reditary	evo'lutionary	con'fectionary

WORDS 'berry' endings:

'barberry	'bayberry	'dogberry	'chinaberry
'cranberry	'dewberry	'snowberry	'gooseberry
'hackberry	'mulberry	'blackberry	'winterberry

PHRASES polysyllabic word endings

1. no alimony
2. difficult repertory
3. conservatory class
4. derogatory message
5. unsanitary conditions
6. great library
7. necessary notary
8. huckleberry bush
9. temporary position
10. elocutionary expert

SENTENCES polysyllabic word endings

1. I enjoyed the ceremony.

2. It's just a temporary setback.

3. Recertification is mandatory.

4. Who is your literary manager?

5. The jury reviewed his testimony.

6. Your performance was extraordinary.

7.   He has tremendous elocutionary skills.

8.   Where did you go to secondary school?

9.   I understand he has monetary problems.

10.   Have you written the valedictory speech?

11.   She had coronary and auditory weakness.

12.   The bakery requires special confectionaries.

13.   When do you start your conservatory training?

14.   The patient complains of hallucinatory dreams.

15.   The religious ceremony is being held in the sanctuary.

STANDARD BRITISH TEXT polysyllabic word endings. *Mark the following and speak out loud.*

ə-nɪ
O matrim<u>ony</u>!

(Farquhar: The Beaux Stratagem)

Isn't Mr. Worthing in his library?

(Wilde: The Importance of Being Earnest)

Health is the primary duty of life.

(Wilde: The Importance of Being Earnest)

We used to rail at matrimony together.

(Sheridan: The School for Scandal)

Business must be preferred always before love and ceremony with the wise, Mr. Horner.

(Wycherley: The Country Wife)

Let us not be accessory to your putting the ladies out of countenance.

(Congreve: The Way of the World)

Miss Tattle, who was by, affirmed that Lord Buffalo had discovered his lady at a house of no extraordinary fame.

(Sheridan: The School for Scandal)

Matrimony has made you eloquent in love.

(Congreve: The Way of the World)

Always saying no when you meant yes!—simple purgatory for
shy and sincere souls!

(Shaw: Mrs. Warren's Profession)

Most men are the contraries to that they would seem.

(Wycherley: The Country Wife)

Sir, I have endeavored not to wrong your well-known generosity
by an ill-timed parsimony.

(Lillo: The London Merchant)

She would needs have it that no man ever does any extraordinary
kindness or service for a woman but for his own sake.

(Steele: The Conscious Lovers)

These are the genuine signs of true receptance, the only preparatory,
the certain way to everlasting peace.

(Lillo: The London Merchant)

I believe it is customary in good society to take some slight
refreshment at five o'clock.

(Wilde: The Importance of Being Earnest)

If your physick be wholesome, it matters not who is your apothecary.

(Congreve: The Way of the World)

If it wasn't for Bunbury's extraordinary bad health, for instance, I
wouldn't be able to dine with you at Willis's tonight.

(Wilde: The Importance of Being Earnest)

Why, madam, a greater expense than all this men lay out upon an
unnecessary stable of horses.

(Steele: The Conscious Lovers)

I shall be in the conservatory, under the second palm tree on the left.

(Wilde: An Ideal Husband)

I always did what it was customary for a gentleman to do.

(Shaw: Man and Superman)

ADDITIONAL RP VOWEL CHANGES

Carried over from Classical American

The following material was covered as part of the previous work on Classical American dialect. If the reader studied Classical American, then proceed to the supplementary material and Standard British Monologues on pages 481-497.

If the reader began directly with Standard British, the following list of adjustments also needs to be incorporated. These elements are covered in brief on the following pages.

Each item listed above is explained on the following pages and practice text is provided. Additional practice material located in the Classical American section is also referenced. Spoken samples are included on the CD.

/ɪ/ prefixes and suffixes, schwa suffixes, and syllabic endings are carried over from Neutral American. See that section for practice material.

VOWELS BEFORE / r /

In Standard British as in Classical American, when the consonant /r/ occurs in the middle of a word, it should be preceded by a pure vowel sound, not a diphthong.

In Standard British only, when the consonant /r/ occurs between two vowel sounds, the tongue tip can 'tap' the alveolar ridge, resulting in a sound similar to a soft /d/, and often associated with the word 'very' (ve_dy_).

The vowel and the consonant /r/ that follows it are separated by a dash throughout, for clarity.

/ ɪ / (wi̱ll)

before consonant / r /

Use the pure /ɪ/ (wi̱ll) sound, rather than the /ɪə̆ / (he̱re) diphthong, before consonant /r/. Words requiring this adjustment can often be recognized by the presence of an /ɪ/ prefix and/or by the initial spelling 'irr'.

AUDIO 86▶ /ɪ/ (wi̱ll) before /r/

      ɪ   ɑ
I always hoped it would be something really he-roic, at last.
      (Shaw: Man and Superman)

    ɪ
For me you have always had an i-rresistible fascination.
    (Wilde: The Importance of Being Earnest)

ˈsɪrə
Here, si-rrah, light me to my chamber.
    (Farquhar: The Beaux Stratagem)

PRACTICE WORDS, PHRASES, SENTENCES page 357-361.

STANDARD BRITISH TEXT /ɪ/ **(wi̱ll) before** /r/. *Mark the following and speak out loud.*

I

Here you escape this ty̱ranny of the flesh.

(Shaw: Man and Superman)

I'll aid you with such arms for their destruction,
They never shall erect their heads again.

(Vanbrugh: The Relapse)

Here they talk of nothing else but love: its beauty, its holiness, its spirituality, it's the devil knows what!

(Shaw: Man and Superman)

Your decision on the subject of my name is irrevocable, I suppose?

(Wilde: The Importance of Being Earnest)

I suppose you will go in seriously for politics some day, Jack.

(Shaw: Man and Superman)

Though the renewing my visit may seem a little irregular, I hope
I shall obtain your pardon for it.

(Vanbrugh: The Provok'd Wife)

It needs a brain, this irresistible force, lest in its ignorance it should resist itself.

(Shaw: Man and Superman)

I little thought, madam, to see your spirit tamed to this degree.

(Etherege: The Man of Mode)

Marriage is honourable, as you say; and if so, wherefore should
cuckoldom be a discredit, being derived from so honourable a root?

(Congreve: The Way of the World)

/ e / (ge̱t)

before consonant /r/

Use the pure /e/ (ge̱t) sound, rather than the /eə̆/ (the̱ir) diphthong, before consonant /r/. Words requiring this adjustment can often be recognized by 'er' or 'err' in the spelling.

AUDIO 87▶ **/e/ (ge̱t) before /r/**

          e
With Ann as the he-roine?

(Shaw: Man and Superman)

      e
We are knight e-rrants, and so Fortune be our guide.

(Farquhar: The Beaux Stratagem)

         e
A pox take you both; fetch me the che-rry brandy then.

(Congreve: The Way of the World)

PRACTICE WORDS, PHRASES, SENTENCES   page 362-365.

STANDARD BRITISH TEXT /e/ (ge̱t) before /r/. *Mark the following and*
    speak out loud.

            e
I don't mean to defend Charles's e̱rrors.

(Sheridan: The School for Scandal)

Why, I ask you nothing but what you may very well spare.

(Vanbrugh: The Provok'd Wife)

If he should marry and have a child, you may be disinherited, ha?

(Congreve: The Way of the World)

Yes, he has told me all about poor Mr. Bunbury, and his terrible
state of health.

(Wilde: The Importance of Being Earnest)

/ æ / (th<u>a</u>t)

before consonant / r /

Use /**æ**/ (th<u>a</u>t) (rather than /**eə̃**/ (th<u>ei</u>r)) before /**r**/. These words can often be recognized by their 'ar' or 'arr' spelling.

AUDIO 88► /**æ**/ (th<u>a</u>t) before /**r**/

'næ-rəŭnɪs
I scorn its n<u>a</u>-rrowness.

(Shaw: Man and Superman)

æ   æ
Ah, nowadays that is no g<u>ua</u>-rantee of respectability of character.

(Wilde: The Importance of Being Earnest)

æ   ə
O, he c<u>a</u>-rries poison in his tongue that would c<u>o</u>-rrupt integrity itself.

(Congreve: The Way of the World)

PRACTICE WORDS, PHRASES, SENTENCES   page 366-370.

STANDARD BRITISH TEXT /**æ**/ (th<u>a</u>t) before /**r**/. *Mark the following and speak out loud.*

æ
What do you think of your p<u>a</u>ragon now?

(Shaw: Man and Superman)

Harry, take this, and let your man carry it for me to Mrs. Fourbes's chamber.

(Etherege: The Man of Mode)

He's firm in his resolution, tells me I must marry Mrs. Harriet,
or swears he'll marry himself and disinherit me.

(Etherege: The Man of Mode)

/ ə / (<u>uh</u>)

before consonant / r /

Use the pure schwa sound /ə/ (<u>uh</u>) with no **'r'** coloring before the consonant /r/. Also use it when adding suffixes that begin with 'able', 'er', 'ing', or when linking to the word that comes after.

AUDIO 89▶ /ə/ (<u>uh</u>) before /r/

                                             ə

I...show the whole church my concern by endeavo-ring to hide it.

                          (Farquhar: The Beaux Stratagem)

             ə (or eliminate schwa)

What on earth do you mean by a Bunbu-ryist?

              (Wilde: The Importance of Being Earnest)

        ə

Call him tyrant, murde-rer, pirate, bully; and he will adore you.

                             (Shaw: Man and Superman)

NO PREVIOUS PRACTICE WORDS, PHRASES, SENTENCES.

STANDARD BRITISH TEXT /ə/ (<u>uh</u>) before /r/. *Mark the following and speak out loud.*

        ə

It is much to s<u>u</u>rrender.

                           (Wilde: An Ideal Husband)

Why are you so timorous?

                           (Vanbrugh: The Relapse)

He is a fool with a good memory.

                          (Congreve: The Way of the World)

/ ʌ / (UH)

before consonant / r /

There are many words spoken with the /ʌ/ (UH) sound before the consonant /r/, rather than with the /ɜ/ (ER) sound before /r/ that is spoken in Neutral American.

AUDIO 90▶ /ʌ/ (UH) before /r/

> ʌ
> What wo-rries me is the idea of trusting you to her.
> (Shaw: Man and Superman)
>
> ʌ
> Illness of any kind is hardly a thing to be encou-raged in others.
> (Wilde: The Importance of Being Earnest)
>
> ʌ
> When a man would enslave his wife, he hu-rries her into the country.
> (Farquhar: The Beaux Stratagem)

PRACTICE WORDS, PHRASES, SENTENCES   page 371-373.

STANDARD BRITISH TEXT /ʌ/ (UH) before /r/. *Mark the following and speak out loud.*

ʌ
The rudest hurricane of wild desire.

(Vanbrugh: The Relapse)

So, this is fine encouragement for me!

(Farquhar: The Beaux Stratagem)

Than I am contented to make him pay for his scurrility.

(Wycherley: The Country Wife)

Pshaw, think no more on him but trust to occurrences for success.

(Goldsmith: She Stoops to Conquer)

/ ̹ɔ / (all)

before consonant / r /

Use / ̹ɔ/ (all) before the consonant /r/, rather than the /ɔ ̆ə/ diphthong.
The jaw and lips are more closed and the back of the tongue arch is higher.

AUDIO 91► / ̹ɔ/ (all) before /r/

> ̹ɔ
> Jack is a noto-rious domesticity for John!
>> (Wilde: The Importance of Being Earnest)
>
> ̹ɔ
> She is only triumphant, successful, victo-rious.
>> (Shaw: Man and Superman)
>
> ɑ or æ   e   ̹ɔ
> Most transcendently; ay, though I say it, me-rito-riously.
>> (Congreve: The Way of the World)

PRACTICE WORDS, PHRASES, SENTENCES   page 374-376.

STANDARD BRITISH TEXT / ̹ɔ/ (all) before /r/. *Mark the following and*
speak out loud.

   ̹ɔ
But if Hell be so beautiful as this, how glorious must Heaven be!
>> (Shaw: Man and Superman)

Some of your stories have taken a good effect on Maria.[1]
>> (Sheridan: The School for Scandal)

Shameful! But the world is so censorious, no character escapes.
>> (Sheridan: School for Scandal)

Tell me not, my good Lord Plausible, of your decorums, supercilious
forms, and slavish ceremonies!

>> (Wycherley: The Plain Dealer)

---

[1] Use the British pronunciation of the name Maria: /mə'raɪ̆ə/

/ ọ / (h<u>o</u>nest)

before consonant / r /

Use the pure /ọ/ (h<u>o</u>nest) sound, rather than the /ɔə̆/ (sp<u>or</u>ts) diphthong, before the consonant /r/.

AUDIO 92 ► /ọ/ (h<u>o</u>nest) before /r/

>   ọ ọ ɪ
> Here endeth my first and last attempt to assert my autho-rity.
>   (Shaw: Man and Superman)
>
> ọ   ọ   ọ   ọ
> Ho-rrid Political Economy! Ho-rrid Geography! Ho-rrid, ho-rrid
>
> German!
>   (Wilde: The Importance of Being Earnest)
>
>   ọ
> What an inco-rrigible liar you are.
>   (Shaw: Man and Superman)

PRACTICE WORDS, PHRASES, SENTENCES page 377-380.

STANDARD BRITISH TEXT /ọ/ (h<u>o</u>nest) before /r/. *Mark the following and speak out loud.*

                        ọ
Sir Robert is still at the F<u>o</u>reign Office, my lord.
                                    (Wilde: An Ideal Husband)

I thought none but lovers quarrell'd with their beds.
                                     (Vanbrugh: The Provok'd Wife)

I'll warrant he has been murdering somebody to-night.
                                     (Vanbrugh: The Provok'd Wife)

Why, I believe I should be obliged to borrow a little of your morality, that's all.
                                     (Sheridan: The School for Scandal)

Pure / æ / (th<u>a</u>t)

before 'm' 'n' 'g' 'ng' 'nk' spellings

In Standard British as in Classical American, pure non-nasal /æ/ is spoken before /m n g ŋ ŋk/ sounds. The back of the tongue should remain relaxed and uninvolved.

AUDIO 93 ▶ **pure /æ/ (th<u>a</u>t)**

æ

Give us an account of the state of love as it now st<u>a</u>nds.
(Etherege: The Man of Mode)

æ

I can play with a girl as an <u>an</u>gler does with his fish.
(Farquhar: The Beaux Stratagem)

ae   ae   ae (or weak form)

I insist on knowing where you deposited the h<u>a</u>nd-b<u>a</u>g th<u>a</u>t

ae

contained th<u>a</u>t infant.
(Wilde: The Importance of Being Earnest)

PRACTICE WORDS, PHRASES, SENTENCES   page 349-352.

STANDARD BRITISH TEXT   pure /æ/ (th<u>a</u>t).   *Mark the following and speak out loud.*

ae

Such reports are highly sc<u>a</u>ndalous.
(Sheridan: The School for Scandal)

Anger helps complexion, saves paint.
(Congreve: The Way of the World)

Hell is full of musical amateurs: music is the brandy of the damned.
(Shaw: Man and Superman)

Jack Handicraft, a handsome, well-dressed, mannerly, sharping rogue, who keeps the best company in town.
(Farquhar: The Beaux Stratagem)

'Liquid' / ju / (<u>you</u>)

In Standard British as in Classical American, when the /u/ sound occurs after 't', 'd', or 'n' in the spellings, /j/ is added before /u/ so that 'liquid' /ju/ (<u>you</u>) is spoken. This is optional after 's' or 'l', and also occurs occasionally after 'z' and voiceless 'th', as in 'Zeus' and 'enthusiasm'.

AUDIO 94▶ liquid /ju/ (<u>you</u>)

> dju
> I am neither the slave of love nor its <u>dupe</u>.
>> (Shaw: Man and Superman)
>
> tju
> Shame and ingrati<u>tu</u>de!
>> (Congreve: The Way of the World)
>
> lju   dju
> Do you al<u>lu</u>de to me, Miss Car<u>dew</u>, as an entanglement?
>> (Wilde: The Importance of Being Earnest)

PRACTICE WORDS, PHRASES, SENTENCES   page 345-348.

STANDARD BRITISH TEXT   liquid /ju/ (<u>you</u>). *Mark the following and speak out loud.*

ju
Inveterate s<u>tu</u>pidity!
>> (Farquhar: The Beaux Stratagem)

My annuity! 'Sdeath, he's such a dog.
>> (Vanbrugh: The Relapse)

No, hear him out; let him tune his crowd a while.
>> (Wycherley: The Country Wife)

He allows you a maintenance suitable to your quality.
>> (Farquhar: The Beaux Stratagem)

Pure / aĭ / (my)

In Standard British as in Classical American, speak a pure, open /aĭ/ (my) diphthong when it occurs before a voiceless consonant, rather than the more closed /əĭ/ (uhee) sound that is often spoken in casual American speech.

AUDIO 95▶ /aĭ/ (my) before a voiceless consonant

>   aĭ   aĭ
> I've now realized for the first time in my life the vital Importance
>
> of Being Earnest.
>
>   (Wilde: The Importance of Being Earnest)
>
>   aĭ
> He seems to be a mighty good-humoured old man.
>
>   (Etherege: The Man of Mode)
>
> aĭ
> I have a frightful feeling that I shall let myself be married.
>
>   (Shaw: Man and Superman)

PRACTICE WORDS, PHRASES, SENTENCES   page 167-168.

STANDARD BRITISH TEXT /aĭ/ (my) before a voiceless consonant in the same word. *Mark the following and speak out loud.*

                  aĭ
Lovers are short-sighted.

                                   (Vanbrugh: The Provok'd Wife)

I confess I do blaze today, I am too bright.

                                   (Congreve: The Way of the World)

Why, I thought thou hadst loved a man with a title, better than a suit with a French trimming to't.

                                   (Wycherley: The Country Wife)

When the lady's instinct was set on me, there was nothing for it but lifelong servitude or flight.

                                   (Shaw: Man and Superman)

/ aʊ̆ / (now)

/aʊ̆ə/ (<u>power</u>)

In Standard British as in Classical American, begin this diphthong and triphthong with the relaxed back vowel /ɑ/ (f<u>a</u>ther), rather than the brighter /a/ sound commonly used by contemporary speakers. The tongue arch gently flattens and the articulators remain relaxed when initiating these sounds.

AUDIO 96▶ /aʊ̆/ (n<u>ow</u>) and /aʊ̆ə/ (<u>power</u>)

                               aʊ̆   ɑ

You don't think him a sc<u>ou</u>ndrel after all?

                                               (Shaw: Man and Superman)

        aʊ̆   aʊ̆

Sit d<u>ow</u>n. Sit d<u>ow</u>n immediately.

                                  (Wilde: The Importance of Being Earnest)

                 aʊ̆   aʊ̆

Was there ever such a f<u>ou</u>l-m<u>ou</u>thed fellow?

                                        (Congreve: The Way of the World)

PRACTICE WORDS, PHRASES, SENTENCES   page 353-356.

STANDARD BRITISH TEXT   /aʊ̆/ (n<u>ow</u>) and /aʊ̆ə/ (<u>power</u>).   *Mark the following and speak out loud.*

                                  aʊ̆

Well, you men are unacc<u>ou</u>ntable things.

                                        (Vanbrugh: The Provok'd Wife)

It holds somewhat above two hundred pound: if you doubt it,
I'll count it to you after supper.

                                        (Farquhar: The Beaux Stratagem)

I don't know how many scandalous tales of me, and all without
any foundation too.

                                        (Sheridan: The School for Scandal)

They have asked me a thousand questions of the modes and intrigues
of the town.

                                        (Etherege: The Man of Mode)

Very Upper-Class Characters

Such characters may be played with a slightly slurred, whiny, nasal sound accomplished, in part, by the jaw's remaining mostly closed while under-utilizing the articulators.

The following may also be incorporated:

* especially short, clipped /ɪ/ (w<u>i</u>ll) endings

* /æ/ (th<u>a</u>t) sounds spoken as /e/ (g<u>e</u>t)

* brighter, longer /ʌ/ (<u>UH</u>) sounds that almost sound like the front vowel /a/

* more precisely 'formed' /əǔ/ (g<u>o</u>) diphthongs

* /aɪ̆ə̆/ (fire) and /aʊ̆ə̆/ (power) triphthongs blending their three elements to sound like one long vowel

* use of voiceless /hw/ on /w/ sounds spelled 'wh'

* more frequent tapping, rolling, or trilling of the consonant /r/ when it occurs between two vowels

This can be heard on Audio 97, a section of which is notated below:

  a   djuə̆rɪŋ 'tempərɪ ə   ʌ ɒ

*This aft^he*r*noo<u>n</u>, during my temporary absence in London on an*

  ɔ (or ə)   əǔ æ (or e)   haɪ̆s

importa<u>n</u>t questio<u>n</u> of romance[1], he obtained admissio<u>n</u> to my house[2]

  ɒ   ɔ   ɒ

*by means of the false pret^hence[3] of being my brothe*r.

(Wilde: The Importance of Being Earnest)

Note: Technically, the tapped /r/ is represented phonetically by the symbol /ɾ/ which is almost identical to the usual consonant symbol /r/. So the tapped 'r' is notated by /d/ in the monologues on pages 493-497 to avoid confusion.

---

[1] Also commonly pronounced: /rəǔ'mæns/, even when used as a noun.

[2] Very upper class pronunciation of 'house' can be: /haɪ̆s/.

[3] Also commonly pronounced: /prɪ'tens/.

COMMON BRITISH-ENGLISH WORDS

WITH AMERICAN-ENGLISH MEANING

Brit. word	Am. equiv.	Brit. word	Am. equiv.
aubergine	eggplant	mousse pudding	pudding
barrister	<u>trial</u> lawyer	nappy	diaper
biscuit	cookie	oven cloth	pot holder
bobby	policeman	pence	penny
bonnet	hood (car)	petrol	gasoline
boot	trunk (car)	pram	baby carriage
braces	suspenders	public school	private school
caravan	trailer	queue	line
caretaker	janitor	roundabout	traffic circle
chemist	druggist	shire	county
cloak room	toilet, bathroom	solicitor	lawyer
constable	police officer	stalls	orchestra seats
crisps	chips	stand for office	run for office
dressing gown	bathrobe	sticking plaster	band aid
dust	garbage	sweets	candy
flat	apartment	swimming	
fish slice	spatula	costume	swimsuit
form, class	grade	surgery	doctor's office
fringe	bangs	torch	flashlight
go on holiday	take a vacation	trunk call	long distance
hair grip	bobby pin	underground	
interval	intermission	(or) tube	subway, metro
jumper	sweater	waistcoat	vest
legal holiday	bank holiday	WC, (or) loo,	restroom, toilet,
lift	elevator	(or) lavatory	bathroom
lodger	roomer	windscreen	windshield
lorry	truck	wireless	radio
mackintosh	raincoat	zed	'Z'

COMMON AMERICAN-ENGLISH WORDS WITH

STANDARD BRITISH PRONUNCIATION

(transcribed without aspiration markings)

again	/əˈgen/	leisure	/ˈleʒə/
	or /əˈgeĭn/	lever	/ˈlivə/
against	/əˈgeĭnst/	lieutenant	/lefˈtenənt/
aluminum	/æljuˈmɪnɪəm/	massage	/ˈmæsɑʒ/
anti	/ˈæntɪ/	missile	/ˈmɪsaĭl/
baptize	/bæpˈtaĭz/	neither	/ˈnaĭðə/
barrage	/ˈbærɑʒ/	nephew	/ˈnevju/
been	/bin/, /bɪn/	omega	/ˈəŭmɪgə/
borough	/ˈbʌrə/	patent	/ˈpeĭtənt/
clerk	/klɑk/	patriot	/ˈpætrɪət/
constable	/ˈkʌnstəbl̩/	potato	/pəˈtatəŭ/
depot	/ˈdepəŭ/		or /pəˈteĭtəu/
derby	/ˈdabɪ/	premature	/ˈpremətjŭə/
either	/ˈaĭðə/	privacy	/ˈprɪvəsɪ/
erase	/ɪˈreɪz/	process	/ˈprəŭses/
figure	/ˈfɪgə/	quinine	/kwɪˈnin/
frustrated	/frʌˈstreĭtɪd/	record	/ˈrekǫd/
futile	/ˈfjutaĭl/	schedule	/ˈʃedjul/
garage	/ˈgærɑʒ/	sensual	/ˈsensjuəl/
glacier	/ˈgleɪsjə/	sexual	/ˈseksjuəl/
herb	/hɜb/	suggest	/səˈdʒest/
hostile	/ˈhɒstaĭl/	tissue	/ˈtɪsju/
inquiry	/ɪŋˈkwaĭɜrɪ/	tomato	/təˈmatəŭ/
iodine	/ˈaĭədin/	vermouth	/ˈvɜməθ/
issue	/ˈɪsju/ or /ˈɪʃu/	weekend	/wiˈkend/
laboratory	/ləˈbǫrətrɪ/	'Z'	/zed/

PRACTICE TEXT

Mark the following selections from Mother Goose for Standard British and speak out loud.

1.	/i → ɪ/	Solomon Grundy, Born on a Monday…
2.	**no 'r' color**	Peter, Peter, pumpkin eater, Had a wife and couldn't keep her.
3.	**consonants** esp. /pʰ, tʰ, kʰ/	A farmer went a trotting upon his gray mare Bumpety, bumpety, bump!
4.	/oŭ → əŭ/	Old King Cole was a merry old soul, And a merry old soul was he!
5.	/ɒ → ǫ/	Hickory, dickory, dock, The mouse ran up the clock.
6.	/ɔ → ǫ/	Jerry Hall, he is so small A rat could eat him, hat and all.
7.	**ask list** /ɑ/	If the diamond ring turns to brass, Papa's going to buy you a looking-glass.
8.	**polysyllabics**	A man in the wilderness said to me, How many strawberries grow in the sea?
9.	**pure vowels** before /r/	Pease porridge hot, Pease porridge cold…
10.	**tapped** /r/	Pease porridge in the pot Nine days old.
11.	**liquid** /ju/ (& days of week)	Monday's child is fair of face, Tuesday's child is full of grace.
12.	**pure** /aĭ/	Star light, star bright, First star I see tonight…
13.	**pure** /æ/	Pat-a-cake, pat-a-cake, baker's man, Bake me a cake as fast as you can.
14.	/ɑŭ/ (relaxed)	Wee Willie Winkie runs through the town Upstairs and downstairs in his nightgown.

PRACTICE TEXT

Mark Standard British sound changes, then speak out loud.

1. Oh! is it a proposal?

    (Wilde: An Ideal Husband)

2. I'll send for't tomorrow.

    (Vanbrugh: The Relapse)

3. Well, Tom, I find you're a marksman.

    (Farquhar: The Beaux Stratagem)

4. How pertinently the jade answers me!

    (Congreve: The Way of the World)

5. No; but seriously, I hate to do a rude thing.

    (Wycherley: The Plain Dealer)

6. I will not be seen in women's company in public again for the world.

    (Wycherley: The Country Wife)

7. I think your frankness does you great credit, Earnest.

    (Wilde: The Importance of Being Earnest)

8. The liberty you take abroad makes her hanker after it.

    (Wycherley: The Country Wife)

9. Well, my own dear, sweet, loving little darling, I really can't see
    why you should object to the name of Algernon.

    (Wilde: The Importance of Being Earnest)

10. He's reckoning his money—my money it was—I have no luck today.

    (Congreve: Way of the World)

11. I know nobody sings so near a cherubim as your ladyship.

    (Vanbrugh: The Provok'd Wife)

12. I could hear but a word here and there; but I remembered they
    mentioned a Count, a closet, a back-door, and a key.

    (Farquhar: The Beaux Stratagem)

13.   I was obliged to call on dear Lady Harbury. I hadn't been there since her poor husband's death. I never saw a woman so altered; she looks quite twenty years younger.

(Wilde: The Importance of Being Earnest)

14.   Here, take away the things; I expect company. But first bring me a pipe; I'll smoke.

(Vanbrugh: The Provok'd Wife)

15.   His master spends his money so freely, and is so much a gentleman every manner of way, he must be a highwayman.

(Farquhar: The Beaux Stratagem)

16.   Though I am a young rake-hell, and have played many a roguish trick, this is so full-grown a cheat, I find I must take pains to come up to't; I have scruples.

(Vanbrugh: The Relapse)

17.   Wine gives you liberty, love takes it away.

(Wycherley: The Country Wife)

18.   My courage should disperse your apprehensions.

(Vanbrugh: The Relapse)

19.   I deposited the manuscript in the bassinette, and placed the baby in the hand-bag.

(Wilde: The Importance of Being Earnest)

20.   Where nights and days seemed all consumed in joy.

(Vanbrugh: The Relapse)

21.   Ay; and what is very extraordinary, in all our disputes she is always in the wrong.

(Sheridan: The School for Scandal)

22.   Providence, thou seest at last, takes care of men of merit: we are in a fair way to be great people.

(Vanbrugh: The Relapse)

23.   People who don't keep their appointments in the Park are horrid.

(Wilde: An Ideal Husband)

24.   Mrs. Clackitt assured me Mr. and Mrs. Honeymoon were at last
become mere man and wife like the rest of their acquaintance.

                                            (Sheridan: The School for Scandal)

25.   You old bawd, how have you the impudence to be hobbling out of
your grave twenty years after you are rotten!

                                            (Vanbrugh: The Relapse)

26.   He's but a half-brother, and I'm your entire friend.

                                            (Farquhar: Beaux Stratagem)

27.   Though I was born to servitude, I hate it.

                                            (Farquhar: The Beaux Stratagem)

28.   This pious charity to the afflicted well becomes your character.

                                            (Lillo: The London Merchant)

29.   Yet they seem to have a torrent of love to dispose of.

                                            (Vanbrugh: The Relapse)

30.   Were I that thing they call a slighted wife, somebody should run
the risk of being that thing they call—a husband.

                                            (Vanbrugh: The Relapse)

31.   I have made you privy to my whole design, and put it in your
power to ruin or advance my fortune.

                                            (Congreve: The Way of the World)

32.   O, ay, letters—I had letters—I am persecuted with letters—
I hate letters—nobody knows how to write letters.

                                            (Congreve: The Way of the World)

33.   Well, I must leave you—and let me beg you, Mrs. Malaprop, to
enforce this matter roundly to the girl;—take my advice—keep
a tight hand—if she rejects this proposal—clap her under lock
and key:—and if you were just to let the servants forget to bring
her dinner for three or four days, you can't conceive how she'd
come about!

                                            (Sheridan: The Rivals)

PRACTICE TEXT

From **MAN AND SUPERMAN**

George Bernard Shaw

Mark Standard British sound changes, then speak out loud.

1. And who the deuce is the superman?

2. Dear lady: a parable must not be taken literally.

3. You are in good spirits today, Commander. You are positively brilliant. What's the matter?

4. I am not a man of honor: I am a man struck down by a dead hand.

5. But the English really do not seem to know when they are thoroughly miserable.

6. Never in my moments of superstitious terror on earth did I dream that Hell was so horrible.

7. You dare boast, before me and my father, that every woman found you irresistible.

8. And he came, sword in hand, to vindicate outraged honour and morality by murdering me.

9. Things immeasurably greater than man in every respect but brain have existed and perished.

10. Sincerity! To be fool enough to believe a ramping, stamping, thumping lie: that is what you call sincerity!

11. You know perfectly well that I am as sober and honest a citizen as yourself. As truthful personally, and much more truthful politically and morally.

12. The confusion of marriage with morality has done more to destroy the conscience of the human race than any other single error.

13. Have you any canonical authority for assuming that there is any barrier between our circle and the other one?

14. The earth is a nursery where men and women play at being heroes and heroines, saints and sinners, but they are dragged down from their fool's paradise by their bodies.

15. But even as you enjoy the contemplation of such romantic mirages as beauty and pleasure; so would I enjoy the contemplation of that which interests me above all things: namely, Life.

16. It is natural that I should have a certain delicacy in talking to my old friend's daughter about her behind her back.

17. I haven't any money, nor the smallest turn for making it.

18. And will all the men call me their dear Ana?

19. You are incorrigible, Jack. But you should not jest about our affection for one another. Nobody could possibly misunderstand it. You do not misunderstand it, I hope.

20. His excellency the Commander puts it with military bluntness; but the strain of living in Heaven is intolerable.

From **A TALE OF TWO CITIES**

Charles Dickens

It was the best of times, it was the worst of times, it was the age of wisdom, it was the age of foolishness, it was the epoch of belief, it was the epoch of incredulity, it was the season of Light, it was the season of Darkness, it was the spring of hope, it was the winter of despair, we had everything before us, we had nothing before us, we were all going direct to Heaven, we were all going direct the other way —in short, the period was so far like the present period, that some of its noisiest authorities insisted on its being received, for good or for evil, in the superlative degree of comparison only.

There were a king with a large jaw and a queen with a plain face, on the throne of England; there were a king with a large jaw and a queen with a fair face, on the throne of France. In both countries it was clearer than crystal to the lords of the State preserves of loaves and fishes, that things in general were settled for ever.

From **GREAT EXPECTATIONS**

Charles Dickens

We were running too fast to admit of more being said, and we made no stop until we got into our kitchen. It was full of people; the whole village was there, or in the yard; and there was a surgeon, and there was Joe, and there was a group of women, all on the floor in the midst of the kitchen. The unemployed bystanders drew back when they saw me, and so I became aware of my sister—lying without sense or movement on the bare boards where she had been knocked down by a tremendous blow on the back of the head, dealt by some unknown hand when her face was turned towards the fire—destined never to be on the Rampage again, while she was wife of Joe.

From **QUEEN MAB**

Percy Bysshe Shelley

THE FAIRY
"The Present and the Past thou hast beheld:
It was a desolate sight. Now, Spirit, learn
            The secrets of the Future.—Time!
Unfold the brooding pinion of thy gloom,
            Render thou up thy half-devoured babes,
And from the cradles of eternity,
Where millions lie lulled to their portioned sleep
By the deep murmuring stream of passing things,
Tear thou that gloomy shroud.—Spirit, behold
            Thy glorious destiny!"

From **THREE SONNETS ON WOMAN**

John Keats

Woman! When I behold thee flippant, vain,
            Inconstant, childish, proud, and full of fancies;
            Without that modest softening that enhances
The downcast eye, repentant of the pain
That its mild light creates to heal again:
            E'en then, elate, my spirit leaps, and prances,
            E'en then my soul with exultation dances
For that to love, so long, I've dormant lain:
But when I see thee meek, and kind, and tender,
            Heavens! How desperately do I adore
Thy winning graces;—to be thy defender
            I hotly burn—to be a Calidore—
A very Red Cross Knight—a stout Leander—
            Might I be loved by thee like these of yore.

KEY TO MARKING STANDARD BRITISH MONOLOGUES
(adjustments or changes from <u>Classical</u> American are shaded)

Rhythm Highlighters	Marking
Stressed syllables *(not marked)*	
Weak forms *(not marked)*	
/ɪ/ (wɪll) prefixes and suffixes	ɪ ɪ ɪ repeat, deny, closet
/ə/ (uh) schwa suffixes	ə ə statement, doorman
Syllabic endings marked /n̦ l̦ m̦/	wooden̦, littl̦e, prism̦
/i/→/ɪ/ unstressed endings (spelled 'y' or 'i')	ɪ ɪ ɪ prettɪy, tallɪy, happɪiness
No 'r' coloring ('sports', 'car' diphthongs also drop the schwa)	heɾe, fatheɾ, shoɾt
Vowel Sound Considerations	**Marking**
Linking words *(not marked)*	
/e/ (gɛt) before 'm', 'n' (in a stressed syllable)	e e e them, when, sent
/æ/ (thæt) before n, m, ng, nk (pure non-nasal vowel)	æ æ æ land, Hamlet, man
/ɔ/ (all) closed/longer, /ɒ/ (hɒnest) closed/clipped	ɔ̦ ɔ̦ ɒ̦ ɒ̦ fall, ought, often, hot
/ʊə̆/ (poor) diphthong (more energized and no 'r' coloring)	ʊə̆ ʊə̆ assure, tour
/aɪ̆/ (mɥ) diphthong (before voiceless consonant in the same word)	aɪ̆ aɪ̆ aɪ̆ bright, night, wife
Liquid /ju/ (you) (after 't', 'd', 'n', optional after 's', 'l')	tju dju nju tune, duke, news
/aʊ̆/ (now), /aʊ̆ə̆/ (power) (initial element changes)	aʊ̆ aʊ̆ə̆ mountain, sour
/oʊ̆/ (go) diphthong→/əu/	əu əu əu go, don't, snow
'Ask' list of words spoken with /ɑ/ (fɑther) sound	ɑ ɑ ɑ pass, craft, dance
Vowels before consonant /r/ (complete observation) (new change: the schwa with no 'r' coloring)	ə ə mutte-ɾer, flatte-ɾer, etc.
Polysyllabic endings: ary, ory, berry, ony spellings	trɪ (or) tə-rɪ secretary, secreta-ry
Consonant Sound Considerations	**Marking**
Consonants generally more vigorous and energized, Voiceless and voiced plosives more 'explosive'	hitʰ, tapʰ, packʰ
Voiced consonant endings (especially before a pause or silence)	dead̲, foun̲d
Consonant /r/ combinations (tr, dr, str)	t̲read, d̲rive, s̲t̲reet
Voiceless /hw/ (optional, used occasionally)	very upper class only

STANDARD BRITISH MONOLOGUES

(with sound changes marked)

AUDIO 97▶ spoken by Stephen Hollis

JACK

It pains me ve-ry much to have to speak frankly to you,

Lady Bracknell[1], about your nephew, but the fact^h is

that^h I do not^h approve at^h all of his mo-ral cha-ract^her.

I suspect him of being untruthful. I fear there can be

no possible doubt^h about the matt^her. This aft^hernoon,

during my temporary absence in London on an important

question of romance[2], he obtained admission to my house[3]

by means of the false pret^hence[4] of being my brother.

---

[1] Bracknell: /ˈbræknəl/ or /ˈbræknl̩/
[2] Also commonly pronounced: /rəʊˈmæns/, even when used as a noun.
[3] Very upper class pronunciation of 'house' is spoken: /haɪs/.
[4] Also commonly pronounced: /prɪˈtens/.

494

text & monologues STANDARD BRITISH

Under an assumed name he drank^h, I've just been informed

by my butler, an ent^hire pint bottle of my 'Pe-rrier-'Jouet[1],

Brut^h, '89; a wine I was specially reserving for myself.

Cont^hinuing his disgraceful deception, he succeeded

in the course of the aft^hernoon in alienat^hing the

affections of my only ward. He subsequently stayed

to tea, and devoured every single muffin. And what

makes his conduct^h all the more heartless is, that he

was perfectly well aware from the first that^h I have no

brother, that^h I never had a brother, and that^h I don't

int^hend to have a brother, not^h even of any kind.

I distinctly told him so myself yesterday afternoon.

(Wilde: The Importance of Being Earnest)

---

[1] Standard British pronunciation of foreign words very often involves a change in stressed syllables from the original language.

AUDIO 98▶ **spoken by Sybil Lines**

MILLAMANT

əǔ   ɔ̧   ɑ   ˈmædɪd   ɒ̧   ɪ
I won't be called names after I'm ma-rri̲e̲d̲[1]; posit^{h}ively̲

əǔ   ɔ̧   aɪ   ɑǔ
I won't be called na̲me̲s̲... as wife, spouse, my dear,

ˈdʒuəl   ɑ
joy, jewel̲, love, sweetheart^h, and the rest^h of the

nɔ̧sjɪəs æ   e   ɑ
nauseous cant^h, in which men and their wives are

əǔ   ɪ
so fulsome̲ly̲ familiar — I shall never bear that^h —

d   əǔ   ɔ̧ ɒ̧
good Mi-rabell, don't let^h us be familiar or fo̲n̲d̲,

ɔ̧   ɪ ɔ̧ əǔ aɪ   ɪ
nor kiss before folks, like my Lady̲ Fadler and

ɑ   ɔ̧ əǔ   ɑ
Sir Francis; nor go to Hyde Park together the first

ɪ   ju æ   əǔ əǔ
Sun̲da̲y̲ in a new cha-riot^h, to provok^{h}e eyes and

e
whispers; and then never be seen there together agai̲n̲[2];

ɑǔ
as if we were proud of one another the first week^h,

ɑ
and ashamed of one another ever after. Let^h us never

ɔ̧ əǔ
visit together, nor go to a play together, but let^h us be

---

[1] This speaker 'taps' the medial consonant /r/ in 'married'.
[2] This speaker pronounces again: /əˈgeǐn/. Another possibility is /əˈgen/.

    e ɪ

ve-ry <u>str</u>ange and well bre<u>d</u>: let^h us be as <u>str</u>ange as if

    i   æ-d ɪ   hw

we had been ma-rr<u>i</u>ed a great wh<u>i</u>le[1]; and as well bred

    ọ æ-d ɪ   ɔ̦

as if we were not ma-rr<u>i</u>ed at^h a<u>ll</u>.

                              (Congreve: The Way of the World)

AUDIO 99► **spoken by Christopher Martin**

THE DEVIL

    e   ɪ   (or ə) əŭ

Men get tired of ever<u>y</u>thi<u>ng</u>, of heave<u>n</u> no less than

                        ɔ̦   ɪ   ɪ   ɔ̦

of he<u>ll</u>; and that^h all histor<u>y</u> is nothing but^h a record

    i ọ   ọ   ɪ

of the oscillatio<u>n</u>s of the world between these two

  ɪk‚s   ˈiphọkh   ˈphendjʋləm

ex<u>tre</u>mes. An epoch is but^h a swing of the pendulu<u>m</u>;

             e   əŭ   ɪ

and each generatio<u>n</u> thinks the world is progressing

  ɪ   ɔ̦   ɔ̦   ɪ   e   ɑd̮

because it's always[2] movi<u>ng</u>. But when you are as

---

[1] Notice use of voiceless **/hw/** in the word 'while' (very upper class choice).

[2] The word always has three pronunciations : /ˈɔlweɪ̆z/ or /ˈɔlwɪz/ or /ˈɔlwəz/

 əʊ æ e   aʊ   'wɪə-dɪd

old as I am; when you have a thousand times wea-ried

     aɪ   ɑ

of heaven, like myself and the Commander, and a

 aʊ   dɪ   ɑ   ɪ

thousand times wea-ried of hell, as you are wea-ried

 aʊ   əʊ ɒ ɪ   ɪ

now, you will no longer imagine that[h] every swing

 ɒ   ɪ æ   ɪ

from heaven to hell is an emancipation, every swing

      ivə'ljuʃn   aʊ

from hell to heaven an evolution. Where you now see

 ɪ ɒ əʊ   ə   e ɪ

reform, progress, fulfillment[h] of upward tendencies,

    e   æ ɒ   ɪ əʊ

continual ascent by Man on the stepping stones of

             ɪ

his dead selves to higher things, you will see nothing

      ɒ ɪ ju

but[h] an infinite comedy of illusions. You will discover

  əʊ aʊ   ɪ   d ɪ

the profound truth of the saying... that there is nothing

 nju

new under the sun. Vanitas vanitatum.

(Shaw: Man and Superman / Don Juan in Hell)

APPENDIX

Short list of useful, indispensable books

A Treasury of Mother Goose. illustrated by Hilda Offen. New York: Simon & Schuster Books for Young Readers, 1984.

Barton, John. *Playing Shakespeare*: London: Methuen London Ltd., 1984.

Berry, Cicely. *The Actor and the Text*. London: Virginia Books, 1992.

Cambridge International Dictionary of English. Cambridge: Cambridge University Press, 2001.

Jones, Daniel. *English Pronouncing Dictionary*. Fourteenth Edition. London: Cambridge University Press, 1991.

Kenyon, John Samuel and Knott, Thomas Albert. *A Pronouncing Dictionary of American English*. Springfield, MA: Merriam-Webster Inc., 1953.

Linklater, Kristin. *Freeing Shakespeare's Voice*. New York: Theatre Communications Group, 1992.

Linklater, Kristin. *Freeing the Natural Voice*. Hollywood: Drama Publishers, 2006.

Onions, Charles Talbut. *A Shakespeare Glossary*. Edited by Robert D. Eagleson. New York: Oxford University Press, 1995.

Parkins, Ken. *Anthology of British Tongue Twisters*: New York: Samuel French, 1969.

Shakespeare, William. *The Riverside Shakespeare*. Boston: Houghlin Mifflin Co., 1997.

Skinner, Edith. *Speak With Distinction*. New York: Applause Theatre Books, 1990.

The Complete Rhyming Dictionary, edited by Clement Wood, revised by Ronald Bogus. New York: Doubleday, a division of Bantam Doubleday Dell Publishing Group, Inc., 1991.

ABOUT THE AUTHOR

Patricia Fletcher has taught Dialects, Voice, and Speech in numerous professional acting programs including: New School for Drama MFA Acting Program/New School University, Actor's Studio Drama School, Mason Gross School of the Arts MFA Acting Program/Rutgers University, Brooklyn College Graduate Acting Program, William Esper Acting Studio, and New Actors Workshop. She is a Designated Linklater Voice Instructor, and holds an MA in Voice and Speech from Antioch University. Patricia has worked as an actor on and off Broadway, and has served as a Voice, Speech, Dialogue, and Dialect Coach for Broadway, Television, and Feature Films. She does extensive private coaching. www.patriciafletcher.com

ISBN 1-41204121-X

Other Titles by Janice VanCleave

Science for Every Kid series:

Janice VanCleave's Astronomy for Every Kid
Janice VanCleave's Biology for Every Kid
Janice VanCleave's Chemistry for Every Kid
Janice VanCleave's Dinosaurs for Every Kid
Janice VanCleave's Earth Science for Every Kid
Janice VanCleave's Geography for Every Kid
Janice VanCleave's Math for Every Kid
Janice VanCleave's Physics for Every Kid

Spectacular Science Projects series:

Janice VanCleave's Animals
Janice VanCleave's Earthquakes
Janice VanCleave's Gravity
Janice VanCleave's Machines
Janice VanCleave's Magnets
Janice VanCleave's Microscopes and Magnifying Lenses
Janice VanCleave's Molecules
Janice VanCleave's Volcanoes

A+ series

Janice VanCleave's A+ Projects in Biology
Janice VanCleave's A+ Projects in Chemistry

Janice VanCleave's 200 Gooey, Slippery, Slimey, Wierd & Fun Experiments
Janice VanCleave's 201 Awesome, Magical, Bizarre & Incredible
Experiments

Janice VanCleave's

Geometry for
Every Kid

Acknowledgements

I would like to offer a warm "thank you" to my current and former students for their enthusiasm, dedication, and joy in the spoken word, and for their valuable feedback on the previous edition. Grateful acknowledgement also, to my colleagues Nancy Mayans and Susan Cameron, and to my sister Susan Lapis, for reading through the manuscript and offering their insightful comments and suggestions, and to Sarah Bisman for taking on the daunting task of proofreading.

I would like, in addition, to thank my teachers of Shakespeare, singing, voice, speech, dialects, and acting, including: Michael Beckett, Linda Benanti, Leigh Dillon, Keeley Eastley, Andrea Haring, Larry Hill, Gordon Jacoby, Raphael Kelly, Dennis Krausnick, Kristin Linklater, Tina Packer, Joe Scott, Roger Hendrick Simon, Bob Smith, Rosemarie Vacca, Daniela Varon, and Walton Wilson, for generously sharing their knowledge and talent.

Special thanks to James Anderson, Susan Cameron, Leigh Dillon, Rebecca Dumaine, Jonathan Fielding, Stephen Hollis, Carman Lacivita, Sybil Lines, Eric Loscheider, Christopher Martin, Nancy Mayans, Evan Mueller, Shane Taylor, and Walton Wilson for their participation in the recording of the CD, Lois Bewley for the drawings, Mark White for *Moose Mirage*, and Allen R. Jones, Director of Education and Technology/New School University, for his invaluable assistance.

I am grateful to William Esper for his support of my work over the years, and to Nova Thomas for her optimism and encouragement in the writing of this book, throughout all its stages of development. I especially thank Christopher Martin, founding Artistic Director of CSC Repertory (Classic Stage Company) in New York, whose direction on the CD, and continuous technical, artistic, and moral support helped make *Classically Speaking* a reality. Lastly, to my parents Robert and Nina Fletcher, and wonderful family, without whom nothing would be possible.

www.trafford.com

North America & international
toll-free: 1 888 232 4444 (USA & Canada)
phone: 250 383 6864 ✦ fax: 250 383 6804
email: info@trafford.com

The United Kingdom & Europe
phone: +44 (0)1865 722 113 ✦ local rate: 0845 230 9601
facsimile: +44 (0)1865 722 868 ✦ email: info.uk@trafford.com

10 9 8 7 6

CLASSICALLY SPEAKING

dialects for actors

NEUTRAL AMERICAN

CLASSICAL AMERICAN

STANDARD BRITISH (RP)

SECOND EDITION

CD included

PATRICIA FLETCHER

Janice VanCleave's

Geometry for Every Kid

Easy Activities that Make Learning Geometry Fun

John Wiley & Sons, Inc.
New York • Chichester • Brisbane • Tornoto • Singapore

Design and production by: WordCrafters Editorial Services, Inc.
Illustrator: Laurel Aiello

This text is printed on acid-free paper.

The publisher and the author have made every resonable effort to insure that the experiments and activities in this book are safe when conducted as instructed but assume no responsibility for any damage caused or sustained while performing the experiments or activities in this book. Parents, guardians, and/or teachers should supervise young readers who undertake the experiments and activities in this book.

Library of Congress Cataloging-in-Publication Data
VanCleave, Janice.
    Janice VanCleave's geometry for every kid : easy activities that
  make learning geometry fun / by Janice VanCleave.
      p.   cm.
    Includes index.
    ISBN 0-471-31142-1.—ISBN 0-471-31141-3 (pbk.)
     1. Geometry—Juvenile literature. [1. Geometry. 2. Mathematical
  recreations.] I. Title. II. Title: Geometry for every kid.
  QA445.5.V38   1994
  516—dc20   93-43049
                                                          AC

Printed in the United States of America

10 9 8 7 6 5 4

This book is dedicated to two ladies who know all the angles of copyediting. They are a pleasure to work with, and I value our professional and personal relationship.

Nana Prior and Jude Patterson

I would be remiss in not extending the dedication to a special young lady who eagerly pretested many of the activities in this book. To my special laboratory assistant,

Kaitlin Patterson

Contents

Introduction

Geometry is the study of shapes. It uses numbers and symbols to describe the properties of these shapes and the relationships between them. This book explores two different kinds of geometry: **plane geometry**—the study of two-dimensional figures—and **solid geometry**—the study of three-dimensional figures. Why is understanding geometry important? Because questions such as What is its shape?, How big is it?, and Will it fit? are all part of everyday life. Geometry provides the skills needed to find the answers to such questions.

From the writings on sun-baked clay tablets found in Babylonian ruins, we learn that the people in this ancient culture surveyed their land. While doing this, they developed rules for measuring geometric shapes. These rules were not as exact as those that are used today. For example, Babylonians calculated the distance around a circle by multiplying its diameter by 3. Elementary schoolchildren today learn that this distance is more accurately determined by multiplying the circle's diameter by pi, which is approximately equal to 3.14.

Have we learned everything there is to know about geometry? No. Like all sciences, geometry is a constantly developing field of study. The more we learn about it, the more questions we think to ask. Comparing the shapes of puzzle pieces or deciding what size pizza to buy are only two of the ways you can develop the geometry skills that are so rewarding.

This book explains geometry's simple language in terms that you can easily learn and use. It teaches geometric concepts using examples that can be applied to many similar situations. The problems, experiments, and other application activities were selected because they can be explained using basic terms. One of the main objectives is to present the fun that can be had with geometry. So grab a pencil and lots of paper, and let the fun begin.

Read each of the 25 chapters slowly and follow all procedures carefully. You will learn best if each chapter is read in order, as there is some buildup of information as the book progresses. The format for each chapter is:

1. What You Need to Know: Background information and an explanation of terms.

2. Let's Think It Through: Questions to be answered or situations to be solved using the information from What You Need to Know.

3. Answers: Step-by-step instructions for solving the questions posed in Let's Think It Through.

4. Exercises: Practice problems to reinforce your skills.

5. Activity: A project to allow you to apply the skill to a problem-solving situation in the real world.

6. Solutions to Exercises: Step-by-step instructions for solving the Exercises.

7. Glossary: All **bold-faced** terms are defined in a Glossary at the end of the book. Be sure to flip back to the Glossary as often as necessary, making each term part of your personal vocabulary.

8. Some chapters also include a Mathematician's Toolbox with step-by-step instructions for making tools to use in the chapter.

General Instructions for Let's Think It Through and Exercise Sections

1. Study each question carefully by reading through it once or twice, then follow the steps described in the Answers.

2. Do the same thing for the Exercises, following the steps described in the Answers to the Let's Think It Through questions.

3. Check your answers in the Solutions to Exercises to evaluate your work.

4. Do the work again if any of your answers are incorrect.

General Instructions for Activity Sections

1. Read the Activity completely before starting.

2. Collect the supplies. You will have less frustration and more fun if all the necessary materials for the Activity are ready before you start. You lose your train of thought when you have to stop and search for supplies.

3. Do not rush through the Activity. Follow each step very carefully; never skip steps, and do not add your own. Safety is of utmost importance, and by reading each Activity before starting, and then following the instructions exactly, you can feel confident that no unexpected results will occur.

4. Observe. If your results are not the same as those described in the Activity, carefully reread the instructions, and start over from step 1.

1
Lineup

Identifying Lines, Line Segments, and Rays

What You Need to Know

A line is a mark made by a pen, pencil, or other tool on a surface. This line can be of any shape and length. It can be straight or curved, such as a tracing around the fingers of your hand.

The geometric definition of a **line** is a straight path that has no definite length and goes on forever in both directions. In geometry, this continuation is indicated by an arrow at each end of the line. A geometrical line can be identified by naming any two points on the line, such as line TA (which can also be called line AT). The name of the line is read: line TA or line AT. It is written as: TA or AT.

A **line segment** is a part of a line. It follows a straight path between two points, called **endpoints**. A line segment is named by its endpoints. The name of the line segment in the example is read: line segment AB or line segment BA. It is written as: AB or BA.

A **ray** is a part of a line with one endpoint. It follows a straight path that goes on forever in only one direction. A ray's name starts with its endpoint. The name of the ray in the example is read: ray HL. It is written as: $\overrightarrow{HL}$.

Let's Think It Through

1. Identify the example that shows a line segment and give its name.

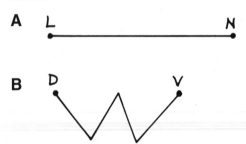

2. Identify the example that shows a ray and give its name.

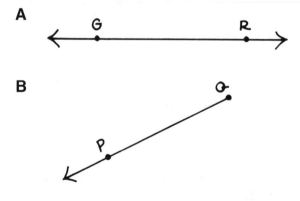

Answers

1. *Think!*

- Do both examples show straight paths? No, only example A shows a straight path.

- The endpoints on the line segment are L and N.

The name of the line segment is line segment LN ($\overline{LN}$) or line segment NL ($\overline{NL}$).

2. *Think!*

- A ray is a part of a line with one endpoint. Which example shows a line with a point at one end? Example B.

- The points on the ray, beginning with the endpoint, are Q and P.

The name of the ray is ray QP ($\overrightarrow{QP}$).

Exercises

1. Study the diagram and name the line segments.

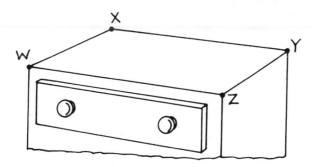

2. Does each example show a line? Answer yes or no for each example.

a.

b.

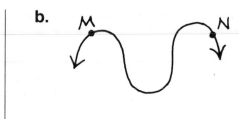

c.

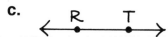

3. Name the ray.

4. Name the line.

Activity: SIDE BY SIDE

Purpose To use lines and line segments to demonstrate an optical illusion.

Materials ruler
          pencil
          typing paper

Procedure

1. Use the ruler to draw a 6-inch (15-cm) line segment any-where on the paper.

2. Mark a point in the exact center of the line. Label the endpoints K and M and the center point I as shown.

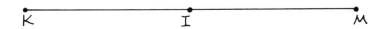

3. Draw two **V**'s pointing toward each other from points K and I. Draw a **V** pointing outward from point M as shown in the diagram.

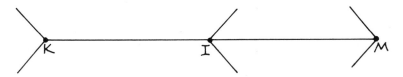

4. Compare the visual appearance of $\overline{KI}$ with that of $\overline{IM}$.

Results $\overline{KI}$ with the **V**'s pointing inward appears to be longer than $\overline{IM}$ even though we know that both lines are the same length.

Why?   Sometimes what we see is not what actually exists. A misleading image seen because of mistakes made by the brain is called an **optical illusion**. The direction of the **V**'s fools the brain into thinking that one line segment is longer than the other. $\overline{KI}$ appears longer because the **V**'s extend outward. The eyes follow these lines, and the interpretation in the brain is that this line segment is longer.

Solutions to Exercises

1. *Think!*

- Line segments have endpoints. The line segments that form the top of the chest are: $\overline{WX}$, $\overline{XY}$, $\overline{YZ}$, and $\overline{ZW}$ (or $\overline{XW}$, $\overline{YX}$, $\overline{ZY}$, and $\overline{WZ}$).

2. *Think!*

- For each example, ask yourself, Does this show a straight path with no endpoints?

  a. *No.*

  b. *No.*

  c. *Yes.*

3. *Think!*

- A ray's name starts with its endpoint.

  The name of the ray is ray SC ($\overrightarrow{SC}$).

4. *Think!*

- A line is identified by naming two points on the line. The name can start with either of the two points.

  The name of the line is line BC ($\overleftrightarrow{BC}$) or line CB ($\overleftrightarrow{CB}$).

2
What's the Angle?

Measuring Angles of Straight-Sided Figures

What You Need to Know

An **angle** is the figure formed when two rays that have the same endpoint or two straight lines meet. The rays or lines are the sides of the angle, and the endpoint where they meet is called the **vertex** of the angle. Three letters are used to name an angle, with the center letter being the vertex. The word *angle* can be replaced by its symbol: ∠. The name of the angle in the example is read: angle BEN or angle NEB. It is written as: ∠BEN or ∠NEB.

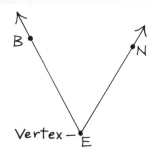

The unit used in measuring an angle is the degree. One degree is written as: 1°.

The measure of a **right angle** is 90 degrees. The corner of a rectangle is a right angle.

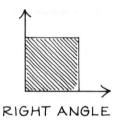

RIGHT ANGLE

The measure of an **acute angle** is less than 90 degrees.

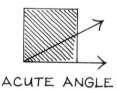

ACUTE ANGLE

The measure of an **obtuse angle** is greater than 90 degrees.

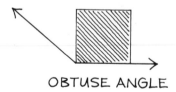

OBTUSE ANGLE

A **protractor** is an instrument used to measure angles in degrees. It is often shaped like a half circle. To measure an angle with a protractor, place the center mark of the protractor on the vertex of the angle and the straight edge on one side of the angle. The protractor will show two numbers on the curved edge where the second side crosses the scale. The sum of these two numbers will always equal 180 degrees. One of the numbers represents an acute angle, and the other an obtuse angle. If the angle is acute, use the smaller number. If it is obtuse, use the larger number. In the example, ray OT crosses the scale at

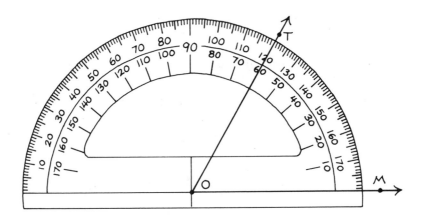

60 degrees and 120 degrees. Since the angle is acute, ∠TOM is 60 degrees.

A ruler or straightedge can be used when the sides of an angle are too short to cross the scale of the protractor. Lay the edge of the ruler along the side, and read the numbers where the ruler crosses the scale of the protractor. In the diagram, the edge of the ruler crosses the scale at 50 degrees and 130 degrees. The angle is obtuse, so ∠CAT is 130 degrees.

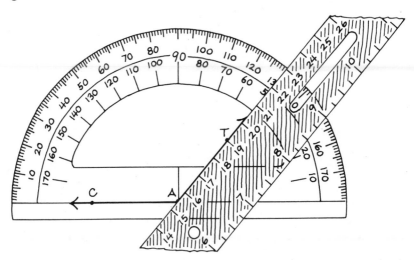

Let's Think It Through

1. Use a protractor to measure the angles in examples A and B.

   A

   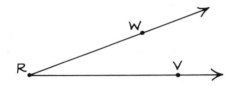

   B

   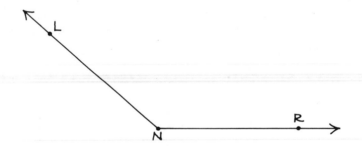

2. Write the name of the angle in example A.

Answers

1a. *Think!*

   • The angle is acute. Which of the angle choices, 20 degrees or 160 degrees, is acute?

   The angle is 20 degrees.

b.

- The angle is obtuse. Which of the angle choices, 40 degrees or 140 degrees, is obtuse?

The angle is 140 degrees.

2. Think!

- What are the angle's three letters, with the vertex letter in the middle? WRV.

- How is the angle read? Angle WRV or angle VRW.

The angle is written as: ∠WRV or ∠VRW.

Exercises

Use a protractor to measure each angle.

1. What is the angle of the bottom left corner of the picture frame?

2. Measure the angle of the lounge chair.

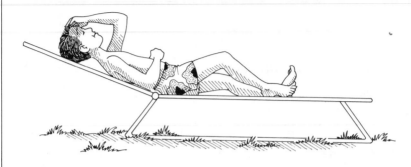

3. Measure and write the name of the angle.

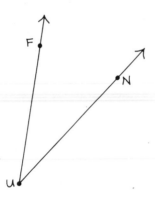

Activity: PAPER ART

Purpose To fold a sheet of paper into the shape of a whale.

Materials ruler
scissors
typing paper
blue crayon

Procedure

1. Measure and cut an 8-by-8-inch (20-by-20-cm) square from the paper.

2. Color one side of the paper blue.

3. Lay the paper on a table, white side up.

4. Fold the paper in half diagonally from point A to point B to form a center fold line.

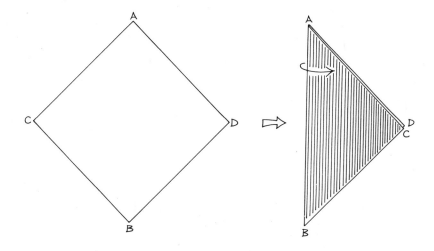

5. Unfold the paper and cut about 2 inches (5 cm) down the center fold line from point A toward point B.

6. Fold the paper so that points C and D meet at the center fold line.

7. Fold the paper again, so that points E and F meet at the center fold line.

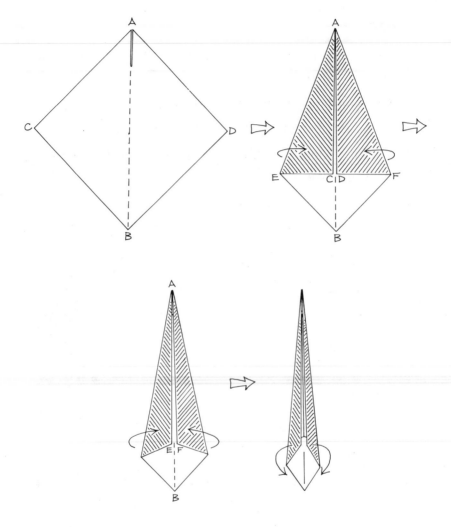

8. Refold along the fold line from point A to point B.

9. Fold the two cut ends outward.

10. Turn the paper over and draw an eye and a mouth on either side of the face, as in the diagram.

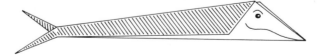

Results   You have made a paper whale.

Why?   Each fold in the paper is made at a new angle. The art of folding paper into shapes that look like objects is called **origami** and was originated by the Chinese about 2,000 years ago. In the seventh century this art form was brought to Japan, where Japanese magicians introduced the seeming magic of making a few simple folds to produce birds, animals, boats, and other pretty forms to delight their audiences. Origami is now a universal word for the art of paper folding.

Solutions to Exercises

1. *Think!*

   • The frame is a rectangle. Rectangles have what type of angles? Right angles.

   • How many degrees are in a right angle?

   The bottom left corner of the frame is 90 degrees.

2. *Think!*

   • The angle is obtuse. Which of the angle choices, 20 degrees or 160 degrees, is obtuse?

   The angle of the lounge chair is 160 degrees.

3. *Think!*

   • The angle is acute. Which of the angle choices, 35 degrees or 145 degrees, is acute?

   Angle FUN (∠FUN) or angle NUF (∠NUF) is 35 degrees.

3

Crossover

Identifying Intersecting, Parallel, and Perpendicular Lines

What You Need to Know

Lines that meet or cross each other and have only one point in common are called **intersecting lines**. In the example, lines CD and EG intersect, with F as the common point.

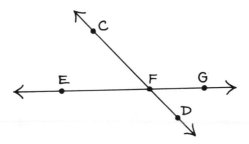

Two lines that intersect to form a right angle are **perpendicular lines**. To indicate that lines are perpendicular to each other, a square can be drawn around the point where the lines intersect, or a single square can be drawn in one corner. In the example on the next page, lines GH and IJ intersect, and as indicated by the square, the lines are perpendicular to each other. They are read: Line GH is perpendicular to line IJ.

They are written as: $\overleftrightarrow{GH} \perp \overleftrightarrow{IJ}$.

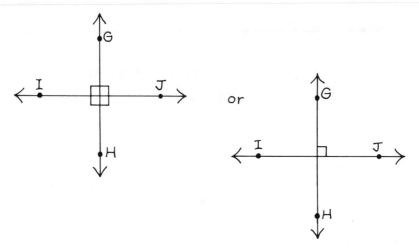

Lines that do not intersect and are always the same distance apart are called **parallel lines**. Lines KB and FN are examples of parallel lines. They are read:

Line KB is parallel to line FN.

They are written as: $\overleftrightarrow{KB} \parallel \overleftrightarrow{FN}$.

Let's Think It Through

Identify the intersecting and parallel lines or line segments in the three examples.

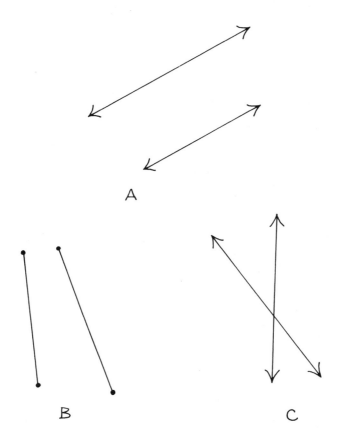

Answer

Think!

- The lines in example A do not meet or cross and are the same distance apart.

A is an example of parallel lines.

- The line segments in example B do not meet or cross and are not the same distance apart. They are neither parallel nor intersecting lines.

- The lines in example C cross.

C is an example of intersecting lines.

Exercise

1. Study the two diagrams and identify the following:

   a. intersecting lines

   b. parallel lines

   c. perpendicular lines

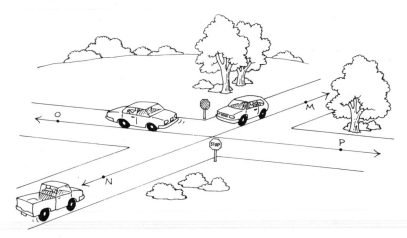

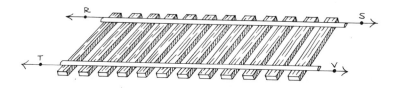

Activity: BALANCING NAILS

Purpose To show how six intersecting and parallel nails can balance on the head of a seventh vertical nail.

Materials hammer
seven 16d nails
2-by-4-by-6-inch (5-by-10-by-15-cm) or larger wooden block
adult helper

Procedure

1. Ask your helper to hammer the tip of one of the nails into the center of the wooden block. The nail should be as firm and vertical as possible without being driven in too deeply.

2. Arrange the nails so that they work as a single unit by following these steps. The numbers refer to the nails as shown in the diagrams:

- Lay nail 1 parallel with the edge of the table.

- Lay nails 2, 3, 4, and 5 over nail 1 so that they are parallel with each other and their heads slightly extend past the sides of nail 1.

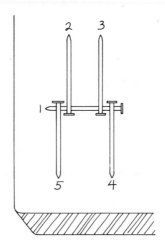

- Lay nail 6 on top of the arrangement so that it is parallel with nail 1 and its tip points in the opposite direction of the tip of nail 1.

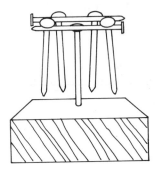

3. Gently and very carefully pick up the group of nails by holding the ends of nails 1 and 6 with your thumbs and index fingers.

4. Place the center of nail 1 on the head of the vertical nail that is in the wooden block. This may take some practice.

Results   The arrangement of nails balances.

Why?   The weight of each nail is the same. Thus, the weights of the two sets of hanging parallel nails counterbalance each other, as do the weights of the two horizontal parallel nails. This counterbalancing of weight allows six nails to balance on the head of one nail.

Solution to Exercise

1a. *Think!*

- Which lines cross?

$\overleftrightarrow{MN}$ intersects $\overleftrightarrow{OP}$.

b. *Think!*

- Which lines do not cross, run in the same direction, and are always the same distance apart?

$\overleftrightarrow{RS}$ || $\overleftrightarrow{TV}$.

c. *Think!*

- Do any of the lines meet or intersect at 90 degrees? No.

There are no perpendicular lines in either diagram.

4
Three-Sided Figures
Identifying Triangles

What You Need to Know

A **plane figure** is a geometric figure that lies on a flat surface. A **closed figure** is a geometric figure that begins and ends at the same point. A **polygon** is a closed plane figure formed by three or more line segments that are joined only at the endpoints, or vertices, with each endpoint connected to only two line segments. In the diagram, figure A is the only example of a polygon.

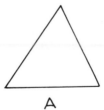

A

B

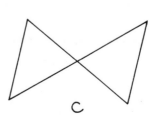

C

The different types of polygons are identified by the number of their sides. A polygon made up of three sides is called a **triangle**. The sum of the angles created by the three sides is always 180 degrees.

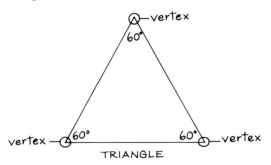

TRIANGLE

Triangles can be identified in two different ways. One way depends on whether the length of their sides is **congruent** (the same). In an **equilateral triangle**, all three sides are congruent. In an **isosceles triangle**, two sides are congruent. In the **scalene triangle**, no sides are congruent.

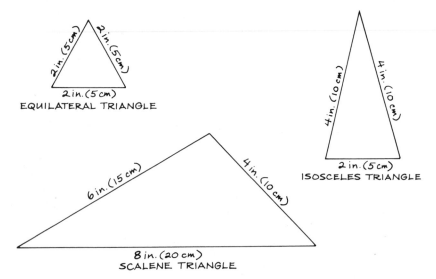

The second way of identifying triangles depends on the size of their angles. In an **acute triangle**, all angles measure less than 90 degrees. In a **right triangle**, one angle measures exactly 90 degrees. (Note in the figure that a small square is placed in the corner to identify the right angle.) In an **obtuse triangle**, one angle measures greater than 90 degrees.

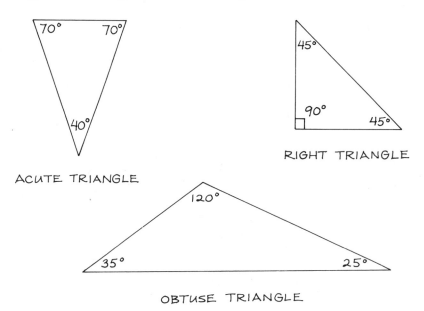

ACUTE TRIANGLE

RIGHT TRIANGLE

OBTUSE TRIANGLE

Let's Think It Through

Look at the pennant in the diagram and answer the following:

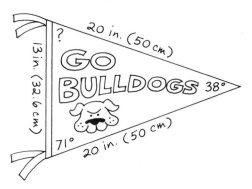

1. What is the measure of the missing angle?

2. What are all the possible names for the triangle?

Answers

1. *Think!*

- The sum of the three angles formed by the sides of a triangle is 180 degrees.

- The sum of the two angles shown subtracted from 180 gives the amount of the missing angle:

$71° + 38° = 109°$
$180° - 109° = ?$

The measure of the missing angle is 71 degrees.

2. *Think!*

- Two of the sides are congruent.

- What is the name given to a triangle with two congruent sides? Isosceles triangle.

- All the angles measure less than 90 degrees.

- What is the name given to a triangle in which all angles measure less than 90 degrees? Acute triangle.

The possible names for the triangle are isosceles triangle and acute triangle.

Exercises

1. What are all the possible names for the boat's triangular sail?

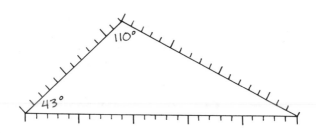

2. Use the angles given and the scale for each side to determine all the possible names for the triangle shown here.

Activity: STRAW TRIANGLES

Purpose   To construct models of acute triangles.

Materials   scissors
4 plastic drinking straws
ruler
6 small paper clips

Procedure

1. Cut the straws into six pieces: make one 2-inch (5-cm) piece and five 4-inch (10-cm) pieces.

2. Open the paper clips as shown in the diagram.

3. To make each triangle, insert one bent end of each paper clip into the end of each straw piece. Adjust the angle of the bent paper clip if needed. Make two triangles by using the following straw length combinations:

- Three 4-inch (10-cm)

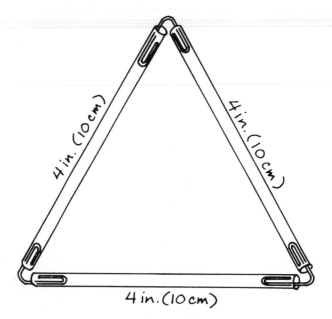

4 in. (10 cm)

- Two 4-inch (10-cm) and one 2-inch (5-cm)

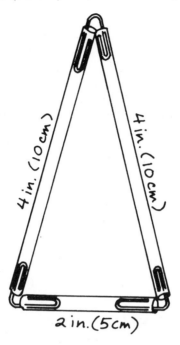

4 in. (10 cm)

4 in. (10 cm)

2 in. (5 cm)

Results   Two acute triangles are formed. One of the triangles is equilateral and the other, isosceles.

Why?   The lengths of the straws determine the angles formed when the straws are connected. The triangle formed by connecting three straws of equal length produces an equilateral acute triangle. The angles of this triangle are congruent and each is 60 degrees. Replacing one of the straws with a shorter straw produces an isosceles triangle. The shorter straw pulls the two longer straws closer together and decreases the angle between them. The other two angles in the triangle increase, but neither is 90 degrees or greater. Thus, both triangles are acute.

Solutions to Exercises

1. *Think!*

- The square in one corner of the triangle indicates that the angle is 90 degrees.

- What are triangles called that have one 90-degree angle? Right triangles.

- The lengths of two sides are congruent.

- What is a triangle having two congruent sides called? Isosceles triangle.

The possible names for the triangle are right triangle and isosceles triangle.

2. *Think!*

- There is one angle greater than 90 degrees. Thus, it is an obtuse triangle. (The missing angle is not needed to identify the triangle.)

- How many sections are on the sçale for each side of the triangle? 12, 18, and 25.

- None of the sides are congruent. Thus, the triangle is scalene.

The possible names for the triangle are obtuse triangle and scalene triangle.

5

Four-Sided Figures

Identifying Quadrilaterals

What You Need to Know

A **quadrilateral** is a four-sided polygon formed by four line segments. There are three basic types of quadrilaterals: the **trapezium**, which has no parallel sides; the **trapezoid**, which has one pair of parallel sides; and the **parallelogram**, which has two pairs of parallel sides.

An **isosceles trapezoid** is a special type of trapezoid whose two nonparallel sides are congruent. Rhomboid, rhombus, rectangle, and square are all examples of parallelograms. A **rhomboid** is a parallelogram that has no right angles and only opposite sides are congruent; a **rhombus** is a parallelogram that has no right angles and four congruent sides; and a **rectangle** is a parallelogram that has four right angles and only opposite sides are congruent. A **square** is a special type of rectangle that has four congruent sides. Even though each of these figures is an example of a parallelogram, the name *parallelogram* is commonly used to identify only the rhomboid.

While a rhomboid is commonly called a parallelogram, it will be called a rhomboid in this book to distinguish it from the other members of the parallelogram family.

QUADRILATERALS

Types	Examples
Trapezium	
Trapezoid family	trapezoid Isosceles trapezoid
Parallelogram family	rhomboid rhombus rectangle square

Let's Think It Through

Study the diagram and answer these questions:

1. How many quadrilaterals are labeled in the diagram?

2. How many of the quadrilaterals are parallelograms?

3. Identify each of the quadrilaterals.

Answers

1. *Think!*

   • Which figures have four sides?

   There are three quadrilaterals: figures A, B, and C.

2. *Think!*

   • How many of these figures have two pairs of parallel sides?

   Two of the figures are parallelograms: A and C.

3. *Think!*

   • Figure A is a parallelogram with four right angles and four congruent sides.

   Figure A is a square.

   • Figure B has only one pair of parallel sides and the two nonparallel sides are congruent.

   Figure B is an isosceles trapezoid.

   • Figure C is a parallelogram that has four right angles and only opposite sides are congruent.

   Figure C is a rectangle.

Exercise

Identify the four labeled quadrilaterals in the diagram.

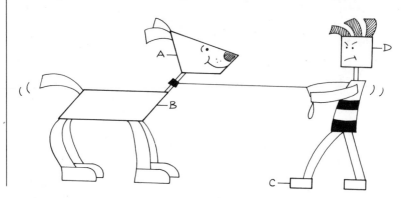

Activity: REARRANGEMENT

Purpose To compare the shapes of a rhomboid and a rectangle.

Materials 1 yellow and 1 blue transparent plastic report folder
marking pen
ruler
scissors

Procedure

1. Lay the yellow plastic folder over the rectangle pattern shown.

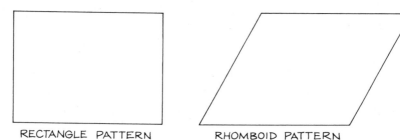

RECTANGLE PATTERN   RHOMBOID PATTERN

2. Trace the rectangle figure onto the plastic. Use the edge of the ruler to make the edges of the rectangle straight.

3. Cut out the traced rectangle.

4. Lay the blue plastic folder over the rhomboid pattern and trace the figure onto the plastic.

5. Cut out the traced rhomboid.

6. Lay the rhomboid on top of the rectangle as shown.

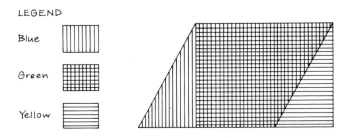

7. Place the edge of the ruler on the right side of the blue triangle and trace this side.

8. Cut off the blue triangle and place it over the yellow triangle as shown.

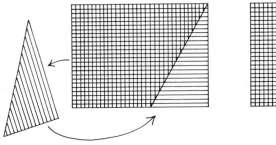
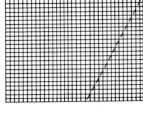

Results The rhomboid is taken apart and rearranged to form a rectangle of equal size.

Why?   The rhomboid is like a flexible rectangle with its top pushed to one side and its bottom pushed to the other. The shape of the rhomboid can be changed into that of an equal-size rectangle by cutting off the blue triangle sticking out on one side and placing it over the yellow triangle on the opposite side. This makes a green rectangle.

Solutions to Exercise

1a. *Think!*

- What is the name given a quadrilateral that has no parallel sides?

Figure A is a trapezium.

b. *Think!*

- A quadrilateral with four parallel sides is called a parallelogram.

- What is a parallelogram with no right angles called?

Figure B is a rhomboid, more commonly called a parallelogram.

c. *Think!*

- What is a parallelogram with four right angles and only opposite congruent sides called?

Figure C is a rectangle.

d. *Think!*

- What is the special name for a rectangle with four congruent sides?

Figure D is a square.

6
Hidden Figures

Determining Different Ways that Polygons Can Fit Together

What You Need to Know

As you learned in the previous chapters, polygons are closed plane figures with straight sides. The simplest polygon, called a triangle, has three sides. Rhomboids, squares, and rectangles are examples of polygons with four sides.

With their straight sides made by line segments, small polygons can fit together to form larger figures of various shapes. Triangles can fit together to form not only larger triangles, but also diamonds, squares, trapezoids, and other multisided figures, such as **pentagons**, which have five sides, and **hexagons**, which have six sides. There are many other possibilities.

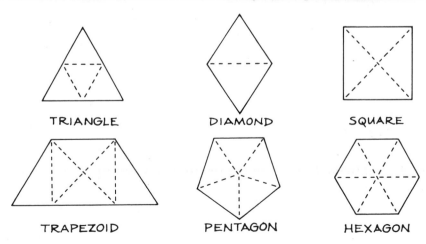

TRIANGLE DIAMOND SQUARE

TRAPEZOID PENTAGON HEXAGON

Let's Think It Through

How many squares are hidden in the figure?

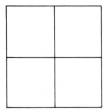

Answer

Think!

- A square has four congruent sides and all its angles are right angles.

- The figure shows one large square made up of four smaller squares.

The total number of squares is five.

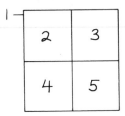

Exercises

1. Study the triangle in the figure to answer questions a and b.

a. How many triangles can you find in the figure?

b. How many hidden diamonds can you find in the figure?

2. Study the figure of the square to determine the total number of squares.

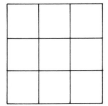

Activity: CUTAWAY

Purpose   To make a tangram.

Materials   ruler
scissors
sheet of construction paper
stopwatch

Procedure

1. Measure and cut an 8-by-8-inch (20-by-20-cm) square from the paper.

2. Follow these steps to divide the square into seven pieces. Number each piece as shown in the diagrams.

   • Cut the square in half diagonally to form two separate triangles, and label the pieces "1" and "2."

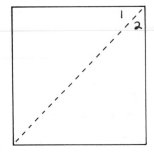

• Cut piece 1 in half as shown and label the second triangular piece "3." Place both small triangles aside.

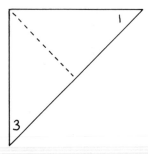

• Fold the corner of piece 2 so that the corner opposite the longest side touches the center of the longest side. Unfold and cut along the fold line. Piece 2 is now a trapezoid. Label the triangular piece "4" and set it aside.

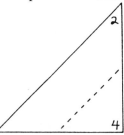

• Fold the trapezoid (piece 2) in half so that the shorter sides match up. Unfold and cut along the fold line. Label the cutoff half piece "5," and set it aside.

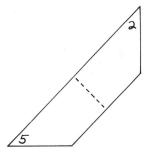

- Fold piece 2 so that the pointed end touches the opposite corner. Unfold and cut along the fold line. Label the square piece "6." Set pieces 2 and 6 aside.

- Fold piece 5 so that side A in the figure touches side B. Unfold and cut along the fold line. Label the triangular piece "7." Set pieces 7 and 5 aside.

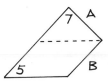

3. Without looking at the diagrams in this book, time how long it takes you to arrange the seven pieces to make the original square.

4. Try making different shaped polygons with the pieces.

Results   The square is cut into seven pieces: five triangles—
two large, one medium, and two small; one square; and one
rhomboid. The time it takes to arrange the pieces into a square
varies with each individual.

Why?   A **tangram** is a Chinese puzzle made by cutting a
square into five triangles, a square, and a rhomboid. The pieces
can be arranged to form the original square as well as a great
variety of other polygons.

Solutions to Exercises

1a. *Think!*

- What is the shape of a triangle? A closed figure with
  three straight sides.
- The figure shows a large triangle with four smaller
  hidden triangles inside.

The total number of triangles in the figure is five.

b. *Think!*

- A diamond shape can be formed by combining two
  equal-size triangles.
- How many pairs of triangles make up the figure?

*The total number of hidden diamonds in the figure is
three.*

2. *Think!*

- The figure shows one square with nine smaller squares inside.
- Each group of four small squares makes one larger square. How many different groups of four squares are hidden in the diagram? Four.
- 1 + 9 + 4 = 14

The total number of squares in the figure is fourteen.

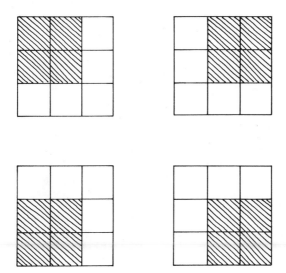

7
Overlay

Identifying Congruent Polygons

What You Need to Know

Congruent polygons are polygons that are exactly the same shape and size. The congruency of two polygons is determined by laying one polygon on top of another to determine if each side and vertex (the point where two sides of the polygon meet) matches with a corresponding side and vertex on the other polygon.

Figures A and B are congruent polygons because they are exactly the same shape and size. If A were placed on top of B, the sides and vertices of both figures would exactly line up.

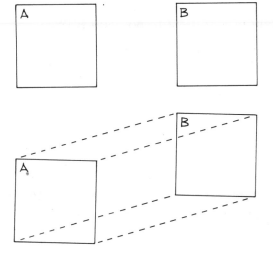

Figures C and D are not congruent polygons. They have the same shape, but C is smaller than D. If C were placed on top of D, their sides and vertices would not match.

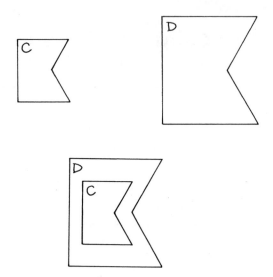

Let's Think It Through

Study figures E, F, and G to answer the following:

1. Is polygon E congruent to polygon F?

2. Is polygon E congruent to polygon G?

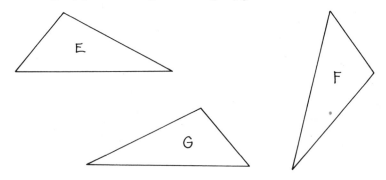

Answer

1. *Think!*

- To compare the figures, use tracing paper to neatly trace polygon E. Slide and rotate the tracing to fit over polygon F.

- Do the figures exactly fit on top of each other with their vertices and sides matching? Yes.

Polygons E and F are congruent.

2. *Think!*

- Flip the tracing of polygon E over, then slide and rotate it so that it fits over polygon G.

- Do the sides and vertices of the two polygons match? Yes.

Polygons E and G are congruent.

Exercise

Use a tracing of polygon A to help you find congruent polygons in the diagram on the next page.

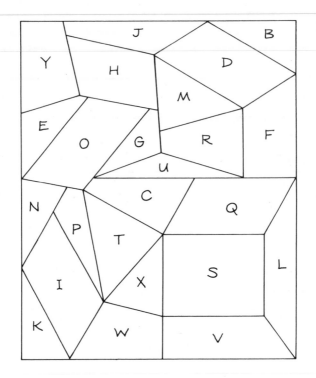

Activity: MATCHUP

Purpose To construct a design with congruent polygons.

Materials pencil
tracing paper
yellow, red, green, and white construction paper
scissors
glue

Procedure

1. Follow the steps below to cut two polygons congruent to figure A from the yellow paper.

- Trace figure A on the tracing paper.

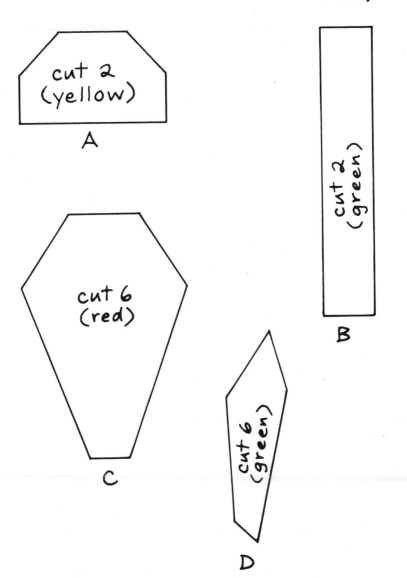

A — cut 2 (yellow)

B — cut 2 (green)

C — cut 6 (red)

D — cut 6 (green)

- Fold the yellow construction paper in half.
- Place the traced pattern of figure A on the folded paper.
- Cut out the design by cutting through the tracing paper and the folded yellow paper.

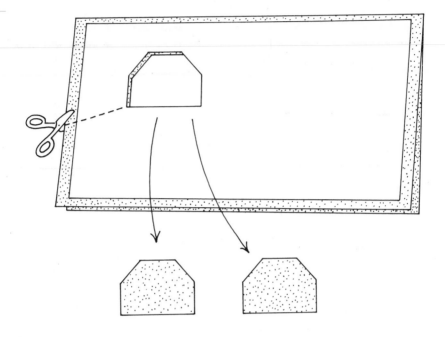

- Keep the yellow congruent polygons and discard the one
  cut from the tracing paper.

2. Repeat step 1 to cut out the indicated number and color of
   shapes B, C, and D.

3. Arrange and glue each of the colored pieces on the sheet of
   white paper as shown in the diagram, using the following
   steps:

   - Overlap the short ends of the two green congruent rect-
     angles to make a stem.

   - Place the shortest ends of the six red congruent hexagons
     together in the shape of flower petals.

   - Flip one of the yellow hexagons upside down and place
     the two in the center of the petals so that the long sides of
     the hexagons touch.

   - Place one of the six green pentagons on the right side of
     the stem to make a leaf that angles upward toward the

petals. Flip a second pentagon leaf over and place it on the left side of the stem opposite the first leaf. Arrange the remaining four green pentagons at the base of the stem to make blades of grass.

Results   A colored flower design is created.

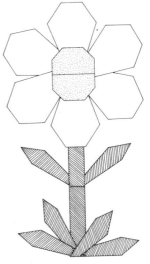

Why?   Cutting out the polygons by cutting through the tracing paper and the folded construction paper produces three congruent polygons, one from the tracing paper and two from the construction paper. Although rotating or flipping the designs can change their alignment, it does not change their shape or size. Thus, they remain congruent polygons.

Solution to Exercise

Think!

- To compare the figures, use tracing paper to neatly trace polygon A. Slide, rotate, or flip the tracing to compare it with the polygons in the diagram.

- Which polygons does polygon A exactly fit on top of so that their vertices and sides match?

Polygons D, I, O, and Q are congruent with polygon A.

8
Five-Square Figures

Making Pentominoes

What You Need to Know

A figure made from five congruent squares is called a **pentomino**. The squares must be arranged so that the entire side of one square lines up with the whole side of the square it touches. The diagram shows figures made with five squares and identifies the correct arrangement of pentominoes and incorrect arrangements that are not pentominoes.

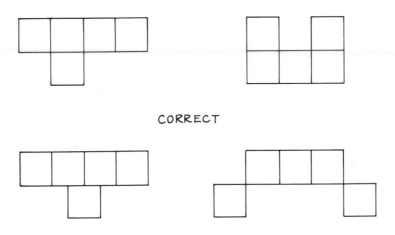

CORRECT

INCORRECT

Let's Think It Through

Which one of the figures is an example of a pentomino?

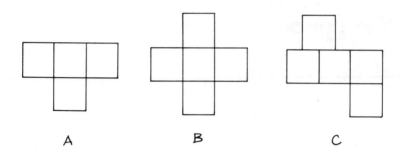

A   B   C

Answer

Think!

- Pentominoes are made up of five squares. Do any of the figures have five squares? Yes, B and C.

- In which figure do the entire sides of touching squares line up?

Figure B is a pentomino.

Exercise

Study the figures to determine how many are pentominoes.

A   B   C

Activity: SQUARE DANCE

Purpose To determine the 12 different possible pentominoes.

Materials ruler
scissors
1 sheet of construction paper
6 sheets of typing paper

Procedure

1. Measure and cut five 1-by-1-inch (2.5-by-2.5-cm) squares from the construction paper.

2. Place the five colored squares on one sheet of typing paper.

3. Arrange the squares into a pentomino.

4. Trace around the outside of each square.

5. Rearrange the five squares on the same paper to form a second pentomino.

6. Again, trace around the outside of each square.

7. Repeat the procedure of arranging the squares into other pentominoes and tracing around them until 12 different pentominoes are drawn, two on each sheet of paper.

Results   Diagrams of the 12 possible pentominoes are created.

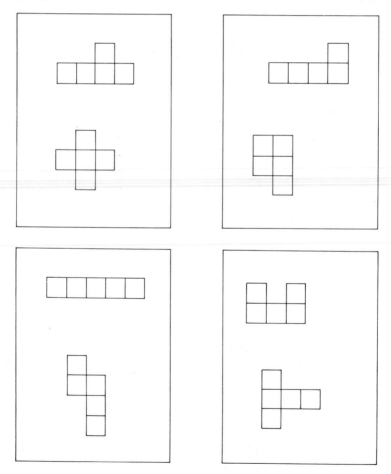

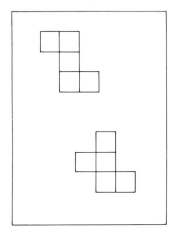 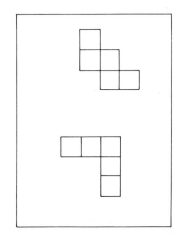

Why?   Only 12 different pentominoes can be created. Rearrangements of the pentominoes, such as flipping them upside down or rotating them, are not counted as new shapes.

Solution to Exercise

Think!

- How many figures are made with five squares? Three.
- In which figure do the entire sides of touching squares line up? B.

Only one of the figures is a pentomino.

9
Curvey Figures
Learning about Curved Geometric Figures

What You Need to Know

Geometric figures that do not have straight sides are called **curved figures**. Curved figures can be closed or open. **Closed curves** are continuous; they do not have a break in the line forming their **perimeter** (the outer boundary of a plane figure). The ends of the lines forming **open curves** do not meet, because the lines are not continuous.

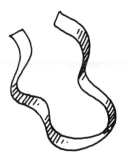

CLOSED CURVE   OPEN CURVE

If the perimeter of a curved figure does not intersect (cross) itself, the curve is said to be a **simple curve**. The perimeter of a **complex curve** does intersect itself. The diagram shows examples of different curved figures, including a **circle**, which is a simple closed curve. Unlike other simple closed curves, the distance between the center of a circle and any point on its perimeter, called the **circumference**, is always the same.

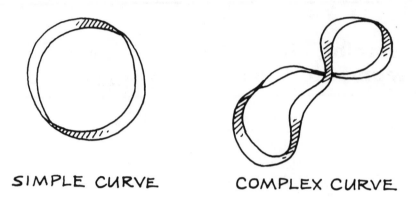

SIMPLE CURVE   COMPLEX CURVE

Let's Think It Through

Match the picture with the correct description.

A

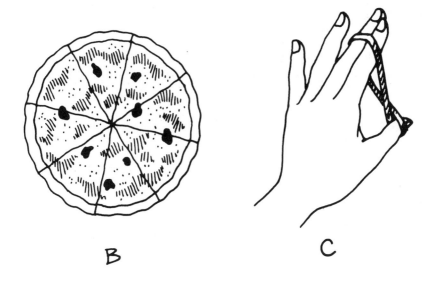

B   C

1. a simple closed curve

2. an open curve

3. a curve whose perimeter intersects itself

Answers

1. *Think!*

- Which curved figure has a perimeter that does not intersect itself and is continuous?

Figure B is a simple closed curve.

2. *Think!*

- Which curved figure is formed by a line that has ends that do not meet?

Figure A is an open curve.

3. *Think!*

• Which curve is formed by a line that crosses itself?

Figure C is a curve whose perimeter intersects itself.

Exercise

Choose two of the following terms to describe each curved diagram: open, closed, simple, complex.

1.

2.

3.

Activity: **TWISTERS**

Purpose   To predict and compare the results of cutting two different closed-curved paper strips down their centers.

Materials   ruler
scissors
butcher paper
pencil
transparent tape

Procedure

1. Measure and cut two separate 2-by-36-inch (5-cm-by-1-m) strips from the butcher paper.

2. Label the strips 1 and 2.

3. Prepare strip 1 by taping the ends together to make a simple closed curve.

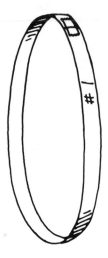

4. Prepare strip 2 by holding the ends, adding a twist to the paper by turning one end 180 degrees, and then taping the ends together to make a complex closed curve.

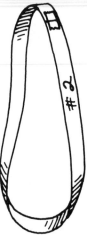

5. Lay strip 1 over the corner of a table. Starting where the edges are taped together, draw a zigzag line back and forth down the strip until you return to the starting point.

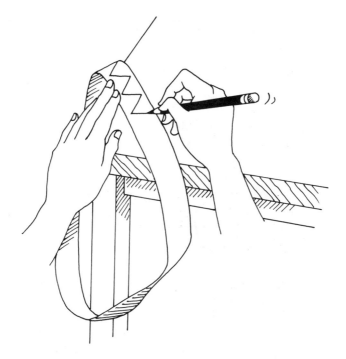

6. Repeat step 4, using strip 2.

7. Without removing the tape, cut along the center of each strip parallel with the edges.

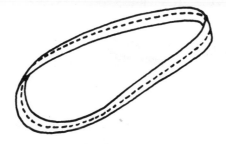

Results   The zigzag marking appears only on one side of strip 1, but on both sides of strip 2. Cutting strip 1 along the center splits the strips into two identical rings, half as wide and equally as long as the original. Cutting strip 2 creates one large ring, half as wide and twice as long as the original, that is also a closed complex curve.

Why?   Twisting the paper 180 degrees creates a complex closed curve known as the **Möbius strip**, named after its discoverer, August Ferdinand Möbius (1790-1868). The reason the Möbius strip does not separate into two rings when it is cut in half is that the twisting produces a ring with only one side—the inside is also the outside.

Solutions to Exercises

1. *Think!*

- Is there a break in the perimeter of the lake? No.
- Does the line forming the figure intersect itself? No.

The figure is a simple closed curve.

2. *Think!*

- Is there a break in the perimeter of the jump rope? Yes.
- Does the line forming the figure intersect itself? No.

The figure is a simple open curve.

3. *Think!*

- Is there a break in the perimeter of the ice pattern? No.
- Does the line forming the figure intersect itself? Yes.

The figure is a closed complex curve.

10
Never-Ending Line

Identifying and Drawing the Parts of a Circle

What You Need to Know

The line that forms a circle has no beginning or end; it is a simple closed curve. Any point on the circumference of a circle is the same distance from the center of the circle. A line segment from a point on the circumference of a circle to its center is called the **radius**. Any line segment that begins and ends on the circle's circumference is called a **chord**. A chord that passes through the center of a circle is called the **diameter**.

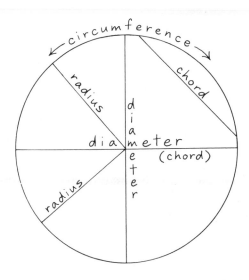

The diameter of any circle is twice as long as the radius of the circle. Every circle has an unlimited number of radii and diameters. For a given circle, all radii are congruent and all diameters are congruent.

Let's Think It Through

Use a compass to draw a circle with a 4-inch (10-cm) diameter.

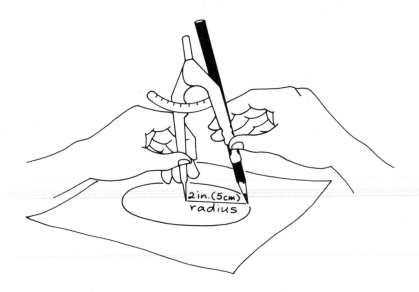

Answer

Think!

- The radius of the circle is half as long as the diameter. What is the radius of a circle with a 4-inch (10-cm) diameter? 4 inches (10 cm) ÷ 2 = 2 inches (5 cm).

- Use a ruler to draw a line the length of the radius, which is 2 inches (5 cm).

- The distance from the point of the compass to the pencil point is equal to the radius of the circle. Place the point of the compass on one end of the line and adjust the position of the pencil so that its point touches the opposite end of the line.

- Draw the circle by holding the compass point steady with one hand and rotating the compass one full turn or 360 degrees with the other hand, as shown in the diagram.

Exercises

1. The diagram shows that Holly and Andrew have worked together to draw a circle in the sand. If the length of rope between the two children is 6 feet (2 m), what is the:

   a. radius of the circle?

   b. diameter of the circle?

2. Use a compass to draw a pie with a radius of 4 inches (10 cm). With a ruler, draw straight lines to divide the pie into eight equal pieces. Study your diagram to answer the following:

   a. What is the diameter of the pie?

   b. How many congruent diameters are shown?

Activity: SPREADERS

Purpose   To produce curved, multicolored patterns.

Materials   one 8-inch (20-cm) coffee filter (basket type)
drinking glass
rubber band
black water-soluble marker
eyedropper
tap water
ruler

Procedure

1. Stretch the coffee filter over the mouth of the glass.

2. Use the rubber band to hold the filter tightly against the glass.

3. Use the black marker to draw a circle with a diameter of about ¼ inch (0.6 cm) in the center of the filter paper.

4. Draw a second circle with a diameter of about ¾ inch (1.9 cm) around the first circle.

5. Use the eyedropper to add one drop of water to the center of the circles.

6. Wait about 10 seconds and add a second drop of water.

7. Continue waiting about 10 seconds and adding one drop of water to the center of the circles until five drops have been added.

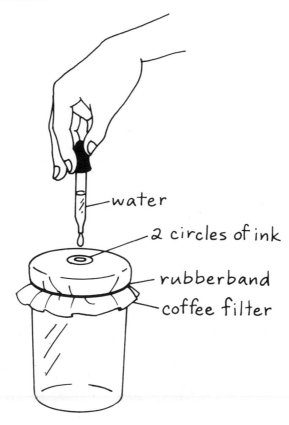

water

2 circles of ink

rubberband

coffee filter

8. Allow the paper to dry. This should take 5 to 10 minutes.

9. Remove the rubber band and spread the paper flat.

10. Use the ruler to measure, in four different places, the diameter of the outer circle produced by the spreading ink.

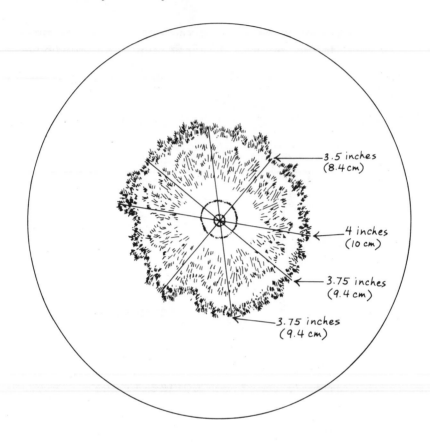

11. Calculate the average diameter of the outer circle by adding the four diameter measurements together and dividing by four as in the example that follows:

3.5 inches (8.8 cm)
3.75 inches (9.4 cm)
3.75 inches (9.4 cm)
+ 4.00 inches (10.0 cm)
_____
15.00 inches (37.6 cm)

15 inches (37.6 cm) ÷ 4 = 3.75 inches (9.4 cm)

Results A multicolored, jagged-edged, circular figure with an average diameter of 3.75 inches (9.4 cm) is produced.

Why?   As the water is absorbed by the paper, the black ink dissolves. The black ink is made from a combination of different colors. In water, most black water-soluble ink separates into the three primary colors of yellow, red, and blue. The colors spread outward to different distances depending on the weight of the chemicals and their **affinity** (attraction) to the paper. This results in a multicolored figure that is the general shape of a circle with an irregular line forming its circumference.

Solutions to Exercises

1a. *Think!*

- The rope is stretched from the center to the circumference of the circle. Thus, the length of the rope is equal to the radius of the circle.

The radius is 6 feet (2 m).

b. *Think!*

- The diameter of a circle is twice as long as the circle's radius. Thus, the diameter of the circle is: 2 × 6 feet (2 m).

The diameter is 12 feet (4 m).

2a. *Think!*

- The diameter of a circle is twice as long as the circle's radius. Thus, the diameter of the circular pie is: 2 × 4 inches (10 cm).

The diameter is 8 inches (20 cm).

b. *Think!*

- How many separate 8-inch (20-cm) lines cross the pie when it is divided into eight equal pieces?

There are four congruent diameters.

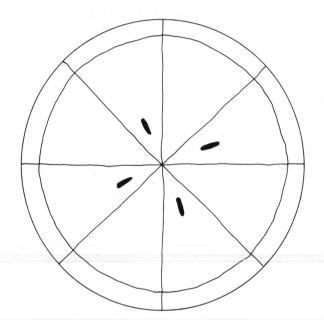

11

Around and Around

Drawing and Measuring Central Angles

What You Need to Know

When the vertex of an angle is at the center of a circle, the angle is called a **central angle**. In the example, angle JAM (∠JAM) is a central angle.

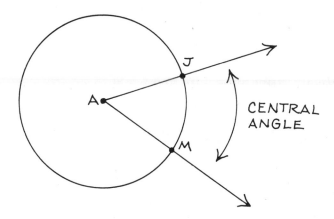

The size of the circle does not alter the size of the angle. The angle between the hands on the small clock is the same as the angle between the hands on the larger clock.

 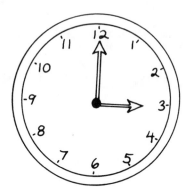

Mathematician's Toolbox: STRING PROTRACTOR

Materials ruler
scissors
string
protractor
transparent tape

Construct a string protractor and use it to measure angles by following these steps:

Procedure

1. Measure and cut a 12-inch (30-cm) piece of string.

2. Thread one end of the string through the hole in the center of the straight edge of the protractor.

3. Tape about 1 inch (2.5 cm) of this end of the string to the back of the protractor.

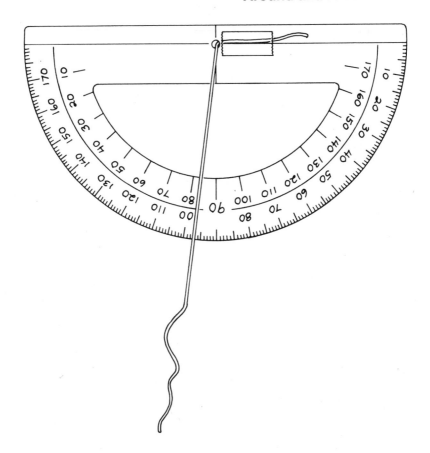

4. Follow these steps to measure the central angle in the diagram with the string protractor:

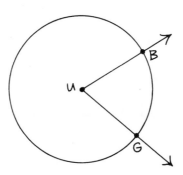

- Place the center mark of the protractor on the vertex of ∠BUG and the edge of the 0-degree line on ray UB (U$\overrightarrow{B}$.)

- Pull the string so that it lines up with $\overrightarrow{UG}$.

- Read the angle where the string crosses the scale of the protractor. There will be two numbers to choose from. If the angle being measured is acute (less than 90 degrees), read the smaller number. If the angle is obtuse (greater than 90 degrees), read the larger number. ∠BUG in the diagram is 70 degrees.

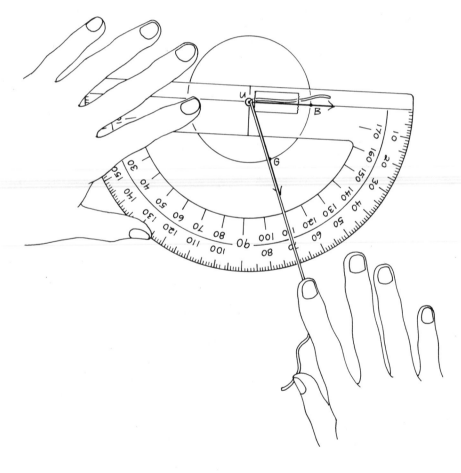

Let's Think It Through

Use your string protractor to measure the central angle, angle SEA, between the second and sixth spokes on the ship's steering wheel.

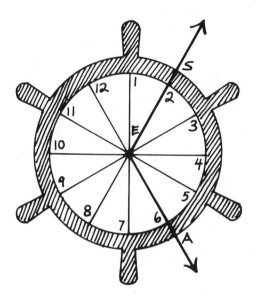

Answer

Think!

- Place the center mark of the protractor on the vertex of ∠SEA and the edge of the 0-degree line on $\overrightarrow{ES}$.

- Pull the string so that it lines up with $\overrightarrow{EA}$.

- Is ∠SEA acute or obtuse? Obtuse.

• Which of the angle choices under the string is obtuse?
∠*SEA is 120 degrees.*

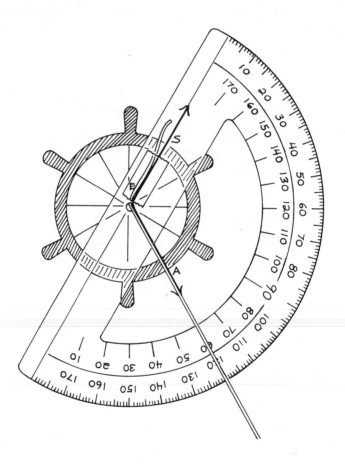

Exercise

How many degrees must the ship turn to be on a course headed directly toward the island?

Activity: 12 O'CLOCK HIGH

Purpose   To use the hands of a clock to estimate direction.

Materials   typing paper
pencil
scissors
paper plate
paper fastener
adult helper

Procedure

1. Lay the typing paper over the pattern of the clock hands and trace them with the pencil.

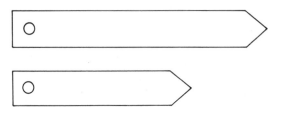

2. Cut out the traced clock hands.

3. Ask your adult helper to use the point of the pencil to punch a hole in the center of the paper plate and through the circle on each clock hand.

4. Use the paper fastener to attach the hands in the center of the plate. Place the shorter hand on top.

5. Write the numbers 1 through 12 around the edge of the paper plate as they would appear on the face of a clock.

6. Imagine that you and a friend are standing side by side, studying the stars in the sky. Your friend gives the following locations for two stars:

   • Star 1 is at 12 o'clock high.

   • Star 2 is to the right at 2 o'clock.

7. Find the approximate location of the stars in the sky by following these steps:

   • Hold the paper plate vertically in front of you.

   • First, move the hands of the clock to 12 o'clock and observe the direction the hands point, noting the size of the angle, if any, between the hands.

- Leaving the longer hand at 12 o'clock, place the shorter hand at 2 o'clock and again note the size of the angle.

Results   At 12 o'clock high the hands point straight up with no angle between the hands. At 2 o'clock the hands should be 60 degrees apart. Follow the short hand as you look up at the imaginary stars, and you'll see the same thing your friend sees at 2 o'clock.

Why?   When both clock hands are pointing to 12 o'clock, the hands point straight up with no angle between the hands.

"12 o'clock high" is used to instruct a person to look at an object directly overhead. Placing the larger clock hand on 12 and moving the smaller hand to any other number on the clock's face creates an angle between the two hands.

The face of a clock is a circle, and like any other circle it measures 360 degrees around. The numbers on the clock break the 360 degrees into 12 even parts. The number of degrees between each number on the clock can be calculated by dividing 360 degrees by 12, which is 30 degrees. This means that the angle between the clock hands placed on consecutive numbers on the clock, such as on 12 and 1, is 30 degrees. At 2 o'clock the clock hands are two numbers apart, making the angle 2×30 degrees, or 60 degrees.

The star at position 2 o'clock in the sky is found by looking straight up and moving your eyes to view a spot overhead about 60 degrees to the right of where you are facing.

Solution to Exercise

Think!

- Measure ∠RIG with your protractor.
- Is the angle acute or obtuse? Acute.
- Which of the angle choices under the string is acute? 60 degrees.

The boat would have to turn 60 degrees.

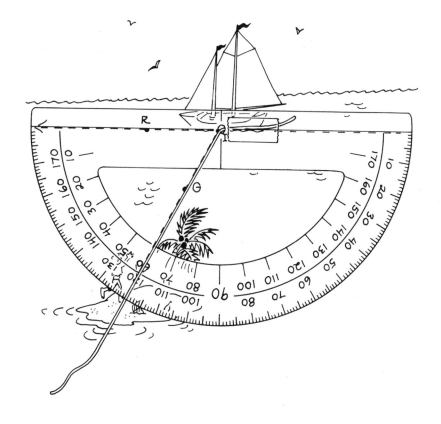

12
Too Odd

Tracing Plane Geometric Figures

What You Need to Know

Some plane figures can be traced with one continuous stroke of a pencil and others cannot. When doing this, the pencil is not lifted from the paper and no line is traced twice. The clue to determining which figures can be traced with this method is the number of line segments that meet at each vertex. If a figure has an even number of line segments meeting at each vertex, as in figures A and B, you can start at any vertex and trace every line segment in the figure only once with one continuous stroke.

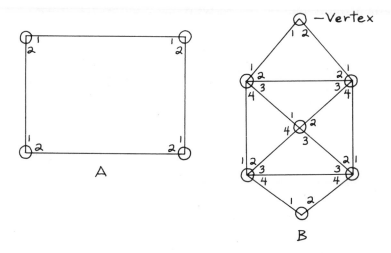

A

B

Some figures have vertices in which an odd number of line segments meet. Figures with only two vertices at which an odd number of line segments meet can be traced with one continuous stroke, but you must start at one of the odd vertices and finish at the other odd vertex. If the figure has more than two odd vertices, it cannot be drawn without lifting the pencil.

Let's Think It Through

Look at figures C and D to answer the following:

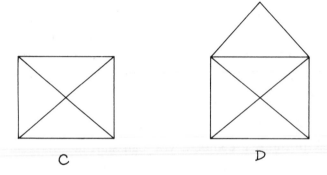

C   D

1. Which figure can be traced with one continuous stroke of the pencil without going over the same line twice?

2. Draw on a sheet of paper the figure(s) that can be traced with one continuous stroke. Use an *S* to indicate the starting point, an *E* to show the endpoint, and arrows to show direction.

Answers

1. *Think!*

- Are there more than two odd vertices in either figure? Yes, figure C has four odd vertices, at vertices 1, 2, 3, and 4. Figure C cannot be traced without lifting the pencil.

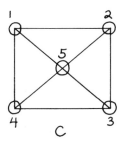

- How many odd vertices does figure D have? Two, at vertices 3 and 4.

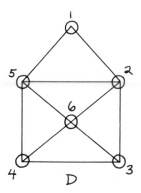

Figure D can be drawn with one continuous stroke of the pencil.

2. *Think!*

- Because it has two odd vertices, figure D can be traced with one continuous stroke if the starting point S is at one of the odd vertices, 3 or 4, and the endpoint E is at the other odd vertex. One of the two possible routes is shown here.

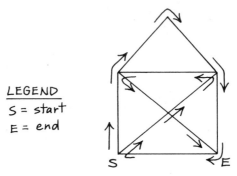

LEGEND
S = start
E = end

Exercises

Study figures E and F to answer the following:

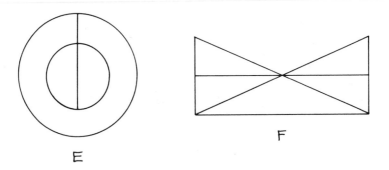

E

F

1. Determine which figure(s) can be traced with one continuous stroke without going over the same line twice.

2. Draw on a sheet of paper the figure(s) that can be traced with one continuous stroke. Use an *S* to indicate the starting point, an *E* to show the endpoint, and arrows to show direction.

Activity: IMPOSSIBLE CHALLENGE

Purpose   To draw a circle within a circle in one continuous stroke of a pencil.

Materials pencil
  paper
  helper

Procedure

1. Challenge a helper to draw a circle within a circle without lifting the pencil from the paper.

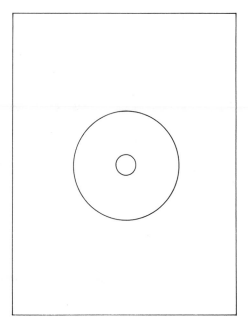

2. When your helper has given up, follow the steps below to show that you can successfully perform this seemingly impossible challenge:

- Fold the paper so that the top right corner is in the middle of the paper.

- Draw a small circle on the front of the paper, beginning at the tip of the folded corner.

- From this circle, draw a straight line about 2 inches (5 cm) long on the back of the folded corner.

- Without lifting the pencil, begin to draw a large circle on the back of the paper, moving the pencil counterclockwise. Do not stop when you reach the edge of the folded corner.

- Continue drawing the large circle on the front of the paper, stopping when you reach the other edge of the folded corner.

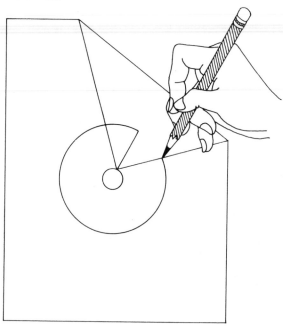

- Hold the pencil in place while you lift the folded corner.

- Finish the circle.

Results   A circle within a circle is drawn with one continuous stroke of the pencil.

Why?   The folded corner of the paper provides a bridge between the inner and outer circles. Once the corner is lifted, the straight line drawn on the back of the paper is not visible on the front of the paper.

Solutions to Exercises

1. *Think!*

- How many odd vertices does each figure have? Figure E has two, at vertices 1 and 3. Figure F has four, at vertices 2, 3, 6, and 7.

- Figures with two odd vertices can be traced with one continuous stroke, but figures with more than two cannot be traced without lifting the pencil.

Figure E can be traced with one continuous stroke.

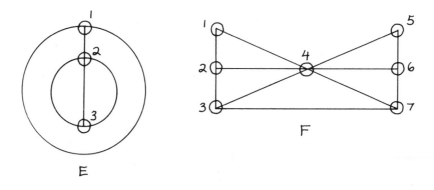

2. *Think!*

- Because it has two odd vertices, figure E can be traced with one continuous stroke if the starting point S is at one of the odd vertices, 1 or 3, and the endpoint E is at the other odd vertex. The following is one of the two possible solutions.

LEGEND

S = start

E = end

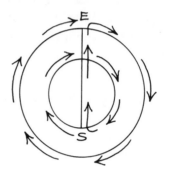

13
Reverse Copy

Determining Lines of Symmetry in Geometric Figures

What You Need to Know

A **line of symmetry** divides a figure into two identical parts that are mirror images of each other, meaning, if a mirror is placed on the line of the folded figure, the whole figure can be seen. If the figure is folded along the line of symmetry, the two halves will exactly match.

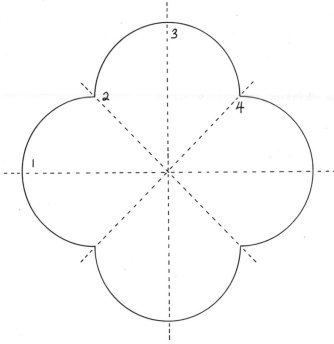

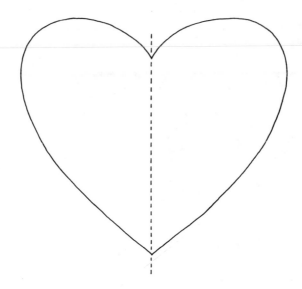

Figures with lines of symmetry are called **symmetric figures**. Some symmetric figures have one line of symmetry, while others have more than one line of symmetry, as indicated by the diagrams on pages 103 and 104.

Let's Think It Through

Determine if the dotted lines are lines of symmetry for the figures on the next page.

1.

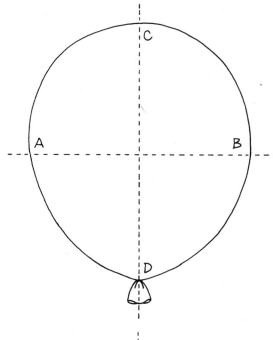

2.

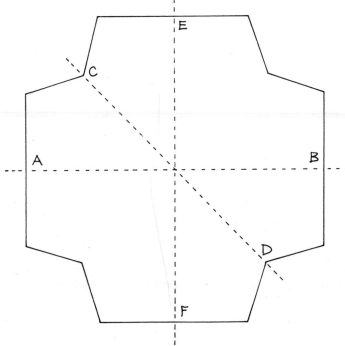

Answers

1. *Think!*

- On which line(s) can the figure be folded to form two halves that exactly match?

$\overleftrightarrow{CD}$ *is a line of symmetry.*

2. *Think!*

- On which line(s) can the figure be folded to form two halves that exactly match?

$\overleftrightarrow{AB}$, $\overleftrightarrow{CD}$, *and* $\overleftrightarrow{EF}$ *are all lines of symmetry.*

Exercises

1. Determine if the dotted lines are lines of symmetry for the figures.

a.

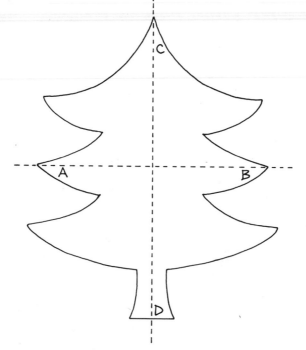

b.

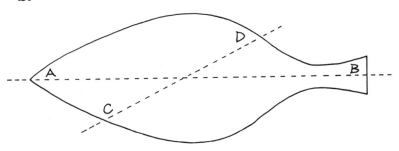

c.

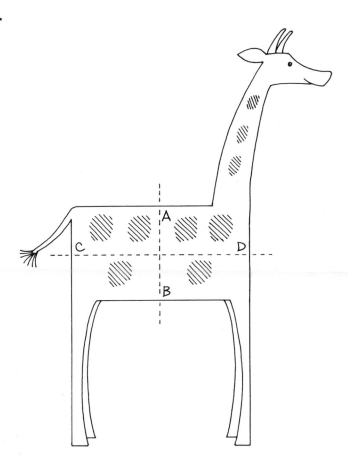

2. Trace the equilateral triangle on paper and cut it out. Fold the cutout to determine how many lines of symmetry the triangle has.

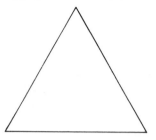

Activity: LACY

Purpose   To create a symmetrical figure.

Materials   compass
typing paper
scissors

Procedure

1. Use the compass to draw a 4-inch (10-cm) diameter circle on the paper. (See Chapter 10 for information about diameter.)

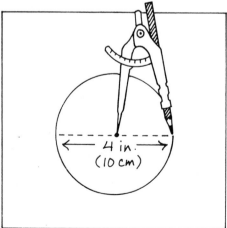

2. Cut out the circle.

3. Fold the circle in half three times.

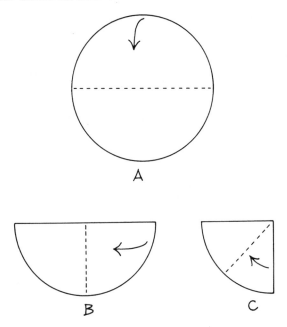

A

B   C

4. Cut four triangular notches in each side and one at the pointed end of the folded paper.

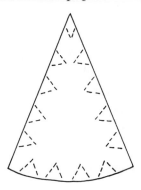

5. Unfold the paper.

Results   A lacy pattern is produced.

Why?   Folding the paper three times produces eight layers of paper. The triangular notches cut along the edges are cut
through each of the eight layers. Thus, the design repeats eight
times around the entire circle. The notches cut on the curved
edge remain triangular, but the notches cut on a folded edge
become diamond shaped when the paper is unfolded. The
notch cut at the pointed end becomes an eight-pointed star in
the middle of the figure. The unfolded figure has four lines of
symmetry.

Solutions to Exercises

1a. *Think!*

- On which line(s) can the figure be folded to form two halves that exactly match?

$\overleftrightarrow{CD}$ *is a line of symmetry.*

b. *Think!*

- On which line(s) can the figure be folded to form two halves that exactly match?

$\overleftrightarrow{AB}$ *is a line of symmetry.*

c. *Think!*

- On which line(s) can the figure be folded to form two halves that exactly match?

None of the lines are lines of symmetry.

2. *Think!*

- On how many lines can the paper be folded to form two halves that exactly match?

The equilateral triangle has three lines of symmetry.

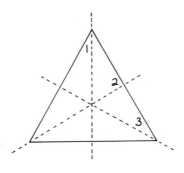

14
Plane Art
Using Plane Geometry to Make Artistic Designs

What You Need to Know

The figures and shapes of plane geometry have been used for centuries to decorate everything from Egyptian pottery and American Indian blankets to modern wallpaper and gift-wrapping paper. In this chapter you will create geometrical art by using line segments to connect numbered points on a plane figure. All of the experiments are based on metric measurements. If you prefer, you may substitute whole inches for centimeters, but you will need to use larger paper.

Let's Think It Through

Use the following steps to draw a curved design by connecting points on an angle:

1. Use a metric ruler and a protractor to draw two 6-cm lines at right angles to each other. Make a dot and number each centimeter division on each ray of the angle as shown in the diagram on the next page.

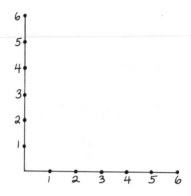

2. Using the edge of the ruler, draw a line segment to connect points on one ray to points on the other ray. Connect the points on **adjacent** (adjoining or neighboring) rays in this way: 1 to 6, 2 to 5, 3 to 4, and so on.

Answer

Think!

- A right angle that has congruent rays is symmetrical, so the curve created by connecting the points on adjacent rays is also symmetrical.

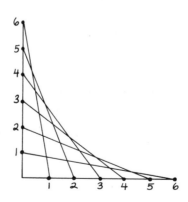

Exercises

Use the steps in Let's Think It Through to draw curved designs that have the following angles and ray lengths. Determine how the shape of the curve changes in each drawing.

1. Draw a 140-degree (obtuse) angle, each ray of which is 6 cm long. Divide the rays into six equal parts as shown in the diagram, then create the curve.

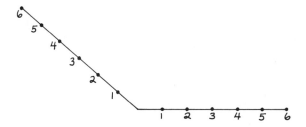

2. Draw a right angle measuring 3 cm along one ray and 6 cm along the other. Divide both rays into six equal parts as shown in the diagram, then create the curve.

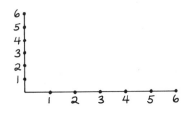

3. Draw a 30-degree (acute) angle, each ray of which is 6 cm long. Divide the rays into six equal parts as shown in the diagram, then create the curve.

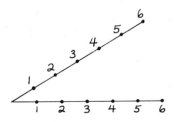

Activity: STITCHERY

Purpose To construct a geometric string design.

Materials metric ruler
protractor
scissors
typing paper
marking pen
pencil with eraser
colored sewing thread
sewing needle
transparent tape

Procedure

1. Use the ruler and protractor to measure and cut a 15-by-15 cm square from the paper.

2. With the pen, draw a 10-by-10-cm square in the center of the paper.

3. Use dots to divide each side into 20 $\frac{1}{2}$-cm parts and number each dot with the pen, as shown in the diagram. This will be called the back side of the paper.

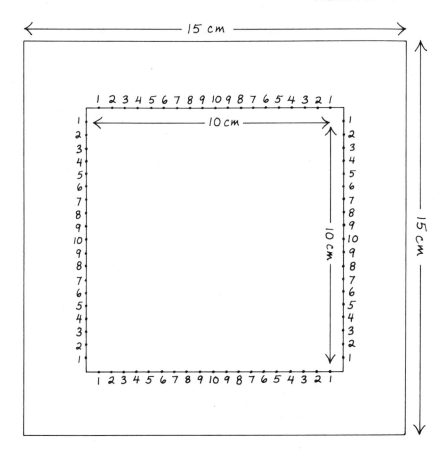

4. During the daytime, turn the paper over so the front side faces you, and place it against a windowpane. The light from outside will allow you to see the marks through the paper. With a pencil, lightly mark and number each division.

5. Thread the needle with about 2 feet (60 cm) of thread. Pull the thread through the eye of the needle so that the two ends meet. Tie a knot in the two ends.

6. Starting on the back side of the paper, begin working in one angle of the square. Insert the needle through one of the points numbered 1.

7. Pull the thread through until the knot in the string touches the paper. Be careful not to pull the knot through the paper.

8. Turn the paper over and on the front side insert the needle into point 10 on the adjacent ray. Pull the thread through the hole in the paper until it creates a straight line between points 1 and 10.

9. Turn the paper over and on the back side insert the needle into point 9 on the same ray. Pull the thread through and across to point 2 on the previous ray.

10. Continue this process until all the points in the first angle have been connected. You will end at point 10 on the ray on which you started.

11. Repeat steps 6 to 10 in the adjacent angle, and continue until all four angles of the square have been connected.

12. When the thread starts to get too short to reach from one point to another, cut it off about 1 inch (2.5 cm) from the back side of the paper. When the design is complete, twist the hanging threads on the back side together and tape them to the paper.

13. Carefully erase the pencil marks on the front side.

Results　The design shown on the next page is created by the colored thread on the front side of the paper.

Why?　As in the diagram made earlier in the Let's Think It Through section, in which line segments were drawn between the points on the rays of a right angle, the colored thread creates a line segment between the points on the stitched design. Try creating and stitching your own geometric designs.

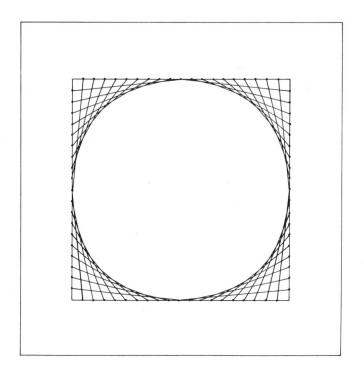

Solutions to Exercises

1. *Think!*

- Both rays are the same length and the angle is obtuse.
- The curve is symmetrical and very slight.

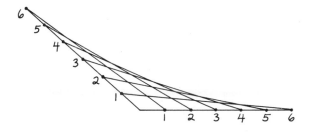

2. *Think!*

- Both rays are not the same length, so the curve is not symmetrical.

- The right angle produces a greater curve than the obtuse angle in the previous example.

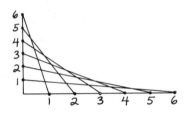

3. *Think!*

- Both rays are the same length, so the curve is symmetrical.

- As angles get smaller, the curves become more pointed. This figure has the smallest angle and the most pointed curve.

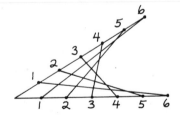

15
What's Next?

Extending and Relating Geometric Patterns

What You Need to Know

A **pattern** is a predictable arrangement of things, such as numbers and/or geometric figures, that have some relationship to each other. To solve a problem, it is sometimes necessary to see if a pattern exists in the problem. In this chapter only geometric figures will be used to create and extend patterns. These figures may vary in size, shape, color, or position, but they work together to form a pattern that can be recognized and extended. An example of predicting the extension of a geometric pattern is shown in the diagram. A large colorless geometric figure is followed by a smaller dark figure of the same geometric shape. The most logical prediction of the next figure would be a smaller dark circle.

 =

Let's Think It Through

What would be the next figure in each pattern?

1.

2.

Answers

1. *Think!*

- What figures are shown in the problem? Ice cream cones with one scoop of ice cream.

- How do the figures differ? There are two different flavors of ice cream.

- What is the pattern? The flavor of the ice cream in the cones alternates.

• The next ice cream cone would be:

2. *Think!*

• What figures are shown in the pattern? Smiley faces.

• How do the figures differ? They vary in size; also the small faces have legs and feet and the large faces wear hats.

• What is the pattern? The size of the faces alternates.

• The next figure would be:

Exercises

What would be the next figure in each pattern?

1.

2.

3.

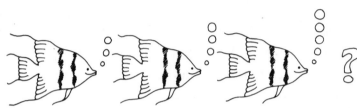

Activity: BOUNCER

Purpose   To demonstrate a repeated pattern.

Materials   ruler
scissors
typing paper
marking pen
transparent tape

Procedure

1. Measure and cut two strips of paper that are 2 × 4 inches (5 × 10 cm).

2. Draw a line across the shorter side of the paper strips 1 inch (2.5 cm) from each end.

3. Tape the top and bottom of one strip to a table.

4. Starting on the bottom line of the taped strip, draw a stick figure about 1 inch (2.5 cm) tall that has both arms down and a ball resting on the bottom line.

5. Place the second paper strip on top of the drawing with the edges of the strips lined up, and tape the top of this strip to the table.

6. Trace the figure onto the top paper, but raise one arm and place the ball in the stick figure's hand.

7. Tape a pencil to the bottom edge of the top paper as shown.

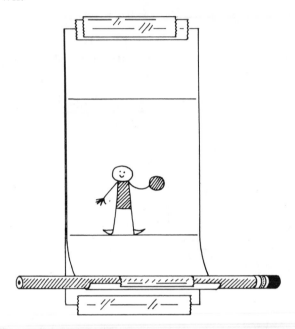

8. Place your hands on the ends of the pencil and roll the pencil up to the top line drawn on the paper.

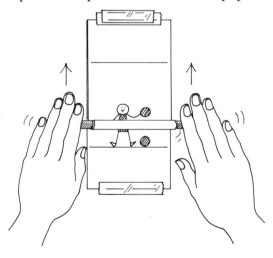

9. Quickly roll the pencil back and forth between the two lines on the paper several times.

Results   The ball appears to bounce up and down.

Why?   The human eye retains an image of an object for a fraction of a second after the object is out of sight. This retention of an image is called **persistence of vision**. When two related images are quickly flashed one after the other, the brain combines the images and perceives that the images are in motion. Rolling the top paper strip back and forth allows one picture to follow the other so quickly that persistence of vision lasts long enough to bridge the time between one image and the next. This creates the illusion that the ball is bouncing up and down.

Solutions to Exercises

1. *Think!*

- What figures are shown? Clown heads.
- How do the figures differ? The heads are facing different directions.
- What is the pattern? The direction of the heads alternates.
- The next figure would be:

2. *Think!*

- What figures are shown? Cartoon dinosaurs.

- How do the figures differ? The dinosaur's body is in different positions.

- What is the pattern? Each dinosaur is in a different position, but the position of the second dinosaur is a mirror image of the first dinosaur. The fourth dinosaur must therefore be a mirror image of the third dinosaur.

- The next figure would be:

3. *Think!*

- What figures are shown? Fish blowing bubbles.

- How do the figures differ? The number and size of the bubbles are different.

- What is the pattern? The next fish in line has one extra bubble that is larger than the largest bubble of the preceding fish.

- The next figure would be:

16
Coverup

Calculating the Area of a Rectangle

What You Need to Know

A plane figure is **two-dimensional** because its surface can be measured in only two directions—length and width. **Area** is the measure of the number of square units needed to cover this surface. This chapter deals with the area of rectangles. To calculate the area of a rectangle, use the formula $A = l \times w$, which is read: area equals length times width.

Let's Think It Through

What is the area of the rectangle shown?

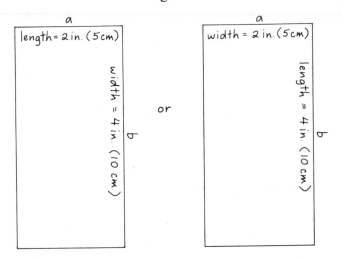

Answer

Think!

- The formula for calculating the area of a rectangle is
  $A = l \times w$.
- Sides a and b of the diagram may be labeled as either the length or the width without changing the results.
- When two units are multiplied, such as in. $\times$ in., a small 2 is placed to the upper right of the unit: in.^{2}. This is read: square inches (cm $\times$ cm = cm^2; and is read: square centimeters).
- The area of the rectangle is:

• **English**	**Metric**
$A = l \times w$	$A = l \times w$
$= 2$ in. $\times 4$ in.	$= 5$ cm $\times 10$ cm
$= 8$ in.^{2}	$= 50$ cm^2
or	or
$A = 4$ in. $\times 2$ in.	$A = 10$ cm $\times 5$ cm
$= 8$ in.^{2}	$= 50$ cm^2

The area of the rectangle is 8 in.^{2} (50 cm^2).

Exercises

1. What is the area of Katherine's scarf?

2. Marlin mows his lawn twice a month. What is the total area that he mows each month?

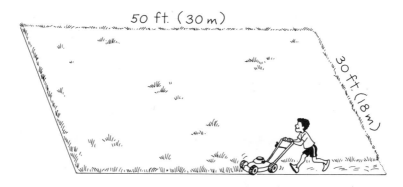

3. Anna Beth is creating a picture using 2-by-2-in. (5-by-5-cm) colored tiles. If she has 60 tiles, does she have enough to fill the frame?

Activity: TWIRLER STICK

Purpose To determine if surface area affects the movement of a spinning object.

Material ruler
new pencil with eraser
small handsaw
scissors
index card
pushpin
round pen
adult helper

Procedure

1. Ask your adult helper to make a twirler stick by following these steps:

- Starting about $1^1/2$ inches (3.8 cm) from the end of the pencil eraser, use the saw to cut notches as close together as possible on one side of the pencil for the next 4 inches (10 cm).

- Measure and cut from the index card two rectangular propellers: a small one $^1/2 \times 2$ inches (1.25 × 5 cm) and a larger one 2 × 2 inches (5 × 5 cm).

- Push the pushpin through the center of the small propeller. Move the pushpin around to enlarge the hole in the paper so that the propeller spins freely on the pushpin.

- Repeat the previous step to prepare the hole in the large propeller.

- Place the pushpin through the hole in the small propeller, and attach the propeller to the twirler stick by sticking the pushpin in the end of the eraser.

2. Hold the twirler stick in one hand and a round pen in the other hand with your index finger on the nonwriting end of the pen.

3. Rub the round pen back and forth across the notches while rubbing your index finger against the side of the pencil.

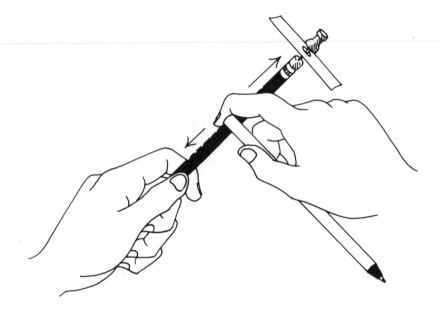

4. Ask your adult helper to take off the small propeller and put on the large propeller.

5. Repeat steps 2 and 3.

Results Both propellers turn, but the smaller one is usually easier to get started.

Why? The pen bumps and hits as it is rubbed across the notches, causing the pencil to vibrate. Moving your finger results in a curved vibrational motion, causing the propeller to spin. The larger propeller has more surface area to be affected by this movement, so it takes more energy to get it started.

Solutions to Exercises

1. *Think!*

- The formula for calculating the area of the scarf is:

  - **English**   **Metric**

    $A = l \times w$ $A = l \times w$
    $ = 1 \text{ ft.} \times 1.5 \text{ ft.}$ $ = 30 \text{ cm} \times 45 \text{ cm}$
    $ = 1.5 \text{ ft.}^2$ $ = 1{,}350 \text{ cm}^2$

The area of Katherine's scarf is 1.5 ft.² (1,350 cm²).

2. *Think!*

- The formula for calculating the area of the lawn is:

  - **English**   **Metric**

    $A = l \times w$ $A = l \times w$
    $ = 50 \text{ ft.} \times 30 \text{ ft.}$ $ = 30 \text{ m} \times 18 \text{ m}$
    $ = 1{,}500 \text{ ft.}^2$ $ = 540 \text{ m}^2$

- Mowing the lawn twice a month means that Marlin covers two times the surface area of the lawn: $2 \times 1{,}500$ ft.² (540 m²).

Marlin mows 3,000 ft.² (1,080 m²) each month.

3. *Think!*

- The area of each tile is:

  - **English**   **Metric**

    $A = l \times w$ $A = l \times w$
    $ = 2 \text{ in.} \times 2 \text{ in.}$ $ = 5 \text{ cm} \times 5 \text{ cm}$
    $ = 4 \text{ in.}^2$ $ = 25 \text{ cm}^2$

- The area inside the picture frame is:

  - **English**   **Metric**

    $A = l \times w$ $A = l \times w$
    $\quad = 10 \text{ in.} \times 20 \text{ in.}$ $\quad = 25 \text{ cm} \times 50 \text{ cm}$
    $\quad = 200 \text{ in.}^2$ $\quad = 1{,}250 \text{ cm}^2$

- Determine the number of tiles needed by dividing the area inside the frame by the area of one tile.

  - **English**   **Metric**

    $200 \text{ in.}^2 \div 4 \text{ in.}^2 = 50$ $1{,}250 \text{ cm}^2 \div 25 \text{ cm}^2 = 50$

- 50 tiles are needed.

Yes, Anna Beth has enough tiles.

17
Same Size
Calculating the Area
of a Rhomboid or Rhombus

What You Need to Know

As explained in Chapter 5, a rhomboid (also called a parallelo-gram) and a rhombus have no right angles. The opposite sides of a rhomboid are parallel, and only its opposite sides are congruent. The opposite sides of a rhombus are parallel, and all four sides are congruent.

RHOMBOID

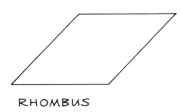

RHOMBUS

The terms *base* and *height* are used when measuring triangles, rhombuses, and rhomboids. (The terms *length* and *width* are

used to describe the same measurements on squares and rectangles.) The formula for calculating the area of a rhomboid or
rhombus is: $A = b \times h$, which is read: area equals base times
height.

Any side of the rhomboid or rhombus may be labeled as the
base (b), but it is customary to label the bottom horizontal line
as the base as shown in the diagram. This method will be used
in this chapter.

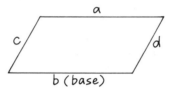

The height of a rhomboid or rhombus is measured by drawing
a perpendicular line between the base and its opposite, parallel
side. The line must form a right (90-degree) angle with the
base. The line segment representing the height can be drawn in
various positions as shown in the diagrams, but it must always
be at a right angle (90 degrees) to the base. The small square
drawn at the vertex of the height and the base indicates that the
lines meet at a 90-degree angle.

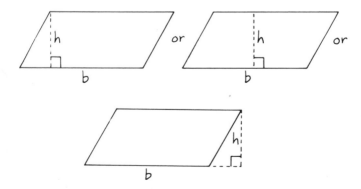

Let's Think It Through

Find the area of the rhomboid shown.

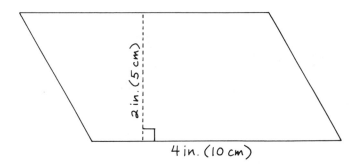

2 in. (5 cm)

4 in. (10 cm)

Answer

Think!

- The formula for calculating the area of a rhomboid is
  A = b × h.
- The base (the bottom horizontal line) measures 4 inches (10 cm).
- The height (the line drawn between the base and its opposite parallel side) is 2 inches (5 cm).

  - **English**

    A = b × h
    = 4 in. × 2 in.
    = 8 in.^{2}

    Metric

    A = b × h
    = 10 cm × 5 cm
    = 50 cm^2

The area of the rhomboid is 8 in.^{2} (50 cm^2).

Exercises

1. Calculate the area of the table leg.

2. Calculate the area of the missing rhombus-shaped puzzle piece in the illustration on the next page.

Activity: HOW HIGH?

Purpose To demonstrate how the height of a rhomboid is determined.

Materials pencil
ruler
index card
scissors

Procedure

1. Use the pencil and ruler to mark two dots on the index card. Make one dot 1¹/₂ inches (3.8 cm) from the upper left corner of the card, and the second dot 1 $^1/_2$ inches (3.8 cm) from the lower right corner.

2. With a ruler, draw two dashed lines across the card, connecting the dots to the corners on the card as shown on the diagram.

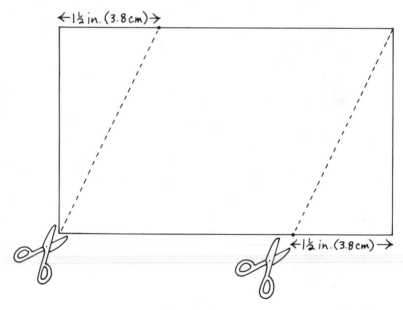

3. Cut along the dashed lines. Keep the rhomboid but discard the triangles.

4. Lay the ruler on top of the rhomboid with the left corner and short edge of the ruler lined up with the left corner and long edge of the rhomboid.

5. Draw a dashed line on the rhomboid along both sides of the ruler.

6. Measure and compare the length of each of the two dashed lines.

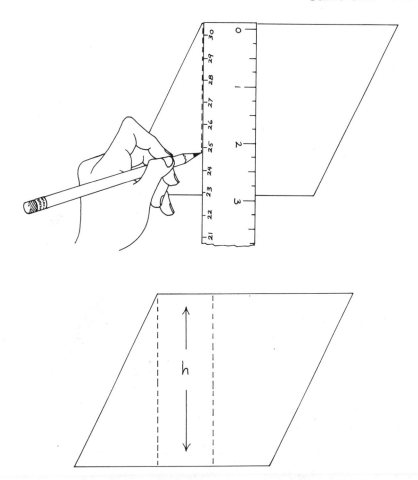

Results   The length of both lines is equal.

Why?   The dimensions of a rhomboid are called the base and height. The height is the perpendicular distance between the base and its parallel side. Thus, as shown in this activity, all perpendicular lines drawn between the base and its parallel side are congruent.

Solutions to Exercises

1. *Think!*

- The formula for calculating the area of the table leg is:

  - **English**   **Metric**

  $A = b \times h$ $A = b \times h$
       $= 36$ in. $\times 4$ in. $= 90$ cm $\times 10$ cm
       $= 144$ in.^{2} $= 900$ cm^2

The area of the table leg is 144 in.^{2} (900 cm^2).

2. *Think!*

- The formula for calculating the area of the missing puzzle piece is:

  - **English**   **Metric**

  $A = b \times h$ $A = b \times h$
       $= 2$ in. $\times 1$ in. $= 5$ cm $\times 2.5$ cm
       $= 2$ in.^{2} $= 12.5$ cm^2

The area of the missing puzzle piece is 2 in.^{2} (12.5 cm^2).

18
Pie?

Calculating the Area of a Circle

What You Need to Know

The ratio of the circumference of any circle to its diameter is shown by the value **pi** (π). To calculate the area of a circle, use the formula $A = \pi r^2$, which is read: area equals pi times the square radius, or area equals pi times the radius times the radius.

The value of π is about $3 \frac{1}{7}$, but there is no exact number equal to this ratio. Calculators give the most accurate value of this number, but 3.14 is the most common value used and it is the number that is used in this book. Using 3.14 as the value for π, the formula can be written more simply as:

area $= 3.14 \times r \times r$.

Let's Think It Through

What is the surface area of the pizza?

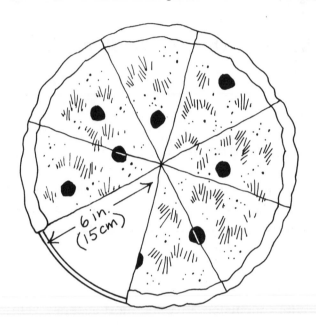

Answer

Think!

- The formula for calculating the area of the pizza is

  A = 3.14 × r × r.

- When multiplying three numbers together, work with two numbers at a time. Multiply the first two, then multiply the product of these two numbers by the third number.

  - **English**

$$A = 3.14 \times 6 \text{ in.} \times 6 \text{ in.}$$
$$3.14 \times 6 \text{ in.} = 18.84 \text{ in.}$$
$$A = 18.84 \text{ in.} \times 6 \text{ in.} = 113.04 \text{ in.}^2$$

• **Metric**

$$A = 3.14 \times 15 \text{ cm} \times 15 \text{ cm}$$
$$3.14 \times 15 \text{ cm} = 47.1 \text{ cm}$$
$$A = 47.1 \text{ cm} \times 15 \text{ cm} = 706.5 \text{ cm}^2$$

The area of the pizza is 113.04 in.² (706.5 cm²).

Exercises

1. Determine the area of the lid on the jam jar.

2. The length of each fan blade from the center of the fan is 4 inches (10 cm). Calculate the area of the circle that the blades sweep with each complete turn.

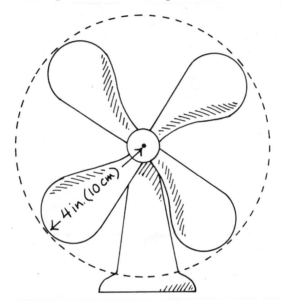

3. Each small square in the diagram has a measurement of 2 × 2 inches (5 × 5 cm). What is the area of the circle?

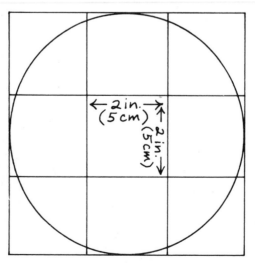

Activity: ROUND OR RECTANGULAR?

Purpose To compare the area of a rectangle made from parts of a circle with the area of the original circle.

Materials compass
typing paper
pencil
scissors
string
transparent tape

Procedure

1. Use the compass to draw a circle with a 4-inch (10-cm) radius on the paper.

2. Lay the paper over the diagram with the center of the circle over the vertex of the rays.

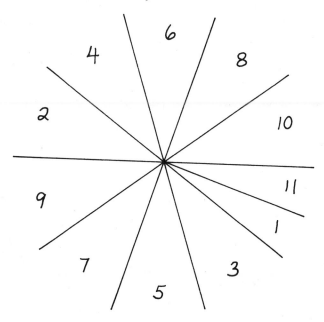

3. Trace each ray, extending it to the circumference of the circle.

4. Number each section in the circle as shown.

5. Use the pencil to shade the bottom half of the circle.

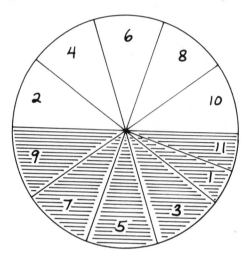

6. Cut two pieces of string equal to the radius of the circle, 4 inches (10 cm).

7. Cut two additional pieces of string equal to one-half the distance around the circle. To do this, cut a piece of string that fits around the circle and then cut the string in half. The length of each string is equal to one-half the circle's circumference, which is equal to $\pi \times r$.

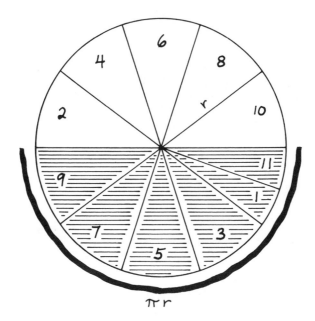

8. Tape the ends of the strings to a table so that they form a rectangle.

9. Cut out the pie-shaped pieces from the circle and arrange them inside the rectangle made by the string, as shown in the diagram.

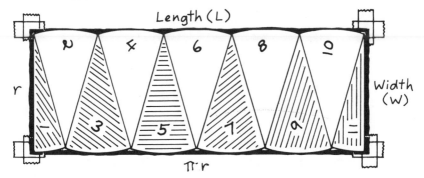

Results   The pieces from the circle fit almost exactly into a rectangular shape.

Why?   The formulas for calculating the area of a rectangle and that of a circle can be compared. The formula for calculating the area of the rectangle made from the pieces of the circle is:

$$A = 1 \times w$$
$$= \pi \times r \times r$$

The formula for calculating the area of the circle is:

$$A = \pi \times r^2$$

While the formulas for calculating the areas of the rectangle and the circle are the same, the areas are only approximately equal because the pie pieces do not fit exactly into the rectangle.

Solutions to Exercises

1. *Think!*

- The formula for calculating the area of the lid is

  $A = 3.14 \times r \times r$.

- If the diameter is 4 inches (10 cm), then the radius is one-half this measurement: $^1/_2 \times 4$ in. (10 cm) = 2 in. (5 cm).

  - **English**

$$A = 3.14 \times 2 \text{ in.} \times 2 \text{ in.}$$
$$3.14 \times 2 \text{ in.} = 6.28 \text{ in.}$$
$$A = 6.28 \text{ in.} \times 2 \text{ in.}$$
$$= 12.56 \text{ in.}^2$$

• **Metric**

$$A = 3.14 \times 5 \text{ cm} \times 5 \text{ cm}$$
$$3.14 \times 5 \text{ cm} = 15.7 \text{ cm}$$
$$A = 15.7 \text{ cm} \times 5 \text{ cm}$$
$$= 78.5 \text{ cm}^2$$

The area of the lid on the jam jar is 12.56 in.² (78.5 cm²).

2. *Think!*

• The formula for calculating the area of the circle is

$A = 3.14 \times r \times r$.

• The length of the fan blade is equal to the radius of the fan.

• **English**

$$A = 3.14 \times 4 \text{ in.} \times 4 \text{ in.}$$
$$3.14 \times 4 \text{ in.} = 12.56 \text{ in.}$$
$$A = 12.56 \text{ in.} \times 4 \text{ in.}$$
$$= 50.24 \text{ in.}^2$$

• **Metric**

$$A = 3.14 \times 10 \text{ cm} \times 10 \text{ cm}$$
$$3.14 \times 10 \text{ cm} = 31.40 \text{ cm}$$
$$A = 31.40 \text{ cm} \times 10 \text{ cm}$$
$$= 314.0 \text{ cm}^2$$

The area of the circle that the fan blades sweep with each complete turn is 50.24 in.² (314.0 cm²).

3. *Think!*

- The diameter of the circle is equal to three times the width of one small square: 3×2 in. (5 cm) = 6 in. (15 cm).

- If the diameter is 6 inches (15 cm), then the radius is one-half this measurement: $\frac{1}{2} \times 6$ in. (15 cm) = 3 in. (7.5 cm).

- **English**

$$A = 3.14 \times 3 \text{ in.} \times 3 \text{ in.}$$
$$3.14 \times 3 \text{ in.} = 9.42 \text{ in.}$$
$$A = 9.42 \text{ in.} \times 3 \text{ in.}$$
$$= 28.26 \text{ in.}^2$$

- **Metric**

$$A = 3.14 \times 7.5 \text{ cm} \times 7.5 \text{ cm}$$
$$3.14 \times 7.5 \text{ cm} = 23.55 \text{ cm}$$
$$A = 23.55 \text{ cm} \times 7.5 \text{ cm}$$
$$= 176.63 \text{ cm}^2$$

The area of the circle is 28.26 in.^{2} (176.63 cm^2).

19
Dotted

Using Graph Paper to Calculate the Area of Plane Figures

What You Need to Know

The area of plane figures drawn on graph paper can be determined by knowing the area of each square on the paper. If the area of figure A in the diagram is one square unit, then the area of figure B is two square units.

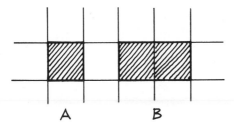

The area can also be calculated by placing dots at each vertex and using "Pick's formula," which is written:

$A = \frac{1}{2} \times b + i - 1$.

This is read: area equals one-half times b (the number of dots on the perimeter of the figure) plus i (the number of dots inside the figure) minus one.

Let's Think It Through

Calculate the area of figures C and D using Pick's formula.

1.

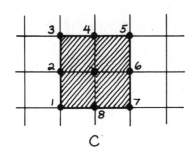

C

2.

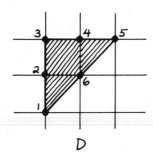

D

Answers

1. *Think!*

- Formula: $A = \frac{1}{2} \times b + i - 1$
  $$b = 8$$
  $$i = 1$$
  $$A = \frac{1}{2} \times 8 + 1 - 1$$

- The steps in solving this problem are:

  1. Multiply the first two numbers. $\frac{1}{2} \times 8 = 4$

  2. Add 1 to the product. $4 + 1 = 5$

3. Subtract 1 from the sum. 5–1 = 4

The area of figure C is 4 square units.

2. *Think!*

- Formula: A = $\frac{1}{2}$ × b + i–1
  b = 6
  i = 0
  A = $\frac{1}{2}$ × 6 + 0–1

- The steps in solving this problem are:

  1. Multiply the first two numbers. $\frac{1}{2}$ × 6 = 3

  2. Add 0 to the product. 3 + 0 = 3

  3. Subtract 1 from the sum. 3–1 = 2

The area of figure D is 2 square units.

Exercises

Use Pick's formula, A = $\frac{1}{2}$ × b + i–1, to find the area of these figures.

1.

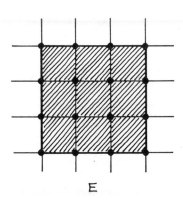

E

2.

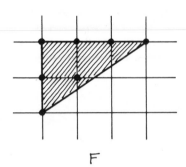

F

3.

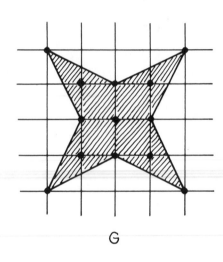

G

Activity: GEOBOARD

Purpose To build and use a geoboard to determine areas of plane geometric figures.

Materials hammer
25 3d finishing nails
block of wood at least 5 × 5 inches (12.5 × 12.5 cm) square
short rubber bands
adult helper

Procedure

1. Ask your adult helper to hammer the nails halfway into the wooden block. The nails should be driven straight, and about half their length should stick out of the wood. Position the nails so that they are 1 inch (2.5 cm) apart in the pattern shown in the diagram.

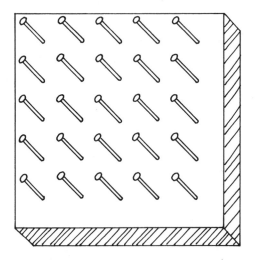

2. Stretch rubber bands around the nails to create geometric figures.

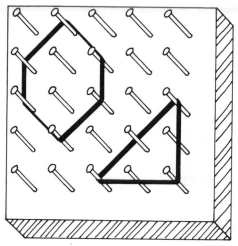

3. Use the formula A = ¹/₂ × b + i −1 to determine the area of each figure.

Results   You have made a geoboard.

Why?   The geoboard provides a quick, fun way of designing and comparing the areas of different geometric figures. Geometric shapes are often used in art. For an extension of this activity, ask your adult helper to construct a larger, colored geoboard. Use colored rubber bands to create geometric designs and display your board. You can change the artistic design as often as you choose.

Solutions to Exercises

1. *Think!*

- Formula: A = ¹/₂ × b + i−1
         b = 12
         i = 4
         A = ¹/₂ × 12 + 4−1

- The steps in solving this problem are:

  1. Multiply the first two numbers. ¹/₂ × 12 = 6

  2. Add 4 to the product. 6 + 4 = 10

  3. Subtract 1 from the sum. 10−1 = 9

  The area of figure E is 9 square units.

2. *Think!*

- Formula: A = ¹/₂ × b + i−1
         b = 6
         i = 1
         A = ¹/₂ × 6 + 1−1

- The steps in solving this problem are:

    1. Multiply the first two numbers. $\frac{1}{2} \times 6 = 3$

    2. Add 1 to the product. $3 + 1 = 4$

    3. Subtract 1 from the sum. $4 - 1 = 3$

The area of figure F is 3 square units.

3. *Think!*

- Formula: $A = \frac{1}{2} \times b + i - 1$
  $b = 8$
  $i = 5$
  $A = \frac{1}{2} \times 8 + 5 - 1$
- The steps in solving this problem are:

    1. Multiply the first two numbers. $\frac{1}{2} \times 8 = 4$

    2. Add 5 to the product. $4 + 5 = 9$

    3. Subtract 1 from the sum. $9 - 1 = 8$

The area of figure G is 8 square units.

20
Spacey

Identifying Space Figures

What You Need to Know

When a geometric figure has three measurements—length, width, and height—it is said to be **three-dimensional** (3-D for short). Three-dimensional figures, like a box of cookies or a basketball, have tops, bottoms, fronts, backs, and sides. Mathematicians call a two-dimensional figure a plane figure, and a three-dimensional figure a **solid** or **space figure**. The five common space figures are the cone, the cylinder, the sphere, the prism, and the pyramid.

The cone, cylinder, and sphere have curved sides. A **cone** has one circular base and is shaped like an ice cream cone without the scoop of ice cream. A **cylinder** has two congruent circular bases (top and bottom) and is shaped like a can. A **sphere** has no flat bases and all points on its surface are an equal distance from its center. A sphere is shaped like a ball.

CONE

CYLINDER

SPHERE

Prisms and pyramids are made up of polygons. In a **prism** the sides are parallelograms and the two parallel bases are congruent. The most common prism is the **cube**, a space figure with six congruent square **faces** (a flat surface or plane region of a space figure). The shape of the bases is used to name other prisms, such as the *triangular prism, rectangular prism,* or *hexagonal prism,* among others.

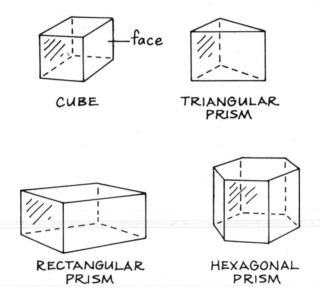

A **pyramid** has triangular sides and a single polygonal base. The shape of the base is used to name the figure, such as the *square pyramid* or *rectangular pyramid,* among others.

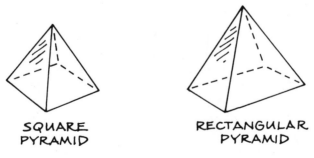

Let's Think It Through

Identify each numbered space figure in the drawing.

Answers

1. *Think!*

- What is the shape of the hat? It has curved sides and one circular base.
- What name is given to space figures with this shape?

Figure 1 is a cone.

2. *Think!*

- What is the shape of the baseball? It is curved on all sides, with no flat bases and all points on its surface an equal distance from its center.
- What name is given to space figures with this shape?

Figure 2 is a sphere.

3. *Think!*

- What is the shape of the can of soup? It has curved sides and two congruent circular bases.
- What name is given to space figures with this shape?

Figure 3 is a cylinder.

4. *Think!*

- What is the shape of the box of cookies? The sides, top, and base are all rectangles.
- What name is given to space figures with this shape?

Figure 4 is a rectangular prism.

Exercise

Each space figure in the first column of the table can be made by folding one of the patterns shown in the third column. Match the patterns with the figures.

SPACE FIGURE	NAME	PATTERN
1.	cube	A
2.	square pyramid	B
3.	triangular prism	C

Activity: 3-D

Purpose To construct a model of a triangular prism.

Materials typing paper
marking pen
scissors
ruler
transparent tape

Procedure

1. Lay the paper over the pattern of the model.

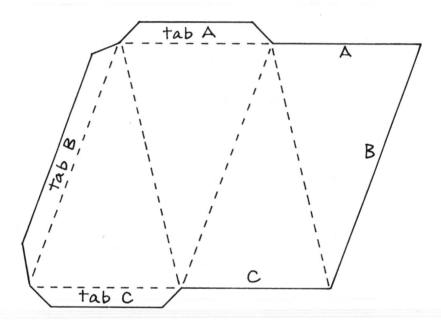

2. Trace the pattern onto the paper with the pen.

3. Cut out the traced pattern along the solid lines.

4. Make the dashed lines easier to fold by following these steps:

- Place the edge of the ruler along one of the dashed lines.
- With the ruler's edge as a guide, use the pen to mark back and forth across the line.
- Repeat the procedure for each dashed line.

5. Fold along each dashed line.

6. Tape the tab sections, matching tabs to sides as follows:

- tab A over side A
- tab B over side B
- tab C over side C

Results   A model of a triangular pyramid is constructed.

Why?   The base of the pyramid as well as the sides are all triangles. The triangular sides and the single polygonal base identify the structure as a pyramid. The triangular base distinguishes the model from other pyramids.

Solutions to Exercises

1. *Think!*

- Describe the number and shape of the figure's sides and bases. Six squares.
- Which pattern has six squares?

Pattern B matches figure 1.

2. *Think!*

- Describe the number and shapes of the figure's sides and base. Four triangles and one square.
- Which pattern has these shapes in these numbers?

Pattern C matches figure 2.

3. *Think!*

- Describe the number and shapes of the figure's sides and base. Three rectangles and two triangles.
- Which pattern has these shapes in these numbers?

Pattern A matches figure 3.

21
Faces

Determining the Number of Faces, Edges, and Vertices of a Polyhedron

What You Need to Know

Each flat surface, or plane, of a space figure is called a face. The line segment where two faces meet is called an **edge**. The corner point where three or more edges meet is called a vertex. A **polyhedron** is a space figure with faces that are polygons.

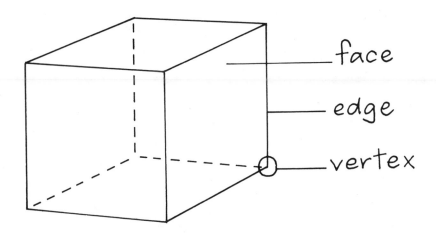

Let's Think It Through

The box shown in the diagram is a polyhedron. Examine the diagram to determine the number of its:

1. vertices

2. edges

3. faces

Answers

1. *Think!*

- The number of vertices in a polyhedron is equal to the number of corners.

The number of vertices for the box is eight.

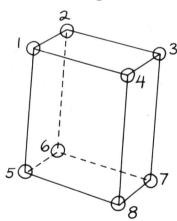

2. *Think!*

- An edge is a line segment where two faces of a polyhedron meet.

The number of edges on the box is twelve.

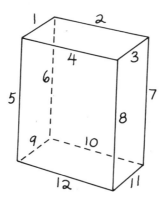

3. *Think!*

- Each flat surface of a polyhedron is a face.
- The box has a top, bottom, left side, right side, front, and back, as shown in the diagram.

The number of faces for the box is six.

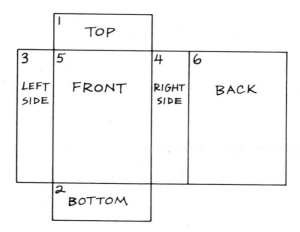

Exercise

Study the closed and open diagrams of each polyhedron and give the numbers needed to complete the table.

Polyhedron	Total Number of:		
	Vertices	Edges	Faces
1. Square pyramid	?	?	?
2. Triangular prism	?	?	?

Activity: FACE PRINTS

Purpose To make prints of the faces of different shaped polyhedrons.

Materials marking pen
ruler
rectangular dishwashing sponge
scissors
3 different colors of poster paint
3 small bowls
2 sheets of white construction paper

Procedure

1. Use the pen and ruler to draw a rectangle and a triangle on one of the largest faces of the sponge.

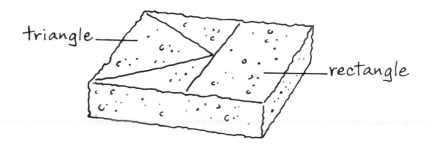

2. Cut out the two shapes drawn on the sponge. The triangle will form a triangular prism, and the rectangle will form a rectangular prism.

3. Pour about ¹/₂ inch (1.25 cm) of paint into each bowl, one color in each bowl. Use a different color of paint for each different shape or size of face.

4. Look at the faces. Dip one of the large rectangular faces of the rectangular prism into one of the bowls of paint, and make a print of this face on the paper.

5. Turn the sponge over and make a print of the opposite face using the same color of paint.

6. Repeat steps 4 and 5 to make prints of the remaining faces of the rectangular prism. Use a different color of paint for each shape of face.

7. Repeat steps 4 and 5 to make prints of each face of the triangular prism. Again, use a different color of paint for each shape of face.

Results   Six prints with one kind of shape are made by the rectangular prism. Five prints with two different kinds of shapes are made by the triangular prism.

Why? The cuts made in the sponge may not produce faces and edges that are exactly smooth and straight, but two general shapes—rectangle and triangle—are produced. Six rectangles make up the faces of the rectangular prism, and the faces of the triangular prism are made up of two triangles and three rectangles.

Solution to Exercise

Polyhedron	Total Number of:		
	Vertices	**Edges**	**Faces**
1. Square pyramid	5	8	5
2. Triangular prism	6	9	5

22
On the Surface

Calculating the Surface Area of Rectangular Boxes

What You Need to Know

The **surface area** of a solid is the sum of the areas of all its faces. The surface area of a rectangular box is equal to the sum of the areas of the six faces that make up the box. Graph paper can be used to draw the flattened shape of the box and calculate the total surface area of the box. For the activities in this chapter, allow the length of one square on the graph paper to equal 1 inch (2.5 cm) on the box.

Let's Think It Through

Use graph paper to determine the surface area of the gift box.

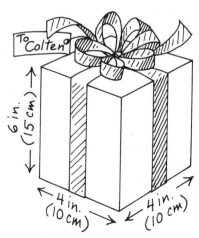

Answer

Think!

- Draw the flattened box on graph paper as in the diagram.

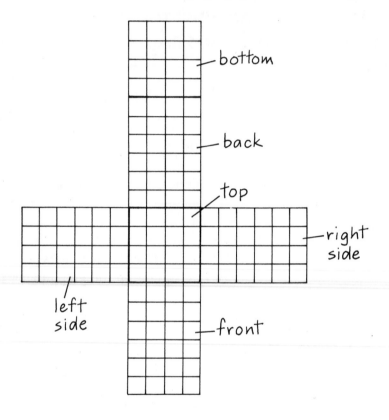

- The length of each square on the graph paper represents a length of 1 inch (2.5 cm) on the box.

- The area of each square on the graph paper represents an area on the box of:

  - **English**

  1 in. × 1 in. = 1 in.²

- **Metric**

2.5 cm × 2.5 cm = 6.25 cm²

- To calculate the surface area of the box, determine the total number of squares in the diagram and multiply the number by the area represented by one square.

Bottom area	=	16 squares
Back area	=	24 squares
Top area	=	16 squares
Front area	=	24 squares
Left-side area	=	24 squares
Right-side area	=	24 squares
Total	=	128 squares

- The surface area of the box equals the total number of squares multiplied by the area represented by one square:

- **English**

Surface area = 128 squares × 1 in.²
= 128 in.²

- **Metric**

Surface area = 128 squares × 6.25 cm²
= 800 cm²

The surface area of the gift box is 128 in.² (800 cm²).

Exercise

Use graph paper to determine the surface area of the open shoe box.

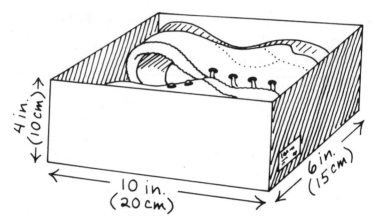

Activity: MORE SPACE

Purpose To demonstrate how surface area can be decreased.

Materials typing paper
pencil
ruler
scissors
transparent tape

Procedure

1. Lay the paper over the pattern of the cube.

2. Use the pencil and the ruler as a guide to trace the pattern on the paper four times.

3. Cut each tracing out of the paper along the solid lines.

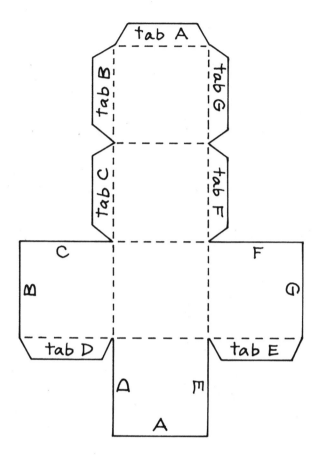

4. With the dashed lines facing you, fold each pattern along the dashed lines. Make all folds without turning the paper over.

5. Tape the tab sections to form four closed boxes, matching tabs to sides as follows:

   • tab A over side A

   • tab B over side B

   • tab C over side C

   • tab D over side D

   • tab E over side E

6. Lay the boxes end to end in a straight line on a table.

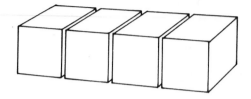

7. Count the visible faces of the boxes and those touching the table.

8. Take two of the boxes and stack them on top of the other two boxes.

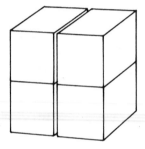

9. Again count the visible faces of the boxes and those touching the table.

Results The boxes positioned in a straight line have 18 visible faces. The stacked boxes have 16 visible faces.

Why? Neither the shape nor the size of the four individual boxes changes. Rearranging the boxes does not change the total size of the figure created, but the shape and therefore the surface area does change. Both figures created by combining the boxes are rectangular prisms, but the figure made up of one layer of boxes has the greatest exposed surface area.

Solution to Exercise

Think!

- Each square on the graph paper represents an area of 1 in.^{2} (6.25 cm^2) on the open shoe box.

- The total number of squares in the diagram of the box drawn on the graph paper is:

Back area	=	40 squares
Bottom area	=	60 squares
Front area	=	40 squares
Left-side area	=	24 squares
Right-side area	=	24 squares
Total	=	188 squares

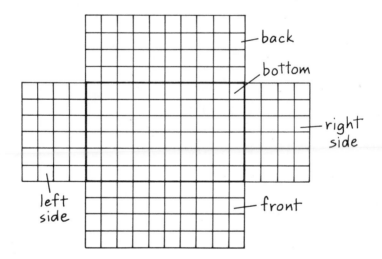

- The surface area of the box equals the total number of squares multiplied by the area represented by one square:

Surface area = 188 squares × 1 in.^{2} (6.25 cm^2)

= 188 in.^{2} (1,175 cm^2)

The surface area of the open shoe box is 188 in.^{2} (1,175 cm^2).

23
Toothpick Magic
Changing Geometric Figures Through Analysis and Reasoning

What You Need to Know

This chapter shows you how to change one geometric figure to another by moving a specified number of lines. Your mental processes of analysis and reasoning will be used and developed. To **analyze** is to mentally separate a thing into the parts of which it is composed. To **reason** is to use one's mental powers to draw conclusions. The strategy used to solve each problem in this chapter will be first to analyze the problem, and then to reason through the steps that need to be taken to make the specified change.

Let's Think It Through

Arrange 12 toothpicks as shown in the diagram. Then, rearrange any four of the toothpicks to change the four congruent squares into three congruent squares.

Answer

Think!

- It takes four toothpicks to make a square. Thus, the four removed toothpicks can be arranged to make one square.

- To make the three specified squares, two original squares must remain unchanged.

- Which four toothpicks when removed from the original arrangement will leave two squares?

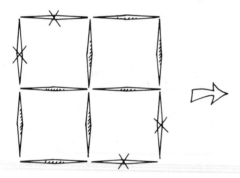

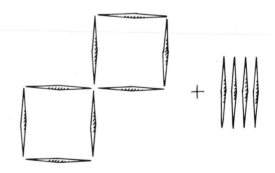

- The third square can be made at any corner of the two unchanged squares.

Two possible arrangements are:

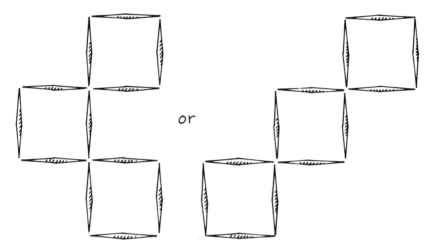

or

Exercises

For each exercise use the specified number of toothpicks to make the original figure. Then, remove or rearrange the toothpicks as directed to create the new figure.

1. Change the nine congruent squares into five congruent squares by removing four toothpicks.

2. Eighteen toothpicks make the six-pointed star. Rearrange six of the toothpicks to create six congruent diamonds.

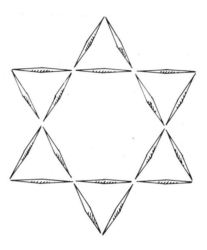

Activity: STAR BURST

Purpose   To watch five toothpicks move by themselves into a six-pointed star pattern.

Materials   5 round wooden toothpicks
12-inch (30-cm) square wax paper
eyedropper
cup of water

Procedure

1. Bend each toothpick into a V shape without breaking it apart.

2. Place the bent toothpicks on the sheet of wax paper in a star burst pattern as shown in the diagram. Put the bent parts as close together as possible in the center.

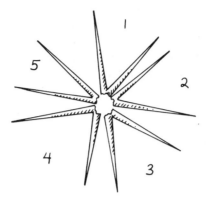

3. Fill the eyedropper with water from the cup.

4. Place four drops of water in the opening in the center of the star burst. You want the water to touch the bent part of each toothpick.

5. Watch and wait until all movement stops.

Results   Each bent toothpick moves so that the angle between the two sides of the V increases. The first pattern that takes shape is a five-pointed figure similar in appearance to a starfish. The angles continue to enlarge until all motion ceases, and a fully developed five-pointed star is created.

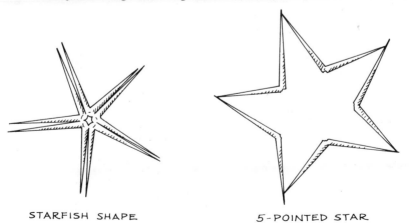

STARFISH SHAPE   5-POINTED STAR

Why?   Water entering the wood where the toothpick is bent causes the wood to expand. This expansion makes the toothpick start to return to its original straight state. Thus, the angle between the sides of each toothpick increases, creating an ever-widening star.

Solutions to Exercises

1. *Think!*

- Remove the middle toothpick from each outside edge of the figure. Five congruent squares are left.

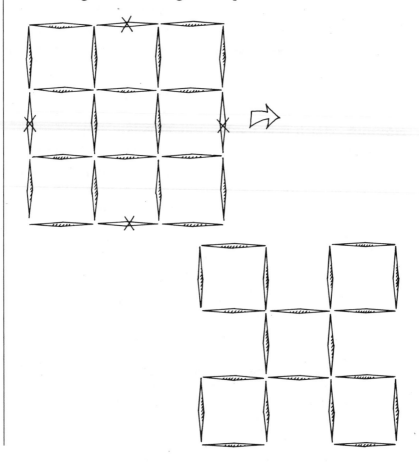

2. *Think!*

- Rotate the six toothpicks that are inside the star so that their ends touch in the center of the figure. Six congruent quadrilaterals are created.

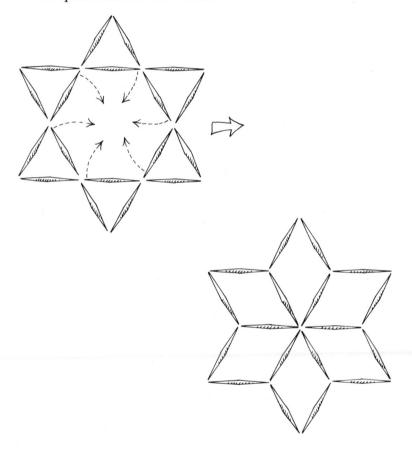

24
Over and Up
Using Coordinates to Graph Figures

What You Need to Know

Figures can be created on a grid by connecting coordinate points in order. **Coordinates** are number pairs that tell the location of a point on a grid. To graph a coordinate, follow these steps:

A. Start at the zero corner of the grid.

B. Move to the right the number of spaces equal to the first coordinate number.

C. Move up the number of spaces equal to the second coordinate number, and mark a dot on the grid.

The diagram shows the steps for graphing coordinates (2, 5).

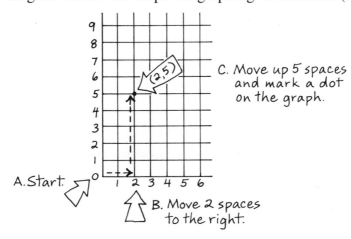

C. Move up 5 spaces and mark a dot on the graph.

A. Start.

B. Move 2 spaces to the right.

Let's Think It Through

1. Graph these coordinates and connect their points in the order given to create a figure: (3, 5), (4, 2), (8, 2), (9, 5), (6, 4).

2. Graph a similar figure, but make it twice as large.

Answers

1. *Think!*

- Follow the steps for graphing coordinates.

- Draw a line to connect each point in the order given. Close the figure by drawing a line from the last to the first point. The arrows in the diagram indicate the order in which each line is drawn.

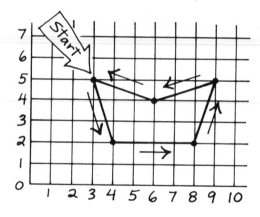

2. *Think!*

- The coordinates of a figure twice as large as the previous figure are determined by multiplying each of the coordinates of the previous figure by 2.

  $(3, 5) \times 2 = (3 \times 2, 5 \times 2) = (6, 10)$
  $(4, 2) \times 2 = (4 \times 2, 2 \times 2) = (8, 4)$
  $(8, 2) \times 2 = (8 \times 2, 2 \times 2) = (16, 4)$
  $(9, 5) \times 2 = (9 \times 2, 5 \times 2) = (18, 10)$
  $(6, 4) \times 2 = (6 \times 2, 4 \times 2) = (12, 8)$

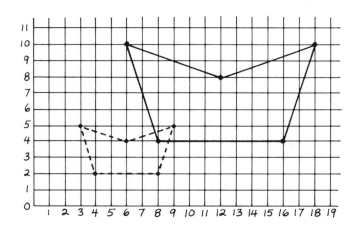

Exercises

1. Graph a figure using these coordinates: (1, 4), (2, 4), (2, 1), (4, 1), (4, 4), (5, 4), (3, 6).

2. Graph a similar figure, but make it three times as large.

Activity: BIGGER

Purpose To use a grid to make an enlargement of a figure.

Materials yardstick (meterstick)
pencil
18-inch (45-cm) square poster board
marking pen
pencil with eraser
crayons

Procedure

1. Use the measuring stick and pencil to draw a 15-inch (37.5-cm) line across the top of the poster board. The line should be 1 $\frac{1}{2}$ inches (3.75 cm) from the top and 1 $\frac{1}{2}$ inches (3.75 cm) from each side of the paper.

2. Draw five more 15-inch (37.5 cm) lines parallel with the first line and 3 inches (7.5 cm) apart.

3. Draw six vertical lines intersecting the horizontal lines, 3 inches (7.5 cm) apart, to form a grid with 25 squares.

4. Number the lines in pencil across the bottom and up the left side, starting with 0.

5. Graph the coordinates of the figure of the boat shown on the next page onto your large grid.

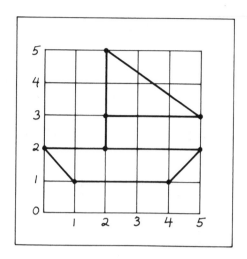

6. Trace over the pencil lines of the drawing with the pen.

7. Erase the grid lines and numbers.

8. Use the crayons to color the figure and add water waves and birds to complete the picture.

Results An enlarged, colored picture of a boat on the water is produced.

Why? The original figure is on a grid made of 25 congruent squares. The figure you made also has 25 squares, but they are bigger than those in the smaller grid. Using the grid with larger squares allows you to use the same coordinates to draw an enlarged version of the original boat.

Solutions to Exercises

1. *Think!*

- Use the coordinates provided to place points on the grid.
- Connect the points in the order given.

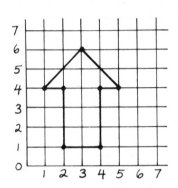

2. *Think!*

- The coordinates of a figure three times as large as the previous one are determined by multiplying each of the coordinates of the previous figure by 3.

$(1, 4) \times 3 = (1 \times 3, 4 \times 3) = (3, 12)$
$(2, 4) \times 3 = (2 \times 3, 4 \times 3) = (6, 12)$
$(2, 1) \times 3 = (2 \times 3, 1 \times 3) = (6, 3)$
$(4, 1) \times 3 = (4 \times 3, 1 \times 3) = (12, 3)$
$(4, 4) \times 3 = (4 \times 3, 4 \times 3) = (12, 12)$
$(5, 4) \times 3 = (5 \times 3, 4 \times 3) = (15, 12)$
$(3, 6) \times 3 = (3 \times 3, 6 \times 3) = (9, 18)$

- See diagram to compare the figures.

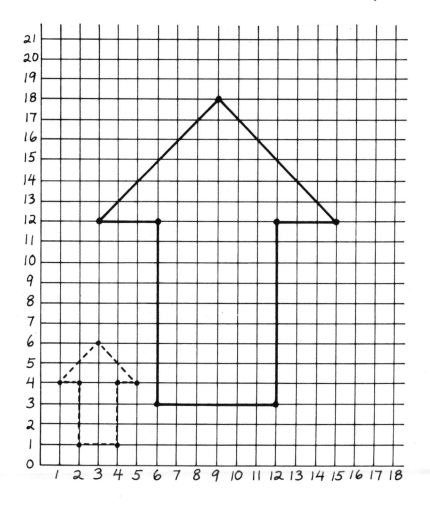

25
Three-Dimensional Drawings

Using Perspective to Draw Three-Dimensional Figures in Two Dimensions

What You Need to Know

Two-dimensional drawings of three-dimensional (3-D) objects can be made by using perspective. **Perspective** is the technique of drawing on a flat surface in such a way as to make the drawing look three-dimensional. The drawing of the pencil box is an example of the use of perspective to give a drawing the look of a 3-D figure. The lines are angled to make the box appear to have depth.

Let's Think It Through

Use a pencil, ruler, and graph paper to draw the following:

1. A rectangular prism

2. A cylinder

Answers

1. Draw the rectangular prism by following these steps:

- Draw a rectangle on graph paper with a width of five squares and a length of three squares. (NOTE: *The measurements are not significant.*)

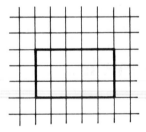

- Draw a second overlapping rectangle of equal size, but start two squares to the right and one square up from the first rectangle, as shown in the diagram.

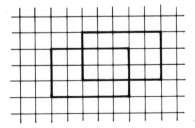

- Draw lines to connect the corresponding vertices of the two rectangles.

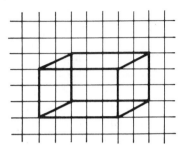

2. Draw the cylinder by following these steps:

- Draw an oval nine squares wide and two squares long. (NOTE: *The measurements are not significant.*)

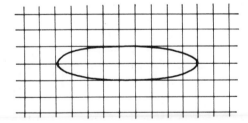

- Draw an identical oval eight squares below the first oval.

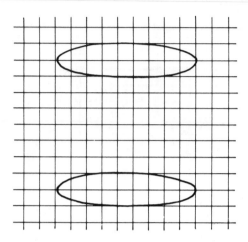

- Draw lines to connect the corresponding ends of the two ovals.

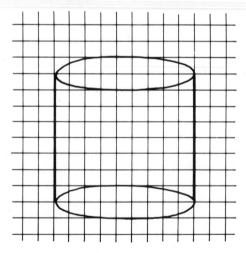

Exercises

1. Draw an open toy box.

2. Draw a cookie jar.

Activity: SWIMMING FISH

Purpose   To show how colors can be used to create a three-dimensional drawing that seems to rise off the page.

Materials typing paper
1 pale blue and 1 pale pink highlight marker
1 red and 1 blue transparent plastic report folder

Procedure

1. Lay the paper over the diagram of the fish in the bowl.

2. Trace the fishbowl with the blue marker.

3. Trace the fish with the pink marker.

4. Place the tracing on a table.

5. Cut one 2-by-2-inch (5-by-5-cm) square from each of the folders.

6. Close your left eye and use your right eye to look through the red plastic at the tracing.

7. Close your right eye and use your left eye to look through the blue plastic at the tracing.

8. With the red plastic over your right eye and the blue plastic over your left eye, look at the tracing with both eyes.

Results   The fishbowl is darker and the pink fish disappears or is only faintly visible when viewed only through the red plastic. Through the blue plastic, the fish is darker and the blue lines of the bowl disappear or are only faintly visible. Looking through the red and blue plastic at the same time produces a 3-D image of a pink fish in a blue bowl.

Why?   What you see is an optical illusion—a misleading image seen when your brain is tricked by your eyes. The illusion in this experiment is caused by the fact that you have two eyes, each of which is sending a different image to the brain. The right eye sees a dark fishbowl and the left eye sees a dark fish. When the brain puts these two images together, a 3-D image results.

Solutions to Exercises

1. *Think!*

- What shape is an open toy box? A rectangular prism.

- Draw a rectangular prism with a width of five squares and a length of six squares, following the instructions given earlier. (NOTE: *The rectangle can be any size.*)

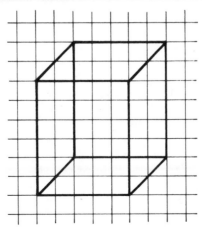

- Erase the lines indicated in the diagram.

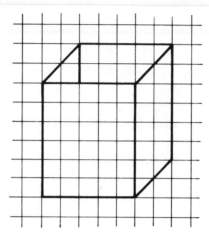

- Trace the drawing onto a sheet of typing paper. Add the label "toys" and a toy plus shading to complete the drawing. Be sure to erase any lines of the box that pass through the figure of the toy.

2. *Think!*

- What shape is a cookie jar? A cylinder.
- Draw a cylinder with a width of eight squares and a length of two squares, following the instructions given earlier. (NOTE: *The cylinder can be any size.*)

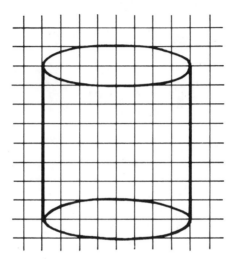

- Erase the line indicated in the diagram.

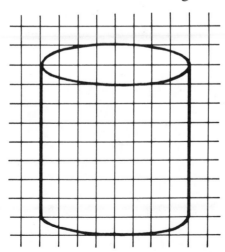

- Trace the drawing onto a sheet of typing paper. To make the lid, add a curved line and a circle as the knob. Write the word "cookies" on the jar so that the word curves as if written on a line parallel with the bottom curve and add shading.

Glossary

Acute angle: An angle that measures less than 90 degrees.

Acute triangle: A triangle in which all angles measure less than 90 degrees.

Adjacent: Adjoining; neighboring.

Affinity: The attraction of one substance to another substance.

Analyze: To mentally separate a thing into the parts of which it is composed.

Angle: The figure formed when two rays that have the same endpoint or two straight lines meet.

Area: The measure of the number of square units needed to cover the surface of a plane figure.

Central angle: An angle that has its vertex at the center of a circle.

Chord: Any line segment that begins and ends on the circumference of a circle.

Circle: A simple closed curve; a plane figure bordered by a curved line called the circumference; every point on the circumference is an equal distance from the center point of the circle.

Circumference: The perimeter of a circle; the length of this boundary.

Closed curve: A curved figure formed by a continuous line.

Closed figure: A geometric figure that begins and ends at the same point.

Complex curve: A curved figure formed by a line that intersects itself.

Cone: A space figure that has curved sides and one circular base; shaped like an ice cream cone without the scoop of ice cream.

Congruent: The same; equal to.

Congruent polygons: Polygons that are exactly the same size and shape.

Coordinates: Number pairs that tell the location of a point on a grid.

Cube: A prism with six congruent sides.

Curved figure: Any geometric figure that does not have straight sides, such as a circle; can be closed or open, simple or complex.

Cylinder: A space figure that has curved sides and two congruent circular bases; shaped like a can.

Diameter: A chord that passes through the center of a circle.

Edge: A line segment where two faces of a space figure meet.

Endpoint: A point at the end of a line segment or ray.

Equilateral triangle: A triangle with three congruent sides.

Face: A flat surface or plane region of a space figure.

Hexagon: A six-sided polygon.

Intersecting lines: Lines that meet or cross each other and have only one point in common.

Isosceles trapezoid: A trapezoid whose two nonparallel sides are congruent.

Isosceles triangle: A triangle with two congruent sides.

Line: The geometric definition of a line is a straight path that has no definite length and goes on forever in both directions; a mark made by a pen, a pencil, or other tool on a surface.

Line of symmetry: A line that divides a figure into two identical parts that are mirror images of each other; the parts match if folded along the line.

Line segment: A part of a line, which follows a straight path between two endpoints.

Möbius strip: A closed complex curve with only one side—the inside is also the outside; discovered by August Ferdinand Möbius (1790–1868).

Obtuse angle: An angle that measures greater than 90 degrees.

Obtuse triangle: A triangle with one angle that measures greater than 90 degrees.

Open curve: A curved figure formed by a noncontinuous, broken line.

Optical illusion: A misleading image seen because of misinterpretations made by the brain.

Origami: The art of folding paper into shapes that look like objects.

Parallel lines: Any two or more lines that do not intersect and are always the same distance apart.

Parallelogram: A quadrilateral that has two pairs of parallel sides; common name for a rhomboid.

Pattern: A predictable arrangement of things, such as numbers and/or geometric figures, that have some relationship to each other.

Pentagon: A five-sided polygon.

Pentomino: A figure made from five congruent squares; the entire side of one square must line up with the whole side of the square it touches.

Perimeter: The outer boundary of a plane figure; the length of this boundary.

Perpendicular lines: Two lines that intersect, forming a right angle.

Persistence of vision: The eye's ability to temporarily hold on to images after the image is out of sight.

Perspective: The technique of drawing on a flat surface in such a way as to make the drawing look three-dimensional.

Pi (π): The ratio of the circumference of any circle to its diameter; 3.14 is the common value used.

Plane figure: A geometric figure that lies on a flat surface.

Plane geometry: The study of two-dimensional figures.

Polygon: A closed plane figure formed by three or more line segments that are joined only at the endpoints, with each endpoint connected to only two line segments.

Polyhedron: A space figure with faces that are polygons.

Prism: A space figure with polygonal sides and two congruent parallel bases.

Protractor: An instrument used to measure angles in degrees.

Pyramid: A space figure that has triangular sides and a single polygonal base.

Quadrilateral: A closed plane figure formed by four line segments; a four-sided polygon; can be a trapezium, trapezoid, or parallelogram.

Radius: A line segment from a point on the circumference of a circle to the center of the circle.

Ray: A part of a line with one endpoint; it follows a straight path that goes on forever in only one direction.

Reason: To use one's mental powers to draw conclusions.

Rectangle: A parallelogram that has four right angles and only opposite sides are congruent.

Rhomboid: A parallelogram that has no right angles and only opposite sides are congruent; commonly called a parallelogram.

Rhombus: A parallelogram that has no right angles and four congruent sides.

Right angle: An angle that measures 90 degrees.

Right triangle: A triangle that has one 90-degree angle.

Scalene triangle: A triangle with no congruent sides.

Simple curve: A curved figure, such as a circle, formed by a line that does not intersect.

Solid: Another name for space figure.

Solid geometry: The study of three-dimensional figures.

Space figure: A geometric figure that is three-dimensional; also called a solid; can be a cone, cylinder, sphere, prism, or pyramid.

Sphere: A space figure that has no flat bases and all points on its curved surface are an equal distance from its center; shaped like a ball.

Square: A rectangle that has four congruent sides.

Surface area: The sum of the areas of all the faces of a solid.

Symmetric figures: Figures with lines of symmetry.

Tangram: A Chinese puzzle made by cutting a square into five triangles, a square, and a rhomboid.

Three-dimensional: Having three measurements—length, width, and height; said of space figures; 3-D for short.

Trapezium: A quadrilateral that has no parallel sides.

Trapezoid: A quadrilateral that has one pair of parallel sides.

Triangle: A polygon made up of three sides; the sum of the angles created by the three sides is always 180 degrees.

Two-dimensional: Having only two measurements—length and width; said of plane figures.

Vertex (plural **vertices**)**:** The point where two or more rays, two or more sides of a polygon, or three or more edges of a space figure meet.

Index